Fresh
from the
Word

Fresh
from the
Word

Devotions for the *300*th Anniversary
of the Brethren

THE BRETHREN CELEBRATE 300 YEARS

About the anniversary logo

This book is one of several Brethren Press publications displaying the mark of the 300th anniversary of the Brethren (1708-2008). It represents the theme, "Surrendered to God, Transformed in Christ, Empowered by the Spirit."

The central symbol represents both wheat and flame. Based on John 12:24-26a, the grains of wheat emphasize surrender as they fall to the ground and die, transformation as they sprout with new life, and empowerment as they bear fruit in new heads of grain. The wheat whiskers point to Christ as they form a cross. The flame expresses surrender in burning and transformation in refining.

Water connotes surrender, transformation, and empowerment through baptism into Christ's death and resurrection, along with being "born of water and the Spirit."

The circle conveys wholeness and unity, as well as the world in which we are empowered to minister. The openness of the circle suggests that we not only need but welcome continued surrender, transformation, and empowerment.

Contents

Introduction

*W*hat characterized the eight men and women who boldly chose to be baptized that morning in 1708? A careful reading of the Scriptures and a commitment to obey the Word of God.

Therefore, what more appropriate way to observe the three hundredth anniversary of that action than to spend an entire year reading the Bible together. This year-long devotional book is a simple but profound way to celebrate our common heritage—and our common commitment to search the Scriptures for God's leading.

We in Brethren Press express our deep appreciation to contributors from six of the groups that trace their origins to Schwarzenau. These six groups include the Brethren Church, the Church of the Brethren, the Conservative Grace Brethren Churches International, the Dunkard Brethren, the Fellowship of Grace Brethren Churches, and the Old German Baptist Brethren. Our instructions to those writers were simple: Write on the assigned Bible text, and speak from your own theological convictions—but with sensitivity to the wide range of people who will be using the devotional book.

You will see that these writings vary greatly in style, faith experience, and point of view. But they are all written by people who call themselves Brethren. The contributors represent many places and ages and vocations. As we began to work directly with them, we took delight in the long-distance connections that developed. There were rounds of friendly e-mails that gave us a window into their lives. These brothers and sisters were eager to join in the project, despite the extra work in busy schedules. We learned that some had to plan their writing around surgery or navigate cancer treatments. One writer e-mailed a beautiful photo of his brand-new baby, along with himself, his wife, and four smiling older children. We are grateful to all of these writers for their contributions.

To represent in a modest way the worldwide identity of the Brethren, we are providing several entries in two languages. Our thanks to the translators who assisted with the editing of these devotions. Anne Holzman edited the Spanish (February 7, April 23, June 12, August 23, October 3, and October 8), with Nancy Sollenberger Heishman giving early assistance on two (June 12 and October 8). Patrick Bugu edited the Hausa (August 20 and September 11). Editing of the Higgi translation (November 4) was done by Samuel Dali. Founa Augustin assisted us with her own Creole translation (March 10). Marcos Inhauser assisted with Portuguese (October 24).

It seemed important to include a few devotions from Brethren history. We are grateful to Frank Ramirez, who searched the Brethren Historical Library and Archives for writings that could be excerpted to accompany specific Bible texts. He prepared 23 of these meditations from the past, adding the sections that brought them into the format of the other entries.

We are indebted to Howard E. Royer and Kenneth M. Shaffer for helping us conceptualize the project. Ken also provided historical expertise all along the way.

Major work on this project has been done by Nancy Klemm, managing editor of Brethren Press. Sometimes she felt daunted by the scope of a project with more than 240 writers, but she was also inspired by each of these contributors. The load was lightened by involvement of the rest of the Brethren Press group, making this truly a team endeavor.

Throughout the development of this book we have been pleased to work alongside the Church of the Brethren Anniversary Committee, which has had the immense task of coordinating a wide range of anniversary projects. For their efforts, and for the privilege of collaborating with them, we thank committee members Jeff Bach, Dean Garrett, Rhonda Pittman Gingrich, Leslie Lake, and Lorele Yager.

We are especially grateful to Donald F. Durnbaugh, a member of the committee until his unexpected death in 2005. Nancy Klemm and I were fortunate to have met with him just months before. During an enjoyable lunch meeting, he handed us pages of suggested contact people and possible writers from the other Brethren groups. Our work was made easier with this head start. Even more significant was the spirit of fellowship we felt when these contact people responded to our invitation with warmth and enthusiasm. This book has benefited from the respect and affection that Brethren from these varied groups have for Don.

Finally, we celebrate the peculiar people known as the Brethren. What kind of anniversary gift does one give to a people celebrating three hundred years? In a spirit of gratitude and love, we in Brethren Press offer this treasury of devotions to encourage us all as disciples of Jesus. As we spend the year together on this journey through the Bible, we pray that we will be reminded of our beginnings, when the Brethren were born out of courage and conviction; we will be strengthened for the present day; and we will be inspired with hope for the future. Thanks be to God.

Wendy McFadden
Publisher

A Brief History
of Brethren Beginnings

*T*he first Brethren baptism took place in the Eder River near Schwarzenau. The exact site and date were kept secret, as was the name of the man (chosen by lot) who baptized Alexander Mack, Sr., their leader and first minister. Mack baptized his baptizer and the remaining six: Anna Margaretha Mack, Andreas Boni, Johanna Nöthiger Boni, Johann Kipping, Johanna Kipping, Georg Grebe, and Lukas Vetter. They did not want their community to be named after any individual; in fact, they chose no name at all, referring to themselves simply as "brethren." Since baptism of adults was considered rebaptism (they had all received Reformed or Lutheran baptism as infants) and was illegal under the laws of the Holy Roman Empire, they also may have had some concern for their safety. Indeed, when rulers of surrounding territories heard of the event, they registered immediate protest with Wittgenstein's sovereign, Count Heinrich Albrecht. He, however, was of pietist inclination himself and defended the recent settlers. The neighboring rulers then denounced the new religious dissenters to the imperial authorities, but that inquiry was not completed until 1720, after the Brethren had left the area.

Although little is known in detail about the young congregation in Schwarzenau, it is clear that early members generated great evangelistic fervor. Large meetings were held in Schwarzenau and surrounding villages. So many people attended meetings in Schwarzenau that these were often held outdoors on a lawn still known as the "Anabaptist yard." Brethren also sent out evangelists to make converts in other parts of Germany, Switzerland, and the Netherlands.

A large branch congregation was founded in Ysenburg-Büdingen-Marienborn, northeast of Frankfurt/Main. As in Wittgenstein, there was considerable freedom of religion, which attracted religious separatists driven from their homes elsewhere. From 1711 to 1715, Mack and others won converts and conducted baptisms among the Marienborn settlers. When Brethren began to bring subjects of Marienborn into their fold as well as the settlers, local authorities forbade such activity under penalty of expulsion.

Unwilling to give up their faith, the Marienborn Brethren left in 1715 and found asylum in the town of Krefeld on the lower Rhine River where Mennonites enjoyed toleration because of their economic contribution to the textile industry. Because Brethren were so similar to the Mennonites in belief and practice, they were considered just another variant of Mennonites. However, whereas the Mennonites were content to perpetuate their belief within their own families, the aggressive Brethren reached out to convert not only the host Mennonites but also members of the established churches, and this invited repression. About 1716 six men of the Reformed confession from Solingen were baptized by Brethren ministers in the Wupper River. These Solingen Brethren were arrested and sentenced to life imprisonment at hard labor at Jülich for refusing to conform to one of the three established faiths. Through the efforts of Dutch citizens, however, they were freed after nearly four years of harsh incarceration.

Persecution continued as Brethren activity extended to northern Germany (Altona near Hamburg), to the Palatinate (Eppstein), and to Switzerland (Bern and Basel). In 1714 the leader Christian Liebe was seized in Bern and condemned, along with Bernese Anabaptists, as a galley slave in Italy. In 1716 he was freed from this draconian punishment. . . .

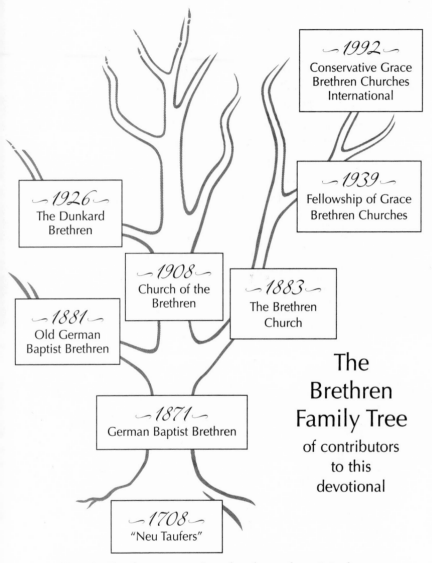

1992
Conservative Grace
Brethren Churches
International

1939
Fellowship of Grace
Brethren Churches

1926
The Dunkard
Brethren

1908
Church of the
Brethren

1883
The Brethren
Church

1881
Old German
Baptist Brethren

The Brethren Family Tree
of contributors
to this
devotional

1871
German Baptist Brethren

1708
"Neu Taufers"

Despite Brethren expansion elsewhere, the original congregation in Schwarzenau remained the largest Brethren congregation. When Count August took office in Wittgenstein in 1719, however, intense pressure was placed upon the Brethren. This, in addition to the recurrent economic problems of the area and increased competition from other religious groups, led the Brethren to decide to relocate. Aided by funds from Dutch Collegiants, forty Brethren families moved to Surhuisterveen in West Friesland in 1720. They remained there until 1729, when almost all of the group emigrated to North America.

The Mack-led group was not the first to leave Europe. Some twenty families from the Krefeld congregation had left for Pennsylvania in 1719, in part because of internal dissension. Most settled in Germantown, north of Philadelphia, a village founded in 1683 by Mennonites/Quakers from Krefeld. Other Brethren settled inland in areas known as Skippack, Oley, Falckner's Swamp, and Conestoga. The dispersion made it difficult for the newcomers to reorganize as a congregation. It was not until Christmas Day, 1723, that Peter Becker, chosen as their leader, officiated at the first Brethren baptisms and love feast in the New World. The "first fruits" were former Mennonites living along the Schuylkill River.

Adapted with permission from "Brethren 1708-1883," Donald F. Durnbaugh, in The Brethren Encyclopedia, *Vol. I, 174-75.*

Part 1

God's Call
to the
Christian Community

The Awareness
of God's Instruction

January 1–January 27

 $\mathscr{T}$ here were those who had an ardent
desire to follow Christ's teachings in all things
and came to the prayerful conclusion that
they had to create some new form of church
community.

Donald F. Durnbaugh (1927–2005)

&

January 1

The Appointed Time for Celebration

Reading: Numbers 9:1-5

Let the Israelites keep the Passover at its appointed time. . . .
[on] the fourteenth day of this month at twilight (Num. 9:2-3a).

Meditation: The Jewish day began at twilight, and, yes, the
new year began at eventide, much like our own New Year's celebration. The Israelites have been traveling for a year and it is
time to celebrate the Passover, an essential part of their life.
They are directed by God to keep the appointed time of celebration. It is the time of year for God's people to rediscover and
recover their orientation and meaning before God and prepare
for the journey led by God's presence in a cloud by day and in
a fire by night (Num. 9:15ff.). These Israelites are a pilgrim
people aware of divine leading; they are a people on the march.

The Passover celebration is set within a review of the past
and a preview of the future, not unlike this day in our own
faith history as we begin the celebration of the three hundredth
anniversary of our founding as Brethren. As we begin this year,
let us not only look back upon the many years of God's faithfulness and guidance, but also look ahead to where God is
leading us now. In our New Year's celebration, let us focus on
the compelling presence of God in our past and prepare ourselves for the life of devotion and action under God's guidance
that lies ahead.

For the day: Prepare yourself by looking back at the life of
God's people and how it has shaped your life. Prepare yourself
for God's new action in the days ahead.

Prayer: God of deliverance, help me to recognize your presence in the past millennia and in these last three hundred years. God of guidance, help me discern where you are leading in the years that lie ahead.

Robert W. Neff

♺

January 2

A Day of Remembrance

Readings: Exodus 12:11-14; Deuteronomy 26:5-9

This day shall be a day of remembrance for you. You shall celebrate it as a festival to the LORD; throughout all your generations you shall observe [the Passover] as a perpetual ordinance (Exod. 12:14).

Meditation: Later in this chapter of Exodus, the children ask the question, "What do you mean by this observance?" (Exod. 12:26). The parents are to answer that this Passover night is when God delivered them out of the hand of the Egyptians (see Exod. 12:12-13). This moment of deliverance, like the death and resurrection of Jesus Christ for the Christian, marks the center of Israelite life. The Hebrews are encouraged to eat the Passover meal with staff in hand and sandals on their feet so that they are ready for the journey (Exod. 12:11).

Life is not stationary; we celebrate on the run in anticipation of God's calling. In the context of an historical celebration, we tend to think the word *remembrance* simply means the recalling of dates, people, and circumstances. However, the Hebrew word for remember, *zakar*, is more about internalizing the past in such a way that all future generations will have the same experience as the first generation had when they left Egypt.

(See Deut. 26:5ff., where the reciters of the confession years after the event relate that they were also in bondage in Egypt.)

In this anniversary year, we as believers are encouraged to internalize our faith so that we may say with the same joy and same vigor as the first Christians, "Jesus Christ is Lord," and with the same zeal as our forebears, "For the Glory of God and Our Neighbor's Good." Having confessed all this, with staff in hand and sandals on our feet, we are ready for the next stage of our journey.

For the day: Remember the saving history of God in the life of God's people and in your own salvation. Internalize your faith in acts of compassion and joy in anticipation of God's new call.

Prayer: God, bring me to a life of devotion and action that grows out of my remembrance of your love and salvation.

Robert W. Neff

January 3

More Than Words

Reading: Luke 2:41-45

Now every year his parents went to Jerusalem for the festival of the Passover. And when he was twelve years old, they went up as usual for the festival (Luke 2:41-42).

Meditation: Hebrews planned celebrations in meticulous detail. Each feature contributed to atmosphere and each symbol conveyed meaning. The participation of all families was a high priority.

For Mary, Joseph, and Jesus, the trip to Jerusalem was approximately a seven-day journey. Imagine the culmination of that exciting pilgrimage: catching the first glimpse of the temple with gleaming, marble columns; joining the gathering throng of people and animals; sacrificing a lamb at the temple where priests dashed its blood against the altar; savoring the aroma of lamb roasted over an open fire; tasting unleavened bread and bitter herbs; explaining to children in each household the meaning of the ritualized meal; making personal the hope-filled story about miraculous liberation from Egyptian slavery.

How do families convey faith and hope to children? How does the church do the same? With words, yes, but creating memorable experiences excels. A gray-haired lady, fondly remembering the aroma of roast beef and homemade rolls baked for love feasts of her childhood, exclaims, "Ah, that fragrance! I think that is why I'm Brethren." Youth talking about times when they felt closest to God mention church camp, youth conference, and a workcamp among people of a different culture. Much of faith is felt before it is conceptualized.

Apparently Jesus' parents were willing to spend time and money to take long trips to commemorate sacred events, to join crowds in celebration, to greet relatives and longtime friends, to create pageantry, to prepare symbolic foods, to sing songs by candlelight, and to say prayers. They would have understood the adage: "Faith is caught not taught."

For the day: Enjoy the memory of high points of your recent celebration of Christmas. Will you take a pilgrimage this year?

Prayer: God of all generations, thank you for journeys and festivals that enrich relationships, enliven hope, enhance joy, and increase allegiance to you. Amen.

Guy E. Wampler, Jr.

January 4

About the Father's Business

Reading: Luke 2:46-50

He said to them, "Why were you searching for me? Did you not know that I must be in my Father's house?" (Luke 2:49).

Meditation: Here's the second trip to Jerusalem's temple in one chapter, and both times momentous things happen to Mary, Joseph, and Jesus. Upon discovering Jesus' absence, would Mary have interpreted the sudden jolt of fear that pierced her soul as the "sword" predicted by Simeon twelve years earlier? A mere pinprick compared to what is to come. Yet Jesus' unusual behavior and enigmatic words stir a troubling mix of anger, fear, and hope in Mary's heart: How could I have known where he would be these three nightmarish days? I should have known he was "in [his] Father's house," shouldn't I? I should have intuited he would be "about the Father's business." The boy's just twelve—been missing seventy-two hours. And he has the gall to act surprised at our desperation! Twelve going on twenty-four, it seems. Is his name going to his head? Do I treasure this? or trounce him?

We parents, ancient or modern, even when holding high and holy aspirations for our children, sometimes find it hard to give them over to their own sense of calling. It's hard to cut the apron strings. From his earliest days, Jesus ate, drank, and slept God. During the Passover, Jesus subsisted on the Holy, becoming so immersed in his heavenly Father that all other concerns drifted away. Where better to learn of God than in the temple where the greatest minds of Israel gathered? Would that all children had this kind of hunger! Would that all of us had more of this hunger ourselves, yearning to know the ways of God and the joy of his salvation.

For the day: Lose yourself in God today. Make a date to spend a full day with God sometime in the next three months. Go on retreat with others or alone. Pray, read, listen, and be silent.

Prayer: Lord, I too want to be about the Father's business. Teach me. Amen.

Daniel M. Petry

January 5

God Weaves the Pattern

Readings: Luke 2:51-52; 1 Samuel 2:26

And Jesus increased in wisdom and in years, and in divine and human favor (Luke 2:52).

Meditation: There are so many threads woven into a life between the ages of twelve and thirty. By inference we know some of the weavings that shaped those hidden years for Jesus. All the vivid metaphors and parables by which he later describes "the kingdom" emerge in the interactions he has with Mary and Joseph and in his observations of the world around him. A deep intimacy with God grew in him, mirrored no doubt in the patterns of prayer that were taught to him and in catching glimpses of his mother's "pondering."

Most likely dark threads were woven in, such as the experience of Joseph's death and the Roman occupation of the land. But what did it all mean? How was he to understand his divine calling? Luke remembers a text from the story of Samuel and gets glimpses for a moment of the divine pattern: "The child

Jesus grew. He became strong and wise, and God blessed him"
(CEV).

These early days of a new year provide time for us to search
for a pattern in the weavings of our own lives. Unexpected
happenings, unwelcome encounters, a medical crisis, blessings
we never counted on—all have produced threads both dark
and light, some disappearing quickly and others emerging in
random fashion. Perhaps we prefer to avoid the hard questions:
Am I more aware of God's presence in my life now than I was
a year ago? If it were a crime to be a Christian, would there be
enough evidence in my schedule or my checkbook to convict
me? Do I hear Jesus, now about his Father's business, saying,
"Come and follow me"?

Broken threads, twisted cords, blotches of color both dark
and light—that's what we see from the underside. Like any rug
or tapestry, one must turn it over to see the beautiful pattern
that emerges.

For the day: Trust that God will take the threads of your life
and weave them all into a pattern of his choosing. There is a
plan for you that far exceeds your imagination.

Prayer: God, grant me to see some sense of direction, some
pattern of growth and identity, that will lead me forward to be
the person that bears your image. Let Jesus stand at the center
of my life, giving me clarity about times to cherish and times
to put aside. Amen.

Dean M. Miller

♼

January 6

Praise the Lord!

Reading: Psalm 148:1-6

Praise him, sun and moon; praise him, all you shining stars!
(Ps. 148:3).

Meditation from our past: I like to study the planets, but I
like to study the sun better. The sun is broadcasting his
rays constantly and we would be surprised to know how
much coal it would take to furnish the Earth as much
heat as we get in 24 hours. . . .The sun is said to be the
center of our solar system and Jesus Christ is the center of
our religious system. . . . Jesus says himself, "I am the
Way, the Truth and the Life and no man cometh unto the
Father but by Me." He is the Truth, the vehicle of transportation and He is the Light, the motor power of transportation heavenward and He is the Highway, the King's
Highway of Holiness upon which nothing unclean is
allowed to travel and where no ravenous beast lurks by
the road-side and He said again, "I will draw all men
unto me, if I be lifted up, etc."

The attractive power of the sun is marvelous. Every
planet is trying to go straight on in a tense line but the
attractiveness of the sun draws it toward the sun and so
every planet makes a curved line which is the line of
beauty. We are inclined to heaven as the sparrows are to
flying upward. We are tending to the flesh toward hell,
but the attractiveness of Jesus Christ draws us to himself
and gives us the beautiful curve line of beauty in the path

of duty. So the beautiful system is exemplified in Jesus Christ. —*I. N. H. Beahm*

From a sermon entitled "The Sunrise," preached to celebrate the 50th anniversary of his ministry, typescript, July 26, 1931.

For the day: Stand beneath the sky by day or night and praise God for one thing that is revealed.

Prayer: With the sun, moon, and stars, I praise you, God of creation, around whom my life is meant to revolve. Amen.

⟋

January 7

Seek the Lord

Readings: Psalm 37:1-11; Matthew 11:28-30

Don't bother your head with the braggarts or wish you could succeed like the wicked. In no time they'll shrivel like grass clippings and wilt like cut flowers in the sun (Ps. 37:1, 2 The Message).

Meditation: Too often we tune in to the impulses of our age, to our surroundings. Envying our neighbor never, never satisfies. We are faced with a multitude of choices that multiply, serve our carnal nature, and result in anxiety and discontent. A consuming desire for wealth, popularity, and power brings strife, lawsuits, prison—and most tragically, impoverishment of spirit and neglect of our neighbor's good. Fun, excitement, over-indulgence merely call for more and more of the same.

First of all—and frequently—reflect upon the invitations of our Lord Jesus, which most certainly bring rest. Work, dependability, and service yield peace and contentment. With simplicity, singleness of purpose, recall that Jesus said, "Come to me, all you who labor and are heavy laden" (for we are laden with self-serving), "and I will give you rest." As we pray for God's will in our lives, we know he answers us. We certainly respond imperfectly to God's invitation. But, is there any more significant endeavor, greater challenge, unending opportunity, and deeper satisfaction than when our God grants us the peace that comes with seeking his face daily? This is what we are created to do! Praise him!

For the day: Take the "long view," always. Pause, look down the road ahead. Faith provides guidance and eager anticipation.

Prayer: Thank you, God, for revealing yourself in the face of Jesus and in his words. Remind us daily to renew our knowledge of you through your Word and regularly seek your refreshing presence. Amen.

Fred W. Benedict

January 8

Love Thy Neighbor as Thy Self

Readings: Leviticus 19:17-19; Romans 13:8-10; Luke 10:27

Thou shalt not avenge, nor bear any grudge against the children of thy people, but thou shalt love thy neighbour as thyself: I am the LORD (Lev. 19:18 KJV).

Meditation: A plain sweater, white canvas sneakers, a warm smile, and a simple song welcomed us every day to *Mr. Rogers' Neighborhood* and Fred Rogers became a PBS legend. Although Fred Rogers passed away in 2003, his work lives on because he did his best to be the kind of person that every child would want for a neighbor.

As a child I watched Mr. Rogers, and as a parent I watched it again. Over the years not much changed with the show; it was the same house, the same trolley to take you to a world of make believe, the same puppets (King Friday the 13th), and the same opening song. In every episode Mr. Rogers asked the same question in his song that not only children but adults as well love to hear: "Would you like to be my neighbor?"

For the day: Build a bridge and get over it! Jesus built bridges between the divergent people of his day. The church must do the same!

Prayer: In the name of Jesus, I make a fresh commitment to you to live in peace and harmony not only with the other brothers and sisters of the body of Christ, but also with my friends, associates, neighbors, and family. I will let go of all bitterness, resentment, envy, strife, and unkindness in any form. I ask for your forgiveness, knowing that I am cleansed from all unrighteousness through Jesus Christ. Likewise, I ask you to forgive all who have wronged or hurt me, as I forgive and release them. From this moment on, I promise to live in agreement, to walk in love, to seek peace, and to conduct myself in a manner that is pleasing to you. In Jesus' name. Amen.

Larry L. Brumfield

January 9

Love Your Enemies

Reading: Luke 6:27-28

. . . Do good to those who hate you (Luke 6:27).

Meditation: Love my enemy? I have enough trouble loving my friends. But who is my enemy? Could it be a neighbor? a family member? a person with whom I disagree about religious or social issues? I hear our political leaders advocate killing our enemies. But Jesus tells us not to kill them. He also tells us to love them. It is not that difficult to refrain from killing the person I detest, but do I also have to love that person? It helps to remember that I do not have to like everyone—just love them, treat them with respect.

We are to love our enemies because, even as we reject God, God loves us. In the Gospel there is hope for redemption for everyone. We must believe that the enemy can be transformed. Though we may see our enemies as people we cannot reason with, as people for whom there is no hope, we can love them by doing good to them, blessing them, and praying for them. That is rather specific.

Being spat upon, stoned, kicked, and punched by Israeli settlers during my work with Christian Peacemaker Teams in Hebron has tested my commitment to this teaching of Jesus. I have tried to respond in love and can say that some of the most exciting experiences of my life have involved enemy love: Israeli Jews visiting Palestinian Muslim families whose homes were demolished by the Israeli military; Muslims welcoming Jews and Christians into their homes; or Muslims, Jews, and Christians planting olive trees together.

"Love casts out fear." If I ask God to give me love for the people I do not like, my fear of them can be overcome. If I can acknowledge the pain my "enemy" has experienced, maybe I can love that person, for I also have experienced pain.

For the day: Whom does the world define as our enemies? Whom do you find difficult to love?

Prayer: God, I cannot love my enemy. I need your help. Please give me love for those people I do not like. I pray for their salvation. Amen.

Art Gish

♂

January 10

Absorb Injustice

Readings: Luke 6:29-30; Romans 12:9-21

If anyone strikes you on the cheek, offer the other also (Luke 6:29).

Meditation: In a world that values winning at all costs and saving face even when it hurts others, this teaching of Jesus may seem irrelevant and disconnected. Surely the words of a bumper sticker that I saw recently would more accurately reflect the world in which we live: "I don't get mad; I just get even."

And yet Jesus said to his disciples: "If someone slaps you in the face, stand there and take it" (Luke 6:29a *The Message*).

We want the world to be fair, so that we all will get what's coming to us, whether punishment for bad behavior or reward for being good. But Jesus said to give more than is deserved: "If someone grabs your shirt, gift-wrap your best coat and make a present of it" (6:29b *The Message*). Practice living the servant life, beyond the law's demand.

God calls us to absorb injustice in our world today, beyond fairness and overflowing with love and grace. The Apostle Paul told the Christians in Rome: "Do not repay anyone evil for evil, but take thought for what is noble in the sight of all" (Rom. 12:17). In other words, do not look for revenge, even if it is well deserved. Rather, trust more fully in God who invites us to overcome evil with good.

For the day: Live within God's Law of Love this day. Absorb injustice through that abounding love.

Prayer: Thanks be to God for love that moves us beyond getting even when life is not fair. Praise be to God for your grace.

May we trust in your love more fully as we seek to live as your faithful disciples, through Jesus Christ we pray. Amen.

Harriet Wenger Finney

January 11

Set the Standard

Reading: Luke 6:31

Do to others as you would have them do to you (Luke 6:31).

Meditation: Today's scripture reminds me of three images. First, I see myself as a young child being taught these words as the Golden Rule in Sunday school—simple in meaning but not always easy to do. Then, I recall a Bible study with people from a wide variety of cultures, customs, and languages. Imagine my surprise when in that setting the scripture suddenly became more complex. My understanding of the passage broadened as those around the table discussed the importance of being aware of other cultural expectations and norms before acting. Without this awareness we expect what we want to be normative for everyone else and we miss the depth of the scripture. The text becomes difficult in both its meaning and application.

The third vision untangles the complexity of the text as believers from many cultures and languages work together toward a deeper understanding. This is God's requirement for us—to strive for an intercultural world as a prelude for an intercultural heaven. This vision requires building relationships where we seek to understand each other as key to the kingdom of God. In this shift, we lose the certainty of our culture and become more involved in God's way.

For the day: Look for different cultures in the community where you live and ponder who from these communities might teach you about your faith. You might even ask!

Prayer: God, open my eyes that I might see, and open my ears that I might hear the words of your wisdom, which comes from the many voices and experiences of your children from around the world. Teach me to learn as you would teach. Amen.

Duane Grady

January 12

Expect Nothing in Return

Reading: Luke 6:34-38

[Jesus said], ". . . for the measure you give will be the measure you get back" (Luke 6:38b).

Meditation from our past: Once upon a time I seemed to be in an immense concourse of people, nothing but people as far as I could see. All seemed to be slowly pressing toward a certain point. Looking intently in the direction of the moving, I could discern a large scales erected. Men were continually being lifted into one side. Some would hold their side down; but many, many would go up into the air. They were weighed in the balances and found wanting. Then it dawned on me that we were in the last judgment, and that I too must be weighed. How would it go with me? I hardly knew. Sometimes I thought I might hold my side of the scales down, but then I doubted. They kept pressing closer and closer. Soon I would be weighed. My heart began to fail. Finally I was at the scales. I was placed in the balances. For an instant I

seemed to hold my own, then I could feel myself slowly but surely rising. "Weighed and found wanting." I was just being condemned, when the judge was halted by someone running in the distance, frantically waving his hand, and calling at the top of his voice. It was a boy who held something under his arm. On he came, pushing fiercely through the crowd as fast as he could. The judge waited. The boy forced himself under the scales. Taking what was under his arm, in both hands, he gave it a toss up into the scale in which I was standing. Down came the scale in balance. "Accepted," pronounced the judge. I looked down at my feet. There lay a loaf of bread. I recognized it as the loaf I had once given to a poor widow.
—*Israel Poulson, Sr.*

> From *"Visions of Israel Poulson,"* History of the Church of the Brethren of the Eastern District of Pennsylvania 1708-1915, *pp. 199-200.*

For the day: Make a list of the ministries supported by your congregation and by you personally.

Prayer: Open my eyes, God of gifts, to the needs around me. Amen.

♂

January 13

Trust in Him

Readings: Psalm 37:35-40; Isaiah 57:20; James 1:11

But the salvation of the righteous is of the LORD: he is their strength in the time of trouble. And the LORD shall help them, and deliver them: he shall deliver them from the wicked, and save them, because they trust in him (Ps. 37:39-40 KJV).

Meditation: Blessings of help, salvation, and deliverance are promised to those who walk uprightly, while destruction is promised to those who are transgressors of God's law. However, life doesn't always seem that simple for us. We observe wicked people who appear to be prospering, while at the same time those who we think are righteous seem to be facing all kinds of challenges and reverses. We need to recognize that God sees things from an eternal perspective, as did the psalmist in Psalm 37. God also has a different timetable than do we. While Satan's reward for those who follow him is always inevitable destruction, sometimes it takes a while for that to occur. In the meantime, life for the wicked can appear to be enticing. However, prosperity for the wicked is always temporary. Whatever happens or doesn't happen in this life, the Bible teaches that there is an afterlife for every human being. Heaven is promised to those who embrace the gospel message, while a place of torment is promised for those who reject God's offer of salvation through Jesus Christ. We can take comfort and hope from the promise that the Lord will help and deliver those who take refuge in him, even though we cannot possibly understand the circumstances around us.

For the day: We are liberated from having feelings of envy toward the wicked. Remember that God is in control, and he knows what is best for us, both for this life and for the next.

Prayer: Dear Father, help me to keep an eternal perspective as I go about my daily activities. Help me to walk in the path of the righteous and avoid the path of the wicked. In the name of Jesus, I pray. Amen.

Robert Lehigh

♫

January 14

Answered Prayer

Reading: Psalm 28:6-9

Blessed be the LORD, for he has heard the sound of my pleadings (Ps. 28:6).

Meditation from our past: Being a minister as well as
   physician, my business called me over considerable territory. In the spring of 1862 Southern soldiers came to my
   house searching for firearms, none of which I kept except
   a plantation rifle. This they took without pay. They came
   from time to time for three years and took my crops and
   horses. When the soldiers came for the last horse they
   rode up with threats and curses. Their language and manner impressed me that they came with intent to kill me.
   Part of the squad went to the field for the last horse and
   part remained with me under their charge. I just stepped
   inside the stable, stood with my hands upwards, and
   prayed to my heavenly Father, saying, "Dear Father, save
   me from these men. Have mercy upon them, and turn
   them from their evil course, and save thy servant."

   I never exercised stronger faith in prayer than at that
   time. It seemed as if I was speaking face to face with my
   blessed Lord. When I stepped out to the soldiers I felt
   that God had answered my prayer, for I could see the
   Satanic look going down out of their faces like the shadow of a cloud before the bright sunlight.

   The soldiers then said to me, "Mr. Wrightsman, can we
   get some bread?" "O yes," said I, "we are commanded to
   feed the hungry." I went at once to the kitchen and

requested my sisters to cut off a large slice of bread, and butter it for each of them. They did so and I took it out into the yard and handed a slice to each. They thanked me for the bread, bowed their heads, mounted their horses and rode away, taking my last horse with them, however. Feeling sure the Lord had saved my life, I felt happy, "thanked God and took courage." This occurred in the summer of 1863. . . . —*P. R. Wrightsman*

From The Brethren in the New Nation, *Roger E. Sappington, comp. and ed. The Brethren Press, 1976, p. 388.*

For the day: When face to face with the enemies of life, trust God in all things.

Prayer: I pray, Lord, that I will see your eyes in my enemy's face. Amen.

January 15

Pray like Kingdom Come!

Reading: Luke 11:1-4

Your kingdom come (Luke 11:2b).

Meditation: In Luke, the kingdom of God is a future hope *and* a reality through the presence and ministry of Jesus. As Jesus told the seventy to say to the sick people that they cured, "The kingdom of God has come near to you" (Luke 10:9). At another time he told the Pharisees, "In fact, the kingdom of God is among you" (Luke 17:21).

When we pray the Lord's Prayer, do we really expect the kingdom to come? Do we ever wonder if the kingdom is already among us, as the body of Christ and members of his church?

If God answered our prayers and the kingdom arrived today, how would things change? Former U.S. President Jimmy Carter commented in *Our Endangered Values* that when we pray the Lord's Prayer, "We are asking for an end to political and economic injustice within worldly regimes." When we say the Lord's Prayer, we are praying for no one to go hungry, for everyone to forgive those who sin against them, for all debts to be forgiven, for no more trials or difficult times.

Are we praying for a time when the church's work to care for the poor and sick, visit the imprisoned, and mourn with the grieving is done—and all that's left to do is gather for worship? Or would such responsibilities really come to an end? Perhaps they would only increase as the tasks of loving and caring for each other become no longer burdensome but joyful—and we are empowered by God's crystal clear presence, no longer glimpsed "in a mirror, dimly" (1 Cor. 13:12).

What a world that would be—and already may be among us.

For the day: Ask what the rest of your day would be like if the kingdom of God arrived right now.

Prayer: Pray aloud the Lord's Prayer in its three versions: Matthew 6:9b-13; Luke 11:2b-4; and Mark 11:25.

Cheryl Brumbaugh-Cayford

♀

January 16

Inconvenient Friendship

Readings: Luke 11:5-8; Proverbs 3:28-29

Suppose one of you has a friend, and you go to him at midnight and say to him, "Friend, lend me three loaves of bread" (Luke 11:5).

Meditation: I have never met a person who likes to sit in traffic. I have never met a person who wishes for a long check-out line at the supermarket. I have never met a person who wishes they could spend just fifteen more minutes in the doctor's waiting room. I have never met a person who wishes to be anonymously inconvenienced. But if the traffic is the result of a first responder saving a life, and the long check-out line is due to a young mother purchasing provisions for her three young children, and waiting for the doctor is the result of the medical staff taking time to explain a diagnosis to another patient, then our inconvenience is lessened. Why? When we see that the reason for our inconvenience is a person, in Christ we extend the gift of friendship. Jesus calls those willing to follow him friends. Yes, he had a relationship with each of the disciples, and, yes, he probably had a personal and abiding friendship, but the friendship Jesus speaks of is a friendship that is also found in our relationship with God. As God is present, patient, and forgiving with us, so we are called to extend that grace to others, even when that other might be a perfect stranger.

For the day: Don't be quick to judge those who inconvenience you; rather, see every opportunity as a way of cultivating patience and extending grace. Who knows, the grace you show to a stranger may lead to a deep and abiding friendship.

Prayer: Gracious God, allow me to accept in friendship the people I see today. Let my words of welcome and farewell sing with an openness that speaks of your presence in my living. And may I live my days confident of your grace as I extend the circle of friendship to others. Amen.

Jeffrey W. Carter

ᒍ

January 17

Ask and Receive

Reading: Luke 11:9-12

So I say to you, "Ask, and it will be given you; search, and you will find; knock, and the door will be opened for you" (Luke 11:9).

Meditation: These verses are part of Jesus' instructions on how to pray. His words teach us to believe that God wants to provide for us. His words also tell us how to approach God—humbly. We are the ones who ask, search, knock on doors. We don't hold the answers. We can't even be absolutely sure we know what we are looking for, or that we are knocking on the right door. It's not our place to make demands, deliver ultimatum, or barge on through. The rightful spiritual attitude for prayer acknowledges that we don't already have the answers; we haven't yet found what we are looking for; we don't possess the key or the strength to open the door for ourselves. And what a blessing that is. We can go to God in prayer right now, as we are. Hallelujah! We don't have to wait until we've figured it all out. In fact, the more certain we are that we hold all the answers we need, the more we block ourselves from seeing what God has next for us. We walk the faith journey with our questions and the reassurance that God blesses our search.

For the day: Live in patience, persistence, and humility. Take your courage from God's faithfulness. Give thanks that you don't have to rely on your own ability to find answers. Practice trusting that God will provide.

Prayer: Gracious God, grant me wisdom to seek you in all I do—to rely on you rather than on myself. Teach me to boldly

ask, persistently search, and firmly knock. And sustain me
when I don't immediately understand your response. Amen.

Audrey Osborne Mazur

♫

January 18

Persistence in Prayer

Readings: Luke 18:1-17; Philippians 4:6-7

*Shall God not avenge His own elect who cry out day and night to
Him, though He bears long with them? I tell you that He will
avenge them speedily. Nevertheless, when the Son of Man comes,
will He really find faith on the earth? (Luke 18:7-8 NKJV).*

Meditation: Thankfully our God isn't like the judge who was
unjust. The only reason the judge dealt with the widow's
request was to relieve himself of her constant requests. He was
not interested in her. Our God hears our prayers and answers
them because we belong to him. He compassionately treats us
like a destitute widow, because we live in a world that is hostile
to him and to us, his children. He promises to avenge us in all
of our needs. So let us come boldly to his throne of grace so
that we can obtain mercy and find grace to help us in the time
of our need.

Many ask why bother to pray at all when God already knows
everything, including our needs? The answer is simple—
because he told us to. Although we never inform God of something that he doesn't eternally know, our prayers often have a
great personal effect. Our faith is encouraged when we talk to
God. And when God answers us—Wow! We have the peace of
God that passes all understanding. Being persistent in our
prayer life will increase our faith and get us through many a
difficult day.

For the day: If Jesus died for you and placed you into his eternal family, then he certainly wants to hear your requests and answer them as well. Keep your prayer life in pristine condition—talk to your heavenly Father often!

Prayer: Father in heaven, lead me in your truth, and teach me, for you are the God of my salvation. Have mercy upon me, O God, according to your loving-kindness, and deliver me out of all my afflictions.

John E. Bryant

$\mathcal{D}$

January 19

On the Loose

Readings: Luke 11:13; Acts 2:1-4

All of them were filled with the Holy Spirit and began to speak in other languages, as the Spirit gave them ability (Acts 2:4).

Meditation: My best friend at the Brethren college I attended was a "charismatic"; he came from a Pentecostal congregation where speaking in tongues was a regular feature of worship. We kidded him about it; he returned the favor by poking fun at the itinerant Brethren preacher who visited Brethren colleges during that era, standing in the courtyard preaching against the Vietnam War. Both expressions of faith came off as a bit "weird" in their own way.

The first Pentecost caused a bit of a stir as well. Bystanders wondered if the Christians had been hitting the bottle—even at this early hour of the day. Turns out the Holy Spirit had been poured out on them in a way that couldn't be contained—not even by one's known language. Barriers toppled as people from all over the Mediterranean suddenly could hear their own tongue being spoken by these locals. Coupled with the astoundingly inclusive love of the Christ-community, these cascading words led to a cascade of new believers, as people were drawn to this amazing community of word and deed.

To be honest, this scares me a bit, this idea of the Spirit being loosed. With this lack of containment comes lack of control, lack of manageable results, lack of being able to anticipate what and where and how and whom God may strike next.

But we contain at a price: If left to its own designs, the Holy Spirit can do for the church today what it did for the early church—loose its tongue and bring it notice. I guess I think both my friend and the itinerant preacher were allowing the Spirit to "be loosed" in their lives, releasing them to praise and preach without inhibition—and garnering some attention in the process.

For the day: Where does the Spirit need to "run loose" in your life and in the life of your congregation?

Prayer: Melt me, mold me, fill me . . . use me.

David R. Radcliff

℘

January 20

Be Thankful

Reading: Psalm 138:1-3

I give you thanks, O LORD, with my whole heart . . . (Ps. 138:1).

Meditation from our past: It has been my experience, Brethren, and I think I have heard some of you say the same, that prosperity does not always make people most truly thankful. Great success in business is apt to foster a feeling of independence. Men may forget God. It was in the days of Israel's prosperity in the goodly land of Goshen in Egypt that they forgot the name of the God of their fathers. When God appeared to Moses in Horeb, he had to tell him from out of the burning bush what his name was, and also by what name he should make him to be known to his brethren in Egypt. Some of the deepest heartfelt expressions of gratitude break forth in times of misfortune. A brother once told me that he was away from home when his barn was struck with lightning and burned to the ground. At his return he beheld nothing but the smoking destruction of his gathered harvest. But when his children came running to meet him, and he saw them all safe, and their mother standing in the door unharmed, he burst into an expression of thanksgiving, which, he confessed to me, surpassed every other emotion of joy he had ever felt. Our best experiences come to us when we are made to realize properly the good that is still left us. —*John Kline*

From Life and Labors of Elder John Kline, *collated by Benjamin Funk. Brethren Publishing House, 1900, pp. 459-460.*

For the day: Make a list of things you are thankful for.

Prayer: God, may I never forget you in good times so that I do not need to rediscover you when things go bad. Amen.

♂

January 21

The Value of Trust

Reading: Psalm 31:1-5

I run to you, GOD; I run for dear life. Don't let me down! . . .
I've put my life in your hands (Ps. 31:1, 5a The Message).

Meditation: As I read and meditated on these few verses, a
vivid image came to mind—that of a young child grasping a
parent's hand as they cross the street at a busy intersection. The
child feels protected, cared for, and safe, with complete trust in
the parent—a trust has been built up over a brief lifetime of
repeated experiences of being held in the parent's arms or holding onto the parent's hand in similar situations. This bond of
trust between the parent and child allows the child to have
confidence that in any given situation it will be protected.

God's chosen people experienced many difficult times, but
in the end God rescued and provided a place of safety and
trust. Since the Lord has consistently provided and protected
before, the psalmist knows without a doubt that God is near
and his hands will provide protection again.

Trust comes through a close relationship with the Lord. To
build that trust takes time and energy. It comes through our
daily time spent alone with God in prayer and meditation.

For the day: Live today into the trust and care God provides,
knowing that God provides for our every need.

Prayer: God of love, hope, and faith, may we be as trusting as
a child this day. May the sunshine of your grace surround and
bless us each moment as we seek to serve you in all aspects of
our daily living. "Into your hands I commit my spirit." Amen.

Ronald D. Beachley

January 22

Flight of Fancy

Reading: Luke 12:22-24, 31

For life is more than food, and the body more than clothing. Consider the ravens; they neither sow nor reap . . . yet God feeds them. . . . Strive for God's kingdom, and these things will be given to you as well (Luke 12:23-24, 31).

Meditation: Sure seems like a bird-brained idea—especially if we take it to mean any one of us can expect to have all our material needs met by just seeking God's kingdom. Koinonia Farms founder, Clarence Jordan, saw this passage in a different light. Jordan was ahead of his time as a proponent of racial equality in the South and was a biblical scholar who wrote the Cotton Patch New Testament—putting the gospel into the vernacular of the rural South. Regarding this text, Jordan noted that birds trying to live under water won't last long, nor will lilies that take up residence on the pavement. Both need to be within their context—the skies and the fields—to prosper. Same with us, according to Jordan. When we begin to live within the kingdom—sharing, caring, focused on relationships rather than resources—then (and only then) will the people of the world have a chance to have their needs supplied by their Maker. It reminds me of an outing with our Gwich'in friend Danny up in Arctic Village, Alaska. Our Sunday walk along a mountain ridge turned into a caribou hunt when several animals were spotted. He eventually bagged five—just the number a family like his would need for the winter. But the next day in the village, along with bringing him congratulations, his neighbors all took home a piece of meat. What a contrast to a society where the mantra of me/more/now seems to reign, shortchanging our neighbors and God's earth as well, as we take much more than our fair share. What a blessing to all when we together begin to live within our intended context— the sharing, justice-seeking community of God's people. On that day all God's children will soar!

For the day: Try living out a new mantra: us/enough/tomorrow.

Prayer: God of all creation, I want to align myself with your purposes for this earth and its people. Open my eyes and my heart to find the way. Through Jesus our leader and Lord, Amen.

David R. Radcliff

January 23

Worry Won't Help!

Reading: Luke 12:25-26

And can any of you by worrying add a single hour to your span of life? (Luke 12:25).

Meditation: Take a moment to imagine for yourself a life free of worry. What would it look like? How would it be different from the life you have? Just picturing a worry-free life makes my shoulders release and my breathing ease. Can you feel the muscles in your face relax?

A life without worry. That's the life God wants for us! Sometimes we convince ourselves that we need to worry—that somehow if we don't devote ourselves to worrying our jobs won't work out, our kids won't be safe, we won't stay healthy. And isn't that what worry really is—an attempt to control what we can't control? When there's nothing else we can do to prevent something terrible from happening, the brain tries its best to take control—through the only tool it has left—worry!

Worry is one more way we stand in God's way. One more way we hang on to control instead of turning our lives over to God's care. God is trying to show us life as it can be. In the face of the unknown and the uncontrollable, we can be empowered through prayer to live outrageously faithful lives—focused outwardly on service instead of inwardly on worry.

For the day: Breathe deeply. Counter worry with prayer. Take charge of those responsibilities that are truly yours to control. Then fill out the rest of the spaces in your day with God's freedom, joy, and grace.

Prayer: Gracious God, I surrender my worry to you. Help me let go of the uncontrollable mysteries that I try so hard to control. Grant me the courage to place my trust in you. Amen.

Audrey Osborne Mazur

January 24

Clothed by God

Reading: Luke 12:27-28

Consider the lilies, how they grow: they neither toil nor spin; yet I tell you, even Solomon in all his glory was not clothed like one of these (Luke 12:27).

Meditation from our past: Sometimes in gardens, I meet the improved, unknown plants, and their very perfumed blossoms. But neither do we meet as strangers,—rather as kindred spirits meet to love, we scarcely need an introduction. Bowing their heads in the gentle air, yielding their sweet odours to my lungs, which naturally expand to receive them, they say to my heart, "we are sent to be your humble servants." I reply, ye all are mine, (mine to enjoy if not to possess,) "My Father made them all."

They tell us, Sister, "there is language in flowers." Be it so. The Scientific never spake more true,—though many natural Philosophers, like a child, read their book backwards, (left handed) and think in nature to find out nature's God,—and in the event, turn 'round not only dumb, but also blind. While the "New born babe," nourished by Revelation, the word of God,—at home in the "Church of God," and abroad leaning on the arm of Almighty power, sees above, around, beneath, a present God, whose voice is everywhere. How consistent the question I once heard a pious man put to a modest young student of Botany: "Do you see Jesus in that flower?" To see the Maker in the thing made, is God's law. For that, the gospel is preached unto us.

. . . Well . . . if my imperfect offering does not much please thee, with thy abler judgment and finer taste, just pleasantly hand it over to some unknowing little one, it may take the withering leaf, and lay it in its Reader to mark some favorite sentence; perhaps where Jesus says, "See ye the Lillies,"—or, "Except ye be converted and become as little children, ye shall in no wise enter into the kingdom of Heaven." —*Attrib. to Sarah Righter Major*

From The Gospel Visitor, *1858, pp. 201-202.*

For the day: Spend some time with a seed catalog, if you have one, and draw a picture of flowers you'd like to see blossom in the spring.

Prayer: God of the garden, even while mine sleeps, I pray that you will preserve and then kindle new life within the deep earth and our hidden hearts. Amen.

&

January 25

God Knows Your Needs

Reading: Luke 12:29-31

Do not keep striving for what you are to eat and what you are to drink, and do not keep worrying . . . your Father knows that you need them (Luke 12:29-30).

Meditation: When my fiancé and I were beginning to think about pooling our financial resources, tension suddenly skyrocketed in our relationship. In particular, the grocery store became a battleground. What can we afford? What is luxury? Instead of rejoicing in our God-given partnership and riches (which are spiritually, if not monetarily, abundant), we joined the ranks of the nations of the world. Instead of focusing on building our spiritual friendship through cooperation, celebration, and creative thinking, we worried. We fought. We thought it was up to us alone to figure everything out. I confess I thought controlling the budget would keep us safe and happy. For awhile, we lost sight of the Love at the center. We forgot our Brethren upbringing to be "in the world but not of it."

Yes, we all go to work, and we buy groceries and prepare food. Without these activities we cannot survive, but they are not the purpose of our lives. When we strive for God's kingdom, when we cultivate loving relationships and practice forgiveness, generosity, and creativity, not only the kingdom comes to us but also our food and drink. Even the rent and the gas money. Jesus reminds us that the Creator *knows* our needs (and probably even knows we like good salsa). Our loving God gives to us abundantly. When our hearts are trained on love, not worry, we can savor the grocery store, the hot stove, and even the dishes as sacred revealers of God's grace and providence.

For the day: God knows what you need. Not just your spiritual needs, but your practical needs. You are not alone. What would be different if you really believed this?

Prayer: God of Life, thank you for your abundant love. Help me to remember to put my faith in you alone. Free me from anxiety that keeps me from loving you and others. In the name of Jesus who frees us, Amen.

Sarah Kinsel

January 26

True Riches

Reading: Luke 12:32-34

For where your treasure is, there your heart will be also (Luke 12:34).

Meditation: When I was younger, I had a metal bank that rang up money I put into it like a cash register. I loved hearing the little bell when I added coins to it. The only downside to the bank was that once the opening was closed, I couldn't open it again until I had accumulated ten dollars. Looking back, I'm not sure if it physically wouldn't open, or if the restriction had been placed by my parents. Either way, I worked hard to save my money to reach the ten-dollar goal. It taught me financial responsibility, but it couldn't offer much for lasting security. In fact, the bank was stolen one night when thieves broke into our home.

Years later, I spent a year in Brethren Volunteer Service, coordinating junior and senior high youth workcamps. Participants voluntarily gave up money they earned through fundraisers or took from personal savings to offer a week of their lives in service. From a financial perspective, they lost money and time. From a faith perspective, the experiences they had as they grew in faithful relationship to God were priceless. Over the course of the year, I saw youth come alive in their understanding and desire to follow Jesus. People willingly gave of their resources to help strangers, and almost always discovered they had received immeasurable blessings in return. These stories and moments of grace have touched my life in powerful ways. Children's smiles, tearful prayers, and renewed hope among those who felt abandoned are glimpses of how I envision the reign of God.

For the day: Money comes and goes, but the ways we give ourselves in Christian love always increase in value. Consider all those things in your life that are priceless.

Prayer: Giving God, thank you for your love for me. Help me to release my dependence on things that cannot last, so that I may be free to reach out to your children with the love of Christ. Amen.

Elizabeth L. Bidgood Enders

January 27

Hope in the Lord

Reading: Psalm 146:1-7

Praise the LORD O my soul! . . . Do not put your trust in princes, in mortals, in whom there is no help. . . . Happy are those whose help is the God of Jacob, whose hope is in the LORD their God (Ps. 146:1b, 3, 5).

Meditation: Psalms 146–150 form a unit, each beginning and ending with the call to "Praise the LORD." The Hebrew word is *Hallelujah*, meaning "Praise to Jehovah." The Hallelujah Psalms praise God as the creator and sustainer of life and extol God's concern for those who live in distress.

We are cautioned not to trust in human rulers (princes who cannot help), but to praise and trust the God of Jacob who is the real source of help. Political leaders, after all, are mortals whose bodies will return to the earth; their plans and promises will disappear with them. The truly happy are those whose hope is "in the LORD their God."

The Lord is called "the God of Jacob." If ever there was a man who was as crooked as a ram's horn, it was Jacob. Even his *name* (meaning *supplanter*) reveals his character. By the time God was finished with him, he was not only made a new man but he received a new name, "Israel," meaning *prince with God*. It is good to know that a stumbling, faltering individual like Jacob could still have *God so love him*, as to even be called "the God of Jacob." The Lord never excused Jacob's wrongdoing—but neither did God leave or neglect Jacob.

For the day: Live today with biblical hope—not a mere blind desire to have something happen, but a firm conviction that God's promises will indeed materialize! (see Rom. 15:13).

Prayer: Eternal God, preserve us from putting our trust in helpless human princes, for they soon die and their philosophies perish with them. Help us, instead, to sing praises to the God of Jacob, who has redeemed us by the blood of Christ and continues to provide for our daily needs.

Harold S. Martin

God Summons Us
to Respond

January 28–February 24

*F*inally, in the year 1708, eight persons agreed together to establish a covenant of good conscience with God, to accept all ordinances of Jesus as an easy yoke, and thus to follow after their Lord Jesus—their good and loyal shepherd—as true sheep in joy or sorrow until the blessed end. . . . These eight persons united with one another as brethren and sisters in the covenant of the cross of Jesus Christ as a church of Christian believers.

Alexander Mack, Jr. (1712–1803)

&

January 28

History Is the Best Teacher

Reading: Psalm 78:1-4

Open your ears to what I am saying, for I will show you lessons from our history (Ps. 78:1, 2 The Living Bible).

Meditation: Yuk, *history!* Everybody's least favorite subject! (Well, not quite everybody's.) History, said the writer James Joyce, is a nightmare. But to Cervantes, history was a sacred thing. It is the story of "how we got here." For people of faith, the history of the Bible is important. But so is everything that happened in Christian history since Bible times. For Brethren, the story of Alexander Mack is important. So is everything that has happened since 1708 in the Brethren movement.

For some people, joining the church is like getting into a waiting car and driving off, setting their own direction and speed. For others, it's probably more like getting on a moving train, already filled with passengers and moving along in a direction already determined. Some people may be unaware of the nature of the church they are joining and presume that the theology, polity, and program of the church are up to them. But for most, the church already has its theology, its polity and program, its history.

Through the ages, Christians have faced many forks in the road. The signposts I have chosen to follow begin with the voice from the cloud that said to the disciples, "This is my Son, my Chosen; listen to him!" (Luke 9:35). In 1708 Alexander Mack posted another sign when he wrote, "If we then begin in the footsteps of the Lord Jesus to live according to His commandment, then we can also hold communion together."

These and many other signs mark the direction of the train I am riding.

For the day: What signposts have marked your path as you have followed in the footsteps of Jesus?

Prayer: God of love, grant me wisdom to know when I am following Jesus and not something else, and grant me courage to take these steps no matter what happens. Amen.

William R. Eberly

January 29

Delivering the Message

Reading: Luke 9:1-10

He said to them: "Take nothing for your journey, no staff, nor bag, nor bread, nor money—not even an extra tunic. Whatever house you enter, stay there, and leave from there" (Luke 9:3-4).

Meditation: Take nothing—you and your words are enough. As Jesus gathers the disciples together and sends them forth, he makes it clear that it's the message that is urgent. Mode of transportation, personal belongings, and lodging are not important. Delivering the message *everywhere* is of the essence, and we, as disciples, are the ministers. We are enough. The message is in us—in our life, our voice, our actions. The truth of God's love is not one that requires accessories. In Jesus' time such items may have been staff, bag, bread, money, and tunic, but today we might consider personal digital assistants, cell phones, luggage, and credit cards parallel impediments. Making the kingdom of God known to all peoples does not require a PowerPoint presentation! It simply requires dedication to sharing the hope, love, and peace that comes from a relationship with God. We need no great wealth, for God assures us that our needs will be met. As followers of Jesus, we are called to a more simple life. We are called to follow Jesus' example. We are vessels of God's love, participants in the kingdom of God.

For the day: Take a break from your cell phone. Leave the extra baggage behind. Live in the generosity provided; do not search for more extravagant or entertaining ways of living. As a disciple you are commissioned to live the message of God's love everywhere you go, in everything you do.

Prayer: O God, fill our hearts, our minds, and our lives with your love. Guide us to a life of fulfillment—a life free of unnecessary baggage, a life through which your love shines throughout the whole world. Help us grow in our dedication to your message. Amen.

Amy R. Rhodes

January 30

Called—But Not Alone

Reading: Luke 10:1-3

Go on your way. See, I am sending you out like lambs into the midst of wolves (Luke 10:3).

Meditation: Have you ever noticed that the last thing you read or hear is usually the one thing you remember? Take this text, for example. The last sentence is "I am sending you out like lambs into the midst of wolves." What is your impression? What if you stopped at ". . . like lambs"? Or what if you stopped after "I am sending you . . ."? Or what if the last words were "I am," after reading the first two verses? Jesus is commissioning new disciples to go forth. It is not just about sending them out in the midst of wolves. It is about Jesus sending them, reminding them that they are not alone. He is also reminding them to remain in prayer, asking the Lord of the harvest to lead them. Do you sometimes feel that you are going into the day "into the midst of wolves"? Remember that Jesus does not send us out alone. "I AM" is sending us and guiding us.

For the day: God calls us forth to serve him, but not alone. We go in community (in pairs) with his blessing (I am sending you). We are to always be in prayer for his guidance (ask the Lord). Go forth and serve the Lord!

Prayer: God of the harvest, open me to you in this day, that I may hear your call to serve you more fully. Keep me focused on your will. I give you thanks for the body of believers that you have placed in my life to journey with me along the way. Lead us to share your saving love and grace. Amen.

Martha E. Beahm

January 31

Travel Lightly in Peace

Reading: Luke 10:4-7

Carry no purse, no bag, no sandals; and greet no one on the road. Whatever house you enter, first say, "Peace to this house!" (Luke 10:4-5).

Meditation: Jesus wasn't just trying to impart knowledge to his disciples (his students). Jesus wasn't just trying to get them to believe in a system that would legitimize them as experts of religious understanding. Jesus was trying to walk his disciples into a full aliveness—into a peace they so embodied that it would spill over onto anyone they touched.

In this passage of scripture, Jesus sends seventy of his students out into the world almost empty-handed. This is part of his teaching method; this is their practicum, their fieldwork, the teaching they have received put into raw application. They are sent without purse, or bag, or sandals. They are not to hop from place to place seeking the most favorable accommodations. They are not to whine.

The students of Jesus are sent to be "out there," where they will be vulnerable, exposed, without worldly resources, power or prestige. Jesus is trying to help them discover the source of real and lasting power, and it can only be found by walking away from illusionary power. The seventy will be forced to face their fears, their weaknesses, their dependencies, their empty religiosity, their demons. They have allowed themselves to be put in a position where they will be forced to depend on the power of God. They will embody peace or be broken.

When the seventy return, the first observable by-product of all this vulnerability will be their joy (Luke 10:17). Such joy is difficult to find within the self-protected sanctuaries of our insulated North American lives. Are we beginning to understand that a barrier to the peace we so long for is built from the weight of all we carry with us?

For the day: Clean out a closet in your home. Give away or throw away anything you have not used in one year. Pray for discernment in determining anything that you carry in your life that binds you.

Prayer: Holy God, help me not to be afraid. Strengthen me to let go of all that I so fear losing. For "fear of loss is the path to the dark side" (Yoda).

Paul E. Grout

February 1

Proclaim God's Kingdom

Reading: Luke 10:8-12

Did you have any idea that God's kingdom was right on your doorstep? Sodom will have it better on Judgment Day than the town that rejects you (Luke 10:11b-12 The Message).

Meditation: I'm glad this is a written devotional rather than a command visit, because the text is uncompromising. It reminds me of those who have knocked on my door with an evangelistic agenda that I didn't want to hear. Imagine knocking on a door and greeting whoever answers with these words: "God's kingdom is right on your doorstep!" Then, if the receiver doesn't respond, you walk away mumbling "in your face," while wiping the dust from your feet. How aggressive, self-righteous, unbending!

Yet there is an important reality in this passage. We, as Christians, have a mission: to proclaim God's love, to show God's love, and to act out God's love. The difficulty lies in the complexity of today's multi-cultural, multi-religious world. Sometimes we may need to approach the door and other times open the door—to listen to others' faith stances and enter into dialogue with them without presuming that we have all the answers. As a follower of Jesus, we may best show his love by feeding the hungry in our communities; by helping a poor child to read; by visiting and writing encouraging notes to those in prison, hospitals, and nursing homes; by welcoming the rejected into our churches; by being patient with the new cashier at the local store; by becoming friends with those whose faith and culture are unfamiliar to us; by forgiving and negotiating with our enemies, instead of killing them. We are called to proclaim God's love boldly, with clarity, commitment, and courage, even if we are rejected. Nobody, especially Jesus, said it would be easy.

For the day: How are you called today to proclaim the gospel message of God's love?

Prayer: God, wake us up! Shake us up! Remind us that we're called to proclaim and practice the gospel in bold and daring ways. Give us courage to do it lovingly. Amen.

Nancy R. Faus-Mullen

February 2

Top Priority

Reading: Luke 10:17-20

Nevertheless, do not rejoice at this, that the spirits submit to you, but rejoice that your names are written in heaven (Luke 10:20).

Meditation: So what's on your agenda for today? You may have a list so long that you don't want to even think about it at this moment, or perhaps you're not quite sure what you will do this day. Whatever and wherever you find yourself, you do know that it's now 2008. Most of us know that this is a significant anniversary year. We could probably name some of the amazing things that the faithful have accomplished in these three hundred years since eight brave souls were baptized in the Eder River. On such occasions it's tempting to name what has occurred in the past and to recall all the things in which we have been involved. On a more personal level, it's not unusual to be asked to "prove ourselves" or to recall what we have done to deserve our current status. And when we come back from a journey or an assignment, we are expected to "report" all that happened.

In this text, when the seventy returned, they were amazed to report that even the demons submitted to them. Eugene Peterson translates the response from Jesus best for me when he writes in *The Message*, "It's not what you do for God [that's amazing] but what God does for you—that's the agenda for rejoicing." So make rejoicing the top priority on your agenda today. As a disciple of Christ, as one who desires to serve and follow, you have been chosen and loved beyond comprehension, and your name is written in heaven.

For the day: Live today with a sense of amazement as you recall the desire God has for you to know that you are loved.

Prayer: Amazing God, remind us again and again that we are chosen and called to be disciples. In all that you call us to do, may we be open to realizing the various ways in which you equip us for the work before us. Through the journey, indeed, we are blessed. Amen.

Christy L. Dowdy

☙

February 3

See God's Work

Reading: Psalm 66:1-7

Come and see what God has done: he is awesome in his deeds among mortals. He turned the sea into dry land; they passed through the river on foot. There we rejoiced in him (Ps. 66:5-6).

Meditation: "There we rejoiced in him," says the psalmist. After crossing the Red Sea to escape Pharaoh's army, the Israelites gave thanks for their deliverance. When an unexpected miracle of God's providential protection occurs, we rejoice. But what of the daily miracles? When the sun rises full and warm in the morning, when a relationship threatened by conflict is restored, when a congregation chooses the hard road of faithful obedience—are these not also signs of God's awesome deeds?

When we recognize these as the work of God, we are moved not only to give praise and thanksgiving, but to realize that we have not come to the place where we are by our own strength or wisdom but by God's help. Even the nations are under God's watchful eye, lest they exalt themselves. In a world of arrogant nations armed with devastating weapons, this knowledge can be deeply comforting.

As God's people, we can rest confidently—and humbly—in the assurance of God's steadfast love. This does not mean that God will attend to our every need or protect us from every danger. It does mean that God cares for us—all of us—and will never abandon us.

For the day: Look around you for the daily miracles. Watch for signs of God's mighty work in your life and the lives of those near you. Give thanks.

Prayer: Thank you, God, for creating, sustaining, and renewing our lives as your people. Thank you for lovingly protecting me and those dear to me. I want to serve you and be part of your redeeming work in the world. Amen.

Bob Gross

$\mathcal{O}$

February 4

My Soul Is Satisfied

Readings: Psalm 63:1-6; Matthew 11:25-30

O God, you are my God, earnestly I seek you; my soul thirsts for you; my body longs for you, in a dry and weary land where there is no water (Ps. 63:1 NIV).

Meditation: The ancient preface to this psalm indicates that it was written by David when he was in the wilderness of Judah. It is, indeed, "a dry and weary land where there is no water." However, David is not writing about the wilderness and its lack of water. He is writing about his desperate need for God. He finds no satisfaction for his soul in the world around him, so he lifts his eyes toward God. He remembers what he saw in the sanctuary, the "tent of meeting" where Israelites gathered to worship. He saw the power and glory of God, and more. He saw God's love. The sight causes David to seek the Lord with all his heart. Thirsting and longing, praising and singing, his soul is satisfied—even when he lies awake all night because of trouble.

My mother has a satisfied soul. As she approached her ninetieth birthday, I asked her to tell me the source of her endurance. At age thirteen, she was forced to drop out of school and go to work. At age forty-three, her husband (my father) died and left her with three young children yet at home. Her youngest child became addicted to drugs and alcohol. Her second marriage dissolved because of abuse.

"What kept you going?" I asked.

She replied, "I have hope. My hope is in the Lord."

For the day: Whatever the burden of the day, remember that the God of all the earth deeply loves and cares for you. He is calling you. Take his hand today.

Prayer: Father in heaven, thank you for sending Jesus to be the atoning sacrifice for my sin. I confess that without him my soul will never be at rest. Fill me with his presence today. Love others through me. Amen.

Jerry Young

February 5

A Day of Radical Moderation

Reading: Luke 3:7-14

Whoever has two coats must share with anyone who has none; and whoever has food must do likewise (Luke 3:11).

Meditation: Fat Tuesday—*Mardi Gras*—might just be the least Brethren day of the year, when many people celebrate the freedom to do whatever they want before the traditional fasting of Lent begins. It's a day of radical immoderation.

In contrast, John the Baptist proclaims an agenda of charity, community, and integrity—a proclamation that is *radical* only in its *moderation*! In Luke 3:7-14, John's message is radical in its orientation toward God and its call to repentance, but John's ethical teachings are really quite moderate. When asked, "What then should we do?" John answers with commands that are remarkable in their ordinariness: If you have extra food or clothing and someone else has none, share! Furthermore, do your job fairly; don't cheat, extort, or threaten. These rules for behavior are about as simple as they come. The fact that they even had to be said is a sad testimony to the sinfulness of John's generation.

Today, the Baptist calls us to nothing less than the ideal Anabaptist lifestyle—a life of *radical moderation* where God's love is shared through the measured generosity of a simple, honest, charitable community. If you hear his words and follow them, this Fat Tuesday could be the most Brethren day of the year.

For the day: How can you bear the fruits of repentance today by committing acts of radical moderation—sharing something simple, giving something away, or tidying up some less-than-perfectly-honest part of your life?

Prayer: God of our ancestors, I recognize that just being part of your family is meaningless if I don't bear the fruits of repentance that you so deeply desire. I hear your prophet reminding me that you want me to radically turn from false freedom and totally embrace the path of honesty and virtue that leads to real freedom in you. I repent, loving God, and turn to you.

James W. Stokes-Buckles

February 6—Ash Wednesday 2008

Repent and Believe!

Reading: Mark 1:14-15

"The time has come," [Jesus] said. "The kingdom of God is near. Repent and believe the good news!" (Mark 1:15 NIV).

Meditation: Jesus came with a perplexing, yet simple, message: Through him the kingdom of God is available (that is "good news"), but repentance and belief are the basic requirements for entering that kingdom.

Sometimes I'm perplexed by Jesus' insistence that we believe. Of course, we believe! But do we? I wonder. Jesus often asked those closest to him, "Do you still have no faith?" And yet he was surprised when he observed faith. Remember his reaction to the Roman army commander in Luke 7:9? I often wonder if we *do* believe what Jesus said about worry, or forgiveness, or loving those who curse and hurt us, or commitment, or material possessions, or eternal judgment.

Perhaps that is why repentance is linked with belief. When we get close enough to observe and hear Jesus, it becomes very clear that he proposes a life that is radically counter to our culture and nature. If we believe him, change (repentance) is mandatory. As Eugene Peterson writes, "[Repentance] is always and everywhere the first word in the Christian life." The hardest thing to change is the way we think. That change, essential if not easy, inevitably leads to a changed lifestyle.

This is Ash Wednesday, a day of repentance. As I write this devotion, I am one week away from surgery that will remove a cancerous tumor. The cancer is very survivable, but without surgery it will kill me in five or six years. Sin and unbelief are survivable, but only when repentance enters the picture. In one week I will submit to the advice and scalpel of my surgeon. When will we submit to the call and command of Jesus? "Repent and believe . . ."

For the day: The kingdom of God is available. Repent, believe, and come on over.

Prayer: Lord Jesus, thank you for making God's kingdom available. On this day of repentance, reveal whatever is keeping us out.

James O. Hardenbrook

♡

Febrero 7

February 7 in Spanish

Arrepentíos o Pereceréis

Lectura: Lucas 13:1-5; 2 Corintios 7:10

Os digo: No; antes si no os arrepentís, todos pereceréis igualmente (Luc. 13:5).

Meditación: Ningún excelente orador repite una frase a su audiencia dos veces o más, a no ser para enfatizar una idea o clarificar un asunto importante. El más grande de todos los oradores sobre la tierra, nuestro Señor Jesucristo decidió repetir 11 palabras, citadas anteriormente, dos veces en el mismo discurso (Luc.13:3 y 5) ¿Con que propósito? ¿Para hablar del amor? ¿Para hablar de la fe? No, para hablar de la salvación de nuestras almas, para darnos la clave de cómo podemos verdaderamente ser trasladados del reino de las tinieblas al reino de la luz admirable y gozar de vida eterna.

Jesucristo dice: "...si no os arrepentís, todos igualmente pereceréis." Surge la pregunta, ¿Qué es arrepentimiento? Será sólo "dar la vuelta y cambiar de dirección" o significará algo más. Arrepentimiento es "sentir culpabilidad y reproche por nuestros pecados contra Dios; verse contrito, arrepentido, impelido al cambio." Hay una gran diferencia entre simplemente cambiar de opinión y verse urgentemente impulsado al cambio.

El apóstol Pablo dice: "Porque la tristeza que es según Dios produce arrepentimiento para salvación..., pero la tristeza del mundo produce muerte" (2 Cor. 7:10). Más adelante en Lucas 13:6-10, Jesucristo hablando en parábolas nos compara con un árbol de higuera que debe producir fruto. Buenos frutos es la señal de arrepentimiento lo cuál nos hace verdaderos hijos de Dios.

Para el día: Examinemos nuestros corazones, evaluemos las intenciones de nuestro corazón y si hay algo de lo cual debamos arrepentirnos hagámoslo sin demora. Dios está dispuesto a socorrernos.

Oración: Dios de gracia y misericordia, en este día decido renovar mi pacto contigo, arrepintiéndome sinceramente de todo pecado y pido que tu Espíritu Santo renueve mis fuerzas y me ayude a ser mejor hijo tuyo cada día. Amen.

Joel Peña

February 7

Repent or Perish

Readings: Luke 13:1-5; 2 Corinthians 7:10

I tell you, no! But unless you repent, you too will all perish (Luke 13:3, 5 NIV).

Meditation: A good speaker does not repeat a phrase two or more times unless he or she is trying to emphasize an idea or to clarify an important point. The greatest speaker ever, our Lord Jesus Christ, used these words twice in this speech. With what purpose? To talk about love? To discuss faith? No, to talk about our soul's salvation, giving us the key to how we can truly be transferred from the kingdom of darkness to the kingdom of light and the joy of eternal life.

Jesus Christ says, ". . . but unless you repent, you too will all perish." So the question is, What is repentance? Is it only to turn around and to change our course of direction? Or does it mean something more? To repent is "to feel guilt and reproach for our sins against God; to feel contrite, sorry, and compelled to change." There's a big difference between simply changing an attitude and feeling an urgent impulse to change our ways.

The Apostle Paul says, "Godly sorrow brings repentance that leads to salvation and leaves no regret, but worldly sorrow brings death" (2 Cor. 7:10 NIV). In Luke 13:6-10, Jesus talks in parables and compares us to the fig tree that should produce fruit. Good fruit is a sign of repentance, which, in turn, makes us true children of God.

For the day: Examine your heart and evaluate your heart's intentions. If there is something you need to repent, do so without hesitation. God is ready to help you.

Prayer: God of grace and mercy, in this day I choose to renew my covenant with you. I sincerely repent all my sins and ask your Holy Spirit to please renew my strength and help me to be a better child of yours every day. Amen.

Joel Peña

℘

February 8

Another Chance

Readings: Luke 13:6-9; Galatians 5:22-23

"Sir," the man replied, "leave it alone for one more year, and I'll dig around it and fertilize it" (Luke 13:8 NIV).

Meditation: The parable of the barren fig tree reminds me of an oddly shaped little peach tree that grew in the yard of my childhood home. It was just the right size for climbing and a wonderful subject for drawing, especially when it blossomed in spring. Unfortunately, it would never bear fruit. Even the few small peaches that took shape would fall to the ground before ripening. One day my father announced it was time to cut it down. How I pleaded for my favorite little tree; I promised to trim it, spray it, and take good care of it for one more year. And, yes, that next year it did bear fruit!

Both of these parabolic trees remind me of the resources it takes for the church to grow and share the good news of Christ's life-sustaining love for the world today. Generations of faithful believers have cared, pleaded, and provided the resources, so that the church might not just entertain us or hold a sentimental place in our hearts, but continue bearing the good fruits of faithful discipleship. The barren fig tree reminds me that the fruits of the church are still needed and attention must be given so those fruits can flourish. This is our chance to continue the fruitful life of the church as we recommit ourselves and our resources to bear love, joy, peace, patience, kindness, generosity, faithfulness, gentleness, and self-control.

For the day: Which of the fruits of the Spirit needs extra attention and nurture for your personal growth this year? What kind of loosening and fertilizing needs to take place in your congregation for new growth to appear?

Prayer: Life-giving One, thank you that the fruits of your Spirit have grown in the church and sustained each of us in barren times. Remind us why your church still lives, and give us the courage to be fruitful disciples. Amen.

Alice Martin-Adkins

☙

February 9

Converting Even the King

Reading: Acts 26:19-23

To this day I have had help from God, and so I stand here, testify-ing to both small and great (Acts 26:22a).

Meditation: Traveling around the Roman world, the Apostle Paul preached the gospel with vigor, sometimes arousing the anger of the crowds, and often escaping by the narrowest of margins. But late in the Book of Acts, Paul finds himself back in Jerusalem, and a false rumor is lodged against him. The angry crowd seizes him and then turns him over for trial.

In today's passage, Paul, who by now has been passed through various jurisdictions and appeared before several authorities, presents his case to King Agrippa. His declaration before the king is this: *I have told everyone—Jew and Gentile— that they need to repent, turn to God, and live a life true to God.* He goes on to tell Agrippa that this is why everyone is in an uproar. It's supposed to be a defense, but it isn't. What Paul is really trying to do is convert the king!

Shortly after this, Paul is sent to Rome, where he meets the end of his life. But for now, Paul keeps talking. He wants everyone he meets to have a new life. It doesn't matter who they are—enemy or friend, pauper or king, small or great. He wants every person to turn from their old life and embrace a new life in Christ. Such is Paul's love for everyone he meets— even a king who would send him to his death!

For the day: Our Christian love is evident when we desire the spiritual well being of everyone. Be aware today of how you show Christian love in *all* your encounters.

Prayer: Few of us, O God, are so focused on sharing the good news of Jesus Christ as Paul was, but we understand that your love is for all people. Help us to share that love with everyone we meet, that they might find encouragement to turn their lives toward you. We pray in Jesus' name. Amen.

Kurt R. Borgmann

February 10

Choose God's Way

Readings: Psalm 1:1-6; Joshua 24:15

How well God must like you—you don't hang out at Sin Saloon, you don't slink along Dead-End Road, you don't go to Smart-Mouth College. Instead you thrill to GOD's Word and chew on Scripture day and night (Ps. 1:1, 2 The Message).

Meditation: Recent devotionals have pointed out that people must always *choose* their way of life and that *choice* will have eternal consequences. Sometimes we get confused or frustrated because these consequences are not immediately apparent or fair (i.e., Why do bad things happen to good people?). Lack of immediate consequences lead many to conclude that there are no real paybacks for choosing "easy street." Over time these false conclusions can creep into churches.

The early Brethren, through Bible study and prayer, found that their churches had strayed from New Testament teachings. Believing that infant baptism was not a biblical ticket to heaven, the early Brethren found that their first choice was to accept Christ's gift and be baptized. This "new baptism" was illegal and had consequences (imprisonment, loss of property, loss of job). These early Brethren also concluded that a change in the heart of a real Christian would show up in their out-ward activities (not only talk the talk but also walk the walk). After more prayer and "chew[ing] on Scripture day and night," these early Brethren "counted the cost" and chose to be obedi-ent despite the consequences.

For the day: Has the doctrine of tolerance caused the church to believe that what's right for me may not be right for you? Is there really more than one choice that will get a person to heaven? Can we allow our friends and family (or ourselves) to choose to be disobedient to scripture and not expect conse-quences? Is there any biblical principle so important that you would choose to "count the cost" and risk your job, your prop-erty, or imprisonment so that this truth can be declared?

Prayer: Holy God, thank you for choosing to send your Son for my sins. As a thankful response, may I choose to be obedi-ent to *all* of your Word. May my "amen" be found in my obedience.

James E. Hollinger

⌀

February 11

Trustful Humility

Reading: Psalm 25:1-10

He leads the humble in what is right, and teaches the humble his way (Ps. 25:9).

Meditation: I can identify with this fellow. He's trying to be humble. According to the prophet Micah, walking humbly with God is to be desired. I want to be humble, but not a squashed tomato! Too often humility seems to mean underrat-

59

ing yourself. Even berating yourself. Rather than self-denigration, I think biblical humility identifies a proper relationship with God.

Biblical humility, actively pursued, is what we see expressed in Psalm 25. The relationship begins in trust. The psalmist sees clearly that his very being is intimately wrapped up with God. He offers his very soul to God. That is the foundation for all that follows. Importantly, his trusting affirmation is not simply pious devotionalism. He knows he is surrounded by "enemies." Some are his fellow countrymen, "wantonly treacherous"— those who, far from humble, are blatant in their abuse of their divinely given lives. Other enemies are internal—memories of his own transgressions, the sins of his youth. Such inner "enemies" can overwhelm faith as well. His prayer is for courage to resist the onslaught of those who care nothing for the Lord's way; he seeks divine forgiveness to free him from the weight of his own past. Sandwiched between his prayer for courage and for forgiveness, he expresses the longing of his devoted soul to be taught, to be led in God's true way.

To be open to God and to what God would teach us is at the heart of humility. It is comforting to know that God does lead and instruct those who are truly open to God in teachable humility. To be taught by a good and upright God leads to ways of love and faithfulness for those whose trust is in God.

For the day: Affirm your fundamental trust in God, but struggle to hear and ingest the truth of God in prayer, scripture, study, and conversation.

Prayer: Good and righteous Lord, keep me close to you that I might learn the truth that leads and the hope that encourages. Amen.

Robert Dell

⊘

February 12

The Brink of Healing

Reading: Luke 14:1-6

Jesus asked the lawyers and Pharisees, "Is it lawful to cure people on the sabbath, or not?" (Luke 14:3).

Meditation: Jesus may have chuckled at the proposition of dinner with the Pharisees, figuring the invitation to be one of those tokens of hospitality designed to fulfill the law of sociability while at the same time spying on the opposition. Jesus provides plenty for the hosts to ponder. Remember, it is Jesus who poses the baited question here! All were seated for dinner, when what to their wondering eyes should appear but a man swollen from the dreaded dropsy.

Sick folk were evidently a serious issue with Jesus, who held in his touch the power of mercy which brought relief and wholeness. Men with dropsy and women bent over for eighteen years and paralytics waiting at curative pools were all worthy of risking the detailed, sometimes ruthless legalities surrounding the sabbath. The Pharisees were unexpectedly silent; perhaps they knew hard words and stiff interpretation could easily betray the God of compassion, and yet they undoubtedly felt nervous about failing to make good defense for the law's technicalities, which they knew and practiced so well.

Their dilemma is our own. Those healed by Jesus were generally nobodies hanging on by the slimmest of hopes. That, however, was enough, for here was one willing to risk pushing law and lawgiver to the brink for the sake of healing and hope. People ahead of things, a new life ahead of the barrenness of tradition and customs.

For the day: How is it in your healing field?

Prayer: *Healer of our every ill, light of each tomorrow; give us peace beyond our fear and hope beyond our sorrow* (Marty Haugen). Amen.

Sandra L. Bosserman

⌀

February 13

Name and Rank

Reading: Luke 14:7-9

. . . the host who invited both of you may come and say to you, "Give this person your place," and then in disgrace you would start to take the lowest place (Luke 14:9).

Meditation: When it came to social ranking, the Pharisees were not the "highest of the high," but they were accustomed to some special perks of status. Among those was a place of distinction at special events. I'm not sure how we take this parable in the twenty-first century, especially among church folk. Nowhere do we have more trouble getting folks to move to the head of the line and the front of the building than at church! The back of the sanctuary is the "new front"—and how we do flock there in droves, where we can hide out in the shadows and leave should the service go too long or too intensely.

Maybe the question for us is where and what we assume to be our granted "spots"—where are we surprised and a little threatened to see someone else dare to place themselves in our worlds? How possessive are we of our positions in home and church home? Being too attached sets us up for "disgrace," says Jesus. Wear title and rank lightly, whether that of parent, preacher, or prelate. What is important is that we show up at the table, deliberately and purposefully, whether it is the family dinner table, the corner café where cronies gather, or the Lord's table at love feast.

A local teen's vehicle boasts a bumper sticker that reads: "Get in, sit down, shut up, and hold on." It serves as a reminder that the car is hers and passengers are the guests, for better or worse! She who issued the precarious invitation is in charge of the ride. There are times we need a similar regard for God's tables. We are guests, albeit the family variety, and any-where in the room, seated next to anyone at all, is close enough to the head of the table for us. All things are ready—come to the feast!

For the day: "You're blessed when you're content with just who you are—no more, no less. That's the moment you find yourselves proud owners of everything that can't be bought" (Matt. 5:5 *The Message*).

Prayer: God, keep us near your heart of humility. Amen.

Sandra L. Bosserman

February 14

A Friend in High Places

Reading: Luke 14:10-11

But when you are invited, go and sit down at the lowest place, so that when your host comes, he may say to you, "Friend, move up higher" (Luke 14:10a).

Meditation: Before our younger son was baptized, he was seat-ed with his dad at a small "overflow" table for love feast. He was "lively" through the time of instruction and confession, and utilized his "learner's permit" privileges during feetwashing. The meal proceeded, and he, who would never have touched bread softened with beef broth at home, ate with relish. The time for introducing the bread and cup proceeded and lasted longer than usual. Perhaps it was our prior conversation in which we had agreed that he would not participate in this part of the service; perhaps it was just exhaustion from being such an "active participant" to this point. At any rate, Kelly's eyes dragged and drooped until, with a mighty thud, his face landed in his not-quite-finished plate. Peers stifled laughter, elders smiled, and his father wiped the little face and pulled the boy against him. At such moments, no higher place exists than to be called to lean on Dad, the one who authorized that it was fitting and proper for Kelly to be present in the first place.

God is like that—no embarrassment demanded for falling asleep in holy settings, just a readjusting to lean when we recognize we cannot hold ourselves up. It's important to sit in a place near enough to God's presence to be summoned to God's side—a place where we can be called to lean or to leap in faith, assured by the trust we learned at the side of the God and Father of our Lord, Jesus Christ.

For the day: Consider today whether the rigors of life allow you to live near enough to God's presence to lean and to leap at God's call.

Prayer: Remind me, dear God, that the place nearest you is the highest place, even the cross of Jesus Christ. Amen.

Sandra L. Bosserman

ᓂ

February 15

Place Cards for All

Reading: Luke 14:12-14

But when you give a banquet, invite the poor, the crippled, the lame, and the blind. And you will be blessed . . . (Luke 14:13-14a).

Meditation: The last installment of the humbling lesson that revolves around food and tables is at hand. This time the table is turned. In earlier portions, Jesus asked, "Where will you sit?" Now the question is, "Who will you invite?"

Eating together had serious implications with the crowd Jesus addresses in Luke 14. It remains so among the households of God. And it's best not to simply swap two-martini lunches with those who scratch your back as you scratch theirs. A better choice is to seek those who "dwell in darkness and the shadow of death" and relocate them to the main table. Know them by name, and make place cards for those who have no place. Carry the crippled, crutch the lame, publish the bulletin in Braille for the unsighted and in bright color for the unsightly. And you will be blessed, as those cemented by hard knocks will soften a bit at the thought of their own name on the guest list, published for all to see.

Such hospitality is not a piece of cake. You will be asked to go out of your way, catering to beggars who shouldn't be choosers. Your pocketbook will be affected as elevators are installed to the sanctuary, and the family recipe will be broadened as you learn to cook both bold and bland, salt and no salt, sweet and sweetener. You will be expected to cater to whims and listen to whiners. You will need to wash little faces and big clumsy feet and give of yourself extraordinarily. But you will experience new freedom at every turn—and energy, purpose, and hope. And you will be renewed as the served turn the tables and reveal God's grace to you in a hundred life-giving ways, renewing strength and faith that God's table and your table are one and the same.

For the day: Open the table of your household—or your household of faith—to someone new.

Prayer: Lord, grant us the will to be your servants and the grace to allow ourselves to be served. Amen.

Sandra L. Bosserman

February 16

Heirs by Grace

Reading: Ephesians 3:1-10

. . . the Gentiles should be fellow heirs, of the same body, and partakers of His promise in Christ through the gospel (Eph. 3:6 NKJV).

Meditation: This scripture reads like a composition teacher's nightmare. Starts and stops, introductions in the middle, run-on sentences, and then a mystery tossed in for good measure. Paul wrote this letter from prison to the members of the very culturally and ethnically diverse church in Ephesus. During Paul's time the barriers between Jews and Gentiles were very rigid. Racially motivated contempt and exclusivism were predominant behaviors of the day. The Jews saw themselves as the group in relationship with God and rightful heirs to the boundless riches of Christ.

Paul's mystery is the heretofore unrevealed idea that all people, Jews and Gentiles alike, are co-heirs with Israel, members together as one body, with a right to share together the promise in Jesus Christ. Paul is clear that God chose to reveal this mystery to him. God gave him stewardship of sharing his uncovered mystery with the Gentiles. Bold, sometimes arrogant and oftentimes painfully blunt, Paul saw himself in the role of a servant whose commission it was to preach to the Gentiles and share the news of the gift of God's grace and compassion.

As God's heirs we have great privileges. God has broken down the barriers that once separated us and by grace reconciles us both with him and with each other. But like Paul we are also his servants charged with stewardship of sharing the good news of the gospel with all people around us.

For the day: As God's heir, you have a great mission before you. Your mission is possible because God is behind you. Be open to opportunities to share the good news today.

Prayer: God of Grace, we thank you for the great privileges you grant to us, your children and heirs. Give us the courage to be good and humble stewards of sharing your good news. Amen.

Asha Solanky

$\mathcal{D}$

February 17

Fear, Humility, and the Grace of God

Reading: 1 Peter 5:1-5

Clothe yourselves with humility in your dealings with one another . . . (1 Pet. 5:5).

Meditation: I am fortunate to work in a congregation that is very supportive and encouraging of its youth. And yet, I am still amazed by the divide that exists between the youth and the adults in the congregation. Both claim they do not know how to talk to the other. Each feels too young or too old to be valid in the other's eyes. And yet, when they open their hearts to each other, the grace of God is incredibly present.

It was the Friday after Thanksgiving. Ten youth, two advisors, and I loaded some plates with cookies and, with song sheets in hand, went to visit some elders of our congregation. Our first couple, who lived with the daily struggle of the husband's Alzheimer's disease, invited us in for some hot chocolate and conversation. They knew we were coming and relished the opportunity to get to know some of our youth better. I'll confess my fears. I was afraid that the older couple might not connect with the youth as they told stories of their lives. And I was afraid that the youth would get bored, not pay attention or, worse, be rude. But a beautiful thing happened. The couple shared stories of the husband's track career and the wife's interest in women of history. The youth engaged while we were there and asked questions after we left. Old and young alike expressed deep appreciation for the visit with each other and asked when we might be able to do it again. I was the one humbled by God's grace.

For the day: Open your heart to those who are different or in a different situation than you are. What do you have to learn from them? What do you have to share with them?

Prayer: Thank you, God, for the opportunity to be in relationship with all kinds of people. Remind me to clothe myself in humility and open my heart to your grace. Amen.

Melissa Bennett

February 18

The Omniscience of Our God

Readings: Psalm 139:1-6; Psalm 94:8-11

I look behind me and you're there, then up ahead and you're there, too—your reassuring presence, coming and going. This is too much, too wonderful—I can't take it all in! (Ps. 139:1-6 The Message).

Meditation: "O Lord, we are not here to inform you of *anything!*" is the way my late uncle Alton Bucher (a Church of the Brethren minister in Lebanon County, Pennsylvania) would begin many of his public prayers. Then he would always acknowledge the fact that God knows us better than we know ourselves. Uncle Alton's prayers undoubtedly were based on the attribute of God's omniscience. Psalm 139 is a key portion of scripture in helping us to understand the awesomeness of God's infinite awareness, insight, and understanding.

God knows every thought we think, he hears every word we utter and is aware of every deed we perform. There is no hiding from his awesome presence, since he was even privy to our formation in the dark concealment of the womb. "Such knowledge is too wonderful for me," declares the psalmist in verse 6, "too lofty for me to attain."

Sometimes, by design, we keep others at arm's length, not allowing them to get to know us. Perhaps we fear they may discover something about us they won't like—secret sins, a tainted past, covert behavior, whatever. However, God already knows everything about us, even the number of hairs on our heads (Matt. 10:30). But despite the ugliness of our sinful faults and failures, our all-knowing God still accepts and loves us unconditionally. *And that's awesome!*

For the day: Sinners attempt to hide *from* God, but believers hide *in* God! May you take comfort in knowing that God is always with you.

Prayer: All-knowing God, help me to be keenly aware of your infinite knowledge, insight, and understanding of me as a person. Keep me from believing that I can think, say, or do anything without your knowledge of it. In light of your omniscience, O Lord, may I live each day carefully and well. In your precious name. Amen.

Paul W. Brubaker

February 19

Discipleship 101

Readings: Luke 14:25-27; James 1:2-4

Whoever comes to me and does not hate father and mother, wife and children, brothers and sisters, yes, and even life itself, cannot be my disciple (Luke 14:26).

Meditation: The crowd diminished that day. Though the message was clear, it wasn't welcomed. If Jesus wanted to divide the faithful from the curious, he was successful. Most in the crowd didn't want this kind of spirituality, but Jesus wasn't interested in gaining followers at the cost of truth. He wasn't trying to build a church by numbers. Jesus was trying to build disciples, and he wasn't shying away from the sacrifice it would take to follow him. Many of us want Jesus to coddle, to pamper, and to indulge us. But today's text does not show the warm and fuzzy side of Jesus. This is a Jesus who demands that we consider the cost of discipleship. Far from the popular notion that Christianity is a life soaked in bubbles and fun, following Jesus is risky business. It is a journey to the cross, a willingness to die for what we believe, to live up to some unpopular ideals: that strength lies in weakness, that good overcomes evil, that to lose one's life is to gain. This is a scary, demanding Jesus, a Jesus who requires our allegiance above all other allegiances. Jesus blessed little children, called God his Father, and gave his mother into the care of John. He loved his family; he expects us to love ours, too, but not at the expense of our allegiance to him.

For the day: Discipleship means putting God first at all costs!

Prayer: Teach us, O Lord, we pray, by your example, to prioritize our lives in such a way as to place you first in all that we say and do. Let our lives be living testimonies of the power of sacrificial love, in Jesus' name. Amen.

David A. Whitten

February 20

Counting the Cost

Reading: Luke 14:28-33

Whoever . . . does not renounce all that he has cannot be my disciple (Luke 14:33 RSV).

Meditation: To hate family and self sounds very un-Christlike. In North American culture, media and marketers teach us to affirm and love ourselves and to gratify our desires. Jesus' words to hate our closest relationships, especially ourselves, cuts against most of what American culture treasures.

In light of God's cost-counting, the perspective changes. God spared no cost to send Jesus Christ, the Son of God, with the message of God's measureless love. Jesus opened God's love to others through his teaching and miracles, and through his uniquely redemptive death and resurrection. In light of this extravagant love, even the closest human relationships of love pale in comparison. Jesus beckons us to love God in return so much that our human loves might seem almost like hate in comparison.

Of course, Jesus loved his mother, his siblings, his followers, even those who wanted him dead. He, who loves and commands love, never taught hate. However, God's measureless love stirs us to love God first, ordering all other loves properly within divine love. In such love for God, our spiritual forebears at Schwarzenau risked wealth, status, power, even their lives, in order to trust and follow Christ into baptism and discipleship. For those who live in the U.S., a land of wealth, power, and violence, the message to count the cost, deny self and take up the cross of Christ frees us to love without measure. May God's gift of costly love help us to love family, neighbors, the needy, even enemies, and to know we are beloved.

For the day: Count first the cost of God's love for you, for your family, for neighbors near and far, even enemies. Count well the measure of your response in faith, discipleship, and love.

Prayer: Holy God, help us to count the cost of your love in Jesus Christ. Grant us grace to take the cross and love others without measure. Amen.

Jeffrey A. Bach

February 21

Riches—Rue or Rejoicing?

Readings: Luke 18:18-25; Matthew 13:44

He became very sad, for he was a man of great wealth (Luke 18:23 NIV).

. . . in his joy [he] went and sold all he had . . . (Matt. 13:44b NIV).

Meditation: As kids we used to play a game called "hot and cold." We had to guess where a gold ring or prize was hidden. Mom would say "you're getting warm" when we drew near to the treasure. Or "you're cooling off" when we moved away. Here we have two souls: one moving very deliberately away from the realm of God and one rushing to embrace it. One rejecting Love's invitation because of the cost, and one gleefully smashing the piggy bank so he can enter in. For one who has discovered mercy, financial resources are a means to a glorious end. For the rich ruler, they are heavy weights that keep him from the God-life—a life he clearly longs to possess. When we've answered the call to follow Jesus, it hasn't felt as cut and dried as it does with our two opposites here. It's more like the hot and cold game, with the Spirit guiding our daily choices. We struggle: Should I buy this book (it could help me on my journey)? Will I celebrate my son's birthday with an expensive meal? Do I, in each decision, answer Love's call to care for the needy? The result is the same. We're always walking away or coming toward the Savior.

For the day: Play the "hot and cold" game as you move through the day making choices about money and time. At every turn, let the Spirit whisper to you about whether you're gravitating to God's treasure or moving away. Let your own spirit tell you when you feel joy or sadness when you make each decision.

Prayer: Lover of all, I am fabulously wealthy in the eyes of the needy, and all too often desperately poor in your sight. Help me be aware of you, moment by moment, and "live simply so that others may simply live."

Paula A. Bowser

☞

February 22

Rewards of Discipleship

Reading: Luke 18:28-30

. . . there is no one who has left house or wife or brothers or parents or children, for the sake of the kingdom of God, who will not get back very much more in this age, and in the age to come eternal life (Luke 18:29b-30).

Meditation: Authentic discipleship requires this much sacrifice? Wasn't Jesus expecting a lot when he responded to Peter? Notice that their dialogue comes at the end of the story of the rich young ruler and before Jesus tells the twelve about going to Jerusalem where he will be crucified and resurrected. To the rich man Jesus has said that discipleship requires selling all possessions and giving the money to the poor. Then Peter points out that the disciples have given up property and family to follow Jesus: "We have left our homes" (v. 28). The Greek word here is *taidia*, which is translated literally "we left what was ours" to follow you. Like many of us who claim to be followers of Christ, Peter reminds Jesus of all that has been left behind to gain eternal salvation. But Jesus is not empathetic with Peter's claim nor ours. Jesus confronts Peter and us with the existential reality of our lives. All our good deeds, all our "family values" language to gain religious and political correctness in today's acculturated church will not save us. Discipleship is about following and being in fellowship with the person of Jesus Christ. It is not hero worship, but obedience. God, in mercy and love, will provide much more if we are willing to make sacrifices in our discipleship journey. Whoever leaves house, wife, sibling, parent, or child for the purpose of discipleship will receive more in this time as well as in the eternal future. The reward of life in the faith community is greater than the sacrifice.

For the day: When we tear ourselves away from the attachments and frills of the good life, there will be even greater abundance through the attachment of grace, God's perfect gift.

Prayer: God of amazing grace, free me and our world from all those things that detract us from living in your dominion and reign. Amen.

Warren M. Eshbach

February 23

First Disciples Called

Reading: Luke 5:1-11

For he was astonished, and all that were with him, at the draught of the fishes which they had taken: And so was also James, and John, the sons of Zebedee, which were partners with Simon. And Jesus said unto Simon, Fear not; from henceforth thou shalt catch men (Luke 5:9-10 KJV).

Meditation: People were attracted to our precious Lord. Wherever he went, they followed. This day was not an unusual one but the proceedings were. Tired fishermen thought that they had a night of failure. They had caught nothing. Nets by now were washed and cleaned when Jesus asked that they try one more time. He suggested that they throw their nets out into deeper water, and when they did, a miracle took place. They caught such a great number of fish that, the scripture says, "their nets began to break."

Seeing the crowds on the land and watching the disbelief on

the faces of these men, Jesus made another pronouncement. He said, "Don't be afraid, Simon. From now on you will be catching men."

If only we could understand that working for the Master, being members of his body the church, means "fishing" for men! This is serious business, and it took this miraculous happening to let these men know just how serious our Lord was to seek and to save the hearts of men. Jesus called these four men here to be his disciples, and he is calling us today in like manner to "fish" for men.

Remember that Jesus does not want to leave anyone out of the "fishing" business. Let us remember that there are no bystanders in God's kingdom program, but also remember that when Jesus calls on you, on me, on us, he demands *all*. He has more in store for us than we can ever imagine.

For the day: Remember that when our Lord touches you, calls you, he will outfit and prepare you for the task to which you will be assigned. His will is all you will ever need.

Prayer: Loving Heavenly Father, open our blinded eyes to see you as you really are, and enable us to be fully what we cannot be without you. Help us to renew our commitment to you as "fishers of men." Amen.

Phill Carlos Archbold

February 24

Do Not Be Afraid

Readings: Acts 9:1-6, 11-16; Matthew 5:11, 43-48; 28:1-10

Ananias answered, "Lord, I have heard from many about this man, how much evil he has done to your saints. . . ." The Lord

said to him, "Go, for he is an instrument whom I have chosen . . ."
(Acts 9:13, 15).

Meditation: Fear is a human reaction to conditions perceived as a threat or risk. It is a basic human emotion closely connecting us to the emotional intelligence of animals. "Fight or flight," in the natural world, allows for the greatest potential level of survival of the individual animal. It is in that fearful place that we find Ananias as he encounters the resurrected Jesus. In any other circumstance, presenting himself before Saul as Jesus suggests would ensure Ananias at least imprisonment, perhaps even death.

An encounter with Jesus changes everything. It should not be a surprise that God-through-Jesus can use even the great persecutor Saul to advance the vision of God. For God, all things are possible. But take note of Ananias's faith in the face of fear. It is that very real encounter with Jesus that gives Ananias the ability to turn off the "flight from fear" sensation that causes us all to seek self-preservation more often than not. There is something about encountering the presence of the Divine that, while not eliminating fears, gives us what we need to function in the face of fear. Quite often in the biblical encounters with God it is a simple "Do not be afraid." Other times, as with Ananias, it is a call to action—some physical response—that aligns the hearer with God's work in the world.

For the day: To what might God be calling you that gives you fear? Name the very real encounters you have experienced with Jesus. How might those encounters inform and give you the courage to participate in the work of God even in the face of fear?

Prayer: O God of all that has been, is, and will yet be, walk with us in our inevitable times of fear. Speak to us words of comfort—"Do not be afraid," and give us the courage to be more like the women at the tomb than the guards frozen in fear. Amen.

Shawn Flory Replogle

Part 2

God, the People, and the Covenant

Signs of God's Covenant

February 25–March 30

$\mathcal{F}$ollowing the first baptism, the eight immediately became zealous in witnessing to their newly found faith. They were convincing because they were convinced.

Donald F. Durnbaugh (1927–2005)

⌐♂

February 25

Praise the Lord!

Reading: Psalm 150

Let everything that breathes praise the LORD! Praise the LORD! (Ps. 150:6).

Meditation: Worrying about the future of our denomination or even the survival of the church takes too much of my time. I keep telling myself it is a futile exercise. Why? Because the scripture tells me so. God's Word says I should be expending my energy praising God for God's surpassing greatness! Indeed, were the whole Creation . . . at least everything that breathes . . . focused on giving God the glory worthy of God's name, we would find the power and confidence to live life to the full! Psalm 150 has been a favorite ever since I was sent to a state music camp at age fourteen where I sang Cesar Franck's anthem Psalm 150. I thought it was the most magnificent piece of music in the whole world! It opened my eyes to God's wonders everywhere and gave me permission to use every musical instrument and every human skill to proclaim God's glory! In her divine little book, *A Pilgrim at Tinker Creek*, Annie Dillard describes her expression of praise for God's surpassing greatness this way, "My left foot says 'Glory,' and my right foot says 'Amen.' " Is your every step made in the light of God's surpassing greatness?

For the day: Walk today with the awareness of God in everything and everybody you see. Use every word and every action to praise God for God's surpassing greatness.

Prayer: Gracious Giver of all life, forgive us for thinking that what we have and what we love are accomplishments of our own hand. Open my eyes that I might see glimpses of your surpassing greatness everywhere I go. Give me grace and courage to praise you with my whole being. Help me to guide others toward the light of your love and faithfulness. Free us from tradition's bondage that hinders our praising you with every instrument and gift you have given us. Amen.

Fred W. Swartz

ℭ

February 26

God Resides in Our Brokenness

Reading: 1 Chronicles 15:1-3, 11-15

. . . for them hath the LORD chosen to carry the ark of God, and to minister unto him for ever (1 Chron. 15:2 KJV).

Meditation: From the corner of my eye, I noticed a bearded man in a wheelchair wearing a worn baseball cap. He arrived one day at our community bicycle shop, a place where donated bikes are refurbished and given to low-income people. He sat quietly outside the entrance, with his right leg propped on a cinder block, and repaired a tire for a young woman. As we shook hands, he said his name was Joe and that he was sleeping by the river and had no place to stay or work. He showed me his right leg; it had been disabled several years ago. His wheelchair was surrounded by white plastic shopping bags filled with all of his belongings, a literal mobile home. Joe demonstrated that he knew how to repair bicycles and that he wanted to be useful. He now comes to the shop and volunteers his skills repairing bicycles for people in need. Joe is one of the best bike mechanics I know, and we rely on him for our toughest repairs.

As I think about Joe, it strikes me that perhaps God's presence is contained within our brokenness. Our brokenness is one of the places where "the Lord has chosen to carry the ark of God." I see Joe as a vessel holding the ark of God. Perhaps in his poverty he was cracked open to allow God to enter, reside there, and reflect acts of love and kindness. In the midst of the poor and marginalized, God is made visible to me.

For the day: Take time to reach out to someone who is marginalized in your community. See where God resides and where God's love surfaces.

Prayer: God of the Abandoned and Marginalized, give me the strength and courage to move, live, and work with our sisters and brothers who are discarded and impoverished in our communities and world. Help me to see where the ark of your love resides in the "least" of our brothers and sisters.

Tom Benevento

February 27

Music, Joy, and Celebration

Reading: 1 Chronicles 15:16-24

David also commanded the chiefs of the Levites to appoint their kindred as the singers to play on musical instruments, on harps and lyres and cymbals, to raise loud sounds of joy (1 Chron. 15:16).

Meditation from our past: You don't sing? And you can't carry a tune? That's hard to believe because you've been making music from the day you were born. That first cry was a sustained sound, with a tone all its own. Your mother and father heard music in the cooing, gurgling noises you made before you could talk. And there was a beat in your pulse from that first day on. Often you would call for Mom-mie or Dad-dy with an accent on the first syllable and with a high note followed by a low one, or sometimes, in anger, the other way around.

Music began for you when you were able to sustain a sound, form a tone, use your natural sense of rhythm (as regular as a heartbeat) and develop little melodies in cadences that are still a part of your speech. You may even have harmonized with another voice. All the elements are there—even if you can't read a note of music and think your voice is a monotone.

Music in worship is just as natural, just as interwoven with all the various ways in which we express our thanksgiving and praise, make our petitions and prayers, or to reach out to touch other persons in the body of Christ. Music is integral to worship and celebration. It may serve as a means or a tool to implement acts of praise, but music is far more than an aid. It is a gift we offer with ourselves when we sense the presence of God. —*Kenneth I. Morse*

From Move in Our Midst, *Brethren Press, 1977, pp. 86-87.*

For the day: Slap your palm against your thigh, and thump out praise for God. Or look for other opportunities to make music to God today.

Prayer: *Move in our midst, Thou Spirit of God;*
Go with us down from Thy holy hill;
Walk with us through the storm and the calm;
Spirit of God, go Thou with us still.

Touch Thou our hands to lead us aright;
Guide us forever; show us Thy way.
Transform our darkness into Thy light;
Spirit of God, lead Thou us today. (K. M., 1941)

February 28

Raining on Parades

Readings: 1 Chronicles 15:25-29; Romans 12:15

And when she saw King David dancing and celebrating, she despised him in her heart (1 Chron. 15:29 NIV).

Meditation: The return of the ark of the covenant to Jerusalem was a big deal. This once central symbol of God's presence among his people had been captured by the Philistines, returned when it became too troublesome, then largely neglected for years by God's people. David was doing something about it. He was bringing it back and restoring it to a prominent place. This was something to celebrate, and celebrate he did. There was even a parade, complete with a marching band, with David serving as both grand marshal and drum major. From her lofty window Michal looked down on the event, and all she could see was a king making a fool of himself, acting "like any vulgar fellow would" (2 Sam. 6:20). Like the church member who rails against an outreach ministry because it leads to scuffs on the church floors by people who "don't know how to behave in church," Michal missed the point entirely and rained on David's parade. But David refused to let his wife's deadening spirit dampen his desire to celebrate God's goodness. In essence, he said to Michal, "I'm going to celebrate even if it does make me look foolish." He was more focused on rejoicing in God's goodness than on how he would be judged in the court of public opinion. We probably should be more like David, and less like Michal.

For the day: Look for someone today who is celebrating an achievement in his or her personal or spiritual life. Rejoice with them.

Prayer: Gracious God, restore unto me the joy of my salvation so that I can celebrate your goodness and rejoice with those who rejoice. Crucify the critical spirit that is within me. Fill me with a contagious joy so that I can be a source of encouragement to others. Amen.

Donald R. Fitzkee

February 29

Our Standing, Not Our Setting

Readings: 1 Chronicles 16:1-6; John 4:21-24

They brought the ark of God and set it inside the tent that David had pitched for it, and they presented burnt offerings and fellowship offerings before God (1 Chron. 16:1 NIV).

Meditation: Once David succeeded in bringing the ark to Jerusalem, the best he could do for it was to erect a makeshift tent. There was no glorious temple to house it or in which to conduct worship. Instead, the Israelites held "tent meetings" as they worshiped God. David appointed some to pray, some to praise, and some to play harps, lyres, cymbals, and trumpets. In his classic commentary, Matthew Henry observes, "David, who pitched a tent for the ark and continued steadfast to it, did far better than Solomon, who built a temple for it and yet in his latter end turned his back upon it. The church's poorest times were its purest." Henry was pointing to the inverse relationship that often exists between prosperity and piety. The early Brethren worshiped in homes and then later in simple, unadorned meetinghouses. Today, many of us worship in air conditioned sanctuaries surrounded by more churchly décor. Our worship facilities certainly have improved, but how about our faith? As we settle into padded pews instead of kneeling on hardwood floors, let the ark in the tent remind us that our standing with God is more important than the setting of our worship. God's ultimate desire is that we "worship in spirit and truth" (John 4:24).

For the day: God desires our devotion, whether we are worshiping in a tent, a temple, or somewhere else. The sincerity, not the setting, is what matters.

Prayer: God, I know you see right through me when my faith is just for show. Forgive me for times I have "played church" to impress others. May your Spirit inhabit me and transform me into the temple I was meant to be. And may my worship be as pure as David's was in that tent. Amen.

Donald R. Fitzkee

March 1

Praise God and Pass It On

Reading: 1 Chronicles 16:7-36

Give thanks to the LORD, call on his name; make known among the nations what he has done. Sing to him, sing praise to him; tell of all his wonderful acts (1 Chron. 16:8-9 NIV).

Meditation: Once the ark was in its rightful place and worship had begun, David composed a psalm of thanksgiving for the occasion. The psalm—portions of which also appear in Psalms 96, 105, and 106—praises God for his splendor and majesty and power, thanks God for his goodness and enduring love, and recounts God's faithfulness to his people. But interspersed with all these expressions directed toward God are exhortations for the people to tell others about God's greatness: "Make known among the nations what he has done." "Declare his glory among the nations." "Proclaim his salvation day after day." David rather naturally moves back and forth between praise to God and proclamation to others. And that seems right. If we truly believe all the wonderful things we say to and about God in our worship, we quite naturally will want to tell others about such a God. Praise to God without a willingness to proclaim to others—whether our proclamation is through words, deeds, or some of each—rings hollow. A faith that sings "A Wonderful Savior Is Jesus My Lord" without adding "We've a Story to Tell to the Nations" falls short of David's balance of praise and proclamation. David's approach? Praise God, and pass it on.

For the day: Tell God how grateful you are for what he has done for you in Jesus Christ. Then tell others—use words if necessary.

Prayer: Thank you, God, for revealing yourself to us through your majestic creation, your written revelation, and your Son, Jesus. Thank you for your faithfulness in the past, your guidance in the present, and your promise of a glorious future. Truly you are worthy of our praise. Empower us and embolden us to declare your glory among the nations and your marvelous deeds among all peoples, starting with the ones we meet today. Amen.

Donald R. Fitzkee

℘

March 2

It's About Time

Readings: 1 Chronicles 16:37-43; Acts 2:42-47

David left Zadok the priest . . . to present burnt offerings to the LORD on the altar of burnt offering regularly, morning and evening, in accordance with everything written in the Law of the Lord . . . (1 Chron. 16:39-40 NIV).

Meditation: It is hard to imagine any generation that has had more free time than ours. We have more labor-saving devices than ever before and spend relatively little time caring for our basic needs. So why do I feel like I have so little time to give to the church? Once David finished celebrating the placement of the ark in Jerusalem, he designated priests to continue regular worship, morning and evening, just as the Scriptures instructed (see Num. 28:1-8). In Acts 2, we read of a church where people met *daily* for worship and fellowship. I don't know where they found the time. Unless it was simply a matter of where they placed their priorities and how they used the time they had. If I looked at my calendar to determine what really made me so busy, I might find that I had more than enough time to do everything that I really wanted to do. I had three hours to watch that football game, three days to spend at the cabin, three weeks for that luxury vacation. When it comes right down to it, it's about time. And priorities.

For the day: "Let us not give up meeting together, as some are in the habit of doing, but let us encourage one another . . ." (Heb. 10:25 NIV).

Prayer: Lord of life, grant me wisdom to put the best ahead of the merely good and to eliminate activities that squander the valuable resource of time. Help me to make regular worship and fellowship with other believers a priority in my life so that my faith can be strengthened and I can be a source of encouragement to others. Amen.

Donald R. Fitzkee

♀

March 3

Open to Call

Readings: Psalm 78:67-72; James 1:19-25

The Lord God chose David to be his servant and took him from tending sheep. . . . Then God made him the leader of Israel, his own nation. David treated the people fairly and guided them with wisdom (Ps. 78:70-72 CEV).

Meditation: I retired from nursing when my husband faced his second bout of cancer. Our pastor's health also began to fail. The deacons asked me to be an advocate for the pastor's family in navigating our difficult health system. There were many doctor appointments, a mountain of forms to complete for disability benefits, trips to Switzerland for treatment, and ultimately our pastor's death. As chair of the church board at that time, the business of the congregation and wider church continued. Then having prepared for the ordained ministry before retirement, I was called to serve my own faith family as its interim! We do not always understand the call that prepares us for life's next chapter. We do know that God provides all that is needed to carry out his work. David was called from tending sheep to lead the Israelites. God made David the leader of Israel and he led them with wisdom (Ps. 78:70-72). God works in mysterious ways his wonders to perform! We may not understand, but we must answer when God calls.

For the day: There is a saying, "Many are called but few are chosen." Today is a day of new awareness and acceptance led by God's grace. Be open to his call.

Prayer: Heavenly and loving Father, open my eyes that I may see, open my ears that I may hear, open my heart to receive your call. Open my mind that I may serve you not just for today, but into eternity. Remove the things that get in the way. Help me to listen and consider your call in my life, and provide me with the courage and will to do your work peacefully and humbly in the name of Jesus Christ. Amen.

F. Joyce Person

March 4

God's Intention

Readings: 1 Chronicles 17:1-6; 2 Samuel 7

David said . . . , "I am living in a house of cedar, but the ark of the covenant of the LORD is under a tent" (1 Chron. 17:1).

Meditation: David's confession, "I live in a house of cedar," could be echoed by many of us today. We live in nice houses. We often store sweaters with cedar balls to prevent moth or other insect damage. Some luxurious homes today even have cedar closets for the same effect on a larger scale. I remember when my parents remodeled our house when I was growing up; they were so happy to put wood paneling on the walls. Now imagine a whole house made of this precious wood! The people of ancient Israel would have considered this an almost decadent luxury.

The story of the beginnings of the temple is probably one of the most stunning biblical stories of stewardship. Imagine a person who is aware of the disparity between her or his wealth and the situation of the church and proposes to make a large gift. The person approaches the head of the stewardship committee, who affirms the idea and prepares to accept the gift. Then God intervenes and prohibits the gift.

The stories of the beginnings of the temple (1 Chron. 17 and 2 Sam. 7) emphasize that the temple story is not about David; it is a story about God. The version of the story as it is told in 2 Samuel 7—"Are you the one to build me a house?"—is clear that the temple is not a courtesy gift from David. The 1 Chronicles 17 rebuff—"You shall not build me a house to live in"—is not so directly a question of David's character. One wonders how many times our own practice of stewardship becomes more about us than about God.

For the day: What are the possibilities that God presents to you today?

Prayer: Lord, open our eyes to the houses we live in. Open our hearts to the situation of God's mission in the world. Open our hands to your will.

Stephen Breck Reid

🕮

March 5

God's House

Reading: 1 Chronicles 17:7-10

Moreover I declare to you [David] that the LORD will build you a house (1 Chron. 17:10b).

Meditation: God honored David's faithfulness by promising that David would have a "house of worship." Our faithfulness too is honored by God when we worship in a house that God has built for preaching and fellowship.

Our houses of worship serve many purposes. Our dedication to the worship of God brings us together every week for praise, prayer, and preaching. Our houses of worship are primarily centers for worshiping God and for the revelation of God that we see in Jesus the Christ. Also, as Trinitarians we receive the Holy Spirit, who unites us in faith and service. Hearing the Word of the Lord and providing service to those in need throughout the world are major themes of our life together.

Our houses of worship also serve us through music, study and education, health and spirituality, and in fellowship and recreation. We believe that it is in a community of people dedicated to discovering the mind of Christ and the guidance of the Holy Spirit that we can find true meaning in life.

Our houses of prayer are gifts of God. We build them to his glory and honor, even though they differ according to the traditions and the situations in which we live. The "house" is where the congregation meets. The structures do not make the congregation; only people who meet there and radiate out from there form the family of God.

For the day: Remember today to focus on the meaning of worship together in the house of the Lord. Remember that we are to welcome all who seek Christ as Lord and Savior.

Prayer: God of grace, we acknowledge that we are all sinners who stand in need of your grace. Help us to discern in our day that we have much to learn from the leading of the Spirit, from the teachings of science, from the traditions of the church, and from the preaching of the Bible. Amen.

W. Robert McFadden

March 6

P.S. I Love You

Readings: 1 Chronicles 17:11-15; 1 Samuel 16:7; 1 John 1:9

And it shall be, when your days are fulfilled, when you must go to be with your fathers, that I will set up your seed after you, who will be of your sons; and I will establish his kingdom. He shall build Me a house, and I will establish his throne forever (1 Chron. 17:11-12 NKJV).

Meditation: Take a moment and contemplate the life and legacy of King David. What thoughts come to your mind? The sins of David? The battles of David? The turmoil of David's family? We are so quick to remember the negatives, aren't we? But dear Brethren, Beloved of God, read these verses and know that God is not like man, for he looks upon the heart (1 Sam. 16:7). God reveals to David that one day he will die ("when thy days are ended"). The body they will place in the ground will house the heart of a man who warred the greatest of battles, striving for holiness of life and fellowship with God. Did David sin? Yes. But O how his heart grieved and drove him to many days and nights of confession, repentance, and the pursuit of a right relationship with his Good Shepherd. Now contemplate the mercies of our God, "I will raise up thy seed after thee . . . I will establish his kingdom . . . I will establish his throne forever." Wow! God conveys to David that he will receive his son Solomon; and yes, his wish to build God a house will come to pass; and know this too, David, the One who will reign forever, the Messiah, the King of kings and Lord of lords, he will come through you. P.S. David, I love you!

For the day: David lost some battles, but he won the war. Part of the reason God gave David this commendation before he died was so you could read it and put it in your heart. There are great rewards for you, too, if you don't quit. You have to decide today if loving God is worth the fight of surrendering your life and will to his.

Prayer: Dear Heavenly Father, thank you for your Word that tells me of the precious promises you have in store for me. Help me, strengthen me by your Word and Spirit, that I too may win the war over the flesh and live a life that is pleasing in your sight.

Gordy A. Harmon

☙

March 7

Good Deeds of God

Reading: 1 Chronicles 17:16-19

Who am I, O LORD God, . . . that you have brought me thus far? . . . You regard me as someone of high rank. . . . For your servant's sake, O LORD, and according to your own heart, you have done all these great deeds (1 Chron. 17:16-19).

Meditation: When the story about David begins, he is an overlooked shepherd boy. He rose to become king over the tribes of Israel, and he was given promises regarding his descendants. We might label this a wonderful success story, but David sees it differently. It is not his own success, but the grace of God that has operated in his life. And David expresses his gratitude in the prayer in 1 Chronicles 17:16-27.

Should we be impressed by David's prayer? It would be quite easy to sit comfortably in a royal palace with twelve tribes promising their support, and to pray a prayer of gratitude for personal blessings. Would David have been so grateful if his wife's love had turned to hate? if his son had tried to kill him? if his daughter had been raped?

In fact, David experienced all these personal tragedies and more. And the event that triggers this prayer of gratitude in 1 Chronicles was a rejection—God's rejection of David's offer to build a temple.

Prosperity and personal success are not the only tie to God. People of faith continue to press on through all of life's variety until they can name each thing that happens as a "good deed of God." Suffering is still suffering; pain is still pain; death is still death. But those who know the story of the resurrection will also know that even God's "no" can be redeeming.

For the day: Dag Hammarskjöld, the Swedish diplomat, wrote, "For all that has been, thanks. For all that will be, yes." Are you able to write that prayer in your own spiritual diary?

Prayer: For the glory of life, O God, and for its wonder, I give you thanks. This day, remember me for well-being. This day bless me with your nearness. This day help me to a fuller life. Amen.

Robert C. Bowman

March 8

Hearing of God

Reading: 1 Chronicles 17:20-22

There is no one like you, O LORD, and there is no God besides you, according to all that we have heard with our ears (1 Chron. 17:20).

97

Meditation: David prayed there is no one like God, "according to all that we have heard with our ears." It makes one wonder what David had heard "with his ears." Had he learned of God from his mother or father? What would he know of faith if no one had spoken to him of God? Is this the reason we are urged in Deuteronomy to speak of our faith "when you are at home and when you are away, when you lie down and when you rise" (Deut. 6:7)?

On the other hand, perhaps David is suggesting more. Perhaps the God he heard about with his ears has finally become real. Perhaps he is confessing his own faith, like Job who declared, "I had heard of you by the hearing of the ear, but now my eye sees you" (Job 42:5). A God we only "hear about" will not take us far. Somewhere we need to find our own burning bush.

Yet, perhaps it is not enough to proclaim God. Nor is it enough to acknowledge the reality of God. Our spiritual horizons suddenly fall away when we realize that no human language we have ever heard "with our ears" can be adequate to speak about God. Our language about God is a feeble way of pointing to something, someone, whom no words can ever contain. You are not, O God, like anything we have ever heard with our ears. You are so much deeper, higher, and more mysterious that we end up, as in Charles Wesley's hymn, "lost in wonder, love and praise."

For the day: This day has its own brand of holiness. May you discover it and worship appropriately.

Prayer: Despite our frailty, we are your people, O God. Bound to you through Jesus Christ, we are called to your service. We thank you and bless you and proclaim the holiness of your name. Amen.

Robert C. Bowman

&

March 9

The Future Hangs on a Promise

Readings: 1 Chronicles 17:23-27; Matthew 16:13-20

Jesus said: "And I tell you, you are Peter, and on this rock I will build my church, and the gates of Hades will not prevail against it" (Matt. 16:18).

Meditation: With all the political posturing in today's culture, it is refreshing to read of Israel's greatest king acknowledging dependence upon God. That's the heartbeat of David's prayer in today's text. God promises David: "I will raise up your offspring after you, one of your own sons, and I will establish his kingdom . . . forever" (vv. 11, 14). When this unexpected good news from God was delivered by Nathan to David, David sat in God's presence pondering its meaning. My dynasty, established forever, in this world, with all its twists and turns? This can happen only if God keeps the promise. Without God in this volatile mix, the dynasty crumbles. So David summons his courage and boldly asks God to "do as you have promised" (v. 23).

Jesus makes a similar promise about "my church." Jesus says to Peter, "And I tell you, you are Peter, and on this rock I will build my church, and the gates of Hades will not prevail against it" (Matt. 16:18). Rocky Peter was often wobbly and uncertain, yet the universal church of our Lord continues to thrive. We Brethren, in Christ's worldwide church, have had wobbly moments. Yet here we are, celebrating three hundred years of service and worship and mission and church planting. We know this has not been our doing. Jesus made a promise to his church and the promise has been kept. Let's sit in God's presence and meditate on the promise and boldly ask our Lord to continue keeping the promise to build the church.

For the day: Choose one of God's promises and live with the promise.

Prayer: Eternal God, may it please you to bless your church built upon the foundation of the apostles and prophets, with Christ Jesus himself as the cornerstone. Amen.

L. Gene Bucher

⌇

10 Mas

March 10 in Creole

Ségnè a té fè David yon promès

Lekti: Sòm 132: 1-12; 2 Samyèl 7:12-16

Ségnè-a té fè David, sèvitè li-a, yon promès, lap toujou kinbé paròl li: Sé yon nan pitit ou yo map mété chita sou fotèy ou-a. Si pitit ou yo kinbé kontra mouin fè ak yo-a, si yo kinbé prinsip mouin bay o, pitit pa yo tou va toujou chita sou fotèy ou-a. (Sòm 132: 11-12).

Meditasyon: Lè nou mété konfians nou nan Ségnè a epi nou swiv tout sa li di nou, lap fè nou viv pi byen é lavi nou ap ranpli ak benediksyon. Sé poutèt pwomès lit é fè zansèt nou David, ké nou menm ki sou tè a kapab jwen tout privilèj nou genyen jodiya, sé pa paské nou mérité li men paské li renmen nou. Lè nou mandé Ségnè a li répònn é sé dévwa nou pou nou rété tann; é lè li fè nou yon promès ou pa bézwen pè paské nap jwen sa nou mandé a. Rété anba zèl Ségnè é na wè jan li renmen nou é na jwen rékonpans nou mérité.

Pou jou a: Mété konfyans nou nan Ségnè epi pa janm sispann di li mèsi. Rélé non li chak jou pou nou ka wè jan gras li ap kouvri nou.

Priyè: Ségnè papa ki nan syèl la, mouin beni non ou pou tout sa ou fè pou mouin. Mouin di ou mèsi pou jan ou renmen mouin. Fè mouin rékonèt grandè ou pou-m kapab toujou mété konfyans mouin nan ou. Antré nan lavi mouin é pa kité mouin sèl. Mèsi pou gras ou é pou tout sa wap kontinyé fè pou mwen. Nan non Jézi piti ou mwen priyé ou. Amèn.

Founa Augustin

⊘

March 10

God's Promise to David

Readings: Psalm 132:1-12; 2 Samuel 7:12-16

The LORD has sworn in truth to David; he will not turn from it: "I will set upon your throne the fruit of your body. If your sons will keep my covenant and my testimony which I shall teach them, their sons also shall sit upon your throne forevermore" (Ps. 132:11-12).

Meditation: If we put our trust in God and live as he would have us live, our lives will be blessed. Because of his promise to our ancestor David, we are able to enjoy many privileges today. We receive God's good gifts not because we deserve them, but because God loves us. Because of God's promise, we know that he will always hear our prayers and answer them when the time is right. We should wait in faith, and without fear, knowing that he will keep his promise. When we stay faithful in the Lord, we will see how much he loves us and we will be rewarded with grace.

For the day: Put your faith in God and never stop thanking him. Call on his name every single day and be showered with blessings.

Prayer: Our Father in heaven, God of mercy and grace, I glorify your name for everything you have done for me. Thank you for your love. Make me recognize your grandness, so that I can always put my faith in you. Thank you for your grace and everything you will continue to do for me. In the name of your Son Jesus I pray. Amen.

Founa Augustin

March 11

Freedom to Change

Reading: 1 Chronicles 28:1-5

I had it in my heart to build a house as a place of rest for the ark of the covenant. . . . But God said to me, "You are not to build a house for my Name . . ." (1 Chron. 28:2a, 3a NIV).

Meditation: "I feel the Lord is calling me to lead a Bible study!" His enthusiasm was obvious and his sincerity beyond question.

"What curriculum would you like to use?" his pastor asked.

"I don't need anything like that; we will just read the Bible and I will lead discussion," was the reply. "I have a heart for leading Bible study."

Most church leaders are happy to accept such volunteers. But is a strong inner calling qualification enough? Or should there be a way of confirming that call? King David called an assembly in order to make an important announcement. His son Solomon would build the temple. In 1 Chronicles 17:3-4,

God had told the prophet Nathan to tell David that building a temple was not in his future.

The New International Version of the Bible translates 28:3 as "I had it in my heart to build a house." David's deep desire was to build the temple. But his personal sense of purpose was altered by a word from Nathan.

It is increasingly common to hear people say, "I have been called by the Lord to do thus and so." When leadership is in short supply, deep personal desire sometimes seems sufficient. But it is not. Even David must change his heart's desire.

It is wonderful to feel an inner calling from God. But even deep desires must be tested and sometimes, as in David's case, changed.

For the day: Test your deepest desires with your sisters and brothers. All of us are prone to occasional self-deception.

Prayer: Wise and gracious God, open our eyes to your intentions for us. Keep us from replacing your will with our own, and help us to be open to your Word spoken through the words of others. Amen.

Michael L. Hostetter

March 12

Legacy of Faithfulness

Reading: 1 Chronicles 28:6-8

Observe . . . all the commandments of the LORD your God; that you may possess this good land, and leave it for an inheritance to your children (1 Chron. 28:8).

Meditation: What future do you want for the children? What legacy do you wish to leave for the young people you love?

When asked such questions, people often say, "I want them to be happy, safe, fulfilled." These hopes are understandable. One does not need to be a person of faith to desire such things for one's children.

King David announces that God has chosen Solomon as heir and king. Solomon, not David, will build the temple. God's choosing Solomon includes the command that "he continues resolute in keeping my commandments" (v. 7). David offers a father's council to his son. "Observe and search out all the commandments of the Lord your God; that you may possess this good land, and leave it for an inheritance to your children after you forever" (v. 8). David desires more than happiness for his descendants. He desires faithfulness. In 1 Chronicles faithfulness and obedience are as much a part of the inheritance as was the land. We also know that faithfulness to Christ is not always safe. Despite our desire to ensure the safety of our children, we know that if our children are faithful, some trouble may come their way.

Faithfulness to God is not to be equated with ease of living—but with fullness of life. What kind of legacy do we really want to leave our children?

For the day: The desire for safety is grounded in fear. The desire of obedience is grounded in faith.

Prayer: Help us, O God, to trust in your care, to risk all for the sake of Christ, and to leave to our children an inheritance of faithfulness. Amen.

Michael L. Hostetter

⊘

March 13

With Single Mind and Willing Heart

Readings: 1 Chronicles 28:9-10; Philippians 2:12-13

Know the God of your father, and serve him with single mind and willing heart (1 Chron. 28:9).

Meditation: Ask someone what comes to mind when they hear the name Solomon, and nine times out of ten, you'll hear the word *wisdom*. In today's text, however, it is not wisdom that is required of Solomon, but a wholehearted devotion and single-minded focus. These qualities were of primary importance for the man chosen to build a house for the Lord God. Solomon's father, King David, assured him that God would reward Solomon's seeking with a relationship of fidelity but predicted dire consequences if he abandoned his God. Sadly, 1 Kings 11:9-13 reports that Solomon left the way of God to worship idols, following the ways of his seven hundred wives!

What does it take to keep a wholehearted devotion and single-minded focus? What can prevent the distractions of daily life, tragedy, confusion, disappointments, suffering, and temptation from derailing our fidelity to God? If even a great king like Solomon lost his spiritual way, so to speak, what hope is there for us common followers of God?

From my few years living here among the Dominican Brethren, I have seen the ancient spiritual disciplines carried out with great fervor and dedication, sustaining brothers and sisters in their walk with Christ, even against great odds and obstacles. Daily prayer, Bible reading and worship, and regular periods of fasting and prayer are standard fare for this vibrant church. Many people here illustrate the spiritual truth that we are active partners with God, called to "work out our salvation with fear and trembling," but always with God willing and acting within us for his good purpose. With such a dynamic partnership, we find that by God's grace we eagerly keep a wholehearted devotion and single-minded focus that enables God to use us for the mighty purposes of his reign on this earth. Hallelujah!

For the day: Focus today on the words of the hymn "Be Thou My Vision": *Riches I heed not, nor vain empty praise; thou mine inheritance, now and always. Thou and thou only, first in my heart, High King of heaven, my treasure thou art!*

Prayer: Gracious God, thank you for the particular ministry you have called me to. Grace me with a wholehearted devotion and a willing mind as I face the challenges of today. Let me hear your words, "Be strong and courageous, and act!" ever keeping my heart focused on your presence. Amen.

Nancy Sollenberger Heishman

March 14

The Plan

Readings: 1 Chronicles 28:11-19; Jeremiah 29:11-14; Ephesians 1:8b-10; 3:7-13

For surely I know the plans I have for you, says the LORD, plans for your welfare and not for harm . . . (Jer. 29:11).

Meditation: Early in my ministry someone gave me the aphorism, "Those who fail to plan plan to fail." Failing to plan meant late night cramming for sermons and sometimes missed deadlines. Planning ahead was a lot less stressful for both pastor and people.

Failure to plan was not part of David's makeup as reported by the Chronicler. Five times in 1 Chronicles 28 we are reminded of the plan David handed his son, Solomon, for the building of the temple. The plan was meticulous. Even the weight of the gold and silver temple furnishings was given to Solomon. Moreover, the plan was "at the Lord's direction." With plans in hand, Solomon could build the temple with confidence.

Jesus has plans for his disciples, too. The plans are not as meticulous as David's plans for the temple, but they are clear. "Go therefore and make disciples of all nations" (Matt. 28:18-20). "You shall love the Lord your God with all your heart. . . . You shall love your neighbor as yourself" (Mark: 12:29-31). "When you pray, say: 'Father, hallowed be your name' " (Luke 11:2-4). Moreover, Jesus gives us assurance for those times and settings when guidance is needed, but there seem to be no specific words from Jesus: "I still have many things to say to you, but you cannot bear them now. When the Spirit of truth comes, he will guide you into all the truth" (John 16:12-13). Our calling as disciples is to plan how we will incarnate Jesus' plans into daily living.

For the day: Reflect on ways you are living within God's plans for you.

Prayer: Thoughtful God, in a world where so much seems haphazard and arbitrary, we give thanks for your plans that are for our welfare and give purpose and hope. Grant that we will find our freedom within your plans; through Christ our Lord. Amen.

L. Gene Bucher

⟨⟩

March 15

God Is with You

Reading: 1 Chronicles 28:20-21

Be strong and of good courage, and act. Do not be afraid or dismayed; for the LORD God, my God, is with you. He will not fail you or forsake you, until all the work for the service of the house of the LORD is finished (1 Chron. 28:20).

Meditation from our past: August 1st [1823] O how sensible I am of my weakness. My memory appears to be very weak can Scarceley retain any of the gospel. My constant prayer to God is that he would write his Gospel upon my heart. And put the same into my mind. That when I stand before the congregation I might not be at a loss to communicate the same to the people; There are a Diversity of sects in this Neighbourhood. I feel as though I could not preach. The people are now beginning to flock in, and the time is just at hand, when I must face them. I appear to be overwhelmed in darkness, and come before the people I must. The time has arrived, I go sensible of my weakness. the words of the text are in the 24th and 14 verse of the Gospel according S. Matthew I speak with much labour. I have now made an end of Speaking, but O how miserable do I feel, now am I sensible of my weakness. I find that it is good for me to be humble; I find that I wanted to be considered by the people a good speaker, if this be a desire as a temptation, I find that it must be taken away from me. I must be anything or nothing for my Redeamers cause—

August 2nd. Thanks be to God I feel humble this morning and I feel in my soul the Lord has not forsaken me. I think I can say this morning that I am willing to be led by the Spirit. —*Peter Nead*

From "Vindicator of Primitive Christianity: The Life and Diary of Peter Nead,"
by Donald F. Durnbaugh. Brethren Life & Thought, *August 1969, pp. 202-03.*
(Reproduced in its original orthography and punctuation)

For the day: Draw a timeline of your life, and mark places where you felt God's apparent absence and a sense of God's powerful presence.

Prayer: God of comfort, I pray for your presence in both darkness and light. Amen.

♂

March 16

The Zion Within

Reading: Psalm 132:13-18

Yes—I, GOD, chose Zion, the place I wanted for my shrine;
This will always be my home; this is what I want, and I'm here
for good (Ps. 132:13-14 The Message).

Meditation: Zion. It's not something I usually think about. This entire verse is about Zion, but what is it really? It's a word we throw around sometimes, but do we really understand what it means for us? I remember hearing the hymn "Marching to Zion" for the first time as a little kid. I remember enjoying its triumphal melody and buoyant beat. I recall getting this image of a mystic city on a hill, sort of like King Arthur's Camelot. Zion (which to most people I know represents heaven) is sort of an ideal—an end goal. But what does Zion have to do with our life this very day?

When I look at this Bible verse I see the description of a wonderful place, a place that God promises us he will create.

What if we thought of Zion as the relationship with God that he truly desires to have with us? When we are completely for God, then he is completely for us and will transform our lives into a beautiful city: a city whose light cannot be hidden, who feeds the poor, a radiant place built for him and his Son, one that is impenetrable to the forces that might destroy Zion.

We know that our journey toward Zion is a lifelong struggle, and at times we may feel very distant and unworthy of God's city in us, but the struggle is worth it. Zion is waiting. Look for ways that God can build a Zion in you with fortified walls, not ones that will go up today and come down once they become inconvenient. Forgive yourself when they weaken.

For the day: Look today for ways that you can march toward Zion in your relationship with God.

Prayer: God, I know that you want to build the city of Zion in my heart. Give me the strength to help you do this. The path to Zion is a hard one—a path that I may stumble on or stray from. Help me to keep my eye on the end goal and to find Zion today in all that I do. Amen.

Jake Blouch

March 17

The Grace to Praise!

Reading: Psalm 135:1-5

Praise the LORD! Praise the name of the LORD; give praise, O servants of the LORD, you that stand in the house of the LORD in the courts of the house of our God (Ps. 135:1-2).

Meditation: As I walked in the front yard I was greeted with *"Dios te bendiga!"* It had been a long time since I visited this small Anabaptist Pentecostal community.

Conflict within their congregation had driven them from their meeting place. This group had lost their sanctuary. They had been turned away from the doors to *their* house of the Lord. They had lost their home. I heard that night just how homeless they knew themselves to be and their longing for a place.

They gathered this midweek evening to hear the Word interpreted to them by their district elder, to pray, to seek direction. They shared their agony, but when it came time to pray, they poured out their requests and were not fearful to ask the Lord for what they desired. Praises and blessings echoed up above their outstretched arms. It was a time of blessing one another and praising God for God's love, God's continued presence, and God's unending mercy.

This community of aliens—a people in exile from their old building and some of them in exile from the land of their birth —could have stood in that courtyard downcast and claiming only that their plea for justice be dealt. They could have stood in that place and uttered their list of righteous complaints.

This group of sojourners praised God, out loud, in their front yard, for the world to see and to hear. Anyone who walked by—their neighbors and even those with whom they had once broken bread but from whom they had parted ways—would know that they had hope. God would neither leave them nor forsake them.

What faith! What courage! In this evening of blessings, bits of wisdom and grace, and praise for God, the house of the Lord had been built. And they praised the Lord who welcomed them into that sanctuary of peace and praise.

For the day: In the midst of your everyday, chaotic existence, give thanks to God, but also praise God for the unknown tomorrow. Praise God for God's blessed hope.

Prayer: God of all nations, we praise you for our lips. Unbind our tongues from that which seals them so that we may unashamedly and boldly praise you not just in times of gladness, but in times of despair. Help us to recognize that you never forsake us or leave us hopeless. We praise your holy name. Amen.

Valentina F. Satvedi

March 18

God's Transformative Power

Reading: 2 Chronicles 6:1-11

Then Solomon said, "The LORD has said that he would reside in thick darkness. I have built you an exalted house, a place for you to reside in forever" (2 Chron. 6:1-2).

Meditation: The Chroniclers here present an unabashedly celebratory account of Solomon's dedication of the temple. Unlike the authors of the Book of Kings, they make no mention of the more ambiguous elements of Solomon's undertaking: the heavy taxes he levied to fund the project, the slave labor he conscripted to complete the work, or the personal glory that he achieved as the benefactor for this magnificent temple. The Chroniclers see the magnificence, the grandeur without the darkness and the dirt. Yet the eyes of the Chroniclers have much to teach us. They write these words in the years following the dedication of the second temple. In the recent past, the people have witnessed the destruction of Jerusalem at the hands of the Babylonians, have seen the great temple of Solomon reduced to rubble, and have endured the exile. Yet somehow they managed to keep alive the stories of their ancestors, to teach their children of the God who brought them out of Egypt, and to rejoice when that same God delivered them out of Babylon. The miracles of the return to Jerusalem and the construction of the second temple have given the Chroniclers new eyes for the past. They see in the dedication of the temple of Solomon a structure that will be more solid than stone and cedar and cypress, a way of worship that will reach beyond the temple walls and the house of David, and a God who will not forsake them. The God they see wrests an anointed dynasty out of a fallen family, a people out of a ragtag group of refugees, and a divine plan out of a tragic story. When the darkness of the circumstances that surround us threatens to drive us to despair, let us remember the eyes of the Chroniclers and hope in the transformative power of God.

For the day: Open your eyes to see not the fallen nature of human efforts, but God's transformative power to conform all things to his will and his way.

Prayer: God of all goodness, embolden us to trust in your unfolding work in the world. Help us to see beyond our own shortcomings, beyond our doubts and despair, that we might hope in your cleansing grace. Amen.

Carol A. Scheppard

March 19

Body Language

Readings: 2 Chronicles 6:12-17; 2 Samuel 8:6-9

He stood on the platform and then knelt down before the whole assembly of Israel and spread out his hands toward heaven (2 Chron. 6:13b NIV).

113

Meditation: The thing that impressed me in this reading was Solomon's body language in prayer. He stood on a platform so that all could see, he knelt down before the whole assembly of Israel (a very unlikely thing for a king to do) and spread out his hands toward heaven. This was not just an oral prayer, it was visible prayer! Here was a leader of a whole nation kneeling down in great honor and respect and subservience to God, suggesting that God is the ultimate King.

Solomon bows down in humility before the true King! Remember that the people wanted a king like all the other nations, and Samuel was displeased. God told Samuel that the people were not rejecting him (Samuel) but they were rejecting God as their King. Perhaps Solomon was trying to say that God is not to be rejected, but to be enthroned in our lives. We must lift our hands up to heaven to receive the blessings of the One we serve. Of course, Solomon allowed the worship of many gods, leading Israel to forsake the one true God and worship false gods. War and a belief in redemptive violence are the false gods of our day. What leaders will visibly repent, humble themselves, kneel in obedience to God, and lift their hands to plead for peace?

For the day: Let go of all inclinations toward violence and war. Walk in peace and trust the call of Jesus that peacemakers are blessed children of God.

Prayer: God of hope and peace, we would, by your grace, pray with our heart, our lips, our body, and our soul to be a visible expression of your kingdom come, a light unto the nations to guide them into the ways of peace. Amen.

Richard F. Shreckhise

March 20

Prayers of Forgiveness

Reading: 2 Chronicles 6:18-31

Hear the supplications of your servant and of your people Israel when they pray toward this place. Hear from heaven, your dwelling place; and when you hear, forgive (2 Chron. 6:21 NIV).

Meditation: Solomon has great faith in God's presence in the temple. He asks that people will pray toward the temple even though God's dwelling is in heaven. The temple is where the people can meet God and express their prayers. Solomon assumes most of the prayers will be prayers of forgiveness. That is not a bad place to start. In the fall of 2006, there was a tragic shooting in an Amish schoolhouse. The Amish shocked the world by beginning their grief process with forgiveness. There can be no closure until there is forgiveness, so why not start there? Might this be just as true in our personal lives as we pray toward God? The place we call the church is often a place where we are most aware of God's presence, so let us come to this place with prayers of forgiveness for our foolishness, our sins, and with a willing spirit to be taught to walk in God's ways. The Apostle Peter denied Jesus three times and was restored by love to walk in the way of God tending his sheep.

Without forgiveness, we would be lost in the darkness of our wrongs.

For the day: Let forgiveness be a daily attitude, a daily practice toward others and from our own hearts toward God. Walk in forgiveness "for the glory of God and my neighbor's good" (Christopher Sauer II).

Prayer: When we come to you, Lord, squabbling with each other, when we are feeling alone and defeated, when we are struggling with natural or self-made disasters, when we need new life and resurrection . . . Lord, we come asking you to hear from heaven, your dwelling place, and when you hear, to forgive. Amen.

Richard F. Shreckhise

March 21

Forgiveness in a New Temple

Readings: 2 Chronicles 6:36-39; Luke 15:11-32

For there is no one who does not sin . . . (2 Chron. 6:36).

Meditation: Temples seem to anchor the presence of God with us. In his dedication prayer for the temple, Solomon expressed hope that the love and mercy of God would be found there. Included in Solomon's prayer is the hope that the temple would mediate divine forgiveness. He and we are fully aware that "there is no one who does not sin." His fervent desire was that God would hear and forgive the repentant prayers of a people gone wrong, no matter how far away from God their sins had taken them. Isn't that what we all hope for in those places where we meet God? Don't we hope that when our confession of our sin is authentic and our repentance genuine, God will somehow grant the strength to begin again and welcome us home with open arms?

In the Christian church, we rejoice that Christ in his resurrected glory has raised up a new temple, the temple of his body, the Church. When each of us functions as a priest for a brother or sister, God does indeed hear and offer forgiveness.

Just as it was once thought that God dwelled in the holy darkness of the temple, so now in the congregation we sense the presence of God who has shown himself in the life, death, and resurrection of Jesus Christ. Through that temple-like congregation, we hear the forgiving words of Christ in answer to our genuine confession and repentance and are drawn into new life—no matter how prodigal our lives have become.

For the day: Live today with the assurance that God does hear our genuine repentance and does respond with the love of a Father who has been waiting with eager longing for our return.

Prayer: Forgiving God, hear the deep confession of my soul. I have sinned against you. My single-most desire is that my life move toward your goal in Christ. Forgive me. Encourage me now to live as one forgiven, in freedom and hope. Amen.

Robert Dell

C

March 22

God's Promise Remembered

Reading: 2 Chronicles 6:40-42

O LORD God, do not reject your anointed one. Remember your steadfast love for your servant David (2 Chron. 6:42).

Meditation from our past: 1733. Because I have been requested by some to describe our trip, I have not been able to reject doing this completely, and therefore will try to describe, as briefly as possible, what I think necessary. . . .

On June 24 we sailed from Rotterdam until a half-hour from there, where we stopped, because of counter winds until July 3. . . . here began seasickness among the passengers. . . . On the 25th a small child died, who had come on board very ill, and was buried in the sea on the next day at eight o'clock. . . .

On August 3, I rose one hour before daybreak in order to see how it was going, as I had decided to watch the compass during the whole trip to see if a change of course took place. As I came to the ladder, all the people were still sleeping, and a bedroll was under the ladder, and the bed-blankets lay high on the ladder. During the night it had rained a little, making it slippery under the hatch, and as I stood on the last rung of the ladder and was about to step on the deck, the persons stretched themselves in their bed and involuntarily knocked the ladder from under me, so that I fell from the level of the deck with my left side striking the ladder. I was almost unconscious and lay there a long time before I could stand up. Then I had to lie on my back for fourteen days until I could get up again, and walk a bit. I was at first afraid that I would become lame but the Great God in His Son be praised, who allowed me to recover without herbs or bandages, so that I hardly feel it any more. . . .

On [September] 17th, a small land bird similar to the yellow water wagtail of Germany alighted several times on the ship, so that the people could see it well. This caused such great joy among the people that they all clapped their hands. . . .

. . . [On] the afternoon of the 29th in Philadelphia. . . . Brethren and sisters came to meet us in small boats with delicious bread, apples, peaches, and other refreshments of the body, for which we praised the great God publicly on the ship, with much singing and resounding prayers.
—*John Naas*

From European Origins of the Brethren, *Donald F. Durnbaugh, comp./tr., The Brethren Press, 1958, pp. 302-308.*

For the day: Are you ready to go where God sends you?

Prayer: Lord, grant me strength to follow where you lead me. Amen.

♉

March 23—Easter 2008

Fulfilled

Reading: Luke 24:44-49

Then he said to them, "These are my words that I spoke to you while I was still with you—that everything written about me in the law of Moses, the prophets, and the psalms must be fulfilled" (Luke 24:44).

Meditation: When was the last time life left you speechless?

In the case of the stunned disciples gathered in the upper room, it was the appearance of the risen Christ that robbed them of their words. It is easy to imagine their bewildered expressions and their racing thoughts. Can it be? What does it mean?

Jesus does all the talking in this text from Luke's Gospel, and what he says is aimed at answering their questions. First, he offers his wounded hands and feet as proof that it is indeed he. Then he moves on to the much more important question: What does it all mean?

What it means, Jesus explains, is that God is faithful. The plan and promises of God are being fulfilled. The crucifixion may have been a terrible tragedy, but it was no accident. It was a way to show the depth of God's love and the strength of God's commitment to humanity. Not even death can defeat our God.

When we grasp what Easter means, we recover our voices and join with Christians everywhere to sing, "Christ the Lord is risen today—Alleluia!"

For the day: Celebrate God's faithfulness and power. Let it free you from fear, so that you can live boldly, serve joyfully, and love deeply every day.

Prayer: God, because you keep your promises, we know what faithfulness is. Help us to be faithful to you and to one another as we receive the power from on high and set out in ministry. And may your victory over death give us confidence and courage every day. Amen.

James L. Benedict

March 24

God's Commands

Readings: Psalm 119:25-32; Mark 12:28-34

And thou shalt love the Lord thy God with all thy heart, and with all thy soul, and with all thy mind, and with all thy strength: this is the first commandment. And the second is like, namely this, Thou shalt love thy neighbour as thyself. There is none other commandment greater than these (Mark 12:30-31 KJV).

Meditation: The psalmist calls us to follow God's commandments, but sometimes our understanding of God's will fails us. As Paul puts it, we see through a "glass darkly." Even our conscience can mislead us. Before the Civil War, Christians sometimes embraced scriptural passages to support slavery. Their conscience told them slavery was right.

Mark Twain's Huckleberry Finn grew up in a slave state. Huck's conscience told him that he was wrong by helping Jim, a runaway slave, escape from his rightful owner. As Huck and Jim rafted down the Mississippi River, Huck's feelings for his good friend overcame his conscience and he helped Jim escape.

Huck did the right thing, but he still thought it was wrong. His feelings won.

Our feelings can also mislead us. Impassioned cries for vengeance echo under every flag, in every war. An eye for an eye. Right and wrong are lost in the fury, and everybody is blinded.

Both head and heart are important in discerning the commandments, but we need more. Jesus provides it in the commandment to love God and neighbor as ourselves. Christians came to judge slavery not by the letter but by the spirit of Christ, expressed by that great commandment. Every other command is to be judged in that light.

For the day: Measure everything by love: your concern for the welfare of others in your head and the kindness in your heart.

Prayer: May the rising sun of each day bring again and again the warmth of your love and the wisdom of your commandments. May your love embrace our passions and guide our reason; may our trust rest with the greatest commandment of all, that we love you and others, as we love ourselves. Amen.

Kenneth L. Brown

♂

March 25

Living Toward Maturity

Readings: 2 Chronicles 34:1-7; Ephesians 4:11-13

[Josiah] did what was right in the sight of the LORD, and walked in the ways of his ancestor David; he did not turn aside to the right or to the left (2 Chron. 34:2).

Meditation: Some people seem to get it right. They serve as good role models, whose lives exemplify spiritual maturity. The

Chronicler describes King Josiah as one who "got it right."

In poetic form the Chronicler identifies three marks of spiritual maturity, all of which are interrelated. Josiah participated in an ongoing conversation with God. Secondly, he chose carefully his own life model. And finally, Josiah would not be distracted from right living.

Most of us can identify such a person (or persons) whose life models spiritual maturity. We may be tempted to try to duplicate that life, but such an effort always ends in failure. We will be more successful if we are able to identify the marks of spiritual maturity that distinguish that exemplary life. Perhaps, in our own way, we can embody those marks of maturity.

Equally risky is the temptation to live intentionally as a model for others. Such a life seldom exemplifies spiritual maturity. Instead, as the Apostle Paul reminds us, such a person lives a life controlled by law, image, and duty.

Jesus, the model and the completion of all spiritual maturity, lived as the Chronicler ascribed to Josiah: conversing with God, rejoicing in the maturity of others, and focusing fully on God's way, truth, and light.

For the day: Live each day toward spiritual maturity, giving thanks for the spiritual maturity visible in the lives of those around you.

Prayer: Guiding and gracious God, thank you for the maturity that has marked the lives of others, past and present, maturity that is most perfectly visible in the life of Jesus. Help us to take from others not so much the path we should walk, but the way we must walk the road you have set before us through Jesus Christ. Amen.

Eugene F. Roop

♂

March 26

Learning from the Past

Readings: 2 Chronicles 34:8-18; Hebrews 12:1-2

The priest Hilkiah found the book of the law of the LORD given through Moses (2 Chron. 34:14b).

Meditation: The temple needed repairing. Most likely the flat roof leaked. As the carpenters and stonemasons cleared out the storage room, they found a book (a scroll) and gave it to the priest. Hilkiah found it to be Torah, God's teaching. Scholars suggest the scroll was at least part of the Book of Deuteronomy. Recognizing the importance of the scroll, Hilkiah took it to King Josiah.

We seldom clean out the "attic" unless we need to locate a leak in the roof or (more frequently) our parents are downsizing. The work goes slowly as we sort through the discoveries such cleaning uncovers. Most of the "valuables" go to the dumpster or Goodwill. Occasionally the sorting uncovers a diary or a bundle of letters. Those we read.

We naturally construct our past out of bits and pieces of our own memory. Putting our hands on additional documents may provide us with new information about or perhaps another perspective on family history. We may discover that we have idealized our past, measuring ourselves by a standard that never existed. Perhaps we have misread our formative relationships, feeling damaged by events we never adequately understood. Quite likely we will discover that the past presents a mixed picture, both of wisdom and folly. Be that as it may, learning more about our ancestors enables us to better understand ourselves. Such knowledge may lead to an increase in wisdom.

For the day: Cherish the opportunity to learn more about your past not to judge your ancestors, but to learn more about yourself.

Prayer: God of our ancestors, open us to learning more about the people, places, and events that formed us. Teach us to welcome moments of discovery, whether they come through documents or conversations. Help us to use such "discoveries" to grow in wisdom through Christ Jesus. Amen.

Eugene F. Roop

March 27

The Sins of the Past

Readings: 2 Chronicles 34:19-21; Leviticus 26:40-46

Our ancestors did not keep the word of the LORD (2 Chron. 34:21b).

Meditation: The work of every generation reflects a mixture of faithful and unfaithful discipleship. This "mixed" past affects our faith and practice today. The faithful service of the past has provided a foundation on which we can build. The sin of past generations leaves wounds that must be addressed. Bigotry against people of color, prejudice against Jews and Roman Catholics, constraints on leadership by women, all this discrimination together with global mission work, Heifer Project, CROP, SERRV, Brethren camps, and alternatives to military service constitute our mixed heritage.

Josiah recognized that he needed to address the unfaithful practices from the past. He began with a ritual of acknowledgment and confession: *he tore his clothes.* He followed that by seeking God's forgiveness. Too often we ignore the sins of our ancestors, contending that we cannot be accountable for their sins. We insist that the prejudice of the past does not affect us.

Inherited prejudice is far more powerful than we usually acknowledge. Most of us worship in racially or economically homogeneous congregations, unsure why that remains the case. At the same time, we assume that our beliefs and practices serve as an essential mark of our distinctive identity. Could it be that some of those practices serve a less noble purpose—excluding others and perpetuating prejudice inherited from our ancestors?

For the day: Do you observe or participate in church practices that serve to exclude others, thus, perpetuating prejudice inherited from our ancestors?

Prayer: Gracious God, we see clearly the flaws of our ancestors. We even acknowledge that the sin of our ancestors may affect us—a little. We confess that for the most part our eyes cannot see and our hearts cannot admit that this is so. Give us eyes to see what lies still hidden from our sight and the courage to respond in confession and change. Amen.

Eugene F. Roop

March 28

Act and Consequence

Readings: 2 Chronicles 34:22-28; Matthew 6:24

Because they have forsaken me . . . my wrath will be poured out (2 Chron. 34:25).

Meditation: For the most part, actions have predictable consequences. Very early children learn the relationship between act and consequence: touching a hot stove burns; falling from a bike hurts. Adults understand that the direct relationship between act and consequence extends far beyond the "law" of gravity.

The biblical sage also extends cause and effect beyond hot stoves and traffic accidents: *Whoever is steadfast in righteousness will live, but whoever pursues evil will die* (Prov. 11:19). The way we live affects our life and our death.

The prophet Huldah takes the act-consequence principle further still: *Because they have forsaken [God] . . . [divine] wrath will be poured out.* Violation of the first commandment has direct and deathly consequences. *You shall have no other gods before me* allows for no exceptions. Jesus makes the same point: *No one can serve two masters.*

We are in no danger, we say. We steadfastly affirm our commitment to God. But be careful. Josiah realized that those most clear and confident about their commitment to God are often blind to their own divided loyalties. Money, beliefs, power, image, family, work, children, country. The list is long. Most of us do not realize how consistently we compromise our allegiance to God.

For the day: Search your heart today for your divided loyalties.

Prayer: God, we reaffirm our commitment to you, three in one: Creator, Savior, and Sustainer. We confess that we compromise this allegiance. Sometimes in the very moment of choosing our actions, we recognize they violate our commitment to you. You see the many times we are blind to our own sin. Open our eyes and forgive our sin. This is our prayer through Jesus Christ our Lord. Amen.

Eugene F. Roop

&

March 29

Keeping the Balance

Readings: 2 Chronicles 34:29-33; Luke 22:17-20

The king . . . made a covenant before the LORD, to follow the LORD (2 Chron. 34:31).

Meditation: A covenant is a relationship marked by mutual commitment, responsibility, and benefit. Each party to the covenant commits him/herself to the other, assumes certain responsibilities within the relationship, and gains benefit from the relationship. Marriage constitutes the most clearly defined covenant in our culture. In marriage the commitment and responsibility are generally spelled out. The benefits of marriage are less clearly expressed. For the most part, previous generations expected companionship and security from the marriage covenant. Today many married couples identify happiness as a primary benefit of marriage.

For adults in the church, in baptism we entered a life-defining covenant. In that act we made a public commitment of faith in Jesus Christ. In that moment we received God's commitment to us through Jesus Christ: *I am with you always, to the end of the age* (Matt. 28:20).

In our life journey, some of us become preoccupied with one aspect of Christian covenant and lose the balance of commitment, responsibility, and benefit. Over-emphasizing responsibility can leave us exhausted as we constantly strive to be more faithful. On the other hand, settling comfortably into baptism's benefit lulls us into cheap grace, grace without accountability. While it is easy to see the imbalance in the lives of others, we too often ignore the fact that our own covenant with God lacks balance in commitment, responsibility, and benefit.

For the day: Think about the covenants you are part of. How well do you balance commitment, responsibility, and benefit?

Prayer: Most gracious God, thank you for the covenant you granted through Christ Jesus. When we take that covenant for granted, remind us of our responsibility to act justly, to extend compassion, and to walk humbly with you. When we strive to secure our covenant with you, help us relax and receive the peace, joy, and rest granted by a life lived in your presence through Jesus Christ our Lord. Amen.

Eugene F. Roop

⁗⋮

March 30

His Word Only

Readings: Psalm 119:33-40; Hebrews 4:12; 2 Timothy 3:16-17

Teach me, O Lord, the way of Your statutes, And I shall keep it to the end. Give me understanding, and I shall keep Your law; Indeed, I shall observe it with my whole heart. Make me walk in the path of Your commandments, For I delight in it. Incline my heart to Your testimonies, And not to covetousness. Turn away my eyes from looking at worthless things, And revive me in Your way. Establish Your word to Your servant, Who is devoted to fearing You. Turn away my reproach which I dread, For Your judgments are good. Behold, I long for Your precepts; Revive me in Your righteousness (Ps. 119:33-40 NKJV).

Meditation: One of the most difficult and challenging aspects of being a new pastor is determining what book of the Bible or portion of a text to preach on next. The text above, with the great emphasis on the personal pronoun *Your* (which is used ten times in eight verses), provides for me a greater determination to ask the Lord what *he* wants me to say from *his* Word. Our Fellowship's motto is "The Bible, the whole Bible, and nothing but the Bible." What if we went back to those basics and just used a concordance (maybe an expository dictionary) and *his* Word alone for sermon preparation? Likewise, for all of us who are devoted to fearing the Lord, what if we in our personal devotions approached *his* Word by asking the Holy Spirit's insight and understanding and not someone else's opinion? Perhaps he would revive us in *his* righteousness.

For the day: Make a renewed effort this day to ask the Holy Spirit for understanding and new insight into his Word.

Prayer: Heavenly Father, in whom belong all the treasures of wisdom and knowledge, forgive us for relying on the opinions of others and for looking at worthless things. Revive in us your righteousness as we seek to follow your Word alone.

Christopher J. Hinshaw

Trusting God's Covenant in Hard Times

March 31–April 27

$\mathcal{A}$lthough on the one hand they found favor with God and the people, they also encountered enemies of the truth. Now and then persecution occurred for the sake of the Word. Some endured with joy the confiscation of their property. Others, however, had to endure bonds and imprisonment. Some spent only a few weeks, but others several years in prison. . . . All were freed, however, with clear consciences through the miraculous providence of God.

Alexander Mack, Jr. (1712–1803)

March 31

With Uplifted Hands

Reading: Psalm 141:1-4

Let my prayer be counted as incense before you, and the lifting up of my hands as an evening sacrifice (Ps. 141:2).

Meditation: Students called it the *"Por Favor"* class. Designed to teach Spanish to meet everyday needs, the lessons centered on basic words and phrases. A simply essential phrase was *por favor*, Spanish for "please" or "if you please." Just those words *por favor*, coupled with hand gestures, became a marvelously effective way to communicate: hands offering a chair, *por favor*; hands beckoning another to come near, *por favor*; hands offering a registration form to fill out, *por favor*; hands inviting another to go first, *por favor*; hands in prayer inviting the entire gathering into praise and communion with God, *por favor.*

Perhaps we humans understand universal hand language better than words. Everyone knows the meaning of a hand knotted in a fist, a hand extended in friendship, a hand held, a hand caressing a fevered brow, a hand that slaps, a hand offering a cup of cold water, hands lifted to the heavens in joyful praise and petition. And so with God. However we may talk with God, however we request God's support, we believe God hears the language of words, lifting of the hands, even the breath of our hopes, and even more, the yearnings of our hearts. "Please, God!" *"Por favor!"*

For the day: Let your whole being pray. Let every word you say, every move of your hands, every breath you breathe, every step you take, every hope of your heart be a prayer of blessing for others and God's support for yourself!

Prayer: God, with Christ and all the saints of all time, we come to you with our hopes and need for your support and love. Whatever we say and however we say it, we believe you will understand and answer! Thanks be you! Amen.

Sonja Sherfy Griffith

ᖇ

April 1

God's Deliverance

Readings: Daniel 1:1-2; James 1:1-4

And the Lord delivered Jehoiakim king of Judah into his hand . . . (Dan. 1:2 NIV).

Meditation: We are conditioned to think of God's deliverance as that which rescues us from peril or adversity. In this case, for Daniel and the Israelites, God delivered them into the hands of their oppressors, the Babylonians. Of course, prophets like Jeremiah had warned that just such "deliverance" was coming as God's judgment on Israel's unfaithfulness to their holy calling. The prophet Habakkuk struggled to understand how a God who loved them and stood in covenant relationship with them could carry out such "deliverance." But God did. Someone has said that history is God's story. Of course, we know that God was not finished with his people. After a season of refinement, God "delivered" them again, this time from the hands of the Babylonians, and granted them permission to return and rebuild their glorious temple and city.

When we enter difficult times personally, or as congregations and denominations, our first response is to pray for "deliverance" from these situations that beset us. The stress of the denominational history of the 1880s may have been one of those times. However, such situations might, in fact, be God's "deliverance," so that we will return to our first love and learn again the things that lead to holiness and find ourselves in a new place spiritually, which may lead to the revisioning and rebuilding of our lives, our families, and our congregations.

For the day: God remains faithful to the covenant established with his people. There is always hope. God desires to restore us to wholeness and holiness. Sometimes the path there leads us through dark valleys. But for the faithful, there is always tomorrow. Be hopeful today.

Prayer: Loving God, who loves with a covenantal love, provide the deliverance we need for this hour that is upon us. Teach us your ways, even in the midst of suffering, so we may again worship, serve, and witness with passion and joy. Amen.

Galen R. Hackman

April 2

Be Not Conformed

Readings: Daniel 1:3-7; Romans 12:1-2

The chief official gave them new names . . . (Dan. 1:7 NIV).

Meditation: As was the practice in Babylon, the king chose from among the deported peoples a few men of outstanding characteristics to be trained for service in his court. The training was extensive and amounted to a reorientation to the culture, history, language, and religion of the Babylonians. To begin this process, the king gave each of the chosen Israelites new names. On the surface, this may not seem like such a big deal. However, the Israelite names had built into them a reference to the God of Israel, while the new names that were given included one of the gods of the Babylonia pantheon. For example, Daniel (includes *el*, Hebrew for God, as in *Elohim*) means "God is my judge"; but his new name, Belteshazzar, includes *Bel*, the name of the Babylonia god equivalent to the Canaanite god, *Baal*. As it turned out, learning the literature and history of Babylon did not pose a problem for the Israelites—they excelled in their learning beyond all others (Dan. 1:18-20)—but it was the reorientation of their faith that gave them trouble.

We live in a world that would like to reorient our faith in the God of the Bible. Though we may gladly learn the languages and histories of our world, we must ever be on guard against the relentless erosion of our faith that would lead us away from God and the principles that please him.

For the day: Pressure to be conformed to this world never lets up. Some such conformity is good in that it enables us to serve the present age. But some take us away from our faith. Walk through this day with open eyes, seeking to see the difference.

Prayer: God of Wisdom and Understanding, we desire to honor you; give to us this day wisdom to know what principles are indeed from you and therefore must be held dear at all costs, and what things are simply a matter of our preference and can be let go or modified. Amen.

Galen R. Hackman

℘

April 3

Resolve

Readings: Daniel 1:8-10; Romans 10:8-15

Now God had caused the official to show favor and sympathy to Daniel . . . (Dan. 1:9 NIV).

Meditation: Daniel made a resolution. He decided that he would remain true to the principles of his covenant with God and not eat the king's food. No doubt it was the best food in the land, but it was unclean by God's standards. As Daniel determined to live by this principle, even in this pagan land, he had no idea of how his resolve would be received by the king. It could mean his death. Nonetheless, he stood his ground. However, God had prepared the heart of the king's official, and Daniel was able to leave a substantial witness for God in this heathen land.

Often we face situations where we need to choose. Do we stand for a principle we know to be God's way, do we speak out for God, or do we cave in to the expectations around us and keep our mouths shut? When faced with these dilemmas, we are often unsure how those around us will respond. We ask ourselves, If I share my faith in this situation, will I be rejected or ridiculed or marginalized? These are natural fears and questions. But at the root, they show a lack of faith in God. Perhaps he has prepared a heart and that heart is just waiting to see or hear some good news. We Brethren desperately need to boldly share our faith.

For the day: Every day holds God appointments—those times when we are placed in situations and with people whom God has prepared. Live today looking for just such opportunities and then share from your heart the Word as God gives it to you. Expect great blessings as you are obedient to God.

Prayer: All seeing God, place me today in situations that you have prepared, and give me insight and understanding and courage to share my faith in love for you and love for those around me. Amen.

Galen R. Hackman

X

April 4

The Ten-Day Test

Readings: Daniel 1:11-14; Luke 7:1-10

Please test your servants for ten days . . . (Dan. 1:12 NIV).

Meditation: Tests abound: academic exams, physical exams, medical tests. Daniel and his three friends put their faith and the promises of God, as they understood them, to the test. This, we are cautioned in Scripture, should not be done carelessly (Deut. 6:16). The four Hebrew men stepped out in faith and trusted God and they were not disappointed. In New Testament language, they walked by faith (Heb. 10:38).

Many Brethren have exhibited strong faith and put God to the test; Alexander Mack, John Naas, Christopher Sauer come to mind. They may have wondered, Will God honor his promises? But they pressed forward nonetheless. At times the way became difficult, as it did on a later occasion for Daniel and his friends. But God was faithful. Today God is again calling us to increase our faith, personally and corporately as congregations. God wants us to rise up and reach out into a world nearly as pagan as the one in which Daniel found himself. Daniel and his friends were confident that God would honor their faith and that he would receive glory. A witness for God is always manifest when people live by faith, especially when they do so against all odds.

For the day: God honors the covenant with us, his people, by blessing our faith in his promises, especially faith that alters our way of living and leads us to boldly and lovingly step out and proclaim God's heart in word and deed. This brings glory to God in places where darkness reigns.

Prayer: God, grant me great faith today. Enable me to lay hold of your promises and live by them so that you might be glorified in my life, community, and church. Enable our congregations to be bold in faith as we live for you and as we reach out to our communities with the healing balm of the gospel.

Galen R. Hackman

April 5

Godly Wisdom

Readings: Daniel 1:15-17; John 15:18-25

To these four young men God gave knowledge and understanding . . . (Dan. 1:17 NIV).

Meditation: Twice in these verses the word *understand* (or *understanding*) appears. Daniel and his four friends had understanding and knowledge that were rooted in their relationship with God. Theirs was Godly wisdom and knowledge, with widespread practical ramifications. They had resolved to "obey God rather than human beings" (Acts 5:29). They did so humbly and respectfully. Nonetheless, they had broken the law and would face the consequences. But their obedience to God resulted in deep spirituality. Daniel and his friends were able to discern God's way in the midst of many other ways. As a result, they had a positive impact on the lives of those around them. Those with eyes to see grew in their openness to God.

Everyone needs mentors on this journey of faith. Some guides or mentors influence us directly through their presence in our lives; others leave a legacy for us through their writings or their life stories. The three hundred years of Brethren history that now lie behind us are filled with people who demonstrated Godly wisdom. Thank God for them.

For the day: Think of the spiritual giants who have influenced your life as a Christian. Perhaps it was a minister or pastor or a teacher or just a friend. Maybe the impact came decades or centuries later through their writings. These are women and men who embody Godly wisdom—a wisdom born out of a lifetime of living in the light of God's covenant.

Prayer: Transforming God, today we ask two things. First, that you would give us hearts to remember those who have been used by you to move us along the journey of faith. Thank you for their lives of faithfulness. And second, we ask that in your counsel and grace, we might be found worthy to be such a person who provides inspiration and story for another on his or her path of faith. Amen.

Galen R. Hackman

April 6

For the Long Haul

Readings: Daniel 1:18-21; Hebrews 11:13-16

And Daniel remained there until the first year of King Cyrus (Dan. 1:21 NIV).

Meditation: Daniel was young when he was carried into captivity by the armies of Nebuchadnezzar. He remained in this foreign land until his death and was, according to tradition, buried in Susa. His last vision occurred during the third year of King Cyrus's reign (536 B.C.). Daniel would have been over eighty years old at the time and had lived under three ruling powers: Babylonians, Medes, and Persians. What was it like for Daniel to live nearly his entire life as a sojourner in this foreign land? He was a stranger and a pilgrim there. Yet, he served his time and his culture well, rising to high levels of leadership in government and serving as an advisor in the courts of three kings. In many ways Daniel would have looked and acted like any other person of importance. However, during all this time, he remained faithful to the covenant God had established with his people. He worshiped only God. It could not have been easy. Danger abounded (fiery furnaces and dens of lions).

Daniel's faith comes down to us today as a challenge and an example. Many of us live in communities and work in environments where it is not easy to live our faith. Tests and temptations abound. And Daniel did this for the long haul, day after day and year after year.

For the day: You are not the first person to face spiritual challenges in the environment, in your family, in the workplace, in your school, community or even the church. Many of our Brethren and Anabaptist forebears faced arduous situations. God calls us to be faithful where we live and work. And God enables us for this calling through the Holy Spirit dwelling within us.

Prayer: Sustaining God, remind me of Daniel's faith and unswerving loyalty when I am called upon today and everyday to live for you as the days stretch into months and months into years. May I be found faithful in the long haul. Amen.

Galen R. Hackman

⌒

April 7

God's Protection and Peace Forevermore

Reading: Psalm 121:1-4

I lift up my eyes to the hills—from where will my help come?
My help comes from God, who made heaven and earth. God will
not let your foot be moved; the one who keeps you will not slum-
ber; behold, the one who keeps Israel will neither slumber nor sleep
(Ps. 121:1-4 An Inclusive Language Lectionary: Readings for Year
B, p. 186).

Meditation: The view of the mountains outside my window is
breathtaking. Each season has a beauty all its own. In spring
there is the delicate budding of leaves all along the vista. In
summer there is the splendor of the trees and grasses fully
dressed in shades of green. In the fall there is a technicolor
landscape of autumn hues climbing up the mountainside. And
even in the winter the stark outline of trees against a fresh
blanket of snow holds its own striking beauty. After a long day
at work I come home and gaze out my window and I am
inspired. My thoughts gradually shift from the mountains to
the Creator and Maker of heaven and earth, of creepy crawly
things, of the sun and the moon, of rivers and lakes, of wind
and rain, and of men and women like me. My spirit becomes
one with creation and I experience this deep and prayerful
knowing that God is the source of any help and strength, any
comfort or courage that I need. Slowly then the joys and the
challenges of my day find their rightful places. The stresses are
put in perspective and the power they wield is subdued. And
for those moments, I am given the gift of peace that the world

never gives and can never take away—a deep peace that is mine for the moment but available to all.

For the day: Take a moment to find the "window" in your life that inspires you and directs you to God. What do you see there today? What of God is there to behold?

Prayer: Holy One, help me to see you in the landscapes of life. Help me to trust your constant care and to experience the deep peace that only you can give. Amen.

Bonnie Kline Smeltzer

April 8

Red Carpet Gold

Reading: Daniel 3:1-7

. . . you are to fall down and worship the golden statue that King Nebuchadnezzar has set up. Whoever does not fall down and worship shall immediately be thrown into a furnace of blazing fire (Dan. 3:5b-6).

Meditation: Wow! This sounds like Babylonian Oscar Night. In trendy Hollywood fashion, the king crafts an exquisite golden statue, summons the notable dignitaries and celebrities, ushers the distinguished guests down the red carpet of infamy, and then, as a part of the gala's program, commands them to express thanks to the academy of one—himself—by falling down in adoration, devotion, and worship.

How tempting it is to get caught up in all the hoopla of the day. The king calls. The gold glitters. The orchestra plays. The red carpet beckons. The excitement builds. The people jump and run. But what is the true source of all this attraction? Will this fascination draw me closer to God? What is misguided devotion? How much will my action cost me? There are so many summonses for attention, so many questions, and so many images that contend for my devotion. Where is God? Is the splendor of Babylon the splendor of *my* King? What if red carpet gold is in fact fool's gold? What if God is somewhere totally unexpected—in the furnace of faith—and is not the bling of Babylon?

Godly discernment is a gift available to every generation. Yet, the allure of apostasy dazzles the mind of the spiritually disconnected. Knowing this, we must anchor our thoughts and our hope in God, pledge our worship to the One who is worthy, and filled with trust, fall in adoration before the Refiner's Fire.

For the day: Consider what dazzles you, and seek to divert your devotion to God, the One who is worthy.

Prayer: God of unshared glory, pour out your discernment. Protect me from shallow allegiance, foolish loyalty, and perilous worship. Usher me into true worship. Grant me astonishing courage—the kind that burns bright and is never consumed. Amen.

Craig H. Smith

April 9

Spiritual Integrity

Reading: Daniel 3:8-15

If you are ready to fall down and worship the image I made, very good. But if you do not worship it, you will be thrown immediately into a blazing furnace. Then what god will be able to rescue you from my hand? (Dan. 3:15 NIV).

Meditation: Men of power feel compelled to force people to praise them, by one means or another. The case of the great king Nebuchadnezzar was dramatic. Every one of his subjects was compelled to bow down in worship before his huge image of gold. It would almost have seemed natural for the three Jews, Shadrach, Meshach, and Abednego, to follow their colleagues in this act. After all, they could have reasoned, was this not merely a civil ceremony? They knew in their souls, however, that the worship of that idolatrous image would compromise their allegiance to their Creator and Lord. Death was preferable to the sacrifice of their spiritual integrity.

Our Brethren forefathers learned by bitter experience the lesson of the three Jews. Commitment to their convictions cost them lands and sometimes lives. Today the temptation to compromise is far more subtle. However, though few believers face punishment for their refusal to bow down to life's idols, all can experience the deep satisfaction of living a life of integrity.

For the day: What are the idols in your life? Worshiping God means refusing to allow anything else to become a god in our lives, whether material possessions, pleasures, or even other people.

Prayer: Holy Father, I renew my commitment to you as the God of my life. I am in this world, but not of it. May I use the things of this world not as objects of spiritual satisfaction, but as the means of using my life to bow down to you and give you glory.

Thomas Julien

April 10

Subject to the King

Reading: Daniel 3:16-23

If our God whom we serve is able to deliver us from the furnace of blazing fire and out of your hand, O king, let him deliver us. But if not, be it known to you, O king, that we will not serve your gods and we will not worship the golden statue that you have set up (Dan. 3:17-18).

Meditation from our past: Now I will freely and publicly confess that my crime is that Jesus Christ, the King of kings and Lord of lords, desired that we do what we are doing—that the sinner shall repent and believe in the Lord Jesus and should be baptized in water upon his confession of faith. He should then seek to carry out everything Jesus has commanded and publicly bequeathed in His Testament. If we are doing wrong herein against the revealed word of the Holy Scriptures, be it in teaching, way of life, or conduct, we would gladly receive instruction. If, however, no one can prove this on the basis of the Holy Scriptures, and yet persecutes us despite this, we would gladly suffer and bear it for the sake of the teachings of Jesus Christ.

. . . Therefore I am making my humble appeal to the gracious lord that he might test according to the Holy Scriptures and investigate thoroughly everything that now goes on in his territory. For he, too, has an immortal soul, and will have to give account one day before Jesus, the supreme liege lord, by whom he was placed in authority in his territory, about the way he governed his territory— .

whether it was according to sacred order or not.
—*Alexander Mack, Sr.*

From The Complete Writings of Alexander Mack, *"Letter to Count Charles August,"*
Wm. Eberly, ed. BMH Books, 1991, p. 18.

For the day: Does your way of life provide enough evidence to convict you of being a Christian?

Prayer: One Lord, one faith, one hope, one prayer to you, God of heaven and earth. Amen.

ᴂ

April 11

Not a Hint of Fire

Reading: Daniel 3:24-27

Nebuchadnezzar then approached the door of the furnace of blazing fire and said, "Shadrach, Meshach, and Abednego, servants of the Most High God, come out! Come here!" So Shadrach, Meshach, and Abednego came out from the fire (Dan. 3:26).

Meditation: Cut off from all they had known and loved, the ancient people of Jerusalem had to rethink—even re-invent—their relationship with God. Prior to the fall of Jerusalem, the ancient people of Judah could not conceive of their beloved city's destruction, convinced as they were that God had chosen the city and its temple as God's dwelling place. But with the city's destruction, a new framework needed to be embraced.

Consider how powerful this story of Shadrach, Meshach, and Abednego would have been to the exiles. The three companions of Daniel hold so firm to their devotion to God that they are willing to endure a fiery furnace. Astonishingly, the three are unharmed. "The hair of their heads was not singed, their tunics were not harmed, and not even the smell of fire came from them" (3:27). Even more astoundingly, the king and his advisors look into the blazing furnace and see not three, but four people walking, and the fourth "has the appearance of a god" (3:25). In the midst of intense fire, God provides an angel of protection for Shadrach, Meshach, and Abednego.

The power of this story is not that it carries a guarantee that our hairs will not be singed as we walk through our own times of trial. No, the power is its amazing affirmation that the Spirit of God walks with us even in the midst of our deepest struggles, encouraging, upholding, strengthening, empowering us. This story challenges us to embrace the pathways of Christian discipleship with faith and courage. The good news is that God is with all who respond to the call to do justice, proclaim peace, extend arms of compassion, go the extra mile in relationships, and walk humbly with the One who loves us with a love that will not let us go.

For the day: Embrace the good news. Even in the midst of difficulty, struggle, and grief, God is with us, strengthening, renewing, and empowering us to live faithfully.

Prayer: Grant us courage, O God, to live courageously, embracing your call to walk in the ways of peace, compassion, servanthood, and right living. Amen.

Joel D. Kline

April 12

God's Power to Deliver

Readings: Daniel 3:28-30; John 19:8-12

Nebuchadnezzar said, "Blessed be the God of Shadrach, Meshach, and Abednego, who has sent his angel and delivered his servants who trusted in him. They disobeyed the king's command and yielded up their bodies rather than serve and worship any god except their own God" (Dan. 3:28).

Meditation: God's power to deliver is for those who continue to trust in God, even in the worst of circumstances. King Nebuchadnezzar threw Shadrach, Meshach, and Abednego into the fiery furnace because they refused to fall down and worship the golden statue that was ninety feet high and nine feet wide. To the astonishment of the king, they were untouched. So the king acknowledged that the power of God is beyond the power of the king himself or the power of any idol. Therefore, Nebuchadnezzar decreed that he would destroy all people and nations who challenged God.

To know God's power is to distance ourselves from the idols of our lives, from whatever calls our primary allegiance away from God. When our trust is with God, over and above the many demands that clamor for our commitment, only then will we experience God's power to deliver us. Even our trust in governmental power and its great symbols must not replace our trust in God. Standing before Pilate, Jesus said, "You would have no power over me except it had been given you from above" (John 19:11a). Like Nebuchadnezzar, the Roman emperors finally came to acknowledge the power of God in Jesus Christ. Neither could understand that God's kingdom does not come by threat of destruction. When Pilate asked Jesus, "Are you the King of the Jews?" Jesus answered, "If my kingdom were from this world, my followers would be fighting" (John 18:36). God's ultimate power and justice are evidenced not by decrees of destruction, but rather by the embodiment of God's grace and love. This is true for all people and nations. Those who trust in God will live in God's love.

For the day: God's ultimate power is seen not in the capacity to compel others to submit, but in the deliverance we come to know when we continue to trust God even in the darkest times of our lives.

Prayer: O Divine Lord, who holds all the powers of our lives in your hand, teach us to trust you in the midst of our greatest fears, to rejoice in your deliverance, and to learn that your kingdom comes by grace and love beyond all of our expectations. Amen.

Donald E. Miller

April 13

God Will Keep You

Reading: Psalm 121:5-8

The LORD will keep your going out and your coming in from this time on and forevermore (Ps. 121:8).

Meditation from our past: It's something to get to the place where you don't know your name or where you are. That's how far I got [after a debilitating stroke]. Babies don't know their names. Babies just lie there and trust. I can do that. I can trust just like a baby. I am ready to take anything God sends—not only what "God sends," but what "God lets happen." That's important.

There are certain things I can't do all right.

I am here in a world of suffering.

I can't even choose what kind of suffering I'll have. But I can choose what my attitude is going to be toward suffering.

No matter how great a person's suffering or loss, he is still free to decide how he will take his condition— whether he will yield to it or stand up to it. In the process he will find that he becomes more concerned about a meaning for life than a meaning for suffering. In finding a meaning for life, he can take whatever happens to him.

Even if there may be nothing to do for oneself or for others, one can still worship. Worship makes thanksgiving possible. Thanksgiving opens the heart for God and for being a blessing to every available person. It will bring an end to any feeling of uselessness. We must trust God to take everything and work it out to his glory. —*Anna Mow*

From Two or Ninety-Two, *Plough Publishing, 1997; Brethren Press edition, 2001, p. 15.*

For the day: Take inventory of your body, what is working and what is not, and praise God for ability and disability.

Prayer: Lord, grant me the courage to change the things I can, the patience to accept the things I cannot change, and the wisdom to know the difference. Amen.

♫

April 14

Commitment to Christ

Reading: Psalm 119:57-64

The LORD is my portion; I promise to keep your words (Ps. 119:57).

Meditation from our past: We indeed have neither a new church nor any new laws. We only want to remain in simplicity and true faith in the original church which Jesus founded through His blood. We wish to obey the commandments which was in the beginning. We do not demand that undoubted divinity be recognized in our church fellowship. Rather, we would wish that undoubted divinity might indeed be recognized in Christ himself, and then in the church at Jerusalem. If this and its divinity in teaching, words, and commandment were to be acknowledged, then it could be determined whether a church has this divine teaching in it or not.

. . . If we remain in the teaching of the New Testament, we expect this outcome, namely, that the fulfillment of our faith will be eternal life. In return for insignificant shame and suffering, we will obtain immeasurable momentous glory. We cannot testify for our descendants—as their faith is, so shall be their outcome.
—*Alexander Mack, Sr.*

From The Complete Writings of Alexander Mack, *"Basic Questions" (1713).*
Wm. Eberly, ed. BMH Books, 1991, pp. 39-40.

For the day: Write down a list of things that have changed in your church over the years, reflecting on the ways in which they have or have not led toward the restoration of the "original church."

Prayer: *We praise thee, O God, for the Son of thy love,*
for Jesus who died, is now gone above.
Hallelujah! Thine the glory, hallelujah! Amen!
Hallelujah! Thine the glory, revive us again.

Revive us again, fill each heart with thy love.
May each soul be rekindled with fire from above.
Hallelujah! Thine the glory, hallelujah! Amen!
Hallelujah! Thine the glory, revive us again.
(Wm. P. Mackay, 1863)

&

April 15

Quiet Integrity

Readings: Daniel 6:1-4; 1 Corinthians 15:9-11

Now Daniel so distinguished himself . . . by his exceptional qualities that the king planned to set him over the whole kingdom (Dan. 6:3 NIV).

Meditation: Quality leadership shows up in many places. One of my favorite songs in the Church of the Brethren is *Full-Measure Man*, written by Brethren folk singer Andy Murray about Cyrus Bomberger. Cyrus's integrity was so well known in his community that when he took his wheat to the mill, the miller would not inspect it to see if the bags were actually full. Cyrus Bomberger could be taken at his word—if he said the bags of wheat were full, they were full. Cyrus's motivations were spiritual. As the song says, "I'm a little too tight to sell my soul for a nickel's worth of wheat."

In Daniel's case, his integrity and his abilities came from his exceptional qualities. It was an integrity that was demonstrated in his job performance—showing up on time, staying focused, doing quality work, not getting caught up in office gossip, treating people fairly. Its source was God's Spirit. Things prospered under Daniel because these heaven-given exceptional qualities enabled him to do things well. Qualities like these go a long way toward earning the trust and respect of others.

Integrity is one of the most sought after qualities in our contemporary life. Everybody wants it, but it seems that fewer and fewer people actually have it. As Christianity moves into its third millennium, a primary task of the church will be to raise up people—both ministers and lay people—who have the quiet integrity Daniel had. In an age of shifting values, the church's ability to minister depends on it.

For the day: Look around you today for those people who demonstrate the "excellent spirit" that was in Daniel. Who are these people in your workplace? Who are these people in your church? How are these qualities present in you?

Prayer: Loving Father, may every aspect of my living be a reflection of the Spirit that dwells in me. Amen.

Timothy P. Harvey

April 16

Flowery Speech

Readings: Daniel 6:5-9; James 5:12

O King Darius, live forever! (Dan. 6:6 NIV).

Meditation: I once saw a movie in which two of the main characters (the "bad guys," as it turns out) were running a scam. With greatly exaggerated and flowery language, the men were advertising a portrait of George Washington in a nice frame and at a reasonable price. What they were actually selling was a 1-cent stamp (depicting President Washington) on a piece of paper with a border. Flowery words notwithstanding, their words greatly misrepresented the product.

It's tempting to use flowery language when we want to embellish something substandard. Whether it's our kids spending more time decorating the cover of their book report than on the actual report itself, or our covering over the fact that we didn't spend enough time preparing our Sunday school lesson because of all of our volunteer assignments, it's easy to get caught up in talking more but saying less. Or worse, saying one thing, but delivering another. To use a common phrase, "talk is cheap."

There was a time when Brethren would not "swear" to tell the truth in court. By today's standards, this may seem strange. What's the big deal with saying, "I swear"? Is it really any different than saying, "I affirm"? Aren't we just arguing about words here?

The difference came because the old Brethren wanted to be known by the character of their living, not their flowery speech. Anyone can learn to be a smooth talker. But a quality life—now there's something to set your sights on!

For the day: Think back over the last several days. How many times did the content of your words not match the quality of your life? Ask God to help you grow in this area.

Prayer: Precious Jesus, may my words and my actions tell the same story. Amen.

Timothy P. Harvey

April 17

He Prayed Anyway

Reading: Daniel 6:10-14

Three times a day he got down on his knees and prayed, giving thanks to his God, just as he had done before (Dan. 6:10 NIV).

Meditation: A college friend once attempted to "audit" a class that was outside his major; he enrolled in the class, but was not required to do the work and would receive no grade. His intentions were good—for the first two weeks he kept up with the reading and attended class faithfully. But as the pressures of other required classes began to build, it wasn't long before the audited class fell by the wayside. By the middle of the semester he was no longer attending the audited class at all.

It's hard to be disciplined in things that are not required of us. We may wish to get up early to read the Bible and pray. We may wish to spend time volunteering at the homeless shelter. We may wish to visit the shut-ins in our church. But the pressures of life easily take over. If we're not intentional, these so-called "optional" spiritual activities never get done.

The interesting thing about Daniel's case is that he could have prayed in a way that no one noticed. Why not just pray quietly as he worked around his home, or walked to and from work? Daniel had every opportunity to not get caught. Yet he refused to change his practice when things were inconvenient.

We don't want to make a law out of our spiritual practices. But do we value those practices enough to do them anyway, even when we could justify not doing them? Can we see that remaining constant in prayer, worship, fellowship, witness, and service—even in the face of outside pressures—both honors God and benefits us? May we be a people who prays anyway.

For the day: Consider your spiritual practices and how the activities of this week may cause you to set them aside. What needs to change so your commitments remain constant?

Prayer: Precious Lord, may my spiritual practices remain steady and true, even as my intentions vary with the wind. Amen.

Timothy P. Harvey

&

April 18

Owning Up to Our Choices

Reading: Daniel 6:15-18

. . . no decree or edict that the king issues can be changed . . .
(Dan. 6:15 NIV).

Meditation: One of the pressing justice issues in our society is how hard it is to break out of the cycle of poverty and homelessness. For those who live near the bottom of the economic scale, bad choices and unexpected expenses have significant ramifications. An unexpected illness, job loss, pregnancy, or fine can perpetuate poverty and homelessness for years—even generations.

Many live with the idea that poverty and homelessness can be changed: "If the right person will just do something." Some blame the system: "If the government would do more to help people out, things would get better." Others blame people: "If they would just get a job, they wouldn't be in the place they are." But when we play the blame game, attention gets diverted from the real issues, and people are left to suffer in their situations.

Whatever our circumstances, it is saddening to realize how many times we are the victims of our own choices. Change may be easy or difficult, but our own choices play a huge part. King Darius certainly never intended harm by his edict, yet it was his own choice that led to Daniel's predicament. The blame was the king's alone. King Darius grieved his bad choice, but had to live with it.

It certainly looked like Daniel's situation "might not be changed" (Dan. 6:17). Whenever we find ourselves a victim of our own choices, it's tempting to think our situation also might not be changed. The thing is, we know how this story turns out—Daniel will survive the lions. The question facing us is, Do we believe we will, too?

For the day: Remember the last time you were a victim of your own choices. Has your situation changed yet? Where has God been as you emerge from your bad choices?

Prayer: Dear God, save me from my own bad choices, that I might live in harmony with you and my neighbors. Amen.

Timothy P. Harvey

April 19

Songs in the Night

Readings: Daniel 6:19-23; John 16:33

They have not hurt me, because I was found innocent in his sight (Dan. 6:22 NIV).

Meditation: One of the callings of a pastor is to walk with people who are living with pain. The pain may be physical, emotional, and/or spiritual. Whatever the cause, when pain arrives it often takes a primary place in a person's life, defining their identity and shaping their behavior. Unless we've been there, it is a challenge to understand someone whose life is defined by their pain.

Daniel had to spend the night in the lion's den. The lions, which threatened his life, were an all-night reminder that his only hope was the power of God. The time in the lion's den was filled with long, unsure hours. Everything was on the line and nothing was under his control.

But even though he was surrounded by lions, Daniel was not without hope. He believed that his ultimate deliverance would come from God. When all he could physically see were threats to his life, in his spirit Daniel could proclaim his hope in God's power.

When we walk with those who are suffering, this too is our hope. The pain and suffering that we experience in our mind and body may threaten to overwhelm us. But our hope is that God, whose Holy Spirit lives within us, will deliver us.

In times of suffering, verse 3 of "My life flows on" describes our hope in God:

> *What though my joys and comforts die?*
> *The Lord my Savior liveth.*
> *What though the darkness gather round?*
> *Songs in the night he giveth.*
> *No storm can shake my inmost calm while*
> *to that Rock I'm clinging.*
> *Since love is Lord of heav'n and earth, how can*
> *I keep from singing?* (Robert Lowery, 1869)

For the day: In the midst of your pain and suffering (or that of another), are you able to hear the "song in the night"? Listen for God's voice in the midst of your present circumstances.

Prayer: God, whatever comes my way, give me the strength to put my trust in you. Amen.

Timothy P. Harvey

April 20

The Parts of the Bible We Don't Like to Read

Reading: Daniel 6:24-28

And before they reached the floor of the den, the lions overpowered them and crushed all their bones (Dan. 6:24 NIV).

Meditation: Yikes! For many of us, the glorious words declaring God's praise in Daniel 6:26-28 might be muted by the rather horrific sounding words of verse 24. Crushed *all* their bones? The *wives and children*, too? What are we to make of verses that don't fit our understanding of God? Several options seem possible.

First, we might ignore them. This one and lots of others—just read over them, pretending that they're not in the Bible. We can choose to limit ourselves to the New Testament, or even the words of Jesus in the Gospels. But does such a choice give us a full understanding of God?

Second, we might realize that some verses (like these) don't describe God's choice. It was King Darius's command that led to the terrible fate of the conspirators. That's well enough for this passage, but it doesn't solve all of our so-called "problem passages." Sometimes the Bible describes God doing things of which we don't approve.

Third, we might acknowledge that God's ways are not our ways. It is a humbling, yet healthy point for us when we realize that God does not always have to make sense to us. But even when God doesn't make sense, we will trust anyway. Might it be that those passages we're inclined to read over or ignore are telling us something we need to know to better understand God?

For the day: What are those parts of the Bible that you find difficult to read? How can you expand your understanding of God to find value in all Scripture?

Prayer: Precious Lord, help me move past my limited understanding of you. I will never comprehend all of you, but let me know more of you. Amen.

Timothy P. Harvey

April 21

The Assurance of Redemption

Reading: Psalm 130

I wait for the LORD, my soul waits, and in his word I hope; my soul waits for the Lord more than those who watch for the morning, more than those who watch for the morning (Ps. 130:5-6).

Meditation from our past: White Oak Country, November 6, 1763

Dear Brother Sander Mack! I thank you warmly for your love and loving admonitions and for your warm greeting. I, Catharine Hummer, your lowliest fellow-sister, my heart and my soul wish you health and happiness of body and soul. I will be patient in the paths of tribulation, for the dear Savior has said that one must pass through many tribulations in entering the Kingdom of God. Therefore I will prepare myself for it as far as the Lord provides grace that I might be found worthy to enter into the Kingdom of God, for the winter of persecution is here.

Contempt and persecution are great, but I comfort myself with the dear Savior and with the small herd of Zion, which has been gathered from all peoples. I am not only persecuted by the world but also hated by those who call themselves believers. They say that what has happened through me is idolatry. They blaspheme about something that they know nothing about. May the Lord have mercy on them and not punish them according to their merits.

Dear Brother Sander, you wrote me that in the end the weightiest will weigh less than nothing, once they are

weighed on the right scales. I am indeed imperfect, but may the Lord put His good spirit into my heart so that when I am weighed I might have the correct weight and be taken out of this sorrowful world into eternal rest, where no enemy can trouble me any more. Let everything be commended to the Lord and may He deal with me as He wishes. His will be done now and in eternity. Amen.
—*Catharine Hummer*

From The Brethren in Colonial America, *Donald F. Durnbaugh, ed.*
The Brethren Press, 1967, pp. 263-64.

For the day: Consider those in your church who may have no advocate, and seek ways to help.

Prayer: Lord, when all abandon me I count on your presence. Lift me up. Save me. Amen.

April 22

Preparing to Pray

Reading: Daniel 9:1-3

Then I turned to the Lord God, to seek an answer by prayer and supplication with fasting and sackcloth and ashes (Dan. 9:3).

Meditation: Daniel's genuine and consecrated heart for the Lord God was evident throughout all of his years as a Hebrew exile in Babylon. Captured as a young man, transported from Jerusalem to Babylon, selected for training to serve in the palace of the Babylonian king, Daniel refused to "defile himself with the royal rations . . ." (Dan. 1:8). Years later, as a trusted advisor to King Darius, Daniel defied the order to worship only the king by openly worshiping the Lord God (Dan. 6:10). For this he ended up in a den of lions. Even in hostile circumstances his heart for the Lord never wavered.

In today's passage we discover two of the characteristics of Daniel's heart that kept him faithful to the Lord: his passion for the Word of the Lord and his passionate prayer life.

Daniel's passion for the Word of God was the basis of his prayer. His actions and his prayer represent thinking that is found in God's revelation in Deuteronomy and Kings as well as in Jeremiah. If God's people sinned and followed other gods, they would eventually be captured and taken into exile in a foreign country. But, if his people repented, the Lord would be gracious to forgive and to restore their nation. As far as we know, Jeremiah never was in Babylon, but his prophetic writings evidently made it there. When Daniel read passages such as Jeremiah 25:11-12 and 29:10, his spirit was moved to passionately pray according to God's Word for restoration. According to 1 John 5:14, "If we ask anything according to God's will, he hears us." Based on God's will as expressed in his Word, Daniel became a passionate intercessor for God's will to be accomplished for his people.

For the day: Our Brethren ancestors had the same kind of unwavering faithfulness to the Lord that was deeply rooted in the Word and in prayer. May the same be said of us!

Prayer: Gracious heavenly Father, thank you for revealing so much of your will to us through your Word and through Jesus Christ, your Son. It is your will that none should perish but that all come to repentance (2 Pet. 3:9). We fervently pray that your will be done on earth as it is in heaven. Amen.

Arden E. Gilmer

&

Abril 23

April 23 in Spanish

Oración de Confesión

Lectura Biblíca: Daniel 9:4-10

De Jehová nuestro Dios es el tener misericordia y el perdonar, aunque contra El nos hemos rebelado (Dan. 9:9).

Meditación: Todos nosotros establecemos prioridades en nuestras vidas. En el caso de Daniel la oración fue algo de gran prioridad, lo cual quedó bien marcado en el transcurso de su vida. En esta occasión el viene delante de Dios con un espiritu de confesión. Al usar el término confesión, lo hace en el sentido general de la palabra; es decir que no se estaba refiriendo solamente a la confesión de pecados sino también a una serie de confesiones las cuales eran partes integrales en toda oración. El inicia su oración confesando lo grande que ha sido Dios con el pueblo de Israel a traves de su historia. Confiesa la fidelidad de Dios al guardar su pacto con un pueblo que había sido rebelde y desobediente. Confiesa la misericordia de Dios para los que le aman y guardan sus mandamientos. Finalmente, confiesa los pecados cometidos. En ésta confesión hay dos cosas muy importantes: primero, Daniel se identifica con el pueblo cuando dice: hemos pecado, y yo soy parte de ese pueblo pecador. Segundo, es muy especifico no solamente al enumerar los pecados sino también al llamarlos por su nombre. Hay situaciones en nuestras vidas en las cuales sentimos la necesidad de expresarle todo al Señor, recordando que no hay nada que nos haga merecedor del perdón obtenido mediante la confesion y el arrepentimiento.

Pensamiento para el día: Deja que tu vida sea un reflejo de la misericordia de Dios.

Oracion: Dios de infinita misericordia, reconocemos nuestras debilidades y errores y los presentamos delante de ti esperando recibir el perdón a través de tu amor y misericordia. Amen.

Gladys Encarnación

♎

April 23

Prayer of Confession

Reading: Daniel 9:4-10

To the Lord our God belong mercy and forgiveness; because we have rebelled against him (Dan. 9:9 RSV).

Meditation: We all establish priorities in our lives. In Daniel's case, prayer was a top priority, which he left well documented in the course of his life. On this occasion, he comes before God in a spirit of confession. The term *confession* is used in a general sense, which is to say that he wasn't referring only to the confession of sins, but also to a series of confessions that were an integral part of all prayer.

He begins his prayer by confessing the great things God has done with the people of Israel throughout their history. He confesses God's faithfulness in keeping a pact with a disobedient and rebellious people. He confesses God's mercy toward those who love God and keep God's commandments.

Finally, he confesses sins that have been committed. This confession has two important parts: First, Daniel identifies himself with the people when he says, we have sinned, and I am among the sinners. Second, he very specifically does not simply list the sins, but calls them by name.

There are situations in our lives when we find it necessary to express everything to our Lord, remembering that there is nothing that makes us deserving of the forgiveness obtained through confession and repentance.

For the day: Let your life be a reflection of God's mercy.

Prayer: God of infinite mercy, we recognize our weaknesses and errors, and we bring them before you in hopes of receiving forgiveness through your love and mercy. Amen.

Gladys Encarnación

April 24

We Have Sinned

Readings: Daniel 9:11-14; Psalm 51:1-12

All Israel has transgressed your law and turned aside, refusing to obey your voice. So the curse and the oath written in the law of Moses . . . have been poured out upon us, because we have sinned against you (Dan. 9:11).

Meditation: It is often difficult for us to acknowledge our sins. It is easy to confess others' sins, but to talk about our own is another matter. We deny them, hide them, excuse them, and tend to resist any suggestion that we should repent of them.

This was the situation that caused Daniel to enter into serious prayer for his people Israel. He made a simple, yet profound, acknowledgment in Daniel 9:11, "We have sinned." The same words are seen in at least two other places in Daniel 9. That kind of confession is an essential part of dealing effectively with our transgressions.

Sin is a transgression of God's law and a failure to obey his voice—which, in today's text, results in a curse (v. 11) and brings great shame and evil to the land (v. 12). The punishment confirms God's earlier Word, "Be sure your sin will find you out." Sin always has a payday. It came in the form of God's judgment, which brought an evil oppression upon the nation. The people acknowledge, "We did not entreat the favor of the Lord our God [and turn] from our iniquities" (v. 13).

It was the same careless attitude toward sin by many people in the state churches of Europe that influenced Alexander Mack and the early Brethren to seek to establish a more faithful church community. It is important to proclaim the love and grace of the gospel of Jesus Christ, while also avoiding *an accepting attitude* toward sinful living. The reading from Psalm 51 gives a good outline for repenting and finding restoration from a life of sin.

For the day: Be aware of entanglement with evil, so that every day you can focus on living for God.

Prayer: Create in me a clean heart, O God, and put a new and right spirit within me (Ps. 51:10).

James F. Myer

April 25

Prayers of a Righteous Person Go a Long Way

Readings: Daniel 9:15-19; James 5:13-16

Turn your ears our way, God, and listen. Open your eyes and take a long look at our ruined city, this city named after you. We know that we don't deserve a hearing from you. Our appeal is to your compassion. This prayer is our last and only hope (Dan. 9:18 The Message).

Meditation: Sometimes we just don't get it. We think we are the master of our world's fate. We blindly think we can right any situation, regardless of our or others' actions. The present strife among ourselves and with other nations has proved us wrong. Daniel's prayer is for his people and their land. He confesses their guilt and pleads for God's attention and compassion. If God would only look and see their pitiful condition, God would act out of who God is.

God is a willing and moving shaker waiting for our petition of believing prayers. Prayer helps us to get right with God and moves us to believe in God's mighty hand to act in restoring people, churches, and nations. But it begins with our own relationship to this awesome God. Daniel prayed to God because of his right relationship with God. Our prayers tell more about us than we care to imagine. They often feel empty, selfish, and condescending. James reminds us that "the prayer of a person living right with God is something powerful to be reckoned with." God is a willing senior partner with us in answering our prayers when our hearts are filled with the love of Jesus. Then, and then only, can we come boldly to the throne of grace addressing God for our and the world's needs.

For the day: Our righteousness depends on our humble submission to an awesome God who can do unbelievable things far beyond our ability to imagine the outcome.

Prayer: Awesome God, help me to submit my will to yours and pray without ceasing, believing that you can do unbelievable things in your time. In Jesus' name I pray, Amen.

H. Fred Bernhard

✑

April 26

Our Prayer

Readings: Daniel 9:20-23; James 4:6

While I was . . . confessing my sin and the sin of my people . . . ,
[God's messenger] said to me, "Daniel, I have now come to give
you wisdom and understanding" (Dan. 9:20-22).

Meditation: Daniel was confessing his sin and the sin of his
people. He was not accusing others of *their* sin. Daniel identified himself with his people. Their sin was his sin, and they
were in need, defeated and in exile. While reading Jeremiah,
Daniel saw that the prophesied time was approaching when
God would bring the Jewish people home. Daniel responded
by humbling himself before God, praying, fasting, and confessing his sin and the sin of his people. The Bible says, "God
opposes the proud, but gives grace to the humble." God
answers prayer. God answered Daniel and sent his Word to
give understanding and reassurance of God's love. Receiving
God's Word did not finish the process, however. God told
Daniel to consider and understand the Word.

For the day: Are you and your people in need? Who are your
people? your nation? your family? your church? Get alone with
God today. Read God's Word and pour out your heart to God.
Thank God for all that God has done for you and your people.
Be totally honest about your needs, your feelings, and your
sin—yours and that of your people. Be still and watch for the
Word God will bring you. Then consider and understand.

Prayer: Father, you have always been faithful to us. You have
never failed us or forsaken us, but we have failed you. Please
lead us in paths of righteousness. We do not trust in our ability

to understand, but we trust in your ability to reveal. We do not trust in our wisdom to follow, but we trust in your wisdom to lead. Thank you. In Jesus' name, Amen.

James O. Eikenberry

✐

April 27

God Keeps His Promises

Readings: Daniel 9:24-27; Isaiah 53:1-6

So you are to know and discern that from the issuing of a decree to restore and rebuild Jerusalem until Messiah the Prince there will be seven weeks and sixty-two weeks; it will be built again, with plaza and moat, even in times of distress. Then after the sixty-two weeks the Messiah will be cut off . . . (Dan. 9:25-26a NASB).

Meditation: God makes promises and keeps them. Much of the Bible is filled with God making promises to his people. Hebrews teaches us about the promises of God by using the example of God's promises to Abraham: "For when God made the promise to Abraham, since He could swear by no one greater, He swore by Himself, saying, 'I WILL SURELY BLESS YOU AND I WILL SURELY MULTIPLY YOU.' And so, having patiently waited, he obtained the promise" (Heb. 6:13-15 NASB). In our passage for today we see God making promises. From Daniel's vantage point, these promises would have seemed like "pie in the sky" impossibilities—things Daniel might hope for and dream about but things that in the "real world" would never come true. The promise of the rebuilding of Jerusalem (v. 25)—it was no more than a pile of ruins. The promise of Messiah the Prince (v. 25)—the nation was defeated and scattered. The promise of Messiah being cut off (v. 26)—sounds more like a defeat than a promise. Today we look back and see that these promises are now history. They came true just as God said. Even the Messiah being cut off can be seen as the wonderful event it is, because through Jesus' death we have salvation. One day we accept the promises of God by faith. One day they become confirmed in history.

For the day: Encouragement comes each day as we walk by faith in God's promises and with a God who makes promises and keeps them.

Prayer: Promise-keeping God, would I walk strong and be encouraged today as I claim your promises and hold them close to my heart.

Jeffrey Brown

Restoration and Covenant Renewal

April 28–May 25

*I*n the evening following the momentous baptisms [on Christmas Day in 1723], the Germantown congregation welcomed the "first fruits"—as the newly baptized were called—through participation in the first love feast in North America.

Donald F. Durnbaugh (1927–2005)

&

April 28

Yearning for Sacred Spaces

Reading: Psalm 84:1-4

How lovely are Your dwelling places, O LORD of hosts! My soul longed and even yearned for the courts of the LORD (Ps. 84:1-2a NASB).

Meditation: As I sat on the edge of the Grand Canyon on a dark and star-studded winter night, I was so overwhelmed by the majesty of God's creation that I lay down on the ground next to the mouth of that great chasm. It was so cold that I would have been concerned for my health if not for what happened next. As I looked far into the sky that night, I heard a whistle of wind start in the west and sing its way through the canyon. The air around me was perfectly still until the wind gently brushed my cheek and continued along the way. What a blessed and sacred space! I thought, as warm tears soon cooled on my face. To me, this is hallowed ground.

Any place where we sense the presence of the Lord is God's dwelling place. From the mountaintops to the valleys, from the depths of the ocean to the city streets—God is there. Some places seem to hold a potency of the Holy Spirit like no other place we know. These places are a gift to us as we walk this Christian journey.

Sacred spaces satisfy a yearning that grows as we serve God's calling to be salt and light. In dark times, our yearnings may begin in despair. Soon they take the shape of joy and strength to endure. For it is in our yearnings that the memories of sacred spaces dwell. Our longing reminds us of the holy anointing that restores us as we enter into God's presence.

For the day: Close your eyes for a moment. Imagine that hallowed place where you feel God's presence most deeply. Allow your times of yearning for sacred spaces to be reminders of God's love and healing balm in your life.

Prayer: God of all creation, I adore you. Thank you for joining me in my sacred space. Here is where I find the strength to continue the work you have called me to do. I ask that you grant me the wisdom to do your will as a light in this dark world. Amen.

Verdena Lee

April 29

Build for God's Glory (and Our Neighbor's Good)

Reading: Haggai 1:1-11

Thus says the LORD of hosts: Consider how you have fared. Go up to the hills and bring wood and build the house, so that I may take pleasure in it and be honored, says the LORD (Hag. 1:7-8).

Meditation: How have we fared? That's a good question to ponder. If we're honest, the response will likely be "pretty well," especially here in North America. I have lived where people talk of "the lake house," "the mountain cabin," and "ocean property." These are all places that we tend and manage and that, at times, tend to manage us. The prophet Haggai lived with those who spent a great deal of time tending to their own well-being. God nudged him to offer an alternative (a dispute, if you will) to such living. God wanted the people to rebuild the shattered temple not because it was a special place for God to reside, not because it was what they ought to do, and not to end the drought they were suffering. The people were to build the temple not inhibited or motivated by fear or out of some exclusive right. The temple was to be a space built simply out of gratitude, thankfulness, and devotion to honor God for who God was, is, and will be.

For the day: Consider how you are faring. In spite of your circumstances, are you helping to create spaces where God takes pleasure? Who is included in such space? What is your motivation to create such space?

Prayer: God of endless time and space, you are not bound by my various parameters. Keep me mindful enough to catch a glimpse of your ever-elusive Spirit calling me to create places of welcome and praise. Stir up my whole heart and mind and give me a vision where I can put the strength of my convictions to create places where gratitude is expressed. By your grace, may it be so.

James H. Chinworth

April 30

Restore God's House

Readings: Haggai 1:12-15; Matthew 28:18-20

*The people feared the LORD. . . . "I am with you, says the LORD."
. . . And the Lord stirred up the spirit . . . of all the remnant
of the people; and they came and worked on the house of the Lord
(Hag. 1:12-14).*

Meditation: The prophet Haggai declared God's call: Restore God's house! Because the people believed it was truly God's

Word and earnestly wanted to do what God required, God gave his life-giving promise to them: "I am with you, says the Lord." And the Lord stirred up their spirits to rebuild the temple in Jerusalem.

The early Brethren heard God's call to restore God's house in a different way. Their focus was not on glorious buildings like the temple. Indeed, when they met beyond their own homes, they built very simple meetinghouses. Their focus was on building up strong and faithful believers in whom God could dwell, through whom God would be at work. They earnestly desired to become courageous disciples who would follow Jesus faithfully in every aspect of life. And God was with them, just as the Lord Jesus had promised would be true when he commissioned his first disciples to make disciples of all nations, stirring their spirits with his life-giving promise: "I am with you always, to the end of the age" (Matt. 28:20).

What stirs your spirit today? How can you heed God's call to restore God's dwelling among us? When you earnestly desire to do what God requires, the Lord will be with you.

For the day: God's presence with you will provide the courage and strength you need to do what God requires. Do it today. Go with God. Restore God's house.

Prayer: Inspire our leaders, Lord, and each of us to restore your church to faithful discipleship. Stir our spirits to do your work. With your presence we will be able to do all things. Amen.

James M. Beckwith

&

May 1

Change: A Mixed Bag with Mixed Shouts

Reading: Ezra 3:8-13

And all the people responded with a great shout . . . because the foundation of the house of the LORD was laid. . . . But many . . . who had seen the first house on its foundations, wept with a loud voice when they saw this house, though many shouted aloud for joy (Ezra 3:11-12).

Meditation: Change is always a mixed bag with mixed shouts. Our text celebrates a new foundation laid for a new temple. After all, the old temple was gone and a new temple was required. But in spite of this reality, not everyone was happy. Along with shouts of joy were shouts of sorrow (Ezra 3:12).

Are there people in sorrow in your home or congregation? We need to acknowledge those who are weeping. It's exciting to anticipate the next three hundred years of our beloved church and the inevitable changes that will occur. But in the anticipation, vigor, and joy, we must not overlook the deep loss some people experience when things change. Let us strive to accommodate both "shouts"—of celebration and of weeping. An anonymous poem captures both "shouts":

> *All growing is changing from one state to another. Leaving a world behind, entering the fear of the unaccustomed: of colors that don't blend, of holy words that jar, of fractures that give rise to visions. We have left one realm but have not yet arrived at the other. . . . That is the changeover in which we experience our nakedness to the point of hurting. But there is no real*

growth without leaping, without crossing ridges and standing wide-eyed and shivering on a new shore.

For the day: Give yourself permission to both anticipate and weep as things change.

Prayer: God of changing seasons, we pray for *this* changing season of life. For us, our congregations, the larger church, remind us that unaccustomed colors are not "wrong" colors or "unfaithful" colors, but colors that signal needed adjustment. Show us signs of your faithfulness even when foundations shake or change. Through Christ we pray, Amen.

Paul E. R. Mundey

May 2

Thanks, but No Thanks

Reading: Ezra 4:1-4

But Zerubbabel, Jeshua, and the rest of the heads of families in Israel said to them, "You shall have no part with us in building a house to our God; but we alone will build to the LORD, the God of Israel, as King Cyrus of Persia has commanded us" (Ezra 4:3).

Meditation: Rebuilding Solomon's temple was no small project. You would think that the building committee would have welcomed any and all help. Here they were, back in Israel for a year or so. With worship they were finding strength, but they also knew they weren't out of the woods. They had taken a big risk in returning to the homeland of their parents and grandparents. Why not get the local community's support? Their request sounded so fitting, so sincere: "Let us help you build. We worship your God." What would your church do? Someone might remember the rest of the story: "Yes, but they worshiped many other gods too" (see 2 Kings 7:24-41). Someone else might say, "Hey, could they be that bad? After all, they weren't exactly willing immigrants. Assyria forced them to leave their homelands too."

Zerubbabel and Jeshua and their committee turned down the offer. When their help was refused, the opponents' true colors became clear. They tried to discourage the builders. They threatened them. Then they blocked the construction with bribes. In short, they practically wrote the book on how to make things miserable for the returning Israelites. Jesus knew something about dealing with opponents also. Can we expect anything less when we work for justice or peace or equality in the name of Christ?

For the day: Say no to the world of greed, violence, and illicit sexuality and you'll be saying yes to life.

Prayer: God, we know faith is not for the fainthearted. Show us how to get over the rough spots, and give us the courage that comes from knowing Jesus as our friend. Amen.

Ronald E. Wyrick

May 3

Where's Your Building Permit?

Readings: Ezra 5:1-5; Zechariah 4:6-7

At the same time Tattenai the governor of the province Beyond the River and Shethar-bozenai and their associates came to them and spoke to them thus, "Who gave you a decree to build this house and to finish this structure?" (Ezra 5:3).

Meditation: May I see your driver's license, please? We know the routine. Most of the time we have done something wrong. Even Brethren get speeding tickets. But what if we weren't speeding? What if the officer singled us out for being Brethren? No, it's not likely. We don't stand out *that* much. The newcomers in Jerusalem were different. They were the new kids on the block and city hall was not going to let them forget it: "Who gave you a decree to build this house . . . ?"

Once I read an essay about the things that would need to turn out right for an extremely poor person to rise above poverty's pernicious grip. Think about it: first you would need job skills, then job availability, transportation, appropriate clothing, and perhaps other abilities and means to your end of profitable employment. Sure, it's possible to overcome the obstacles. Many immigrants and many poor have proven it.

Now think back to that temple-building project. With everything in place—good leadership, a workable plan, contractors, building suppliers, a royal decree—work came to a standstill when obstacles proved too much for the settlers to overcome. God waited until the right time and spoke again. Haggai and Zechariah got the project going again. But the obstacles kept coming. Isn't it amazing to think how many obstacles there are in everyday life even for the most fortunate of us? The God of hope doesn't take away obstacles. The God of hope shows us it is possible to walk through them.

For the day: Help someone who is facing obstacles.

Prayer: Lord, give me strength and wisdom today so I can pass the tests I will face. In the name of the One who faced more than I will ever know. Amen.

Ronald E. Wyrick

$\mathcal{G}$

May 4

Work That Prospers

Reading: Ezra 5:6-17

May it be known to the king that we went to the province of Judah, to the house of the great God. It is being built of hewn stone, and timber is laid in the walls; this work is being done diligently and prospers in their hands (Ezra 5:8).

Meditation: A book by an evangelical Christian who served at the highest levels of government in the U. S. claims that government leaders who benefitted from overwhelming evangelical support laughed behind the scenes at evangelical leaders (and, worse, that the government failed to put its money where its mouth had been in the campaign). Such is politics. At times Brethren have stayed as far away from politics as possible. At other times we have tried to influence the politicians. Always, when we have been at our best, we have prayed for those who must make decisions that change so many lives.

The returning Israelites knew two things: God had blessed them through Cyrus, king of Persia, and God expected much from them. They worked accordingly. In spite of opposition, they recognized God's purpose in their work. When all else failed to block the work on the temple, local officials wrote to King Darius himself in the capital city of Babylon. Surely that would stop the construction. It would take months for the king's reply. Somehow God allowed the work to proceed even during the long wait for the king's reply.

Many years later when Jesus told his disciples to be as wise as serpents and as gentle as doves, he may have remembered the story of these builders who persevered in the face of their opponents (see Matt. 10:16).

For the day: Ask God to guide your work and to make your efforts creative and bold.

Prayer: Dear God, guide the work of my hands today. No matter how simple or how profound others may think my efforts, would you give me the will to do my very best? In the Carpenter's name, Amen.

Ronald E. Wyrick

May 5

Strength in Remembering

Reading: Psalm 137:1-7

Let my tongue cling to the roof of my mouth, if I do not remember you, if I do not set Jerusalem above my highest joy (Ps. 137:6).

Meditation: "I woke up and was really scared. I couldn't remember where I was or why I was here." Those words of my mother reflected the pain of the ongoing battle with cancer that had once again landed her in the hospital unexpectedly. She was confused and her life felt out of control and unfamiliar, some of the most frightening things any of us can experience. It was only when my sister came into the room and she heard that familiar voice that she began to relax and find some clarity.

This is not unlike the experience that the Israelites were having. They found themselves in a foreign place, without any of the familiar landmarks. They felt alone and scared and cried out to God in their fears. But their memory and their songs that spoke of who they were as a community of faith became the source of strength. "Let my tongue cling to the roof of my mouth, if I do not remember you, if I do not set Jerusalem above my highest joy," says the psalmist.

Remembering the Promised Land, the place where they knew God's presence in a very real and tangible way was the source of hope as the Israelites lived in a place where nothing any longer made sense.

My mom knew she was confused, but knowing it didn't make it go away. In those times when life just doesn't make sense, when it is simply out of our control, what do we hold on to?

The psalmist's cry invites us to remember—whether it is special moments as a family, or special scriptures, or meaningful moments of worship, song, and prayer. And in the remembering we find a touchstone. We can remember and in remembering we will find strength for what is ahead. God is not just in Jerusalem, and God is not just present in the good times.

For the day: May you be as willing as the psalmist to cry out to God, speaking the truth even when it is a painful truth, so that, in speaking your heart's desire to God, you might begin to remember the joy of walking in God's love wherever you find yourself.

Prayer: O God, sometimes I feel alone, even forgotten. In the times of confusion or pain, help me to cling to you and the promise that you will always be near. Draw me close so that I might once again know the strength of walking in your loving presence. Amen.

L. David Witkovsky

May 6

Fasting into God's Presence

Readings: Nehemiah 1:1-4; Acts 13:1-3

When I heard these words I sat down and wept, and mourned for days, fasting and praying before the God of heaven (Neh. 1:4).

Meditation: Nehemiah, a king's cupbearer; Anna, an elderly widow and prophet in Jerusalem (Luke 2:36-38); Paul and other church leaders in Antioch; some early Brethren, prior to the first baptism in 1708—what do they all have in common? They, along with others in our time who have deep concerns, have participated in fasting and praying as a way of bringing those concerns to God. Combining fasting with prayer seems to open the way for us to feel God's presence in a special way.

For some, fasting is an established and regular practice. More often it is practiced when we lose our sense of direction, feel "in over our heads," or experience a "wintertime" of the soul. To have a deep need for sanctuary or the sincere desire to be in solidarity with important issues may be a call for fasting and prayer. It may be the chosen way to prepare for a time of difficult decision-making. Ultimately, the hope is that fasting and praying will lead to a better understanding of God's will and bring about a right relationship with God. Like Nehemiah, Anna, Paul, and those early Brethren, many have turned to fasting and praying to seek that right relationship and to find a way to enter into what God is doing and would have them do.

For the day: Is this the day for you to deepen your relationship with God by combining fasting with prayer?

Prayer: God, putting on hold my three-meal-a-day regimen seems like a bigger challenge than I had in mind. However, if fasting would be a way to bring me into closer relationship with you and let me more sincerely enter into what you are doing, guide and lead me to take that step. Amen.

Elaine M. Sollenberger

May 7

Confession

Reading: Nehemiah 1:5-11

O Lord, let your ear be attentive to the prayer of your servant, and to the prayer of your servants who delight in revering your name. Give success to your servant today, and grant him mercy in the sight of this man! (Neh. 1:11).

Meditation from our past: At a regular appointment in my home church, at a point where usually from six to eight ministers were present, the senior elder extended the liberty [to preach] by saying he had nothing on his mind. The assistant made the same declaration, which was repeated by number three. My place was about fourth or fifth. When it came my turn, I said aloud, "Well, brethren, I can wish the freedom, but I can not say that I have nothing on my mind; in fact, I'd be ashamed to say so, if it were the case." In response, a deacon directly in front of me remarked aloud, "That's so." When it occurred to him what he had done, he acted as if he wished he were under the table.

I then rose and said: "I presume I'm in for it now. First, permit me to explain. According to our method, nobody knows who is to preach at this appointment, there being generally from six to eight of us present. I make it a rule of my life whenever I attend any of our appointments, to go prepared to preach, so that in case I should be called upon, I may not be put to shame by making a bungled effort; but I do not have to preach every time I go to church, simply because I am prepared to do so. A sermon will not spoil for want of being delivered. It may be salted down and kept for weeks. More sermons are spoiled by premature delivery than by being deferred."

Then I took my seat, again extending the liberty, which was returned to me by the full board, with the unanimous consent of an interested audience, probably in order to test the extent of my preparation. —*Henry R. Holsinger*

From History of the Tunkers and the Brethren Church *(1901), pp. 239-40, note.*

For the day: Are you ready if needed to share the Lord with others?

Prayer: Fill me with your Spirit, Lord God, that I might speak when called up in word and deed. Amen.

May 8

God's Gracious Hand Is upon Me

Reading: Nehemiah 2:1-10

And the king granted me what I asked, for the gracious hand of my God was upon me (Neh. 2:8b).

Meditation: What a wonderful feeling that God's gracious hand is upon us. Certainly that gives an inner confidence, helps pave the way, and sustains us against the odds. Nehemiah, a palace servant, felt a burden on his heart to raise up the walls of Jerusalem. With such an awesome task, he could have easily felt overwhelmed.

Yet Nehemiah senses that God's gracious hand is upon him. How often we are faced with challenges that seem too great! How easy it can be to get discouraged! Yet Nehemiah's testimony reminds us of God's strength and support.

Christian discipleship doesn't guarantee ease in moving forward; in fact, we may have to face great odds. Nehemiah's testimony reveals that through God's presence one can accomplish much in the face of resistance. Our Brethren heritage calls us to count well the cost and act upon our faith.

In this anniversary year, may we be blessed with the sense of the gracious hand of God upon us as we face the challenges to be faithful disciples.

For the day: As you face challenges, consider how God's gracious hand is upon you.

Prayer: O God, may I draw on you for strength today to help me be faithful in doing that to which you are calling me.

David S. Young

♌

May 9

What God Puts on Our Hearts

Reading: Nehemiah 2:11-16

I told no one what God had put into my heart to do for Jerusalem (Neh. 2:12b).

Meditation: Perhaps it is hard for us to identify with Nehemiah when he makes a secret inspection of the destroyed walls. Following what God put upon his heart, Nehemiah goes on this nighttime expedition with light provisions and just a few men to inspect the ruins.

Yet were not early Brethren in a similar position as they felt compelled to open the scriptures and baptize adult believers? God placed this effort upon their hearts. Faith always entails risk, hoping against hope, and acting when it seems nothing can be done. What Nehemiah does, and does so wisely, is to secretly inspect the odds. With the challenges so great, we might have to face sacrifices required to live faithfully in an affluent, secular culture.

As Brethren, on this anniversary, we may need to make an inner inspection of our faith journey to count well the cost. Just as Nehemiah faced rebuilding the walls, may God grant us the spiritual energy to renew the church and engage in Christ-centered mission.

For the day: May you live today by what God puts on your heart. Consider the odds and be willing to make the sacrifices.

Prayer: Lord, help me to be faithful to what you have placed on my heart, so that I may live the mission you have for my life.

David S. Young

May 10

Prayer Rebuilds

Reading: Nehemiah 2:17-20

Come, let us rebuild the wall . . . (Neh. 2:17).

Meditation: Nehemiah models impressive leadership. His attention to detail and to prayer, as well as his careful organization, are noteworthy. But it strikes me also that he models something akin to the practical wisdom of James who declared faith empty if it is merely wishful encouragement to "be warmed and filled." When Nehemiah reached Jerusalem, he surely worshiped in the temple. But his prayerful thinking went beyond those walls. The city walls reduced to piles of stone spoke of a people's despair and hopelessness. The people were resigned to loss and aliens to hope. Who could ever possibly restore lives destroyed by forces too powerful for them?

"Just pray harder" is not always the answer to overwhelming problems. Sometimes the answer is to work harder. What a transformation when the people started to build! They worked hard—for the common good! Nehemiah saw to it that they had the necessary materials, knew what to do, and had a job assigned. They became part of the divine help they received. Their faith was restored.

When homes are destroyed, when crops fail, when cities are destroyed, someone needs to help the people become part of the answer to their prayers: help to find the materials to build a well; provide materials and guidance to build a clinic where persistent disease can be eradicated; help to organize to overcome legal obstacles to their freedom and well-being. Prayer and faith must build walls, too.

For the day: Today, look for things that you can do to help someone overcome problems that shrink life's possibilities for them. Pray for them, yes, but pray that you can find a way to help them stand on their own feet.

Prayer: Lord, help me see what will make a real difference for those who are trapped in community destruction, unending disease, or in other ways that seem beyond help. Give me very practical eyes. Amen.

Robert Dell

May 11

Giving Thanks to God

Readings: Psalm 138:1-5; Romans 8:15-17

On the day I called, you answered me, you increased my strength of soul (Ps. 138:3).

Meditation: I remember sitting on the porch of my favorite retreat center, reading from the Psalms, as a confidence came over me that God was truly with me and how that knowledge instilled a sense of strength to face whatever might lie ahead. I recall it as a quiet confidence that God's love was as real as the morning sun that peeked over the mountains before me. And a sense of gratitude overwhelmed me.

That is the confidence that the psalmist invites us to have. He voices a deep sense of gratitude for the reminder that he is not alone to face what is ahead. As he steps into the future, he can do so confidently because he trusts God's loving-kindness. He remembers having strength to face tough times in the past, a strength not of his own making, but a strength from beyond himself.

I am truly grateful that the weight of the world does not rest on my shoulders. I am grateful that God is so timelessly dependable, the One that I can return to each day for the strength to face the new day. I don't know what the day ahead will bring, but as I take time to remember God's unfailing love surrounding and leading me, I step forth with a spirit of gratitude that empowers me for whatever might be ahead.

For the day: How might you open yourself more fully to God's love today? Share with God the longings of your soul, confident that God seeks a relationship with you that brings with it healing and strength.

Prayer: O faithful God, I return just now to the well of your love. I come to drink deeply that my soul may be refreshed and that I may face the day ahead with gratitude and strength. May I be a source of strength for someone else whose life is heavy today. Amen.

L. David Witkovsky

ᐱ

May 12

Teach Me Patience—Now!

Reading: Psalm 70

Hasten, O God, to save me; O LORD, come quickly to help me (Ps. 70:1 NIV).

Meditation: Dual citizenship is not easy. Divided loyalties produce stress. It is hard to be a member of both God's kingdom and this secular world. We are torn apart by two sets of values. We feel attacked by the strain of seeking harmonious choices. Sometimes we feel the conflicting pressures so strongly that we cry out in desperation. O God, come quickly, help me now!

People who choose to please God and be directed by him have always been, will always be, subject to attack while in this world. There is no novelty in our persecution today. It is nothing new to pray to God for help; and as we see in Psalm 70, the Now Generation did not invent impatience. In times of distress, God's men and women have always, will always, cry out to God for immediate intervention and a swift succor. Over time we have learned that a cry to our heavenly Father is a valid and effective cure. For that we rejoice and praise him.

But have we learned to wait for God? We know he is always near, always ready to help, but have we learned that his schedule is not our schedule, that the clock of the kingdom is not the clock of the world? Perhaps time is the point of greatest conflict between our two domiciles. The kingdom is the present and the yet to come; this world knows only now.

For the day: Try not to focus on this world's time, but on God's eternity. Remember that God is with you now, but that your final and definitive deliverance will be when God decides.

Prayer: Lord, I want to serve you and follow Jesus. I give you
my full allegiance.
But, Lord, I walk in this world and feel the pressure
of time.
Help me keep my eyes on your eternal kingdom.
Help me, Father, help me now, before the now
of this world engulfs me.
Maranatha, Lord, come quickly.

Mark Logan

May 13

Facing the Bullies

Reading: Nehemiah 4:1-6

*So we rebuilt the wall, and all the wall was joined together to half
its height; for the people had a mind to work (Neh. 4:6).*

Meditation: Nap time turned into a nightmare for my daughter, Katie, for a few weeks at the beginning of her preschool
year. She came home upset and it took us a couple of days to
get her to tell us why. A girl, older and larger than Katie, had
been kicking her at nap time and keeping her from sleeping.
"Did you tell her to stop?" I asked.
"No!"
"Have you told your teacher?"
"No," Katie said, softly. Katie was a little too shy to do
either of those things and I knew it. There's nothing more
infuriating than seeing your child be the victim of a bully.
Adults too are not immune from bullying, as today's scripture illustrates. Furious that the Jews might rebuild the walls of
Jerusalem, Sanballat and Tobiah resort to taunts and ridicule to

try to distract the workers and delay the rebuilding project. Imagine the anger Nehemiah felt at the bullying of these men. But instead of hurling taunts back at his enemies, Nehemiah prays and vents his anger to the One he knows will listen. Nehemiah's prayer motivates his people and gives them the strength and resolve to get on with the work.

Bullying in church can take many forms: the parking lot conversations after a meeting, gossip, withholding contributions, etc. Whether one is a child or an adult, a bricklayer or an architect, a board member or a pastor, it takes intestinal fortitude and trust in the One who ultimately protects us to face the fears, ridicule, and negativity that can lead to discouragement. Respond, not with ridicule and anger, but with prayer.

For the day: Live boldly knowing that you are a child of the living God who will protect you from harm and give you strength for the day's work.

Prayer: Protecting God, we thank you that you are always willing to listen to our deepest fears, anger, and frustration. Give us a mind to do your work, even when we are discouraged. Help us to trust in you for strength and protection. Amen.

Joan L. Daggett

May 14

Too Much Rubbish

Readings: Nehemiah 4:7-11; 1 Peter 5:6-11

The strength of the burden bearers is failing, and there is too much rubbish so that we are unable to work on the wall (Neh. 4:10).

Meditation: I saw a cartoon the other day where a woman is sitting at her desk piled high with papers. "I wish someone would make a desk that flushes," she says. I agree! Just when I think I'm beginning to get myself organized, more piles of paper seem to appear. Junk mail, junk e-mail, even junk faxes! And, of course, the catalogs—lots of catalogs. The higher the piles get, the more it all becomes useless, just "rubbish" that I have to sort through and throw away to get any work done!

Rubbish caused the workers in today's scripture to become overwhelmed and discouraged. Seeing the workers' resolve unshaken, Nehemiah's enemies return to the scene and make threats to attack the builders and destroy the work completed so far. This time, however, their threats seem to work. The workers begin to lose their confidence. Instead of seeing the vision of a rebuilt Jerusalem, the builders can see only the overwhelming amount of rubble that lies between them and God's plan for their future.

It is easy to become discouraged when life gets overwhelming with work to do, people to care for, expectations to meet. In the midst of all the cares and rubble of our lives, God stands ready to help you lift these burdens. *Cast all your anxiety on him, because he cares for you* (1 Pet. 5:7).

For the day: Using a piece of scrap paper, write down one thing that gets in your way of serving God. Place it in your Bible at today's scripture, and pray for God to show you how to rid your life of this "rubbish." Tonight, take the paper from your Bible and throw it in the garbage as a symbol of your commitment to let go of this obstacle.

Prayer: Help me to let go of all the "rubbish" and anxiety in my life that keep me from doing your work, O God. Grant me your peace, and empower me to do your will. Amen.

Joan L. Daggett

⟨⟩

May 15

Arming Ourselves

Readings: Nehemiah 4:12-15; Ephesians 6:10-19

Do not be afraid of them. Remember the LORD, who is great and awesome (Neh. 4:14).

Meditation: For many believers shaped in the tradition of God's shalom, passages like this one can be troubling. It seems to recommend violence in response to threats. Peace-seeking though our people may be, we are enmeshed with a world seduced by violence, where murderous threats are being breathed around us every day. The Jewish people in Nehemiah are trying to pull themselves back together after the exile, rebuilding the city of Jerusalem and strengthening a Torah-loving community. In the midst of their effort, they are assailed by threats and ridicule all around. In response, Nehemiah calls them to arm themselves and prepare to fight.

We too may find scorn and ridicule as we seek the New Jerusalem, God's vision of well-being for every person. How do we "arm ourselves" today to protect the inbreaking of God's reign? We do as Jesus did. Not with weapons of steel or fire. We cannot help but hear Ephesians 6 singing behind this passage, exhorting us to arm ourselves with the armor of God: the belt of truth, the breastplate of righteousness, the shoes of prophetic proclamation of God's peace. Our Lord responded to real threat and violence with astonishing vulnerability and power. We cannot help but follow. In the end, the pervasive threats, which may in truth have been no more than scorn and empty talk, are defused as the people refuse fear's paralysis and as they strengthen themselves in God's presence.

For the day: Threats may rise around you, and doubts may live in your heart. Strengthen yourself in prayer and find courage in God's presence. The New Jerusalem arrives each moment in our hearts and waits merely to be grasped.

Prayer: Awesome and Great God, though there may be enemies all around, let me rely on your strength and power. Take action on my behalf, Lord. Let me guard the New Jerusalem with my great love and my growing heart.

Matthew R. Guynn

May 16

God Fights for Us

Readings: Nehemiah 4:16-23; Romans 12:19-21

Wherever you hear the sound of the trumpet, join us there. Our God will fight for us! (Neh. 4:20 NIV).

Meditation: Surely this story is a familiar one to us—if not in the exact details, then in the world in which we live. We are told we must stand ready to defend ourselves, against terrorists or communists or against evil's current incarnations. Surely the zealots, who wished Jesus would bring a military solution, would have celebrated these phrases about "spears, shields, bows, and body-armor." But Jesus repudiated the zealots! I believe Jesus would lift up the phrase "Our God will fight for us." (See Millard Lind, *Yahweh Is a Warrior*.) What does it mean for God to fight for us? All are entangled in violence, whether it be systems of violence (global war) or personal violence (domestic abuse). If God is to be our warrior, then we must believe that God will lift physical weapons if God wills it. God the warrior works in mysterious ways. Not through the sword of steel, but the sword of the Spirit. Not through grenades, but through the gentle seeping of living water, which softens hearts. Not through napalm and bombing campaigns, but by curing sickness and casting out demons. God does not give us the task of eradicating enemies. Jesus calls us to a new height in the human story: the unconditional love of enemies. Let us draw inspiration for engaging evil and the need to be watchful "from the break of dawn until the stars come out." But then let us watch for signs of God's ways of fighting. Let us be taught how to act.

For the day: Each time violence appears today, give it over to God. Remember that all people are entangled together in patterns of violence. Ask, Is this your will, Lord?

Prayer: God, please show me hints today of your path toward wholeness of life. How can I struggle against evil but not kill or demonize others?

Matthew R. Guynn

May 17

Courage to Do "Great Work"

Reading: Nehemiah 6:1-14

. . . they all wanted to frighten us, thinking, "Their hands will drop from the work, and it will not be done." But now, O God, strengthen my hands (Neh. 6:9).

Meditation: While serving as a cupbearer for the Persian king, Nehemiah learned that Jerusalem lay in ruins and was defenseless because the wall protecting the city was badly damaged. He committed himself to the task of rebuilding and repairing the protective wall around the city. In these verses, the wall is almost finished. Sanballat, Tobiah, and Geshem, the governors of surrounding states, are threatened by the resolve shown by Nehemiah and his workers and have formed an informal coalition to derail the building project. They begin with ridicule; then they offer him letters of false friendliness while seeking in reality to trap and kill him. When all that fails, their methods become more complex, aggressive, and life threatening. Although Nehemiah is fearful, he is not distracted from what he refers to as his "great work." Through it all, he *prays for strength*, he *maintains his focus*, and he *continues to build*.

Nehemiah's model is a good one for us:

• His relationship with God is strong and familiar, and he prays constantly for strength and guidance.

• He discerns God's will for his life; he embraces the task he is called to and he commits his life to it.

• In the face of criticism and obstacles, he doesn't stop and equivocate. He keeps working.

For the day: Ask yourself three questions: 1) Is my relationship with God so familiar and deep that I can recognize God's leading and discriminate it from all the other voices vying for my attention? 2) What is the wall I'm called to build in my life? What is my "great work"? 3) Who and/or what are the Sanballats, Tobiahs, and Geshems that distract me as I attempt to do the work I am called to do?

Prayer: Lord God, remind me today that you call me to great work just as you did Nehemiah. In quiet moments today, give me a glimpse of the work you specifically call me to, and give me the will, the courage, and the focus to do it. Amen.

Martha Stover Barlow

⟨⟩

May 18

Remaining Faithful

Reading: Nehemiah 6:15-19

*When all our enemies heard about this, all the surrounding
nations were afraid and lost their self-confidence, because they
realized that this work had been done with the help of our God
(Neh. 6:16 NIV).*

Meditation: What would be our response if people were trying
to sabotage or even kill us for being faithful to God? That is
what Nehemiah faced. Sanballat, governor of the province of
Samaria, and Tobiah, the Ammonite, did not want a wall to be
built. They harassed the workers and sabotaged their work.
Tobiah sent letters to Nehemiah to intimidate him, apparently
hoping Nehemiah would stop out of fear. Sometimes this happens in churches when the board, a commission, or a group
decides to do a new ministry. A major giver or well-respected
leader will oppose the decision and threaten to withhold funds,
leave, or, if the idea was supported by the pastor, insist on firing
the pastor. Nehemiah and the workers remained faithful to
what they believed was the will of God. God rewarded their
faithfulness by their finishing the wall. We who are involved
with trying a new ministry need to be faithful to what we
believe is God's calling. However, in light of Jesus' teachings,
our love for each other also dictates a respect for those who
don't agree, recognizing that they may see "remaining the
same" as being faithful. We must be open to the possibility
that we misunderstood what God was calling us to do. Following Nehemiah's example, we will follow through and decide
along the way if God is blessing the new ministry. Trusting in
the Spirit of God, we can continue to move forward, present-

ing the love of God in new or different ways consistent with the teachings of Jesus.

For the day: Trust that when you use your talents and skills for the kingdom of God, God is with you and will guide and bless you.

Prayer: Lord, help me to be faithful in showing and giving your love to all people. Amen.

Gene F. Hipskind

⌒

May 19

Courage in Adversity

Readings: Psalms 27:1-14; 62

I would have despaired unless I had believed that I would see the goodness of the LORD in the land of the living. Wait for the LORD; Be strong, and let your heart take courage; Yes, wait for the LORD (Ps. 27:13-14 NASB).

Meditation: The opening verses of Psalm 27 describe David's spiritual confidence when times were good. The Lord had been his light and strength throughout his life. His enemies had stumbled and fallen, and the Lord had lifted him up to his presence and set him upon a rock.

Beginning with verse 7, however, the tone changes abruptly. Now the psalmist is writing in the midst of fresh troubles. He feels the Lord's anger and fears abandonment. David faces accusers who are plotting against him. Perhaps David is describing the betrayal by his own son, Absalom, who sought to take away his throne. He yearns for his life to revert to a more level path (v. 11), instead of the present stresses and upheavals caused by jealous foes. But even in the depths of his despair, he has learned that one can survive if he waits for the goodness of the Lord to be shown to him. David is confident that God is still in control but wants David's faith and patience to grow as he waits for the answer to his prayers.

For the day: It is usually easier for us to theologize about the goodness of God when things in our lives are going well. And we can more easily accept the difficult times when they are in the past. Yet the psalmist shows that we can survive our present difficulties when we put our trust in the Lord, knowing that God is our defense.

Prayer: Lord, help me to learn from your Word about your goodness to your children, so that those truths may undergird me in times of trouble.

Homer A. Kent, Jr.

May 20

Be Thankful

Reading: Leviticus 23:33-43

You shall rejoice before the LORD your God for seven days (Lev. 23:40b).

Meditation: The Festival of Booths, also known as *Sukkot* ("Booths"), celebrated the final harvest of the year in ancient Israel. Jews today continue to observe the command to "live in booths for seven days," even if they live far from any agricultural center. The Jewish custom is to build a temporary shelter—a small, fragile hut of leaves and branches—and to eat meals within the booth, perhaps as the ancient Israelites once did during the harvest season.

Those of us who are surrounded by an overabundance of food may sometimes forget to be thankful. We may also forget that there are many people in our world who experience hunger on a daily basis. According to the organization Bread for the World, a child dies every five seconds from a hunger-related cause. Sukkot reminds us to be thankful for the abundance of food and to share some of that abundance with others, as we are able.

Beyond its significance as a harvest festival, however, Sukkot reminds us of the fragility of life. The biblical writer we know as Qohelet (author of Ecclesiastes) acknowledges the transience of our lives and in response commends us to "eat, drink, and enjoy ourselves" (Eccles. 8:15), because our life on earth is fleeting.

As Christians, let's develop an "attitude of Sukkot." Mindful of the fragility of all life, Sukkot teaches us to express thanks to God for our daily bread. In doing so, those of us who have plenty should remember to share our abundance with those who do not receive enough.

For the day: Be mindful that your life is like a temporary booth constructed in the wilderness. Even as you recognize the transience of life, you are called not to despair, but to rejoice before the Lord.

Prayer: Gracious God, teach me to be thankful for my many blessings, to share my abundance with others who are in need, and to remember the impermanence of my earthly life.

Christina Bucher

⟨𝒪⟩

May 21

We've Got the Whole World . . .

Reading: Deuteronomy 16:13-17

They shall not appear before the LORD empty-handed . . .
(Deut. 16:16c).

Meditation: Being a country boy—and not being real fond of
water sports anyway—for some reason it didn't cross my mind
to bring a bathing suit when invited by a city girl to my first-
ever birthday "pool party" as a young adult. I felt at once
ridiculous and relieved—dumb for not "getting it," relieved
that I was spared the pool part of the party.

There's nothing quite like showing up somewhere unprepared. It's like those dreams we preachers have about not having a word written just before having to preach the big sermon. I'm sure teachers and musicians and workshop leaders
have similar nightmares. It's not like you don't know it's coming—you just don't do what you need to do to be ready.

Our text today is about arriving at the harvest festival without an appropriate offering to present to the Lord. It reminds
one of Jesus' several parables about people being ready—or
not—when the guest of honor or owner or ruler returns. It's a
common biblical theme—that of honoring what God has
given us or entrusted to us by making an appropriate response,
usually by being a good steward, whether of the gospel or of
the earth's goodness.

With what have we been entrusted or what have we been
given about which we may be less than prepared for a reckoning? To play on the Old Testament image of coming with the
earth's bounty in hand, I can't help but think that today we've
got the whole world in our hands. There's not a corner of it

that we haven't touched—and bruised. Forests and coastal wet-lands? Over-cut. Fish stocks and aquifers? Over-drawn. Climate and polar regions? Over-heated. Will God not hold us account-able for what we have done with this wonderful creation? What can we do to "appear before the Lord" as grateful and responsi-ble stewards?

For the day: What part of the "whole world" will you affect by your simple consumer choices today?

Prayer: Lord, help me handle with care all the goodness you've created.

David R. Radcliff

May 22

Going Back to Go Forward

Reading: Nehemiah 8:1-6

Ezra opened the book in the sight of all the people, for he was standing above all the people; and when he opened it, all the people stood up (Neh. 8:5).

Meditation: Sometimes people have to start over—like the people of Israel returning to Jerusalem from exile in Babylon. But people starting over need to be reminded of where they came from in order to know where to go. They need to hear their own "old" story in a new way. So the Israelites gathered in the square before one of the city gates. The priest Ezra stood on a raised wooden platform. He opened "the book of the law of Moses" and read from early morning until midday, and the "ears of all the people were attentive." They were discovering God in a new way for their time.

In 1708 Alexander Mack and the earliest Brethren were

starting over too. It wasn't dramatic like this scene from Nehemiah. They were only a few, not a great gathering. It wasn't in the public square, but quietly in homes. They were coming out of a period of empty formalism in worship and church life. Eagerly they opened the scriptures and read them in a new way. They too had "attentive" ears. They were discovering God in a new way for their time.

Sometimes we have to go back to go forward. For the Jews it was back to the law of Moses. For the first Brethren it was back to the New Testament. God is in the past, the present, and the future. When we go back, we are reminded of what God has done so we can see what God is doing and recognize what God will do.

For the day: Read the Bible to learn of God's reality so that you can see God at work in this day and in the days to come. Open yourself to what you see and be filled with God's Spirit.

Prayer: *Open my eyes that I may see. Open my ears that I may hear. Open my heart and let me prepare. Illumine me, Spirit divine!* (Clara H. Scott, 1896).

James H. Lehman

May 23

Teach the Word

Reading: Nehemiah 8:7-12

So they read from the book, from the law of God, with interpretation. They gave the sense, so that the people understood the reading (Neh. 8:8).

Meditation from our past [on why we need periodicals]:
Some one will say: We have the Gospel, and that is suffi-

cient for us. Truly we have abundant cause to be thankful to God, that he has given and thus preserved unto us the blessed Gospel, not only in the original language, but in so many different translations, that every one may read it in his own tongue. But we would ask: Are there now none among the many, who, reading their Bible, if they were questioned like the Eunuch, "Understandest thou what thou readest?" would have to answer with him: "How can I, except some man should guide me."

Says another: Yes, we must have preachers to expound the scriptures unto us, to teach, to exhort, to reprove and to warn the people according to the Gospel, but this must be done by their word of mouth, and not by writing and printing. Say we: Not so fast, dear friend, or dear brother. Remember, that, if the first preachers of the Gospel had not preached by writing too, we would have no written or printed Gospel at all.

Seeing then, that we have apostolic example, of writing such things which may be profitable for doctrine, etc., and that we are not to put the light under a bushel, but on a candlestick, so that it may give light unto all that are in the house, we trust no more need be said even about print.

But we are asked: What do you want to print, and what is your object? We will try to answer in a few words. We are as a people devoted to the truth, as it is in Christ Jesus. —*Henry Kurtz*

From The Monthly Gospel-Visiter, *Vol. 1, April 1851, pp. 1-2.*

For the day: Count the number of books by and about Brethren in your home or the number and versions of Bibles. Ponder what it would be like to not have that written history.

Prayer: We thank you, God, for those who blazed a trail before and left a record for us to consider. Amen.

May 24

Made for One Another

Reading: Nehemiah 8:13-18

Go out to the hills and bring branches of olive, wild olive, myrtle, palm, and other leafy trees to make booths, as it is written (Neh. 8:15).

Meditation: The gathering of the people of Israel, which began at the Water Gate and spread throughout Jerusalem, reminds me of the love feasts of the nineteenth century. Brethren came from far around, and they stayed for a whole weekend of preaching, singing, visiting, eating, and more preaching. Then they concluded with the feetwashing, the Lord's Supper, and the bread and cup—the love feast itself—this expression of Christ's love embodied in the community.

Here in Jerusalem the people had stood for hours listening to the public reading of the "law of Moses," and they wanted more. So on the second day the leaders began to study the law, and they rediscovered the festival of "booths" described in Leviticus. People were sent into the hills to bring back branches of olive, myrtle, palm, and "other leafy trees." All over the city people made booths—on roofs, in courtyards, in the courts of the temple, in the squares before the city gates—and lived in them for seven days. "And there was very great rejoicing."

Faith is not just an individual matter between God and me. Human beings are deeply communal people. God made us for one another. We find our deepest reality—we find God—when we come together. The people of Israel knew this when they celebrated the festival of booths. The early Brethren knew it when they came together for love feast. We know it now when we pray, worship, serve, weep, and rejoice together.

For the day: Do not be afraid to take time for others. Be willing to suspend the busyness of your life and build booths of something lovely and leafy and live for a time in rejoicing. Return then to your tasks refreshed.

Prayer: O God, you made us so we need you and one another. Give us the grace to know and love all people. Turn us to one another and to you so that your love may flow from us in great rejoicing.

James H. Lehman

𝒞

May 25

Delight in God's Law

Reading: Psalm 19:7-14

The law of the LORD is perfect, reviving the soul; the decrees of the LORD are sure, making wise the simple; the precepts of the LORD are right, rejoicing the heart; the commandment of the LORD is clear, enlightening the eyes; the fear of the LORD is pure, enduring forever; the ordinances of the LORD are true and righteous altogether (Ps. 19:7-9).

Meditation: God's revelation of the divine nature is both general and specific. Psalm 19 begins with the general manifestation of God's glory in creation (vv. 1-6). It then moves to the particular gift of the Mosaic law (vv. 7-14). An astute pagan can discern the greatness of the Creator from nature, but those who obey the divine law understand the mind and will of God. This psalm is a prayer of praise to God for revelation and a plea to be preserved against great transgression and hidden faults. It is quoted by Alexander Mack, Sr., ("Rights and Ordinances," 1715) to encourage the follower of Jesus to contem-

plate all of God's commandments day and night, to keep them
with a pure heart, to let them provide counsel, and to pray for
the guidance of the Holy Spirit in understanding their truth.

From the beginning, the Brethren have sought to live out
the truth of God's revelation with humble spirits and obedient
lives. Jesus' words in John 14:15, "If you love me, you will
keep my commandments," provide the crucial interpretative
principle through which to view the scripture. We must not be
merely hearers of the Word, but doers as well. Doing the Word
means that we are out of rhythm with society and the values of
the majority. Obedience is the test of love. As we accept and
live out the moral imperatives of the Christian faith, we witness most clearly, albeit imperfectly, to the life and faith of the
One whom we follow.

For the day: How do spiritual disciplines (such as scripture
reading, family devotions, private prayer, fasting, and other
sacred endeavors) help you to know and to do God's will?

Prayer: Let the words of my mouth and the meditation
of my heart be acceptable to you,
O LORD, my rock and my redeemer (Ps. 19:14).

David K. Shumate

Part 3

Images of Christ

Images of Christ in Hebrews

May 26–June 29

*Y*ou should look alone to Jesus your Redeemer and Savior. If you have learned from Him the teaching as it is outwardly commanded in the Testament, so that you will remain steadfast in it, . . . you must become used to taking His cross upon yourself daily with denial of your will.

Alexander Mack, Sr. (1679–1735)

♂

May 26

The Wisdom of God

Readings: Proverbs 8:22-31; James 3:13-18

I [Wisdom] was daily [God's] delight, rejoicing before him always, rejoicing in his inhabited world and delighting in the human race (Prov. 8:30b-31).

Meditation: Do you know someone who is truly wise—someone who can give counsel that inspires people to become more than they are? Proverbs 8 pictures God's wisdom as a woman who provides instruction that leads to godly living. The New Testament writers drew upon this picture of wisdom to explain who Jesus is—the eternal, powerful, revealing, transforming wisdom or Word of God. As divine wisdom, Jesus is the "master worker" who set the universe in place and who also restores broken lives. His powerful Word preserves the creation and sustains the weary and discouraged. He brings us healing and enables us to know God. He is the incarnation of God's delight in us. We Brethren believe that God's wisdom, embodied in Jesus Christ, is present to us today through the Spirit of Christ. We believe that really knowing Christ means living as he lived. But we can do this only through the power of the Spirit. As James points out, God's powerful wisdom produces not domination but self-giving. Those who have been shaped by it will reflect in their lives the pure, peaceable, merciful character of God. As those who live stressful lives in a disordered world, we need this wisdom. And the world needs us to embody it in lives of mercy and love.

For the day: Make time to sit at the feet of Jesus and listen to his instruction. Open yourself to his delight in you. Where might his wisdom touch your life or the lives of others today?

Prayer: Wise and loving God, help us to rediscover the joy of being your people. Draw us close to your heart, and form us every day a little more in the image of Christ, so that we can be agents of your wisdom in a hurting world. Amen.

Brenda B. Colijn

May 27

Where Often Is Heard an Encouraging Word

Reading: Hebrews 1:1-5

But in these last days [God] has spoken to us by a Son, whom he appointed heir of all things, through whom he also created the worlds (Heb. 1:2).

Meditation: DR was still shaking, but a smile leaked from his lips. He had just climbed a 40-foot tree, stepped off a 3-foot by 3-foot platform into space, zipped 1000 feet on a line at 35 miles per hour—and survived some of the debilitating anxieties that had led to his being in a prison mental hospital for more than a decade.

He also happened to discover a clothespin on his jacket, which meant he was tagged for special encouraging words from the rest of his group at the challenge course that helps groups build teamwork, trust, and problem-solving skills. Individuals surreptitiously slip a clip onto the clothing of another. At various points throughout the day, we halt, locate the clothespins, and take turns encouraging that person.

The person writing to the Hebrews has noticed a clothespin on the faith community's jacket. The writer plucks it off and encourages the Hebrews with a recitation of the absolute supremacy and sufficiency of Jesus Christ as revealer and mediator of God's grace. In the face of persecution, believers needed reassurance that no matter how harsh the symptoms, the path they had chosen—the way of peace and radical community— was one that was right for them.

No matter how harsh his symptoms, we encouraged DR. That day, he was eventually able to choose not to let those symptoms define him. He chose to rise up (the tree) and fly beyond the limitations they imposed on him.

For the day: What has encouraged you today to rise from your bed and live toward God's ways?

Prayer: When my courage to face the day fails me, God, clip onto me, and let me find the sign that reassures me you are near.

Lee-Lani Wright

ʘ

May 28

In the Beginning

Reading: John 1:1-5

In the beginning . . . God created the heavens and the earth (Gen. 1:1). In the beginning was the Word (John 1:1a).

Meditation: The Book of Genesis takes its title from the opening words of the book. Genesis means "beginning." Genesis 1:1 is concerned with the beginning of creation; that is, how did this earth we live on, the skies overhead, the creatures, including humans, get started? The answer to this question is simply—God. Genesis says that it all began when God said "Let there be light" (Gen. 1:3).

The Gospel of John also opens with "genesis." But now the

concern is not with creation. John takes us back before creation, even before time: "In the beginning was the Word."

What is this Word that, as John tells us, was with God and, in fact, was God? What does John mean when he says of this Word that everything that exists came into being by the Word? What is this Word that brought life into being? We have to read on to verses 14 and following to find the answer John gives: Jesus. Jesus is the Word made "flesh." That's what the word *incarnation* means.

From time to time, I hear Christians, some of them preachers, talk about how important it is to read the "Word," to live according to the commandments found in the "Word of God." And when they use "Word" this way, they mean the Bible. There are many churches that take pride in calling themselves "Bible churches."

What they ignore or forget or don't understand is that Christian faith is based not on a book, but on Word-made-flesh. As important as the Bible is (and for us Brethren, especially the New Testament), it isn't what our faith is based on. Our faith is defined by who Jesus was and still is.

For the day: Live this day as if Christ Jesus lives in your flesh.

Prayer: Thank you, God, for Jesus, Word-made-flesh. Amen.

Kenneth L. Gibble

May 29

To Infinity and Beyond . . .

Readings: Hebrews 1:6-9; Psalm 45:2-7

But about the Son he says, "Your throne, O God, will last for ever and ever, and righteousness will be the scepter of your kingdom" (Heb. 1:8 NIV).

Meditation: Who would have thought that while reading these verses addressed to the Hebrews I would think of my math classroom? Hebrews 1:8 speaks of God's throne lasting forever and ever. While this scripture provoked the memory of teaching my beginning algebra students about infinite numbers, I also felt awe and wonderment at God's great love for us, a love that is both unconditional and infinite. While the text in Hebrews speaks of *righteousness* being the scepter, Psalm 45 (from which this Hebrews text comes) says *justice* is the scepter. Both texts call us to higher living, to a Christlike way of being and serving others. With justice and righteousness being the scepters of Jesus' kingdom, we too must seek to actively pursue these values. What a joy it is to be a part of the kingdom of God today where justice and righteousness prevail. What a beautiful invitation we have to follow Jesus and to advocate for justice and righteousness as worthy values for our culture. What a beautiful gift we've been given to live our lives aware of God's infinite love for us and to share this love with those around us.

For the day: What is righteous? What is just? How great is Jesus' love for all of us? What can you do today to share love, justice, and righteousness with those around you?

Prayer: Loving, just, and righteous God, lead us today to be mindful of your love for us and our responsibility to others and your majestic creation. Empower us to work for justice and righteousness in our communities, country, and world. Let us be witnesses to your infinite, loving light. May it be so. Amen.

Aaron R. Lahman

May 30

The Work of God's Hands

Reading: Hebrews 1:10-12

In the beginning, Lord, you founded the earth, and the heavens are the work of your hands; they will perish, but you remain . . . (Heb. 1:10-11a).

Meditation: "Do all your work as if you had a thousand years to live, and as you would if you knew you must die tomorrow" (Mother Ann Lee, 1816).

A friend shared this quote with me as we walked together following the news of spiritual writer Henri Nouwen's death in 1996. We were very aware in that moment of the fleeting nature of life. We also felt that we had brushed against something timeless in Nouwen's gift to us, something that resonated with God's own nature in and beyond time.

That we are the "work of God's hands" speaks to these two aspects of our identity. We are part of God's creation, all of which is changing, perishing. But we are also those who create with God and thereby become the work of God's hands as in bearing in the world God's nature and intention. The Apostle Paul in his beautiful hymn of love in 1 Corinthians 13 proclaims, "Love never ends." In our love we join what is eternal in the midst of all that passes.

Three hundred years is both a long time and a drop in time's bucket. What springs eternal from our living as Brethren? Surely there is something here of our manner of seeking to live close to the love of God in Jesus. There is something of the way we've embodied love in peacemaking and service that has graced our world these three centuries with the fragrance of God. Our living remains both that which is fleeting and passing and that which yet invites us to become in the day before us a part of God's eternal work.

For the day: "Do all your work as if you had a thousand years to live, and as you would if you knew you must die tomorrow."

Prayer: Creator God, I thank you for all the ways my living can join your work in the world you love. Amen.

Glenn Mitchell

May 31

Seeing His Glory

Reading: John 1:1-18

The Word became flesh and lived among us, and we have seen his glory, the glory as of a father's only son, full of grace and truth (John 1:14).

Meditation: Upon being baptized perhaps too early in life, I searched around for a discipline that would help me live out my vows and decided to work at memorizing significant portions of scripture. My wise parents advised me to start not with Genesis 1, but with John 1. Little did I know then that I had focused on some of the choice words of all literature and the theological worth of such great expressions.

Now, seventy five years later, fresh meanings abound as I ponder the incarnation and the ability to see the glory of God in the earthly life of Jesus. John ably highlights the life of Jesus with just two simple words, *grace* and *truth*. Will you try with me to view these two qualities in another word picture of Jesus? In John 15:5 Jesus says, "I am the vine, you are the branches." There is an eleven-year-old grapevine at the corner of our garden that illustrates Jesus' words. Following the annual winter pruning of the vine, which appears to be good as dead, warm spring days bring on the new growth upon which the grapes will come into being. The sturdy trunk has two branches well formed on the trellis, which in the recent season produced a bushel of tasty and nutritional fruit. Let the one branch represent *grace* and the other *truth.*

Grace speaks strongly of compassion, forgiveness, love, service, and peace. Truth can be rightly described as reality, simplicity, genuineness, sincerity, honesty, and fullness. These two aspects of the glory of Christ, now firmly attached to our very beings, are pictured with these words: "From his fullness we have all received, grace upon grace. . . . grace and truth came through Jesus Christ" (John 1:16).

For the day: Repeat through the day, better still—sing, the words of the old gospel chorus by Albert Osborn, "Let the beauty [glory] of Jesus be seen in me." This is indeed a bold and challenging goal not unlike the goal Jesus asks of us in his Sermon on the Mount, "Be perfect."

Prayer: All gracious God, help me to exchange my greed for Christ's grace and my fickle falsehood for refining truth. Amen.

Glenn E. Kinsel

June 1

Just What They've Been Waiting For . . .

Reading: Hebrews 1:13-14

But to which of the angels has [God] ever said, "Sit at my right hand . . ."? Therefore we must pay greater attention to what we have heard (Heb. 1:13).

Meditation: For those with a lifetime in the church, these opening chapters of Hebrews seem unneeded. The writer works hard to convince the readers that in God's Son something of great importance—ever greater than angels—has come into the world, and we'd best pay attention. We already know that!

Yet while this argument seems superfluous for many of us, it is custom-made for our time. Indeed, our era mirrors those days of the early church when the identity and importance of Jesus were very much at issue. Jesus is no longer a taken-for-granted aspect of our world.

So once again we are obliged to "make the case" for Christ—and his relevance to our world and our lives. While the writer compares Jesus to the angels to show his relative importance, to whom might we compare him today? What are those entities in our time with "angelic" power and influence whom Jesus trumps —and what chance has this of gaining people's "attention"?

We can take our pick. According to the book *Applebee's America*, people in our society have grown weary of looking to the usual cast of powerbrokers for meaning and direction: politicians, media stars, corporate types—even clergy. But this doesn't mean people have given up looking—no, they're just looking in other places. They are looking to trusted friends for counsel on important decisions; they are looking to religious experiences that offer meaning in an increasingly meaningless existence.

Seems to me they'd be looking for someone like the Jesus of Hebrews—a pioneer who committed his life to a higher cause without reservation (see Heb. 12) and one who issues a call away from materialism and toward relationships (see Heb. 13).

For the day: Is this the Jesus you present in your interaction with your neighbors? Does the life of your congregation reflect this Jesus?

Prayer: Let me show the world the Jesus they've been waiting for.

David R. Radcliff

June 2

God's Promise

Reading: Jeremiah 31:31-34

I will put my law within them, and I will write it upon their hearts; and I will be their God, and they shall be my people (Jer. 31:33b).

Meditation: I was thirty-nine years old when God's call came to move from Virginia with my husband and three children to the Dominican Republic to serve as mission coordinators for the Church of the Brethren. I had taken a semester of Spanish twenty years earlier while attending McPherson College, but I could recall only a few words. I often tell my friends that no amount of money could get me to repeat those first few months of living in the Dominican Republic. Because I knew Polish I would answer in Polish whenever a Dominican church member or neighbor would talk to me in Spanish. It was *rough* trying to learn Spanish myself as well as help my children adjust to the new culture and language. But God promises to be with us and to write his law upon our hearts. In those dark times when I felt alone and afraid, the scriptures I had memorized long ago helped me to not give up *hope*. After six months of private Spanish lessons and a lot of patient Dominicans helping me, not only could I communicate in their language, but I even had one sermon to share as I visited churches.

Today I am a pediatric hospital chaplain and have the opportunity to speak Spanish daily. There are many Hispanics moving into our area who are often afraid and concerned when their child must be hospitalized. I am able to pray with them and offer hope in the midst of crisis. Little did I know how

God's promise to be with me would bear fruit later in my life. Now I can see the tremendous blessing in following God's call—wherever it may lead.

For the day: Listen for ways God is calling you to deepen your walk of faith by trying something new or something that you never thought you could do. Trust God to be with you each step of the way.

Prayer: Loving God, you promise to forgive us, to never leave us, and to shepherd us through the trials of life. Thank you for your Word that abides in my heart and helps me know your loving presence each day. Keep me receptive to the new avenues you create where I can share your love and the good news of Jesus with others. Amen.

Rebecca Baile Crouse

June 3

Priestly Blessings

Reading: Hebrews 7:1-3

Without father, without mother, without genealogy, having neither beginning of days nor end of life, but resembling the Son of God, he remains a priest forever (Heb. 7:3).

Meditation: The Bible has relatively little to say about the priestly figure Melchizedek. We know nothing about his parents or other relatives. We do not know when he was born or when he died. We are told that he encountered Abraham and performed a priestly function by blessing him. The writer of Hebrews compares Melchizedek to Christ and indicates that as a priest of the Most High God he is a priest forever.

It happens. We encounter people we know nothing about. They may do something for us. They may teach us something or steer us in a good direction. They may even bless us. I was visiting a woman in the hospital when an elderly couple came to visit her. Somehow the two became separated on their way to the hospital room and the husband could not find his wife. We had hospital security and personnel looking all over the hospital for her. We knew nothing about these anonymous members of the hospital staff, but they were willing to drop their busy schedules and help out with the search. Finally we found the woman standing patiently in an area where she thought she and her husband had agreed to meet. When the couple reunited, there was initial frustration about the mis-communication, but they indeed felt blessed by those who had helped to make the lost once again found. We may not be priests of the Most High God, but we can bless one another through acts of kindness as we treat one another with the human respect and dignity that God requires of us.

For the day: Be mindful of the ways in which you are blessed by others today. In addition, be attentive as to how you may bless other people.

Prayer: God of blessing and God of grace, help me to be open to unexpected things today. Instill within me an openness that will allow me to receive your blessing from others, even those I may not know. May I find your blessing in all aspects of life. Amen.

David A. Leiter

June 4

Not a One-Way Street

Reading: Genesis 14:17-20

Blessed be Abram by God Most High, maker of heaven and earth; and blessed be God Most High, who has delivered your enemies into your hand! (Gen. 14:19-20).

Meditation: Early in the history of television, a program called *What's My Line* included a panel of knowledgeable people who were asked to identify a person's occupation. In a game of biblical personalities, most of us would have trouble identifying Melchizedek, only mentioned several times in scripture. In our text, he is identified as the king of Salem (later to become Jerusalem) and "priest of the Most High God." He brings bread and wine to greet Abram and bless him after he has successfully recovered all that was taken from the king of Sodom (which included Lot, his family, and all of their possessions). By receiving the blessing, Abram recognizes that Melchizedek represents the same God that Abram worships. Melchizedek's words are a reminder that praise is not a one-way street. Abram has been blessed by God and God in turn is to be blessed for helping Abram. It is a formula we know well, for we often sing by memory, "Praise God, from whom all blessings flow."

We understand the call for praise in a major happening like Abram's. We tend to be less enthusiastic in practicing praise for all blessings that flow our way. William Beahm, teacher and mentor for many Brethren, performed a Melchizedek blessing for me. During a pastoral visit in the hospital where he was fighting his cancer, he took my hand and, in the midst of great pain, looked up through the hospital paraphernalia, and with a strained trace of twinkle, spoke words that burned a praise phrase into my soul. "Earle," he said, "be thankful when your plumbing works." A simple reminder that the two-way street of praise is an acknowledgment meant for all blessings, great and small.

For the day: Bless the Lord, O my soul, and forget not all his benefits.

Prayer: Lord, teach us how to help each other identify and acknowledge your blessings large and small, and then in turn, how to bless you from whom all blessings flow. Amen.

Earle W. Fike, Jr.

June 5

Open to Change

Reading: Hebrews 7:4-17

Now if perfection had been attainable through the levitical priest-hood . . . what further need would there have been to speak of another priest . . . ? (Heb. 7:11).

Meditation: We are creatures of habit and tradition and some-times reluctant to change. I grew up on a farm during the transition from horse power to tractor power. The trend was clear, but my father loved those beautiful draft horses so much that we kept one team even after most of their usefulness on the farm was gone. It was fun, however, to hitch them to the mill sleigh on a snowy day or night for a sleigh ride to enjoy the winter beauty of our country roads. Later in life there was a parallel for me in my own reluctance to give up the dictating machine and typewriter for the word processor and computer. Resistance to change is not an unusual trait for humans; this is exactly what the author of Hebrews was confronting as he addressed his audience sometime in the late first century A.D. Apparently some Jewish Christians were still seeking *perfection* (N. T. Wright in his commentary on Hebrews suggests the Greek term can also be translated *completeness*) in the old priestly tradition and not through *the power of a life that cannot be destroyed—Jesus, the Messiah* (v. 16). Re-read the passage and note the meticulously developed and forceful argument the author presents to these doubting, or just tradition bound, Jewish Christians to accept the perfect sacrifice and the true High Priest. Maybe we can draw some comparisons and lessons from the author of Hebrews' concern and message to our individual faith journeys today.

For the day: Does the comfort of tradition and a reluctance to entertain and accept new ideas and possibilities inhibit your growth in the Spirit or the vitality of your Christian faith community?

Prayer: O God, your creation is ever changing and being renewed. As your creatures we too desire change and renewal in body and spirit through the guidance and blessing of your Holy Spirit. Amen.

H. Lamar Gibble

June 6

No Limits

Reading: Hebrews 7:18-24

The former regulation is set aside because it was weak and useless (for the law made nothing perfect), and a better hope is introduced, by which we draw near to God (Heb. 7:18-19 NIV).

Meditation: Who wants to waste time and effort on someone or something that won't stick around for very long? You end up feeling drained and empty in the end. It's easy to get overly consumed in the accumulated memories of what once was, and dreams and promises of what might be. But when plans don't meet our expectations, it's enough to prompt us to look for something more worth our effort.

The new Christian converts from the Jewish community were beginning to question the move they made from a faith with history and tradition. In the chaos of their day it just seemed so hard to hold on to this new faith that Paul was spreading. It didn't have connections to generations of converts. Family and friends just didn't seem to understand. They felt like they had to explain their actions when it was so hard to put into words the inspiration and hope that first drew them to make such a daring move. You would think Paul would take the opportunity to remind them that Jesus also was rooted in the Jewish tradition, himself. But Paul does one better—he reminds his audience that Jesus offers something more solid than a passing social convention or religious tradition. Here is someone who breaks out of the confines of our expectations. He is someone who could not be bound by the ultimate "limiter," death.

For the day: Forget what used to limit you. Today is a fresh day brimming over with opportunities. There is new hope to live into the life God intended.

Prayer: God of fulfilled promises, empower me to be free of imperfect living. Renew me to live in the fullness of your promise for a full and meaningful life. May my life this day reflect back a small portion of the limitless love that you have shown for me.

Steven W. Bollinger

⊘

June 7

He Is Able

Readings: Hebrews 7:25-26; 11:39-40

Wherefore he is able also to save them to the uttermost that come unto God by him (Heb. 7:25 KJV).

Meditation: From the beginning of Hebrews, the author has been building the case for Christ's better priesthood—its necessity, its completeness, and its eternal nature. This is the High Priest we need and want; he becomes us, he fits our need. These verses tell of the eternal excellence of his work; he is able to save to the "uttermost"—a complete saving. Joseph was told after the annunciation, "He shall save his people from their sins" (Matt. 1:21 KJV), not *in* their sin, but *from* their sin. As the old hymn says, "be of sin the double cure, cleanse me from its guilt and power."

Even the most skilled cardiac surgeon in the world cannot repair every heart, but this Great Physician, this eternal High Priest, for all those who come to God by him, can save to the uttermost. It is in this life an ongoing salvation. He lives now and makes intercession even today for us. David anticipated this uttermost salvation when he said, "I shall be satisfied, when I awake, with thy likeness" (Ps. 17:15 KJV).

This invitation is to whosoever will come, to anyone laboring and heavy laden with sin. It is for all who hear his call and follow him, even for me. The old priesthood could not promise this complete salvation; this new High Priest will stop short of nothing less. What a hope, what an uplifting, when we are weary of sin in our lives.

For the day: Be assured of Jesus' perfect priesthood. The One who came as the lowest is now made the highest, interceding to bring those nearer who were farthest and save them to the uttermost.

Prayer: Our Father, I thank thee that Jesus intercedes today—Jesus who was separate in every way from sinners, yet comes near to sinful man. Save me today from my selfishness and sin that I may be of benefit to others and finally saved in heaven. In Jesus' name. Amen.

Reuben D. Hess

June 8

More Than Enough

Reading: Hebrews 7:27-28

Unlike the other high priests, he has no need to offer sacrifices day after day, first for his own sins, and then for those of the people; this he did once for all when he offered himself (Heb. 7:27).

Meditation: During this month, millions of young people—including my youngest child—will walk across a stage in cap and gown, take in hand well-earned diplomas, and step forth from childhood into young adulthood. And millions of parents, looking on with pride and relief, will ask themselves, "Have I done enough?"

It is a nagging question we encounter in many areas of life: Have I studied enough to pass this test? Have I worked hard enough to get the promotion? Have I saved enough for my retirement? Many people even live with a sense of "not enough" when it comes to their relationship with God. They think they haven't been good enough, faithful enough, forgiving enough, or generous enough to deserve God's favor.

And it is true for all of us—we haven't done enough. But

the good news of the gospel is that our relationship with God is not based on whether or not we do enough. It is based on Jesus, who did more than enough, once and for all, when he offered himself up on the cross.

For the day: Let God's "more than enough" love in Jesus Christ quiet your every fear. Discover in God's grace the peace that nothing else can give or take away.

Prayer: Lord, your love is sufficient for all our needs. Remove our fear and replace it with faith. Then let our gratitude be revealed in worship and service. Amen.

James L. Benedict

June 9

Known by Christ

Reading: John 4:21-26

The woman said to him, "I know that Messiah is coming" (who is called Christ). "When he comes, he will proclaim all things to us." Jesus said to her, "I am he, the one who is speaking to you" (John 4:25-26).

Meditation: The story of the woman at the well is a story of spiritual healing. In this one encounter, Jesus transforms the Samaritan woman's life and she has a new faith.

One of the major themes of the Book of John is that the Christ can be recognized by the signs of wonder and amazement that are recorded in the text. Here we read about the woman who goes to the well, completely unaware that her life is about to be totally transformed by Christ, the giver of life. As a Samaritan, she is an unlikely candidate for an encounter with Jesus. At the well she finds not just a man, but rather the giver of life whom she has heard about. She meets Jesus, who knows her better than she knows herself. This knowledge is a sign for her about the true nature of Jesus. Jesus brings her a sense of wellness—a unity of mind, body, and spirit—that will allow her to find wholeness.

Too often we also feel that we are "unlikely" candidates for Jesus' healing. Yet, as Christians we all seek Jesus' healing touch in our lives. Whatever pain, sorrow, or illness that we experience, we know that Jesus, the great healer, walks with us, bringing us hope. Wellness is more than just physical health. Wellness includes our right relationship with God and our neighbor. Like the woman at the well, we rely on the healing touch of Jesus.

For the day: As you encounter the difficulties that life can often bring, remember that Jesus is the great healer and the giver of life, offering wellness and hope.

Prayer: O God, the great healer and giver of life, we come before you with many burdens. Some of us have physical pain. Others are carrying guilt, sorrow, or other emotions that hold us back. Whatever challenges we face, we know that you can give us a sense of wellness and bring us healing. May your Spirit be among us and bring us hope. Amen.

Kathryn Goering Reid

June 10

Mediator of a New Covenant

Reading: Hebrews 9:11-15

For this reason he is the mediator of a new covenant, so that those who are called may receive the promised eternal inheritance, because a death has occurred that redeems them from the transgressions under the first covenant (Heb. 9:15).

Meditation from our past: A covenant is not a wedding but a marriage—and those are two quite different concepts. A wedding is a point event; it happens and is over and done with. My wedding took place on July 9, 1955. But don't ask me when my marriage took place; it is too early to say. It is on the way. . . .

Now the wedding was a very important event. It put the marriage into motion, set the nature of the relationship, and defined to whom I was married and to whom not. Marriages need weddings…but a wedding and a marriage are not the same thing.

Just so, what happened at Sinai was not, in and of itself, God's covenant with Israel; and what happened in the death of Christ was not, in and of itself, the new covenant in his blood. Of course, throughout their way together, covenant partners will want continually to recall the event of sealing that set them upon that way—just as husband and wife need to support and invigorate their marriage by recalling their wedding vows.

We have seen that the Lord's Supper includes a good deal of symbolism pointing us back to the event that inaugurated the covenant of the body of Christ. In fact, our study makes it apparent that, under the erosions of church history, while the Supper was being distorted and truncated, it was these backward-pointing elements that remained strong—to the point that the Supper has become little more than a commemoration of an event of the past. But because that past is intended to connect with the living present, it ought never be forgotten that the resurrection is as essential a part of the new covenant inaugural as is the crucifixion. Without the resurrection, the cross would have marked the end as well as the beginning of the covenant—the groom murdered on his wedding day. The original celebrations of the Supper recognized the importance of the resurrection; it is not as clear that our modern celebrations do. —*Vernard Eller*

From Could the Church Have It All Wrong? *The Vernard Eller Collection,*
copyright © 1997 House Church Central, *www.hccentral.com/eller1.*
Used by permission of Vernard Eller.

For the day: What relationships do you have to other people, to financial institutions, to organizations? How does your commitment to these relationships compare to the active or inactive place of God's covenant with you?

Prayer: God of history, God of covenant, I thank you for your saving grace in the past, the present, and the future. Amen.

♉

June 11

Our Benefactor

Reading: Hebrews 9:16-24

Where a will is involved, the death of the one who made it must be established. . . . For Christ did not enter a sanctuary made by human hands, a mere copy of the true one, but he entered into heaven itself, now to appear in the presence of God on our behalf (Heb. 9:16, 24).

Meditation: Translating the remarkable prose of the unknown writer of Hebrews is no simple task. Written to people of Jewish heritage, the author uses metaphor and language familiar in their worship practices under the old covenant to explain the different character of worship under the new covenant in Christ.

Translating the word *covenant* as "will" is how it is for us. Reading this "new will," we, the inheritors, discover the good news that, on our behalf, the love of God in the life and death of Christ has made us beneficiaries blessed with direct access to worshiping and experiencing God. What an inheritance!

A man risked his life to rescue a young, eight-year-old boy from a riptide. Traumatized but safe, the boy said, "Thank you for saving my life."

Looking the boy straight in the eye, the man replied, "That's OK. Just make sure it was worth saving."

In Romans 12, the Apostle Paul gives us a clue on how to receive and honor this new inheritance. We are to present ourselves as a living sacrifice. Peterson's translation in *The Message* says, "So here's what I want you to do, God helping you: Take your everyday, ordinary life—your sleeping, eating, going-to-work, and walking-around life—and place it before God as an offering. Embracing what God does for you is the best thing you can do for God." What a responsibility!

For the day: Alexander Mack said we are "to be known by the manner of our living." It turns out that the way we live is also our worship of God.

Prayer: Lord God, the inheritance you have provided on our behalf through Jesus is more than I regularly honor. Help me to do better. Amen.

Earle W. Fike, Jr.

⌀

Junio 12
June 12 in Spanish

Un Sacrificio Hecho "Una Vez Para Siempre"

Lectura: 1 Juan 2:2; Hebreos 9:25-28

El es el Sacrificio por el perdón de nuestros pecados, y no solo por los nuestros sino por los de todo el mundo (1 Juan 2:2).

Meditación: Así como fue menester que el santuario terrenal se purificara con sacrificios de animales, también fue necesario que el santuario celestial se perfeccionara con el mejor sacrificio, el que Cristo hizo de si mismo para presentarse ahora ante Dios en favor nuestro. Su venida dio paso a la gran era mesiánica, hacia la cual avanza toda la historia.

Está establecido que los seres humanos mueran una sola vez, y después venga el juicio. Del mismo modo que el hombre muere una vez debido al pecado también Cristo murió una vez como el perfecto sacrificio por el pecado. Y así como después de la muerte el hombre enfrenta el juicio, también Cristo después de su muerte, aparecerá trayendo salvación del pecado y su juicio.

Traerá la perfección, de la salvación comprada para nosotros en la cruz, en toda la plenitud de su gloria a quienes lo esperan, como los israelitas esperaban por el sumo sacerdote mientras estaba en el lugar santísimo el día de la expiación (2 Tim. 4:8; Tito 2:13-14).

Para hoy: Acepta confiadamente en tu corazón el sacrificio por el perdón de nuestros pecados.

Oración: Dios misericordioso, gracias por enviar a tu hijo mediante sacrificio perfecto para salvarnos con su preciosa sangre para el perdón de todos nuestros pecados. Amén.

Félix Antonio Arias Mateo

&

June 12

A Sacrifice Made "Once for All Time"

Readings: 1 John 2:2; Hebrews 9:25-28

[Christ] is the atoning sacrifice for our sins, and not for ours only but also for the sins of the whole world (1 John 2:2).

Meditation: While it was necessary that the earthly sanctuary would be purified with sacrifices of animals, it was also necessary that the heavenly sanctuary would be made perfect with the best sacrifice, that which Christ offered in presenting himself before God on our behalf.

His coming brought about the great messianic era, toward which all of history advances. It is established that human beings are to die only one time, and afterwards comes the judgment. In the same way that the human dies one time because of sin, Christ also died one time as the perfect sacrifice for sin. And just as after death the person faces judgment, Christ, after his death, will appear bringing salvation from sin and judgment.

He will bring the perfect salvation bought for us in the cross of Calvary, in all the fullness of his glory, to those who wait, just as the Israelites awaited the high priest while he was in the holy place of atonement (2 Tim. 4:8; Tit. 2:13-14).

For the day: Accept with trust in your heart Christ's sacrifice for the forgiveness of our sins.

Prayer: God of mercy, thank you for sending your Son as the perfect mediating sacrifice to save us with his precious blood for the forgiveness of all of our sins. Amen

Félix Antonio Arias Mateo

&

June 13

A One-Time Sacrifice

Readings: Hebrews 10:1-10; 1 Peter 1:15-16

We have been made holy through the sacrifice of the body of Jesus Christ once for all (Heb. 10:10 NIV).

Meditation: The writer of Hebrews presents Jesus Christ as superior in every way to every created being and function—the prophets, Moses, angels, the Old Testament priesthood. Furthermore, his sacrifice on the cross is superior to the sacrifices of the Old Testament. The gospel makes clear the infinite contrast between the sacrifices offered by Old Testament priests and the self-sacrifice of Christ.

Hebrews 10 pictures the law as a shadow, not the reality of what God planned (v. 1). The law required the repeated offering of the sacrifice, but no matter how many times repeated, sacrifices could not make the worshiper perfect (v. 1). Nor could they satisfy God's just demands (v. 8). Unknown to the Old Testament saint, the law involving sacrifices was to be set aside; it was only temporary (v. 9).

The law did not remove sin but served as a constant reminder of sin. Because of its required repetition, the annual sacrifices made sin more obvious (vv. 2-3). What's worse, those sacrifices were incapable of taking away sin (v. 4).

Ah, how wonderful the contrast! God sent his Son to offer himself as a sufficient and sinless sacrifice. Jesus came only to do the Father's will (v. 7), that is, to pay the complete penalty for our sin so that the Father's plan could be accomplished for us. That plan for the followers of Jesus is that they be "made holy" (v. 10) through his once-for-all sacrifice. God's purpose is that Christians are to be set apart from sin and separated to holiness.

For the day: Having accepted Christ's sacrifice for your sin, is your life demonstrating the holiness God intends?

Prayer: Thank you, Lord, for your sacrifice for me. Please enable me by your Holy Spirit to live a life of holiness that you may be glorified.

Jesse B. Deloe

♂

June 14

A Full Understanding

Reading: Hebrews 10:11-14

But when Christ had offered for all time a single sacrifice for sins, he sat down at the right hand of God . . . (Heb. 10:12).

Meditation: When I was counseling at a junior high camp at Camp Colorado, communion was scheduled as a part of evening worship. We counselors waited until the campers had received communion, wanting to make sure there was enough bread and juice to go around. Of course, there was enough. As I stood in the dark looking at the fire, I took a sip and a bite and quickly realized we had put too much juice in the glasses and made the pieces of bread too large; there was more than one sip and one taste! As I started thinking about how much juice and bread we had really used, I briefly acknowledged that it was neat to actually feel nourished by the bread and cup instead of getting just a little taste. But, unintentionally, I was reducing the experience, and God was determined to make a point. Soon I was taking a drink rather than a polite communion sip. The juice was sweet and filled my mouth, wetting my throat as I swallowed. I expected each mouthful to empty the cup. Yet after each mouthful that didn't, I was more and more overwhelmed with the deep understanding that God's love and grace are as endless as the communion cup seemed to be.

Reflecting on the bread and cup as symbols of the forgiveness of sin through Jesus' sacrifice is one thing; truly understanding that God's love and grace are endless is another much richer, life-giving lesson.

For the day: Reflect on a significant communion experience. How did the Holy Spirit relate to you and your faith community through the experience?

Prayer: God, forgive us our tendencies to reduce you to something our minds can easily grasp. Overwhelm us with the hope that your love and grace give. Amen.

Becky Ullom

June 15

The Great "I Am" and the Gracious "I Wills"

Readings: Hebrews 10:15-18; Psalm 8

I will remember their sins and their lawless deeds no more (Heb. 10:17).

Meditation: The author of Hebrews reminds us of God's great once-and-for-all sacrifice found in the life, death, and resurrection of God's Son, Jesus. The author quotes the great covenant promises of God from the Book of Jeremiah. I don't know about you, but reading these quoted passages is awe-inspiring. Here on one side of the covenant we have God, the Sovereign Creator. The psalmist ponders the same: "When I look at your heavens, the work of your fingers, the moon and the stars that you have established; what are human beings that you are mindful of them?" (Ps. 8:3-4). On the other side of this covenant, we have humankind, guilty of making a mess out of pretty much everything God has created. But please note the covenant: It is from the Creator to the created; it makes no demands, it requires no sacrifices for wrongdoing, it is certainly not mutual. It is God's initiation. It is stated very clearly by four initiatives from God (cf., Heb. 10:16-17). "I will!" God declares a new relationship with creation. "I will!" God instills in the hearts of his people the ultimate law, the love for God and neighbor. "I will!" God places in the minds of God's people the loving and gracious covenant for all time. "I will!" And finally, God wipes clean the slate of our broken lives, graciously and mercifully, forgetting our sins and lawless acts. "What are human beings that you are mindful of them, mortals that you care for them? Yet you have made them a little lower than God, and crowned them with glory and honor" (Ps. 8:4-5). It doesn't seem right to me for God, the Creator, to bend over backwards to redeem his wayward people. But that's just it; the great "I am" has in Jesus Christ announced the gracious "I wills." I don't know about you, but I am truly awe-inspired.

For the day: Sing praise today—O Lord, our Lord, how majestic is your name in all the earth (Ps. 8:1).

Prayer: O Living, Loving, Gracious Redeemer, help us to live our lives in humble recognition of your gracious acts of reconciliation in Jesus Christ, our Lord. Amen.

David A. Whitten

June 16

Seek God's Leadership and Discipline

Readings: Proverbs 3:5-12; Hebrews 12:1-13

Trust in the Lord with all your heart, and do not rely on your own insight. In all your ways acknowledge him, and he will make straight your paths (Prov. 3:5-6).

Meditation: All too often in our modern world we are inclined to say, "I can handle this myself." The sage who authored Proverbs reminds us that this all-too-human inclination should be resisted, and we should place our trust in the Lord. Unfortunately, this is another example of something that is easier said than done. And yet, no one has ever said that following the teachings of the Lord is easy. It takes much prayer, self-control, dedication, and discipline to live up to our best intentions. Since we are not perfect and do not always act as we would desire to act, subsequent verses remind us not to be angry or discouraged when we are reproached and disciplined by the Lord. Discipline is often necessary to remind us of our real goals and to encourage us to change our course of action. If we can discipline ourselves and accept the Lord's discipline in a positive and resourceful manner, the results will benefit everyone. These results can lead to wisdom and understanding, which in turn, produce happiness and satisfaction.

For the day: Trust the Lord to provide strength and insight to do what is pleasing in his sight.

Prayer: O Lord Almighty, please help me to be humble and faithful; and give me the strength, courage, and will to place my trust in you. Amen.

J. Kenneth Kreider

✑

June 17

Endure the Race

Reading: Hebrews 12:1-3

Therefore, since we are surrounded by so great a cloud of witnesses, let us also lay aside every weight and the sin that clings so closely, and let us run with perseverance the race that is set before us (Heb. 12:1).

Meditation from our past: The Book of Hebrews is, in one respect, the most extraordinary book in the New Testament. It sets forth Christ the Lord to us in a somewhat new light, and new relation. . . . The other books tell what Jesus has done to redeem the world from sin. This book tells what he is now doing to save his people.

. . . the Olympic games [were] celebrated by the ancient Greeks once every four years. From these the figure of running a race, given in the text, was borrowed. A man cannot run long and well with a load on his back. You have no doubt seen the fabled demigod Atlas pictured with the world on his shoulders. I have often thought of that old Grecian representation of avarice, as being something like a true picture of many professors of the Christian religion at the present day. You see the old myth struggling along with this big round world on his back, apparently casting his eyes upward at times as if he might be longing to reach the top of Mount Olympus, the home of the gods: but alas! his head is bowed and his back bent under the mighty pressure, and he never got there. It will fare no better with the man who tries to carry this world with him to heaven. The apostle says: "Let us cast off every weight" that would hinder our progress. —*D. P. Sayler*

From Life and Labors of Elder John Kline, collated from his diary
by Benjamin Funk, p. 301

For the day: As a disciple of Jesus, what possession, emotion, situation, or item from the past is weighing you down?

Prayer: God of all, we offer to you those things that weigh us down, that we might more perfectly run the course you have set for us as your people. Amen.

June 18

Endure Trials and Discipline

Readings: Hebrews 12:4-7; Romans 5:3-4

For whom the LORD loves He chastens (Heb. 12:6 NKJV).

Meditation: Times of testing and training can hit us at any moment in our walk with Christ. It's so easy, even with our firmest belief in Christ's love for us, to feel discouraged and downtrodden, forsaken and forgotten. But I encourage you to hold on to the joy you received when you first came to know of the love and salvation of Christ, for it is in those times of trials and discipline that our God is molding us, refining us, so that we may be like shining stars to those who are still searching for the joy we have within us.

I do not encourage as one who has not gone through a share of trials. In my short lifetime, I have experienced many pains; the most recent and profound is the death of my mother, Diane. The grief, the hurt, and the chaos right before and after her death were overwhelming. I felt neglected by God. "Why?" and "How could you!" flooded my head and for a time weakened my faith. Yet, as I filled myself with the hope and joy found in the Word of God and in the prayers and encouragement of my brothers and sisters in Christ, I reclaimed the joy that was mine when I first believed. Then my God comforted me.

As I look back, my desire for the Lord has grown from that time. And as a direct result, I have gained maturity toward the image of Christ. I am more aware of and more compassionate toward people who are suffering and struggling with their faith. From my trial, I have a testimony that ends with a joy that I can share with the world.

For you who are experiencing a time of testing or training (trial or discipline), again, I encourage you to hold on. Whatever you and I go through, with the knowledge of Christ's love for us and the encouragement of the body of believers, we can endure and his love will carry us through. Our Lord will not give us more than we can bear, and all that is given to us molds us into his image.

For the day: Fill your mind with scriptures on Christ's love and provision for you. When you are in times of testing, listen to great songs and hymns of faith. Call or visit with friends and family who can minister to your heart and soul with prayer, hugs, laughter, and ice cream!

Prayer: Lord, I know that you love me. I believe you will never forsake me. I understand that you are molding me to be more like Christ. Yet I am tired and weak. Speak to my heart. Encourage and comfort me. I will hold fast to your promise that you will never give me more than I can bear. I love you. Amen.

Michaela Camps

✐

June 19

The Necessity of Discipline

Reading: Hebrews 12:8-11

For the moment all discipline seems painful rather than pleasant; later it yields the peaceful fruit of righteousness to those who have been trained by it (Heb. 12:11 RSV).

Meditation: The scripture reminds us that discipline is both necessary and beneficial. It channels our energies, guides our direction, and helps us to grow and mature. It pulls us back from wrong choices and helps us to stay on course. Although it may seem painful and hurtful at the time, discipline strengthens the spirit, provides clarity, and generates endurance for future adversity.

We are constantly bombarded by messages that stress immediate gratification through the accumulation of wealth and goods. Jesus taught that we should not be deceived into pursuing false values. The godly are not deceived into following goals that lead them astray. They stay the course and hold to the discipline that keeps them faithful and true. Yet, these treasures are not gained without patience and persistence. As did Paul, the disciplined follower will "stay the course" and run the race to the finish line.

How does the Holy Father discipline us? He provides us with a community of fellow believers who holds dear the teachings of his Son, supports us when we falter, and lifts us up when we fall. He provides understanding and insight through prayer and Bible study. He guides us into discerning the direction to go and the consequences of getting lost. And at the end, he provides us with the satisfaction of having successfully finished the course.

For the day: Knowing that you are held fast in his loving care and supported by the body of believers, you can gain the confidence to stay the course, reach the goal, and achieve the peace promised by Christ to all his faithful followers.

Prayer: Holy Father, strengthen us when our devotion grows weak, guide us when we become lost, and walk with us as we seek to follow your will. Amen.

Emmert F. Bittinger

June 20

Walking in Faith

Readings: Hebrews 12:12-13; Isaiah 35:3

Therefore, strengthen your feeble arms and weak knees. Make level paths for your feet (Heb. 12:12-13a NIV).

Meditation: Christians can easily be distracted by all that lies along the path that God has chosen for us. Knowing what God wants of us and living within his Word are challenged by today's desire-filled lifestyles. Living the Christian life is not an easy walk. The scripture tells us that the weary believers' hands will hang down and their knees will grow feeble as they struggle to walk along the path of righteousness. We are born in sin, and the burden of sin will always be present on our life's journey. Sin is the greatest weakness that we have; the trial and temptation of our personal desires can lead to our separation from God.

Why does it often seem like God makes life difficult for us? It is his way of molding us into people of faith and character. We may not realize it, but the difficult times that we go through make us stronger for the journey ahead. When life seems unbearable we are not to become discouraged. The struggle between our spiritual well-being and sin will always be there, but it is our faith in God that will see us through the difficult times. By being strong in times of adversity, we not only clear the path for those who are weak in their faith, but we will be led to our own restoration and healing.

For the day: Rejoice in your suffering for you will be strengthened by it. Trust in the Lord and he will clear the path to your destination.

Prayer: Loving God, help me to live with a willing and faithful heart. Let your light shine upon the path that I must walk, and give me the wisdom to choose my steps wisely. Amen.

Ernie Thakor

June 21

Walk Humbly

Reading: Philippians 2:1-4

Do nothing out of selfish ambition or vain conceit, but in humility consider others better than yourselves. Each of you should look not only to your own interests, but also to the interests of others (Phil. 2:3-4 NIV).

Meditation: I often wonder how God wants us to live out humility. Do we refrain from boasting? Do we try to include those who society says do not deserve inclusion? Do we live in a manner pleasing to God's creation? Humility—living humbly as Christ did—can be described in endless ways. But one example sticks in my memory: I was traveling to Honduras on a Faith Expedition when I was fourteen, and accompanying the group on the trip was a cook, Rosita. She woke up before the sun to prepare our twenty-two-person breakfast, washed every dish, and began again to repeat the process for lunch and supper. Each meal we invited Rosita and her daughter to *ensamblarnos* (join us), but each time she refused and waited until we were done to feed herself and her daughter. I was amazed at such humility. Sometimes in our culture we are slow to think first of our neighbor. In the endless rush, we have so many priorities of our own! If we're lucky we can fit in a Bible study, a devotion with Christ, a prayer. When do we find time for devotion with our neighbor, a prayer for an enemy, a kind act for a stranger? Paul tells us in Philippians that if we are Christians, we will make the time to do these things.

For the day: Be guided in your living by the teachings of Christ. Walk humbly, and look to the interests of others as Christ did for us. Acknowledge the times you are encouraged, comforted, and find fellowship.

Prayer: God of today's sunrise and today's promise, steer our day and our lives. Give us the humility to recognize your joys in our lives. Allow the divinity in each person to shine through and help us to see the needs of others in the choices we make today. Help us to live in your image. Amen.

Chrissy Sollenberger

June 22

The Humility of Christ

Reading: Philippians 2:5-11

And being found in appearance as a man, he humbled himself and became obedient to death—even death on a cross! (Phil. 2:8 NIV).

Meditation: Consider the story of Annie, an orphaned girl who had nothing. No parents, nothing to call her own and no one to love. Through a series of miraculous events, Annie is taken in by Daddy Warbucks and by the end of the story she has everything she could dream of: clothing, a home, and someone to love and care for her. This is truly a "from rags to riches" story, the frequent theme of movies and books. However, Paul reminds us of a very different theme—"from riches to rags." The life and ministry of Jesus exemplifies humility and obedience. Jesus, being the nature of God, had it all, robed in majesty and glory. Yet, because of the condition of the world, Jesus humbled himself, became a person, and lived among the sinners, the sadness, and corruption of the world. Never has anyone gone so far in humility. Never has there been an example like what we find in Jesus Christ. If we are to be like Christ, then we must humble ourselves and live daily with an attitude of humility. This certainly isn't an easy call because, in doing so, we may not be recognized as the brains behind a great idea, or the one responsible for a project that was completed. However, Jesus wasn't one to boast of his accomplishments either, but allowed others to shine.

For the day: Live humbly today as Jesus lived. In other words, think the thoughts that Jesus thought and live not for yourself, but, by having the mind of Christ, think of others first.

Prayer: Creator God, I give you this day and pray that I will have the mind of Christ, recognizing opportunities to put aside my selfishness for the sake of others. Teach me to be humble and walk in the way of Christ. Amen.

Jerriann Heiser Wenger

June 23

Take Refuge in God

Reading: Psalm 118:5-9

Out of my distress I called on the LORD; the LORD answered me and set me in a broad place (Ps. 118:5).

Meditation: Today's date, God willing, is our fifty-second wedding anniversary. In those years God has given us many experiences of refuge. We remember the time our car died in a flooded arroyo somewhere in the desert Southwest. We were driving at night. We didn't know much about arroyos, and we stalled in the rushing water. A friendly trucker pushed us out and the Chevy restarted, but we were exhausted from the ordeal. Down the road we spotted the welcome lights of a motel. They were still open, and they had a vacant room. We had found a refuge.

The original Brethren came to America looking for freedom to worship and safety from persecution. Freedom—the opportunity to live and expand—that is "a broad place," as the psalmist puts it. But the early Brethren knew that their refuge and true home was in God. "It is better to take refuge in the LORD . . ." (Ps. 118:8-9). This is the story, this is the song of all God's people. It's no wonder Psalm 118 was Martin Luther's favorite.

As we Brethren enter our fourth century, God is still our refuge and our home—a place to hide and a place to stand. The one to run to and the one to rest in. "I am convinced," wrote Paul after twenty-five years of experience, "that [nothing] in all creation . . . will be able to separate us from the love of God in Christ Jesus our Lord" (Rom. 8:38-39). God's liberating love in Christ Jesus—that is the ultimate refuge, our true home, the final freedom.

For the day: Faith has its risks, but it offers—in the end—rest and delight. Today take the risk.

Prayer: *Other refuge have I none; hangs my helpless soul on thee . . . . All my trust on thee is stayed, all my help from thee I bring* (Charles Wesley, 1740).

Jerry and Julie Flora

⌒

June 24

Like Jesus

Reading: Colossians 1:15-20

We look at this Son and see the God who cannot be seen
(Col. 1:15a The Message).

Meditation: Colossians is not an easy book to read. Perhaps
that is why there are only two selections from this brief epistle
included in this year-long devotional book. Bible scholars can
help our understanding, when, for example, they tell us that in
verses 15-20 of the first chapter of Colossians Paul is probably
quoting from a well-known hymn extolling the lordship of
Christ.

Phrases like "firstborn of all creation," "firstborn from the
dead," and "head of the . . . church" are early Christian
attempts to answer the question that the faithful have been
asking ever since the disciples asked it on a boat on storm-
calmed Galilee: "Who then is this?" (Luke 8:24-25).

Maybe you have wondered, as I have, how many articles,
poems, books, and other writings have attempted to describe
what God is like and who Jesus was. Whatever the total, it is
surely more than anyone could read in several lifetimes.

But sometimes I wonder if simplest isn't best when it comes
to such things. I have to go back thirty years to a moment
when I got the best answer to the kind of question scholars
and theologians have struggled with for centuries. It was given
by my daughter who had yet to reach her third birthday.

I was tucking Katie into bed one night when she said, "I
love you, Daddy." For some perverse reason I asked, "Why do
you love me?"

"Because I like you," she said.

FRESH FROM THE WORD

"I love *you*," I told her. "I love you because . . . because God made you and gave you to me and Mommy."

"What's God?"

I stammered and finally came out with: "Well . . . God made everybody and loves everybody."

"You mean . . . like Jesus?"

Oh yes, child. Yes.

Like Jesus.

For the day: If you want to know what God is like, look at Jesus.

Prayer: *More like Thee, O Savior, let me be. More and more, O Christ, like Thee. Amen.* (Frank M. Davis, 1839–96)

Kenneth L. Gibble

℘

June 25

Show Hospitality and Courage

Readings: Hebrews 13:1-6; Genesis 18:2-5

Do not forget to entertain strangers, for by so doing some people have entertained angels without knowing it (Heb. 13:2 NIV).

Meditation: While Abraham's tent was pitched near the great trees of Mamre, he was visited by three strangers. Abraham was eager to show hospitality to the men, offering them rest, food, and an opportunity to wash up. Today, as in biblical times, meeting another person's need for food and shelter is a practical way of serving others and doing God's will.

The Bible tells us we are obliged to be hospitable. Whether we know the stranger to be deserving or not is not as important as whether we are faithful to following God's will. Abraham's willingness to provide drink and food could have meant the difference of life or death for three men traveling through an arid countryside.

In our communities, which may be filled with very real dangers, God's Word calls us to see the presence of angels in the strangers, foreigners, and dis-empowered among us. While we may not be serving an angel, we would be aiding a child of God. By avoiding potential danger, or playing it safe, we may miss a great opportunity to be backyard missionaries, extending the love of Christ.

For the day: Honoring the scripture's instructions on hospitality means not restricting who can be helped. Open yourself to the possibility of helping one of God's children whom our society might choose to overlook.

Prayer: Dear God, Creator of all humankind, in a world that teaches us to fear those who may be different, help us to remember that our friends were once strangers to us. Help us to remember that lives can be changed when we see the stranger as a brother or sister in Christ. Amen.

Dean Wenger

June 26

True Leaders to Emulate

Reading: Hebrews 13:7-9

Remember your leaders, who spoke God's message to you. Keep before you the outcome of their life and follow the example of their faith (Heb. 13:7 REB).

Meditation: Most of us have sung hymns with a song leader. Many of us have sung in a choir or played in an orchestra, band, or ensemble. When a hymn leader is tuned into the

Spirit and we're led to breathe and sing all together, it is a transcendent experience. As a cellist and singer, I have been taught by countless conductors and teachers. Exceptional role models have inspired me to be even better! My first and best cello teacher, Marijane Carr Siegel, encouraged me to listen carefully to superb cellists for the sound I wanted to learn; she said that only by visualizing this in my head could I ever become the musician I sought to be. Pablo Casals taught his students to play every single note moving in some direction (for example, increasing or decreasing in intensity, dynamics, tone, etc.) Yo-Yo Ma connects eyeball to eyeball with his ensemble and audiences and makes each phrase emote with feeling as he shares his music. Clearly, leaders can prompt us to excel beyond what we might even dream possible.

This scripture invites us to stop and examine the lives of those gifted spiritual leaders who went before us. We are invited to learn from them as we make decisions in our lives. We are reminded to turn to these role models as guides for our own lives. So, despite the fact that many have already been birthed into heaven, we can emulate them as we follow in their footsteps.

For the day: Slow down and take the time to reflect upon those wise ones who have gone before you. Seek insight from your elders. Be discerning as you take each step on your day's journey. In this way their mentoring presence lives on for and with you and in you.

Prayer: Spirit of the Living God, you have promised to be present in our every breath and to be with us in our daily challenges and decisions. We are not alone. I am not alone. Many have gone before me and I am nurtured and strengthened by their wisdom and example. Be with me now in this moment. May your light shine brightly on my path, guiding my every step. Amen.

Barbara Daté

&

June 27

A New Sacrifice

Reading: Hebrews 13:10-16

Through [Christ], then, let us continually offer a sacrifice of praise to God, that is, the fruit of lips that confess his name. Do not neglect to do good and to share what you have, for such sacrifices are pleasing to God (Heb. 13:15-16).

Meditation: Writers of New Testament letters often emphasize that Jesus' actions and words were grounded in Hebrew law and tradition, yet pointed toward a new path. These verses draw a parallel between blood sacrifices to God and the death of Jesus on the cross as sacrifice for sin. While the belief that ritual killing of an animal can resolve sin and be pleasing to God seems strange today, in Jesus' time this was faithful religious practice based in the law of Moses. Those nurtured in this tradition immediately saw the connection between a sacrificial goat carrying the sins of the people outside the camp and the crucifixion of Jesus—also beyond the city gates. Jesus' sacrifice at the periphery invites us to join him and those who suffer at the edges of society.

Jesus made animal sacrifices irrelevant and unnecessary. Post-resurrection offerings to God can now be life-giving actions that reflect a redefined relationship: offering expressions of belief and praise to God, suffering with Christ alongside those at the margins, and living a generous, shared life in community with others.

For the day: Sing or hum a favorite praise song or hymn. Be attentive to how praise to God in words and music, as well as dance or art, has the capacity to uplift and energize your spirit.

What other offerings might you make this week to reflect responsiveness to God's call in your life?

Prayer: May the fruit of our lips be joyous praises to you, O God. And, as we share life with open hands and find our place with those at the edges, may these offerings join us with the transforming power of your Spirit at work in the world. Amen.

Mervin B. Keeney

June 28

Make It Your Own

Reading: Philippians 3:10-16

I want to know Christ and the power of his resurrection and the sharing of his sufferings by becoming like him in his death (Phil. 3:10).

Meditation: My high school Latin teacher would urge us not just to do our homework but to do more. Pressing her fist forward in a gesture of persistence and determination, she'd say, "Make it yours!" From Mrs. Changnon I learned as much about learning as about Latin. We can know about something, then we can know it, then we can own it. Owning makes it a part of us forever. *Veni, vidi, vinci!*

Paul wanted not just to know about Christ but to "know Christ." That was the goal he hadn't yet attained, but "I press on to make it my own."

Accomplishment sometimes gets in the way of progress, and learning can interrupt knowing. After following Jesus for awhile, we can become proud, complacent, or tired. Not Paul. After his life of faith and service, after all he had accomplished, Paul knew that he did not yet fully know. He would not rest on his proud past. "Forgetting what lies behind and straining forward to what lies ahead, I press on toward the goal." He would keep his eyes on the future and the goal of knowing Christ.

No matter how long we've been at this Christian life, we, like Paul, must begin anew to know Christ. As a church with a proud past, we must forget what lies behind and strain forward to what lies ahead in the life of faith.

For the day: Every day with Jesus is a new day, with new life, new love, and history waiting to be made.

Prayer: Christ, remind us that we don't yet fully know you. May we forget the past at least long enough to "strain forward" to a boundless future in your love and power.

Fletcher Farrar

June 29

Transformed in Christ

Reading: Philippians 3:17-21

But there's far more to life for us. We're citizens of high heaven! We're awaiting the arrival of the Savior, the Master, Jesus Christ, who will transform our earthly bodies into glorious bodies like his own. He'll make us beautiful and whole with the same powerful skill by which he is putting everything as it should be, under and around him (Phil. 3:20-21 The Message).

Meditation: What is it that absorbs our time and dedication? The list for most of us is long and varied: families, social clubs, cliques, church committees, PTA, sports teams, and so on. Each of these groups demands a different set of commitments and actions as a part of membership. The things that we do for these groups are just as long and just as varied: typing minutes, baking brownies, fundraising, doing laundry, and running ourselves ragged! In those moments of weariness, many of us wonder, Where can we go and what can we do to be transformed? The invitation to the church at Philippi is an invitation into a citizenship of abundance and full life through Jesus Christ. It is a way of life that takes away the self-glorifying, self-gratifying, self-centered focus of our earthly lives and transforms it into something more. We are transformed into a community that reflects the power and the grace, the hope and the love of Christ. The challenge is to become co-imitators of Christ by becoming co-laborers and co-conspirators in the community of those making all things new, ushering in the kingdom of God in the here and now, putting everything as it should be, under and around our Lord and Savior, Jesus the Christ.

For the day: Let your actions be a bold declaration of your own imitation of Christ and your membership in his heavenly community.

Prayer: Transforming God, break me from my earthly attachments and enliven me with the power that is found in you. Help me to imitate the bold love and compassionate grace of Jesus for all of those around me. In a spirit of unity with all creation I pray. Amen.

Cindy E. Laprade

Images of Christ
in the Gospels

June 30–July 27

$\mathcal{T}$ he Son of God . . . was pleased to be
born of a poor, unnoticed virgin; in a manger
his infant body is seen; he denies himself
of many of the comforts of life.

Peter Nead (1796–1877)

❧

June 30

It's Working

Reading: Isaiah 11:1-3

The spirit of the LORD shall rest on him, the spirit of wisdom and understanding, the spirit of counsel and might, the spirit of knowledge and the fear of the LORD (Isa. 11:2).

Meditation: I encountered a long line as I checked in at the airport for my flight to Annual Conference 2006 in Des Moines, Iowa. The airline had appointed an employee to facilitate the movement of the line. She was effective at her job but she could sense that the line was not moving fast enough for some of us. At one point she stopped what she was doing, looked out at all of us in line, and said, "It's working! It's working! Don't look so despondent. Don't look so gloomy. It's working!" The prevailing mood changed immediately. We chuckled and smiled and, strangers that we were, began to talk with one another in line.

In Isaiah 11:1-3, the prophet encourages the people to understand that God is at work in their lives. God has appointed a Messiah from the house of David who will be led by the spirit and who will delight in the fear of God. In the previous chapter, there is a judgment speech that would cause anyone to be despondent and feel a sense of gloom. The first three verses of Chapter 11, however, attempt to counter that gloomy sentiment by offering words of encouragement because a leader filled by the spirit is in their midst. This leader, the Messiah, will demonstrate to the people that God is at work in their lives. It's working! God is working! Indeed!

For the day: Look for ways in which you can see God at work in your life and in the lives of those around you.

Prayer: God of grace and power, instill in us hope for today and tomorrow. Provide for us assurance that the Messiah, your Anointed One, will deliver us from the gloom and despondency that can overwhelm us from time to time. Give us courage and boldness to demonstrate to others that you are at work in the lives of all of your people. Amen.

David A. Leiter

July 1

Filled with God's Spirit

Reading: Luke 4:14-15

Then Jesus, filled with the power of the Spirit, returned to Galilee. . . . He began to teach in their synagogues and was praised by everyone (Luke 4:14a, 15).

Meditation: Having overcome the temptations in the desert, Jesus returns to his home province and launches into his ministry. He does so not with the arrogant air of indestructibility so common to young men, but humbly and "filled with the power of the Spirit." These verses so remind me of young pastors fresh out of seminary, truly yielding to the Spirit and warmly received by all. Thank God for the honeymoon! And thank God that for a season, at least, Jesus "was praised by everyone." When the Holy Spirit fills a human being, it attracts those who hunger and thirst for God. There is a mighty, saving power at work.

What with scandals and fallen church leaders, church fights and disheartened saints, we sometimes lose sight of this wonderful fact: When a person is filled with the power of the Spirit, good things happen. Miracles take place. People are attracted, transformed, and redeemed! Praise God whenever and wherever the church and its leaders are doing well. Praise God whenever and wherever people look upon the face of Christ and are drawn to him. It's not always this way, of course. Verse 16 reminds us that Jesus' next stop is Nazareth and wholesale rejection. But wherever the Holy Spirit and faith come together, good reports spread through all the surrounding country.

For the day: Where do you see the Holy Spirit at work in your life? in your church? Is it time to shake the dust of your most recent Nazareth off of your shoes and allow God's Holy Spirit to fill you once more with the power of faith, hope, and love?

Prayer: Come, Holy Spirit, power of God. Fill me. Fill my church. Use me in such a way that the world will be drawn to Christ and that once more he will be "praised by everyone"! Amen.

Daniel M. Petry

July 2

With Real Authority

Reading: Luke 4:31-37

They were astonished at his teaching, because he spoke with authority (Luke 4:32).

Meditation: Fruit, nearly forbidden for a Brethren child, was found by this boy in my grandmother's storage room. It was a huge old book, the official U. S. Army field artillery manual of 1917. It might have belonged to my uncle, collected when he was a boy, but Grandma let me have it. Of most interest to me, beyond the care and firing of French 75s, were the chapters describing the care and feeding of horses and mules. I always wanted a horse of my own, but never got one. Because our family was in the business of growing and selling hay, Dad thought a horse would eat into the profits. Even so, thanks to the manual, I fancied myself as something of an authority on horses among my horseless peers. Decades later my daughter wanted a horse, and a nearby rancher, eager to reduce his feed costs, let us borrow one for a summer. I soon learned that reading a book about horses and having a relationship with a horse were two different things. That mare taught me a lot more about horses than the book ever could.

The folks in Jesus' day thought they knew a lot about God. But they had learned it all from a book. Jesus, on the other hand, when he came preaching and healing, knew about God intimately from relationship. He spoke and acted with authority from this deeper kind of knowledge. For us, Bible study, devotional reading, church-going, and the like are good but empty activities unless they lead us into a deeper relationship with the One who has made us. Only through this personal relationship are we able to speak and act with spiritual authority.

For the day: Consider how each moment of your day can be used to deepen your relationship with God.

Prayer: O Loving God, lead me ever from "head" into "heart" knowledge of your will and way that I might become more than I am—more like you have created me to be. Through Christ, Amen.

Ernest J. Bolz

July 3

The Great Reversal

Readings: Luke 6:17-23; John 15:1, 2

You're blessed when you've lost it all. God's kingdom is there for the finding. You're blessed when you're ravenously hungry. Then you're ready for the Messianic meal. You're blessed when the tears flow freely. Joy comes with the morning (Luke 6:21-23 The Message).

Meditation: A profound truth is hidden in our scripture text, a central theme that escapes us too often. With the spiritual eye we discern a great truth of Jesus—the difference between the kingdom of God and the kingdom of this present world—the "great reversal." Our good is bad, while our bad is good. Our good, we think, is pleasure, ease, comfort. But through God's good Spirit, our ailments, discomforts, oppositions, and hurts work in us a powerful change for his glory, and finally our everlasting good! That God means our hurts for our learning and for our good is only comprehended by faith and strengthened by devotion. Surely this is the lesson of Job, of Paul's troubles, of Israel's troubles, and if we can accept it—Israel's and God's church everywhere in their present troubles. Praise God daily because he sees, he knows, he cares, he disciplines—he purges—to bring forth more fruit to his honor and for his glory. Through death, life comes. If we are his, we bear up under anything and in everything give him thanks, for we know that all things were made for him and all praise is due him!

For the day: God's work mixed with our faith enlarges our vision. Now we know that all joy we experience is a mild "prelude" to that which is coming!

Prayer: God, help us to dig deep below the surface. Strengthen our faith that we may see more clearly your smile behind our tears and feel your comforting hand on our troubled spirits. We know that everything we receive is meant for our good, for "all things work together for our good." Lord, help us to share your truth with people everywhere. Amen.

Fred W. Benedict

ℕ

July 4

The Gold Standard

Reading: Luke 6:24-31

Do to others as you would have them do to you (Luke 6:31 NIV).

Meditation: Some proverbs often attributed to the Bible, such as "God helps those who help themselves," aren't actually in there. The Golden Rule, however, is: "Do to others as you would have them do to you." It's a succinct standard for human behavior that has echoes in virtually every religion around the world. Jesus uses it to sum up his topsy-turvy prescription for the world—the "upside-down kingdom," we often call it. Woe to the rich and comfortable? Love your enemies? Don't demand what's rightfully owed to you? The disciples probably thought Jesus had slipped on a salmon and hit his head. But Jesus is thinking quite clearly. He brings it right back to that Golden Rule: "Do unto others . . ." It raises questions for those of us who live in wonderfully free, privileged circumstances today. One of the other proverbs that is indeed actually in the Bible says, "From everyone who has been given much, much will be demanded; and from the one who has been entrusted with much, much more will be asked" (Luke

12:48b NIV). What are we doing for those who are hungry and poor? How are we using our power against those who desire to harm us? Are we generous with our possessions and with our love? Can we afford not to be?

For the day: Take a few moments today to list at least some of your abundant blessings. Spend time in prayer, thanking God for them, and ponder how you might use them to bless others, too.

Prayer: Ruler of the upside-down kingdom, help me continually to take a fresh look at my priorities, to take stock of my rich blessings, and to live generously. Enable me to do unto others as you would do. Amen.

Walt Wiltschek

July 5

Loving Our Enemies

Reading: Luke 6:32-36

But love your enemies, do good, and lend, expecting nothing in return (Luke 6:35a).

Meditation: The tiny part of the Christian movement that we call Brethren began at a time when war was fresh in the minds of the residents of what is now Germany. Likewise, war and terrorism are fresh in our minds as we face the fourth century of our denomination's existence. The passage for today from Luke's Gospel calls us again to seek to love those who are labeled as our enemies. When was the last time you heard anyone outside of the Christian movement call for us to love our enemies? Oh, yes, we occasionally hear someone call for a re-examination of our policies toward our enemies because those policies are creating more enemies. But this line of thinking has little to do with loving the enemy. As Christians we are called to do the difficult work of seeing God in all people, even those who do not seem to be very Godlike. We need to heed and discuss this call as much today as did our forebears in 1708. God, grant us the courage to struggle to understand this call for unimaginable love.

For the day: One way to imitate the Creator is to be merciful and forgiving to both enemy and friend.

Prayer: God of all people who on earth do dwell, help us to sow seeds of love where hatred lurks and reigns. Grant us wisdom and courage for the living of these days. Amen.

Charles Boyer

July 6

The Authority of Jesus

Readings: Luke 20:1-8; John 7:14-17

Tell us, by what authority are you doing these things? Who is it who gave you this authority? (Luke 20:2). My teaching is not mine but his who sent me (John 7:16).

Meditation: Jesus did not boast about his authority. When called "Good Teacher," he responded: "Why do you call me good? No one is good but God alone" (Luke 18:18-19). In Luke's story this humility did not prevent candid responses to chief priests, scribes, and elders who supervised temple activities. Their questions revealed they were more interested in getting rid of Jesus than in understanding the sources of his teaching. He answered their question with one of his own. He asked whether the baptism of John came from heaven or was of human origin. Their fears of answering the question came from the popularity of John the Baptist. When they said they could not answer, Jesus refused to tell by what authority he was teaching.

The Gospel of John tells another story about Jesus teaching in the temple. In this account the religious leaders were astonished that one who had not been taught could have so much learning. Jesus' answer stirred my adolescent questions about the divinity of Christ. My revival event occurred when I was with Christian students from Midwest colleges at Estes Park in Colorado. One morning, with beautiful sky-framed majestic mountains as our backdrop, we sang "God who touches the earth with beauty, make me lovely too." Our leader interpreted the words of Jesus: "My teaching is not mine but his who sent me. Anyone who resolves to do the will of God will know whether the teaching is from God or whether I am speaking on my own."

I was thinking almost out loud: "Try out the teachings of Jesus; then you may know that they and Jesus come from God."

For the day: For me John 7:16-17 has become my "golden rule" text along with John 3:16-17. Get your Bible and look up these texts. What teachings of Jesus are "golden rules" for you.

Prayer of Francis of Assisi: Lord, by your authority make me an instrument of thy Peace. Where there is hatred, let me sow love; where there is injury, pardon; where there is doubt, faith; where there is despair, hope; where there is darkness, light; where there is sadness, joy. Grant that I may not so much seek to be consoled as to console; to be understood as to understand, to be loved as to love. For it is in giving that we receive, pardoning that we are pardoned, dying that we are born to eternal life. Amen.

Dale W. Brown

July 7

Anointed by God

Reading: Isaiah 61:1-4

The spirit of the Lord God is upon me . . . ; he has sent me to bring good news to the oppressed, to bind up the brokenhearted . . . (Isa. 61:1).

Meditation: Have you ever stood in the presence of someone who embodies the spirit of God? Energy, enthusiasm, and appreciation for the moment often radiate from their being. As a student at McPherson College a number of years ago, I was privileged to be shepherded by Zandra Wagoner, the campus minister. The God within Zandra touched our lives as she spoke, led devotions, counseled us, and stood in our presence. The spirit of God was upon Zandra; she brought us the good news, bound our broken hearts, and extended liberty to those of us in physical, mental, and emotional captivity. She played a pivotal role in my desire to live a spirit-filled life.

Each of us must choose either to live with the spirit or to be depleted by the absence of spirit. Choosing to be anointed by the spirit means we have work to do. It means we offer gladness instead of mourning, praise instead of a faint spirit, and choose to build up instead of tear down. Doing so, however, does not guarantee that our actions will be mirrored. We will still walk through the valley of the shadow of death. Despite the darkness, however, and sometimes personal attacks, we are called to draw near to the spirit and to offer the cup of cold water. A spirit-filled life is not an easy life, but it is a life that extends God's grace and love to all, including ourselves.

We have been anointed! We are called to live with the spirit and work by the spirit! Now get to work!

For the day: Live with the great spirit, walk with the great spirit, extend the spirit's grace and love to others along life's journey.

Prayer: Creator God, anoint us with your love that we may live as beacons, as light and leaven in the midst of death and destruction. May we radiate your grace and peace. Amen.

Jennifer Bosserman

July 8

Gathered for Healing

Reading: Mark 1:29-34

And the whole city was gathered around the door (Mark 1:33).

Meditation: At the age of twenty-nine, my father was diagnosed with multiple sclerosis (MS). Now, nearly thirty years later, he is a man who has the courage to face and engage each day even though he cannot walk, feed himself, or even brush his own teeth. I'll confess, a chronic, progressive illness like MS can leave a daughter wondering about the healing stories of the Gospels. I am skeptical of instantaneous physical healing like we see in this story from Mark 1—probably because I have longed for my dad to experience such healing and continue to grieve for his daily struggle.

At the same time I am intrigued by, almost drawn to, this scene at Simon's house, especially to the crowd gathered around the door. While some might interpret this crowd as a mob who needs healing or who simply wants to watch the action, I picture this crowd as witnesses embodying the healing power of Jesus—people who mow the lawn, prepare food, clean the house, build ramps, and carry the people in body and

prayer. Simply walking with someone through the daily difficulties of chronic illness may not be able to "fix" the physical
ailment, but it provides the most amazing gift of God's presence and healing and grace.

For the day: Look for ways to be a vessel for God's healing.

Prayer: Healing God, I give thanks for the community of faith
for reaching out a hand and lifting up those who need your
healing, comfort, and love. Help me to find ways to be your
healing presence in my church and my community. Amen.

Melissa Bennett

July 9

Start Where You Are—And Go Out from There

Reading: Mark 1:35-39

*Let us go on to the next towns, that I may preach there also; for
that is why I came out (Mark 1:38 RSV).*

Meditation: Jesus was not a preacher who stayed in one place
to minister to the same people week after week. He went to
different towns and villages and saw different needy individuals
and families every day. He was always plowing new ground,
sowing seed in fresh soil. His plan: to seek the lost, the sick,
the blind, the bewildered, the sin-burdened, the oppressed and
lead them to God's love, healing, forgiveness, release; to set
them free to live fully as children of God, as servants of the
kingdom of God, as men and women born anew.

Missionary Paul of Tarsus did the same thing.

The Schwarzenau Brethren, baptized into newness of life,
did the same thing.

The 300-year Brethren, living in contemporary North and South America, Asia and Africa, are citizens in the midst of a lost, sick, and violent generation, thirsty for the living water of life, hungry for the bread of God's love.

For the day: Are you ready to be called and sent? Are you ready to serve? Will you take God's gifts to your neighbors?

Prayer: O God, you have given my household and me new life in Christ. Lead me to serve in a needy world. Help me take the light of Jesus' love into the dark places near where I live. Amen.

Merle Crouse

July 10

Reach Out in Loving Action

Reading: Mark 1:40-45

And Jesus, moved with pity, touched him and said, "I want to! Be healed" (Mark 1:41 The Living Bible).

Meditation: Leprosy was a terrible disease. Lepers were considered unclean and to be avoided at all cost. Shunned and humiliated by the people in their community, lepers were made to live alone in a life of misery. Imagine the bravery of the leper in this story. He heard that Jesus was coming to his town. Risking continued humiliation and shunning for his daring, the leper came close to Jesus and said, "If you want to, you can make me well again" (v. 40 LB). Jesus was not repulsed by the sight of the leper, responding instead with understanding and compassion. He saw the human soul in desperate need, reached out, and said, "Be healed."

As we journey along our life's path, we, too, encounter human souls in desperate need. How do we respond? We can ignore . . . shun . . . humiliate . . . as did the community members of the leper. Or, as ones who have experienced the love of God, we can reach out in gentle compassion, but we also need to reach out in loving action. Brethren have long held unity, love, and servant action as values to be embraced and lived out daily. Our forebears gave us the example of serving others with kindness and love. In the spirit of our heritage and with a servant heart, let us reach out and find a way to ease the suffering of someone this day.

For the day: Live today as a blessed child of Jesus Christ. Live as one who will keep eyes and ears open to the needs around you. Reach out with both gentle compassion and loving action.

Prayer: O God of understanding compassion, guide us in each day's encounters with others. Make us attune to those in need. Stir our hearts to reach out in gentle compassion and loving action.

Donna McKee Rhodes

July 11

Christ Amidst the Crowd

Reading: Mark 2:1-2

A crowd gathered, jamming the entrance, so no one could get in or out . . . (Mark 2:2 The Message).

Meditation: Picture the people jammed into that tiny little room with Jesus, standing so close together that no one can get in or out. Our lives are like that, too, sometimes—so crowded that it's difficult to move. Our time gets crowded with projects and appointments, errands and expectations. Our homes are crowded with possessions and purchases, tools and treasures.

Our hearts are crowded, too, with our own unresolved sorrows, the needs of others, the uncertainties of the days to come. When our lives are so crowded, it is difficult for the things of God to enter our lives. I presume Jesus' life must have been like this often: people crowding around him, demanding his attention and his time, bringing him their sorrows, their sickness, their pain.

Yet in the midst of it all, Jesus appears calm, unruffled. The Gospel tells us simply that he is there "teaching the Word." Somehow in the midst of all this mayhem, Jesus goes quietly about doing what he is there to do, as if standing on his own private island in the battering sea.

Jesus had learned the art of simply "being there." He found his sure footing in the Word of God. In the crowded chaos of our lives today, God's Word offers us an anchor, a resting place, a refuge. God's Word does not take us out of the world, but lets us stand securely in it.

If we are doing God's work, life may crowd in around us. But that doesn't mean we have to crowd God out. All the more reason to let ourselves be taught—by the Teacher whom crowds gathered to hear.

For the day: What is crowding God out of your life? Take time to seek refuge in the Word.

Prayer: No matter how crowded my life, help me to make room for you, O God, through the power of your Holy Word. Amen.

Melanie Jones

&

July 12

Healed by Faith

Reading: Mark 2:3-5

When Jesus saw their faith, he said to the paralytic, "Son, your sins are forgiven" (Mark 2:5).

Meditation: Why did Jesus say "Son, your sins are forgiven" to the paralyzed man who was dropped in front of him? Was Jesus implying the man's condition was the result of sin? That's what people thought in those days (and many still mistakenly think so today!). If that's what the man believed, perhaps his conscience had paralyzed him. Was that why Jesus said what he did? Was he assuring the man that God was not angry with him but still loved him? Did this assurance help the man become whole? Are we, too, paralyzed at times, shackled by self-imposed guilt? Are we afraid to truly "live" because we may have hurt someone or perhaps failed at something in the past? Do we, too, need to be assured of God's forgiveness and acceptance so that we are free to do and be our best? No matter what wrongs we think we have committed, no matter what we may have failed to do, Jesus keeps saying to us, "Son, Daughter, your sins are forgiven." That is his way of reminding us that God's extravagant love embraces us regardless of past mistakes and neglect. We are forgiven again and again. God never gives up on us and Jesus doesn't want us to give up on ourselves and become immobile. He wants to free us so we can stretch all of our muscles and dance a life of joy.

For the day: It's a new day. Think new thoughts. Don't be afraid. Try new things. Remember the words of Jesus: "Child, the past is over; your sins are forgiven."

Prayer: O Great Healer, help me accept your forgiveness today for past errors and omissions. Help me believe that you love me just as I am so that I can serve you unshackled.

Jean Lersch

✑

July 13

Tell No One

Reading: Mark 7:31-37

And immediately his ears were opened, his tongue was released, and he spoke plainly. Then Jesus ordered them to tell no one; but the more he ordered them, the more zealously they proclaimed it (Mark 7:35-36).

Meditation: Miracle workers often want the attention of the crowds. Witness the healers on television. But Jesus was different. He took this man aside, who was deaf and who had a speech impediment. He took him away from the crowd. Then he sighed as he looked up to pray. What did his sigh mean? Was he weary? Was there something in the moment that disappointed him? Or was it because he felt the pain in this suffering human being?

People sometimes try to fix things in other people so they don't have to feel their pain. But this isn't Jesus' way. He enters into people's suffering—into our pain, yours and mine, understanding it better than we do. Think of how much is lost when you cannot hear. Think of how much misunderstanding and pain you endure if you cannot speak. Was Jesus grieving this suffering and loss?

Jesus' prayer was simple, "Be opened." And it was so! And the people who were with him were "astounded beyond measure." How wonderful to have your world suddenly opened up beyond anything you can imagine! Jesus is asking us to "be opened" each day to the riches of love and beauty that lie just outside the reach of our own often unseeing eyes and unhearing ears.

Jesus then ordered those who were with him to tell no one. Why would he say that! Isn't it obvious that they should give testimony, broadcast from the transmission towers! Jesus knew something that we in our media-crazed age forget. Healing cannot be contained. The good news of grace and love will come out. You don't need to hit the airwaves. People will share it. Jesus himself is the proof. The man who ordered them to tell no one is now known to everyone.

For the day: Pay attention as you go through the day. See the beauty around you. See the love hidden in your harried co-workers. Hear the joy bubbling below the surface of your own anxiety. See Christ in each person you meet.

Prayer: *Open my ears that I may hear. Open my heart and let me prepare. Illumine me, Spirit divine!* (Clara H. Scott, 1895, adapted).

James H. Lehman

⚘

July 14

The Suffering Servant

Reading: Isaiah 53:4-6

Surely he has borne our infirmities and carried our diseases; yet we accounted him stricken, struck down by God, and afflicted. But he was wounded for our transgressions (Isa. 53:4-5a).

Meditation: WANTED: A couple of trucks big enough to move the town of Hamilton, Washington. The town, sited along the mighty Skagit River, experiences such regular and devastating flooding as to cause FEMA to consider shifting the entire enterprise. Perhaps that's an answer, if it's located in a place that was never suitable for a town site. But there are signs it's not the case. The hillsides visible from the streets are bare. There's no vegetation to absorb and slow the moisture when the heavy winter rains hit, and too much water inundates the riverbed.

When my grandfather lived there in the 1930s, the houses weren't built on stilts. The river's wide green power was flanked by dense fir forests that attracted loggers like him.

Yes, I said logger. In the Pacific Northwest, such a pedigree can be bane or blessing, depending on the company you keep. I've felt chagrined by his profession. But rethink. Power equipment, helicopters, and clear-cutting have strip-mined the hillsides with a vengeance unknown to loggers like my grandfather, who were adept with manual cross-cut saws and horse teams. Such sustainable practices have been eclipsed by greater extraction efficiency. Now the town is regularly battered by what are increasingly being recognized as ecological transgressions.

Hence my uncustomary reading of Isaiah's Suffering Servant texts: Have we turned to our own way, gone astray from God such that this earth, this home that serves our needs, is wounded because of our transgressions, and thus carries our diseases? Brethren have historically partnered with soil and the earth to bring blessing to neighbors. How can we recover that partnership and publicly recognize this suffering servant, this earth, as God's own?

For the day: In your daily rounds, where do you see the earth being wounded? What voice might you raise to ease the suffering?

Prayer: Plant in me, Creator God, a voice. Plant in us a voice like healing water, a voice to turn back suffering.

Lee-Lani Wright

&

July 15

The Full Extent of His Love

Reading: John 13:1-2a

It was just before the Passover Feast. Jesus knew that the time had come for him to leave this world and go to the Father. Having loved his own who were in the world, he now showed them the full extent of his love (John 13:1 NIV).

Meditation: This verse in the Gospel of John marks a turning point in Jesus' mission in the world. He had come from God and lived among us (1:14). Now it was time for him to return. "His hour had come," as many translations suggest. This "leaving the world and going to the Father" signifies Jesus' crucifixion, resurrection, and ascension. Jesus knew it was time. And he was ready.

It was to be the day before the Passover in Jerusalem. That was the day they killed the lambs for the Passover Feast. A few years later the Apostle Paul sensed its appropriateness when he said, ". . . For our paschal lamb, Christ, has been sacrificed" (1 Cor. 5:7).

What better way to show the world God's love?

I have been a part of the Brethren movement all my life. That has kept me close to the story of Jesus. It is a story that has shaped my identity as a human being. It's a story that has grounded me in a community of belief and ethics, giving me direction and guidance. But it also has stretched me to understand God's wonderful and mysterious ways.

Even as I hear this story again and again, I am aware of how much I have yet to understand about God's ways. But until then, I marvel in the divine love that is revealed in Jesus. It is a love so full and rich that one day it will draw us all back together again.

For the day: Consider the ways that Jesus' presence among us is both a gift and a mystery.

Prayer: O God, we marvel at the wondrous gift of your Son Jesus Christ. He came to us in human history, lived among us, redeemed us through the sacrifice of his life, and has returned to you. We thank you for resurrection power in our lives and the church that continues as Christ's body. Amen.

Edward L. Poling

July 16

The Example of Christ

Reading: John 13:2b-11

So he got up from the meal, took off his outer clothing, and wrapped a towel around his waist. After that, he poured water into a basin and began to wash his disciples' feet, drying them with the towel that was wrapped around him. He came to Simon Peter, who said to him, "Lord, are you going to wash my feet?" Jesus replied, "You do not realize now what I am doing, but later you will understand" (John 13:4-7 NIV).

Meditation: "You what? You wash each other's feet?" How many times over the years have we Brethren heard this remark from people inquiring about the practices of our faith, whether from a nonbeliever or a member of another denomination. And how do you respond? My guess is we have a tendency to be almost apologetic and stress that we really don't *wash* the feet of our brother or sister, we just splash a little water over their feet and then dry them. And we may add a little teaching point: "We do it because Jesus did."

Certainly that is a wonderful reason. Emulating our Lord in

as many ways as possible has always been a touchstone for the Brethren. Beyond that, however, we wash one another's feet for the same reason Jesus did: to demonstrate our willingness to serve one another and all of God's creation as humble servants, putting the needs and personalities of others above our own. Isn't that what Jesus did? Aware of the horrific suffering he would soon endure, he chose to spend his last night on earth with his dear friends and to kneel before them in humble service.

The disciples didn't understand that night. It was only later as they finally grasped the truth of who Jesus was—and is— that they were able to give of themselves in humble service to the world and the good news of Jesus Christ.

We wash one another's feet to model in our own life an attitude of humble service to the world around us. And as we are humbled, we bring glory to God in all that we do today and in all the tomorrows until his return.

For the day: Humble yourself in the sight of the world, and the Lord will lift you up.

Prayer: Loving God, may the example of your Son, Jesus Christ, serving in the role of a humble servant, provoke in me a greater awareness of the opportunities I have to serve your creation. Amen.

Charles Beekley

July 17

Followers Everyone

Reading: John 13:12-17

For I have set you an example, that you also should do as I have done to you (John 13:15).

Meditation from our past: When I came into the church, I
was young, and when I took hold of our elder's hand and
he led me into the water where there was a strong stream
flowing, he said, "Don't be afraid, Jesus went before."
And I walked down there, and between heaven and earth
I made a covenant with God to live faithful to Christ
Jesus until death. And didn't I come up out of the water
the same as my dear Savior did? When we came to communion, didn't I rise from the supper the same as my Savior did? Didn't I gird myself the same as he did? Didn't I
wash my sister's feet and thus obey the command to wash
one another's feet? When we come down to the breaking
of the bread and the passing of the cup, however, then
man steps in between us and our Savior. Though man
never suffered, or shed a drop of blood for us, he takes his
hand to break the bread for us, as if God hadn't given us
any hands. We have been using our hands right along,
claiming to come in the Spirit, and following him. He
brake the bread and gave unto them and said, "This do in
remembrance of me." Of course I have been told there
was no sister there. Well, there was no sister there in feetwashing. Excuse us from that if you want to use that
scripture. But Paul comes to us with the words read at
every communion. "Be ye followers of me as also I am of
Christ." There were certainly sisters there, and Paul could
tell them to be followers of him as he was of Christ. He
followed Christ in breaking the bread, and therefore I
think I have a right to ask these delegates to permit us sisters to break bread one to the other. We do not ask to
break it to the brethren, but we want to fulfill that command, and be in touch with Jesus Christ. We want the
letter and the spirit to go together. —*Julia Gilbert*

From The Love Feast, *Frank Ramirez. Brethren Press, 2000, pp. 152-53.*

For the day: Recall your first communion and reflect on its meaning for you at the time.

Prayer: *Lord, I want to be a Christian in my heart, in my heart. Lord, I want to be a Christian in my heart. In my heart, in my heart, Lord, I want to be a Christian in my heart* (African-American spiritual, 1907).

☙

July 18

Whoever Receives Me

Reading: John 13:18-20

Truly, truly, I say to you, he who receives whomever I send receives Me; and he who receives Me receives Him who sent Me (John 13:20 NASB).

Meditation: Servant, slave, flunky, lackey, go-fer—they all imply a subservient individual who carries out the business of someone who holds a more responsible position. When we are the bearer of some tough news to a third party, we might defend ourselves with the qualifier "Don't shoot the messenger!" That rarely stops the recipient from visiting his anger or dissatisfaction on the courier! In general, folks want to hear news "from the horse's mouth." We want to speak with the boss, the woman in charge, the main man, the head honcho. We may downgrade the importance of a contact when it arrives secondhand, or discount the urgency of an epistle if it is once-removed from the source. Jesus impressed upon the twelve the importance of their work. As bearers of the good news of God's reign, the disciples likely thought of themselves as mere runners; they were likely received as such. Yet they were agents of reconciliation and ambassadors of peace. It was critical to the disciples' self-understanding to realize that, in encountering others, Jesus was making a contact through them. For someone to dismiss, discount, or rebuff the disciples was to reject Jesus himself. How important it becomes, then, that we first seek to perceive that which is "of God" in others. Receiving is reciprocal work: each has a stake in the transaction. What might we do or say today that would make Jesus interesting, enticing, appealing, alluring, compelling to others?

For the day: The character of our discipleship may become the gateway or "the highway" for those whose lives we touch. Today's goal is to become more Christlike, that others may more clearly see—and more readily trust—the Man for Others.

Prayer: Throughout this day, Lord, may I see you in the eyes of everyone I meet. And may everyone who looks into my eyes see you. Amen.

Wallace B. Landes

July 19

What Do You Want?

Readings: Matthew 20:20-23; John 14:12-14

But Jesus answered, "You do not know what you are asking. Are you able to drink the cup that I am about to drink?" (Matt. 20:22).

Meditation: I recall sitting in worship many years ago, feeling purposeless and numb. During moments of silent prayer, I asked God to help me "just feel again." Within hours I was plunged into the worst emotional and spiritual pain I ever experienced; my life turned inside out and upside down. Yes, I had received what I asked, but pain wasn't exactly what I had in mind! Jesus promises that if we ask in faith, we will receive.

We rest in that assurance—but sometimes we rest lazily and become careless in our asking. Sometimes our requests are repeated almost by rote; other times our asking is selfish—worded as if we pray to a magician who grants our every whim. Jesus' response to Mary told her then (and calls us now) to be careful—to "count the cost" of what we ask. Perhaps it is a matter of listening first for God, and then discerning how our deepest needs partner with God's yearning for "the kingdom among us." The culture around us teaches that our wants are all that matter, or that some future reward (like sitting at Jesus' right and left) is more important than working in God's realm now. In contrast, Jesus suggests that we pay attention, use the good minds God has given us, and work in the present.

For the day: In your prayers today, take time. First, thank God for the multitude of gifts you receive each day. Listen carefully for God's yearnings for your life. Then respond by clearly asking how you can "continue the work of Jesus."

Prayer: Giving God, donor of all of our days, thank you for life and for _____ and _____ [fill in gifts specific to you]. Teach me to wait patiently and listen for your call in my life. Help me understand what I ask of you. Amen.

Carol Joy Bowman

July 20

True Greatness—Service

Reading: Matthew 20:24-28

Instead, whoever wants to become great among you must be your servant, and whoever wants to be first must be your slave (Matt. 20:26b-27 NIV).

Meditation: The mother of James and John made the request to Jesus, "Make my two sons sit at your right hand and your left hand"—to be interpreted as seats of prominence, distinction, authority, and privilege. All symbols of earthly greatness. The other disciples were angry and expressed it publicly. This gave Jesus the opportunity to set the true standard for greatness once and for all. The essence of greatness is service! Those who truly wish to be great are servants. Now why is this so important to remember?

The fact that you are reading this devotional today may assume that you have some level of comfort and security. However, many, many other people don't. That fellow in your town's local jail may need a visit—your visit. That neighbor who lost her job may need some encouragement—your encouragement. That elderly member of your congregation may need help—your help. That abandoned child may need a home—your home. That town drunk may need an encouraging word—your word. Now, if you choose to serve the needs of the imprisoned, the unemployed, the elderly, the abandoned, and the addicted, you are giving hope and inspiration to those who need it most. And this is a great thing. Lives are changed this way. And the benefit is mutual. If Jesus did it, should we not do the same?

For the day: Choose to serve today not because you want to be great, but because great things happen in faithful service.

Prayer: Lord, please forgive my self-centeredness. Grant me the humility and willingness to serve and the passion to do so. Amen.

Dennis Webb

July 21

Rely on God

Reading: Isaiah 43:1-7

When you pass through the waters, I will be with you; and through the rivers, they shall not overwhelm you; when you walk through fire you shall not be burned, and the flame shall not consume you (Isa. 43:2).

Meditation from our past: But even those who are called of God may not have easy sailing. The Lord's promise is, "When thou passest through the waters, they shall not overcome thee." As we look back over the short history of this work [in Africa], we can see that we have already passed through flood waters. But praise God, they have not overcome us, for we have only advanced as God opened the way. . . . Just as surely as He has called you, if you do not lose faith, He will lead you in mighty triumphs to His place for you. At this time, when God is calling many to lay their lives upon the altar for service in this land, others cannot be expected to have the same faith for you that God will give you for yourself. There is only one kind of faith. True faith as a grain of mustard seed will move a mountain into the sea. Many Christians have great faith but it is MISPLACED. Instead of it being centered in God, it is centered in their own efforts, or those of other persons. God asks us to believe Him and expect Him to keep His word. We are praying for you volunteers. We were once in the same position. REMEMBER JESUS CHRIST! —*James Gribble*

From Undaunted Hope: Life of James Gribble, *Florence Newberry Gribble, M.D. The Brethren Publishing Company, 1932, pp. 338-39.*

For the day: Recall times or circumstances when you chose not to rely upon God. What was the result of that decision?

Prayer: In you only I put my faith and my hope. To you only I pray. Amen.

&

July 22

Who Am I?

Reading: Matthew 16:13-16

He said to them, "But who do you say that I am?" Simon Peter answered, "You are the Messiah, the Son of the living God" (Matt. 16:15-16).

Meditation: The question itself is daunting. Jesus' query, "Who am I?" leads to another question: "Who are you?" How does my friendship with Jesus and my loyalty to him change my identity?

Several years ago my wife and I were called to enter Brethren Volunteer Service. We, and our two-year-old son, ended up working on the northern Eastern Shore of Maryland in a community for the homeless. It's called Meeting Ground. While we were very excited for this opportunity to serve, the actual experience of service didn't start as we anticipated. The work wasn't hard, but for some reason both my wife and I began to feel disoriented, apprehensive, worthless. Prior to this experience we had known who we were. We had strong family roots, firm professional identities, a network of friends. Among the homeless, we found that our identities were eroding. One cold, gray, spring morning, in the gravel parking lot at the shelter, I ended up bearing my soul to the founder of this community, a man fifteen years my senior. As I finished, he raised his head, looked directly at me, and gave a knowing nod. "That happens to people here," he responded. "It's called ego destruction."

So much for comfort! At least it was the truth. Turns out, it was truth I could live into. The confession I make about Jesus is likewise a testimony about myself. Frequently the desires I have for myself govern what I confess about Jesus. But isn't that putting the cart before the horse? Hitched up like that, there is little wonder we grow so slowly toward God.

For the day: My way or the highway? The biblical way is the highway.

Prayer: Jesus, lead me to see you and to see others, that I may in truth come to see who you are calling me to become. Amen.

David R. Miller

July 23

Tell Everyone

Reading: Matthew 16:17-20

Then charged he his disciples that they should tell no man that he was Jesus the Christ (Matt. 16:20 KJV).

Meditation: Jesus revealed to Peter that God himself had filled Peter's mind with who Jesus was, not Peter himself.

Peter's name (*Petros*) means rock, and Peter was living up to his name. Jesus declared that he was talking about himself being the rock on which the church would be built. It was the Messiah's program upon which God would build his church. That church would be built in the future, and Satan would not be able to destroy it.

God's dealings with Israel alone had come to an end. Jesus

Christ shed his blood on Calvary for the forgiveness of sins of all people. He was resurrected so that we also may have eternal life. It was then time to build his church—from Pentecost to now.

Peter was given the keys, or authority, in the church as needed. He was a trusted steward. He was to bind and loose people as God commanded. Those who accept the means of salvation through Jesus Christ are bound to grace and loosed from the law. Those who are unwilling to accept the saving grace of Jesus Christ are loosed to eternal damnation.

As a sign of how the church would be built, Cornelius accepted the binding of grace, and Gentiles also became recipients of God's salvation.

For the day: We know that Jesus Christ is the chief cornerstone—of our foundation, our faith, our trust, our church, our all—every day of our life.

Prayer: We praise thee, Lord Jesus, that you are the humble, solid, and immovable "rock of our salvation." With full trust in you, we give all honor in prayer to you, Amen.

Lowell H. Beachler

July 24

From Rock to Stumbling Block

Readings: Matthew 16:21-23; 1 Corinthians 1:18-25

[Jesus] turned and said to Peter, "Get behind me, Satan! You are a stumbling block to me; for you are setting your mind not on divine things but on human things" (Matt. 16:23).

Meditation: The Apostle Peter, the great rock on whom Jesus has built his church, is now a stumbling block for Jesus and his mission. And because he stands in the way, Jesus tells him, "Get behind me, Satan." Perhaps this is an allusion to Jesus being tempted in the desert by Satan or to Peter's stubbornness in accepting Jesus' fate. In any case, Jesus thinks that Peter is standing in the way because he is focusing too much on human things rather than divine things. From the beginning, Brethren have believed that the church is built on the redemptive suffering and death of Jesus on the cross, and any persecution that they would encounter would be the cost of their discipleship. Brethren did suffer imprisonment, banishment, loss of property, and separation from loved ones for their beliefs. This stand is reflected in the words of an early hymn by Alexander Mack, Sr.:

> *"Count well the cost," Christ Jesus says,*
> *"When you lay the foundation."*
> *Are you resolved, though all seems lost,*
> *to risk your reputation,*
> *your self, your wealth, for Christ the Lord*
> *as you now give your solemn word?* (1720)

Instead of focusing on the "earthly things" they had lost and being a stumbling block to their own faith or the faith of others, Brethren considered the "divine things" they would gain by continuing to follow the ways of Jesus.

For the day: Focus on ways that you have set your mind on "earthly things" and thus served as a stumbling block for your faith or the faith of others. Now focus your mind on "divine things" and continue to follow the ways of Jesus in your daily life.

Prayer: Lord, though I may suffer persecution for my faith, help me to see your divine will in my life. Amen.

Bruce E. Huffman

July 25

Transfiguration

Reading: Matthew 17:1-4

Jesus took with him Peter and James and his brother John and led them up a high mountain. . . . He was transfigured before them, and his face shone like the sun, and his clothes became dazzling white. . . . Then Peter said to Jesus, . . . "[I]f you wish I will make three dwellings here, one for you, one for Moses, and one for Elijah" (Matt. 17:1-4).

Meditation: Aided by Matthew's account that precedes today's reading, we hear Peter exclaim, "God forbid it, Lord!" when Jesus voices his conviction that he must suffer and die at the hands of the religious leaders. And we listen as Jesus tells his disciples that some standing before him "will not taste death before they see the Son of Man coming in his kingdom" (Matt. 16:28b).

And now, with Matthew's continued help, we accompany Peter and his brothers, James and John, as they are taken to a high mountain where Jesus is transfigured before them. His appearance changes dramatically. The anticipations (*figura*) of the coming Messiah are fulfilled (*figured*) in him. Sunlight surrounds his face. Even his clothes glow with light. And suddenly Moses and Elijah appear and are in deep conversation with him.

It is tempting to share Peter's heartfelt wish to hold on to this uplifting moment by some fitting means. But let's remember that we are embarked on a continuing journey. The mountain of transfiguration must be climbed anew each day. Thankfully, our daily climb is spurred onward by a grace-filled promise. For once again we find ourselves with other disciples on a mountaintop. And we hear Jesus say, "And remember, I am with you always, to the end of the age" (Matt. 28:20b).

For the day: Greet this day with joy and overflowing gratitude! For the enabling Spirit of Jesus that graces our mountaintop moments also upholds us in times when we live in the shadowed valley below.

Prayer: O God, empower us to be obedient followers after Jesus so we may help extend the ministry of reconciliation, which is the light, the hope, the joy, and the freedom of our discipleship. Amen.

Warren F. Groff

July 26

On the Mountaintop

Reading: Matthew 17:5-8

Suddenly a bright cloud overshadowed them . . . (Matt. 17:5).

Meditation: On the evening of April 3, 1968, a man got up to speak in Memphis, Tennessee. He had come to lead a peaceful demonstration in support of the city's sanitation workers. That night, the night before he was gunned down by an assassin's bullet, Martin Luther King, Jr., entitled his remarks, "I've Been to the Mountaintop." Near the end of his speech, he spoke of threats that had recently been made on his life. Then he said: "I don't know what will happen now. We've got some difficult days ahead. But it doesn't matter with me now. Because I've been to the mountaintop."

Each of us has had our own times on the mountaintop, surely less dramatic than that one, but just as real. I remember the mountain at Camp Swatara, the Church of the Brethren camp I attended as a kid. I remember watching the sun set behind the mountain as we sat on Vesper Hill. I remember climbing to the top of the mountain and sitting on the huge stones that we called "the Rockpile." I can still picture the vista below.

In every major world religion, mountaintops are associated with God's presence, with divine revelation. Is it because mountaintops bring us close to heaven? Is it because, standing there, we look down into the valley and see the world as we suppose God might see it? Is it because up there we can look down on our problems and worries and put them into proper perspective? Is it because, standing on the mountaintop, we may hear echoes of a holy song that, in the words of a hymn, lift us "above earth's lamentation"?

I honestly don't know. I only know that I have had my own mountaintop experiences and you have had yours.

For the day: Recall a mountaintop experience especially meaningful to you. Where did it take place? What happened? How did it affect you?

Prayer: Thank you, Lord, for the mountaintops in my life. Amen.

Kenneth L. Gibble

July 27

When Silence Is Golden

Readings: Matthew 17:9-13; Luke 2:19

Tell no one about the vision until after the Son of Man has been raised from the dead (Matt. 17:9b).

Meditation: My mother often told me, "Don't tell everything you know!" I wondered why. After all, people seemed interested in what I had to say, and I received a boost from sharing with them. Reading the story that follows Jesus' transfiguration, I hear Jesus telling his disciples something similar: "Tell no one . . ." Isn't it strange that Jesus didn't want his disciples to tell what they had experienced with him on the mountain?

When I am constantly sharing my own experiences and viewpoints, I leave little opportunity for what I can learn from them and for God to speak to me in them. Henri Nouwen, in *The Way of the Heart*, writes that silence does several things. First, it makes us pilgrims. Second, it guards the fire within. And third, silence teaches us to speak. We learn from silence to respond, not merely react. With silence, we listen carefully. What we experience around us in the world and within our own souls needs to be pondered in order for us to recognize the meaning and understanding. When we take time to ponder, we discover questions that can lead us into deeper truth. When we ponder, we can ask what God the Holy One says to us through our experiences. When we ponder, silence becomes a golden avenue not only to enriching our own souls, but also to empowering us to speak more carefully and genuinely to other souls.

For the day: Take time to ponder what you experience from the world around you and from within your own soul. Ask what the Holy One is saying to you and discover the rich resources in pondering.

Prayer: Today, O God, I offer to you my inner thoughts and passions, my troubled spirit, and my uncertain commitments. I also offer to you my experiences of service and blessing. As I offer these, I would ponder what you speak to my life through them. Lead me to ponder with reverence and respect for your Holy Spirit's clarity and relevance. Through Jesus Christ who taught disciples to ponder. Amen.

Robert E. Alley

Images of Christ in Us

July 28–August 31

*J*esus Christ is our exampler, and it becometh
us to pattern after him—to walk in his
footsteps; if so, we shall be careful, and never
boast of our state. . . . If we have the spirit
of Christ, we shall be meek and lowly
of heart; and then it is, that our walk and
conduct will testify that we are the children
of God.

Peter Nead (1796–1877)

July 28

The Full Effect of Endurance

Reading: James 1:1-4

My brothers and sisters, whenever you face trials of any kind, consider it nothing but joy, because you know that the testing of your faith produces endurance; and let endurance have its full effect, so that you may be mature and complete, lacking in nothing (James 1:2-4).

Meditation from our past: It happened once that the jailer refused to bring us any water, so that I, W[illiam] Grahe, received no water from him for five weeks. The idea was that he would deliver to us old, stale beer for which we would have to pay the price of good beer. I could enjoy or use water better than that beer. In the meantime a well opened itself in my room, because when it rained the water often fell through the eaves trough past my window. I fixed a little board so that it was held tightly between the bars, and placed a vessel on it. In this way I could catch enough water to pass quantities of it in a narrow glass through a hole made in the wall near the floor to a brother who was next to me in another room. One time another brother who was far from me was very thirsty. He made a small trough which he could cut an inch thick and push through the thick boards and also receive water from another brother. Finally the jailer saw that he could not torment us in this way and brought water again on his own accord. —*Wilhelm Grahe*

From European Origins of the Brethren, *Donald F. Durnbaugh, comp./ed. The Brethren Press, 1958, pp. 250-51.*

For the day: Pray for all those unjustly imprisoned around the world.

Prayer: Afflict me, Lord, that I might not forget sisters and brothers around the world tormented for their faith. Amen.

C⁊

July 29

Ask in Faith

Reading: James 1:5-8

If any of you is lacking in wisdom, ask God, who gives to all generously and ungrudgingly, and it will be given you (James 1:5).

Meditation: Have you ever asked God for guidance in a difficult situation? If so, you were praying for wisdom. Have you ever asked God to help you understand what is right and what is wrong? If so, you were praying for wisdom. All of us seek guidance and understanding when we pray. But James warns us that we must pray with sincerity. We must truly *want* God's guidance and understanding. We must not doubt that God is the real source of wisdom, and we must be willing to accept God's response and act on it. If we are not ready to accept God's response, then we are double-minded. We are, as the text says, "like a wave of the sea that is driven and tossed by the world."

The first eight Brethren were ready to receive and act on God's guidance. They are described as "fasting and praying" in the days leading up to the first baptism. Through prayer and fasting they came to understand that they needed to be baptized according to the New Testament. But since each of them had been baptized as an infant, they knew that what they were called to do was considered illegal by the authorities. The wisdom they received from God was dangerous. In deciding to act, they could not afford to be double-minded.

For the day: Seek wisdom and be ready to accept God's guidance. Live with an openness to whatever God calls you to do.

Prayer: Loving God, guide me this day in all that I do. Help me understand your will and accept it in my life. Strengthen my faith so that I can respond to your call without fear or doubt. Amen.

Kenneth M. Shaffer, Jr.

July 30

Live Simply

Readings: James 1:9-11; Matthew 6:25-34

For the sun rises with its scorching heat and withers the field; its flower falls, and its beauty perishes. It is the same way with the rich; in the midst of a busy life, they will wither away (James 1:11).

Meditation: It is difficult to read these verses without thinking that James has no use for wealth. Very few of us see ourselves as wealthy because we can always find someone else who has more money than we do, instead of seeing the many people in the world who have less than we do. Wealth, however, is more than just money. It can also be measured by how many "things" we have in our lives—cars, computers, cell phones, clothes, etc. Acquiring and caring for money and possessions can keep us busy all the time. There is no time for what is really important: love of God and love of neighbor. But money and possessions are not permanent. Therefore, James calls the wealthy to be humble and those who lack material goods to celebrate.

We Brethren hear the words of James as a call to simple living. His words remind us of Matthew 6:25-34. Throughout much of the 1800s Brethren were advised against having grand homes with expensive furniture, carpeting, and paintings. Women were not to wear jewelry, and men were not to carry gold watches. Wealth was not considered important among the early Brethren. Alexander Mack was described as a rich miller who gave away his possessions to those in need and became poor himself. Today we Brethren are still called to center our lives on Jesus and our neighbors and not on money or things.

For the day: Consider the place of money and possessions in your life. Are you so busy pursuing things that there is little room for God? Determine how you can simplify your life.

Prayer: Gracious God, forgive me when I lose sight of what is truly important in life. Give me the strength to want fewer possessions and to seek life in your kingdom.

Kenneth M. Shaffer, Jr.

July 31

Endure Temptation

Reading: James 1:12-15

But one is tempted by one's own desire, being lured and enticed by it (James 1:14).

Meditation: All of us are tempted to do things that hurt others or ourselves, and if we give in to such temptations, we often want to blame someone else. In Genesis 3 Adam blames Eve and Eve blames the serpent. At times we even want to blame God for somehow causing us to be tempted. But James warns us not to blame God. Temptations come from our own desires. We are the cause of our temptations, not God, not other people. For example, if we overeat, it is because we want to eat more than our bodies need. We cannot say God tempted us just because God gave us the food and created us to need food. Furthermore, we cannot say those who prepared the food tempted us. It is our own desire that typically causes us to overeat.

Early Brethren struggled with temptations too. Johann Lobach was baptized by the Brethren in 1716 and later imprisoned for nearly four years for his faith. In his autobiography he notes the temptations and sins of his youth. He describes his tendency to arrogance and pride, his temptation to go into debt so as to dress fashionably, his "lust of the flesh," and "lust of the eyes." He felt he had transgressed all of the Ten Commandments. Later in life, however, he was described as "a blessing for many souls." Alexander Mack wrote that believers can "walk amid much temptation with great joyfulness of faith." While we are the cause of our own temptations, we can endure and overcome them.

For the day: Consider the things that tempt you most. How do you resist the desires that could cause you to sin? Allow the joy of your faith to help you endure those temptations.

Prayer: Forgiving God, give me the strength to resist temptations. Make me aware when my desires will do harm to others or myself, and let my love for you guide my actions.

Kenneth M. Shaffer, Jr.

&

August 1

Everything Is from God

Reading: James 1:16-21

In fulfillment of his own purpose he gave us birth by the word of truth, so that we would become a kind of first fruits of his creatures (James 1:18).

Meditation: Have you ever noticed how the light of the sun changes as the seasons change? Sometimes the light is intense and other times gentle. Have you ever noticed how lights in the night sky change as the year progresses? All these beautiful lights are gifts from God. James describes God as the "Father of lights." James goes on to remind us that this creator of light has given us the gospel ("the word of truth"), which enables us to become followers of Jesus (the first fruits of God's creation). But there is also the "implanted word." Does James mean that the gospel is somehow implanted in our hearts? Perhaps he means that the *need* for the gospel is implanted in each of us. Whatever the case, we must listen to the implanted word. And to listen we must be "slow to speak" and "slow to anger" and avoid wickedness. Such things get in the way of all the good gifts God has given us.

James' use of the terms "word of truth" and "implanted word" may be similar to Alexander Mack's use of the terms "outer word" and "inner word." The outer word refers to the written word (Bible), and the inner word is the working of the Holy Spirit within us. We need the Spirit to understand fully the written word and we need the written word to understand fully the testimony of the Spirit. We need both the Bible and the Spirit in our lives, and both are good and perfect gifts from the Creator of lights.

For the day: Take time to notice the lights in the heavens—
the sun, the moon, the stars. Even if it is cloudy, allow God's
light to shine on you and give thanks.

Prayer: Creator of light, I thank you for all the blessings you
have bestowed on your creation. Help me to appreciate your
gifts more completely and to listen more intently to your written word and to the word implanted in me.

Kenneth M. Shaffer, Jr.

August 2

Blessed in Doing

Reading: James 1:22-27

*But those who look into the perfect law, the law of liberty, and
persevere, being not hearers who forget but doers who act—they
will be blessed in their doing (James 1:25).*

Meditation: Local churches in my community participate in a
program where each church opens its doors to the homeless.
Each month during the winter one church is available as an
overnight shelter. Breakfast is also provided. A congregation
often must alter its schedule during the month to accommodate those who have no warm, safe place to sleep. This is just
one example of how Christians can be "doers of the Word."
James is emphatic that the followers of Jesus must do more
than pray and worship. Our commitment to Jesus must also
include compassion for others, and compassion should moti-
vate us to act. If we do not, James says our "religion is worthless." Being doers of the Word includes caring for widows and
orphans and keeping ourselves "unstained by the world." We

can be stained by the world when we adopt the standards of the world rather than the compassion of Jesus.

It is most appropriate that meditations for Brethren include texts from the Letter of James. Historically Brethren have subscribed to James' statement that "faith without works is . . . dead" (2:26). Alexander Mack insisted that both faith and works are needed. Peter Nead, a Brethren elder and writer in the 1800s, quoted James and said it was wrong to teach that we are saved only by faith. For three centuries Brethren have been motivated by compassion to help those who are suffering and in need.

For the day: Consider how you have been blessed by being a doer of the Word. Did you expect to be blessed when you helped someone? What motivates you to be a doer of the Word?

Prayer: Compassionate God, help me to see how I can do more for those in need. Fill me with compassion for those who suffer, and show me appropriate ways to respond.

Kenneth M. Shaffer, Jr.

August 3

Sing for Joy

Reading: Psalm 92:1-5

For you, O LORD, have made me glad by your work; at the works of your hands I sing for joy (Ps. 92:4).

Meditation: How often do you give thanks to God? According to the psalmist we should give thanks at least twice a day—in the morning and at night. The psalmist also suggests that we should give thanks and praise God for God's "steadfast love" and "faithfulness" and for God's great works. We can always depend on God's love and the many gifts God gives us. Note the psalmist's emphasis on music when we give thanks—the lute, the harp, and the lyre. Obviously music and singing played a significant role when the Hebrews praised God. The early Brethren also placed a high priority on singing when they gathered for worship. They published their first hymn book in 1720. The title page, *Geistreiches Gesang-Buch* (Spiritual Song Book), indicates that the hymns were for praising God. We too must sing for joy when we consider the great works of the Lord.

As we remember the birth of the Brethren movement, let us give thanks to God for inspiring the first eight men and women to take the bold step of forming a new church community. Let us also thank God for those who have continued to nurture the church over the past three hundred years. Let us celebrate and sing for joy, and with the help of God's steadfast love and faithfulness, let us pass our faith community on to others.

For the day: After the first eight were baptized, they were "immediately clothed inwardly with great joyfulness." Does your relationship with God and the church fill you with joyfulness? How do you express that joy?

Prayer: Ever faithful God, I thank you for your steadfast love, which sustains me each day. I also thank you for sustaining the Brethren movement for three hundred years and pray that you will guide us as we move into the future.

Kenneth M. Shaffer, Jr.

August 4

Sheep or Goats?

Reading: Matthew 25:31-46

Then the righteous will answer him, "Lord, when was it that we saw you hungry and gave you food, or thirsty and gave you something to drink?" (Matt. 25:37).

Meditation from our past: The children of God will not only be kind and charitable to their brethren in the Lord, but also to the children of men in general. They will at all times as far as it lieth in their power, alleviate the wants and distress of their fellow mortals. . . .

At the final day of reckoning, every good deed shall receive an ample compensation; for in that great day, when our Lord Jesus Christ shall occupy the great white throne, and the separation is made between the righteous and unrighteous, he will say unto those upon his right hand, "Come ye blessed of my Father, inherit the kingdom prepared for you from the foundation of the world. For I was an hungered, and ye gave me meat, [etc]. . . . Then shall the righteous answer him, saying Lord, when saw we thee an hungered, and fed thee? [etc]." . . .

It appears from the above, that the righteous could not see wherein they conferred such favors upon their Judge; and we may conclude, that the righteous who, in this life, performed charitable deeds towards the children of God, have done them out of love to them, and because they were the Lord's disciples; and that they did not perform those good acts with an expectation of meriting or purchasing the kingdom of heaven; but from motives of love towards them because they were Christ's disciples. —*Peter Nead*

From Theological Writings on Various Subjects, *Peter Nead, 1866, pp. 166, 168-69.*

For the day: Reflect on the way an act of service reveals the heart of Jesus, and seek ways today that you can reveal Jesus' love that others might see.

Prayer: Open my eyes, Lord, that I might see the needs of my sisters and brothers all around me, and that in seeing them, I might see you as well. Amen.

ᕲ

August 5

Acts of Favoritism?

Readings: James 2:1-4; Matthew 6:28-34

My brothers and sisters, do you with your acts of favoritism really believe in our glorious Lord Jesus Christ? For if a person with gold rings and in fine clothes comes into your assembly, and if a poor person in dirty clothes also comes in, and if you take notice of the one wearing the fine clothes and say, "Have a seat here, please," while to the one who is poor you say, "Stand there," or "Sit at my feet," have you not made distinctions among yourselves, and become judges with evil thoughts? (James 2:1-4).

Meditation: My church is only a short walk from my house, but I have to cross a busy street to get there. Since there is no signal, sometimes I wait quite a while for a break in traffic to cross. However, I have noticed that on those rare days when I am dressed in a full suit, drivers will stop—regardless of the traffic backing up behind them—and motion for me to cross in front of them. When I wear everyday casual clothes, no one ever stops for me! I'm the same person, but people treat me very differently according to my clothing.

For the day: How can I show greater honor to the "least of these" who cross my path, those who are "poorly attired" in terms of clothing, worldly success, attractiveness, talents, or other traits I admire? What can I do to extend a wholehearted welcome to the people who aren't currently valued as highly as others in my neighborhood, in my church, in my country?

Prayer: O God, you are the Creator of every soul I will encounter today. Let me always remember that. Help me to sense your guidance in each interaction. Help me to truly honor others, and give me the strength to set convention aside when love demands it. Thank you for the challenges that help me grow in this great adventure of living. Lead me into ever-widening circles of love for all your people. Amen.

Shawn Kirchner

August 6

Rich in Faith

Reading: James 2:5-7

Has not God chosen the poor in the world to be rich in faith and to be heirs of the kingdom that he has promised to those who love him? (James 2:5).

Meditation: The renowned priest and professor left his prestigious university to stay with the severely handicapped in a community where those who were cared for and those giving care lived together. The man with whom he was paired could not speak or see or hear. His body was misshapen and he could not walk. His only motor skill was to hold a fork. His name was, of all things, Adam.

This gifted teacher, who was accustomed to the most brilliant students, was as trapped in his great ability as Adam was in his disability. He had no idea how to deal with Adam. For three weeks he lived in fear and anxiety. It took much of the day just to bathe and dress Adam, offer him his meals, and attend to his needs. And then something began to pass between the teacher and Adam. The teacher sensed something deep in the man. Adam had a human spirit.

For the poor, many of the things that we think essential are stripped away—money, clothing, shelter, adequate medical care. They are left vulnerable. Their condition leaves no extra energy for deception. They cannot put up a front. They cannot conform to fashion. They cannot help being who and what they are. They do not have control. This is why the poor often have a faith that the rich and privileged can only imagine.

Jesus is drawn to the poor. People of privilege, like the Pharisees and rulers of Jesus' day, have all the answers. They have power. The poor have nothing. Like Adam the only thing they have left is the ability to respond. They are stripped down to their human spirit. It is here that God meets us. It is here that God's kingdom emerges. The poor are as naked and open as Adam.

For the day: Think about your weaknesses and uncertainties. Do you sometimes cover them up? Let God come to you where you are vulnerable.

Prayer: Remind us that we are not in control. Free us from the illusion that money and power are the measure of our value. Show us that your love comes to us when we are "poor" in spirit.

James H. Lehman

August 7

The Royal Law

Readings: Leviticus 19:18; James 2:8-11

You do well if you really fulfill the royal law according to the scripture, "You shall love your neighbor as yourself." But if you show partiality, you commit sin . . . (James 2:8-9a).

Meditation: There is an unfortunate tendency in the hearts of many churchgoers and pastors (myself included) to size up newcomers to the fellowship on the basis of what they might bring to us rather than what we might give to them. After asking a few of the traditional (but often insensitive) questions like, Where do you work? Are you married? Do you have a family? What church did you used to attend?, we quickly decide whether this person will be a positive resource or a negative drain on our energies. We either happily decide "A great catch; a good, solid family!" or sadly conclude "Definitely EGR—Extra Grace Required." We want and actively pursue the former but are just as happy if the latter doesn't show up again next Sunday.

James reminds us that loving neighbor—every neighbor!—as fully as we love self is the Royal Law of Jesus. James is the only one in scripture who so names this teaching, but we find echoes of Leviticus 19:18 in all four Gospels, so we know it was central to Jesus' message (see Matt. 22:39; Mark 12:31; Luke 10:27; John 13:34). When we prescreen people according to their observable value or lack thereof, we are guilty of showing partiality and are transgressors of the law. Christian, you did not so learn Christ!

For the day: Move into this day intent on giving love, help, and encouragement to every neighbor you encounter, regardless of what they may or may not have to offer you. Receive every new face in your church with open arms. Even the EGRs may surprise you, soon or late, with gifts of grace.

Prayer: Lord Jesus, forgive our tendency to make distinctions and show partiality. May we welcome every neighbor, even the challenging ones, with the openhanded love we have learned from you. Amen.

Daniel M. Petry

August 8

The Law of Liberty

Reading: James 2:12-17

So speak and so do as those who will be judged by the law of liberty. For judgment is without mercy to the one who has shown no mercy. Mercy triumphs over judgment (James 2:12-13 NKJV).

Meditation: According to James, what is this "law of liberty" by which we will be judged? It is not how accurately we assess the world's sin or respond by what people deserve. Rather, seeing through the lenses of God's mercy allows us to see new possibilities for showing the love of God. The story of God's people and his relationship with them is more about his merciful choices than his judgments according to what they deserve.

The invitation to know God through Jesus is described as grace or unmerited favor on God's part toward you and me. To know God through Jesus is to know firsthand the transforming power of his mercy in our lives. It liberates us from hiding behind judgment and empowers us to make our faith in God visible by acts of mercy. When we live in judgment of ourselves or others, we limit our experience of God. Mercy opens up new possibilities for relationships without holding others captive by what they deserve.

We live in a world where judgment justifies ideological and state-supported violence. Victims of natural disasters, rapidly transmitted diseases, and gang or sectarian violence are simply seen as newsworthy items. Broken homes and dysfunctional relationships have become the norm. In the midst of a sin-ridden world, God's people must live out the "law of liberty" in unprecedented acts of mercy.

For the day: Recognize that today your freedom in Christ allows you to consider new options to problems and issues. What new choices does the mercy of God give you for wrestling with them?

Prayer: Lord, help me to see through your eyes and beyond the limits of my judgment. May I experience anew the power of your grace acting through me as I extend your mercy to those who have done nothing to deserve it.

Philip Franklin

August 9

A Dynamic Faith

Readings: James 2:18-20; Ephesians 2:5-10

But do you want to know, O foolish man, that faith without works is dead? (James 2:20 NKJV).

Meditation: Faith and works. Through the centuries this pair of words has created conflict and caused division. "Only believe!" quotes the faith side (Mark 5:36). "Lord, when did we see you hungry?" responds the works crowd (Matt. 25:37). "By faith the walls of Jericho fell!" (Heb. 11:30). "Do good to those who hate you" (Matt. 5:44). And on it goes. However, both sides would agree that no one desires or yearns for a dead faith. James gives a clear argument for the evidence of a living and dynamic faith. This faith involves 1) *our intellect*: the knowledge of belief and faith, 2) *our emotions*: these cause the demons to tremble, and 3) *our lived life*: our living response to God at work within us—including our good works. In his letter to the Ephesians, Paul establishes that our salvation is by our faith, not by our works, yet he affirms the dynamic life of faith by linking good works to God's own workmanship of us, saying we are "created in Christ Jesus for good works." Faith and works are not opposite sides of an argument at all, but intricately linked through God's own creation of us as new creatures in him. What a privilege to participate with God in the plan for both ourselves and those on the receiving end of our good works.

For the day: Be God's workmanship today, choosing to walk in the paths of good works that are provided for you.

Prayer: O God who knows my inward spaces and the dead spots in my faith, stir me to reach beyond my intellectual knowledge and my feelings of you. Help me see the many opportunities to be your hands and feet in a world that so desperately needs your touch, that through this outward revealing of my faith, you may be glorified. Amen.

Pam Warner Franklin

August 10

An Active Faith

Reading: James 2:21-26

You see that faith was active along with his works, and faith was brought to completion by the works (James 2:22).

Meditation from our past: [The college student] studies the great Missionary movement and feels the weight of these unsaved worlds resting upon him. The question is assuming alarming importance. It is not merely the task of saving those heathen countries but of saving our own Christian America. . . .

But knowledge alone will not suffice; he must also act on that knowledge. . . . Christian living is more powerful than Christian preaching. When we scan our horizon and see the wonderful tasks awaiting us, let us not forget our every day living. Even though the foundation to character was laid while in college, we must keep on building till the structure is finished and pronounced "Well Done."

Let us not lose our vision of Christ going about doing good, comforting the sad, cheering the down cast, bringing light to the blind and food to the hungry. His days were filled with deeds of love and sacrifice and helpfulness, yet he had the greatest task ever undertaken—the establishing of God's kingdom on earth. May our lives equal our intellects. May we never lose sight of the central and most important thing in the student's wonderful outlook, so that the reflection of right living may brighten and beautify the field of our chosen work. —*Evelyn Trostle*

From "A Student's Outlook," Evelyn Trostle. Rays of Light, *Vol. XII, No. 4, 1911 (McPherson College), pp. 5-7.*

For the day: Take time today to write a letter of encouragement to a college student.

Prayer: God, bless me in my doing today. Amen.

August 11

The Tongue of the Wise

Reading: Proverbs 15:1-4

A soft answer turns away wrath, but a harsh word stirs up anger. The tongue of the wise dispenses knowledge but the mouths of fools pour out folly (Prov. 15:1-2).

Meditation: To be distinguished from the merely educated, the wise person is one who dispenses true knowledge, not just data and information one might learn in school. In these verses, knowledge refers to the acknowledgment of God, the power and nature of God, and the will of God. The well-known verse "A soft answer turns away wrath" (v. 1) is important knowledge for the wise, as is the understanding that God knows our every action and thought, good or bad (v. 3). The tongue of the wise, like that of a mature and loving parent, dispenses true knowledge, the knowledge of God and God's requirements for us. We often see the wisdom of the admonition to use soft words, because a disagreement that might easily be resolved is made worse by a harsh response. Many times we may be right to claim that harsh words are deserved, but wisdom requires us to respond softly. Whether in personal relationships, in communications within the community, or in relations among nations, we can see the wisdom of using "soft" words and are aware that anger and conflict are exacerbated by harsh words. Just as we know from experience that our harsh words hurt others, we can be certain that God also sees and grieves over our lack of self-control and our failure to follow God's will for us.

For the day: True wisdom for those who love God will reflect God's expectations for the way we should live.

Prayer: Help me, O Lord, to be open to your leading so that I may know your will for me. May my tongue—and my life— reflect the wisdom and love you have called me to share with others. May all my words be soft and loving.

Phillip C. Stone

⊘

August 12

Words that Make or Break Us

Reading: James 3:1-4

For all of us make many mistakes (James 3:2).

Meditation: It's good to know that I'm not the only one who struggles with keeping a civil tongue in my head! James 3:2 graciously states that we all make many mistakes. For example, some stumble by saying things they shouldn't (sins of commission), while others stumble by *not* saying things they should (sins of omission). Remember back to when you were in school. Can you recall a time when a teacher praised you for a job well done? Can you remember a time when you were singled out for a negative behavior? Which memory comes to mind the easiest? For many of us, it's the negative comment that we hold on to.

James 3:1 suggests to me that our generation is not the only one affected by what words do to us. But how are we to respond?

A governor's aide told a mom who was concerned about her child's learning disabilities that he would pass along her concern to the governor, ". . . but you're just a mom in tennis shoes." That lady, Patty Murray, ran for the U. S. Senate from the state of Washington and won. Her winning slogan was "Just a mom in tennis shoes!"

As Senator Murray demonstrated, the messages we hear don't control which path we choose. James 3:4 says that the tongue is like "a ship steered by a rudder." We can be deflated or energized by the tongue and what we say or what others say about us. Controlling the impact of our words before they control us appears to be the work of past generations, the current generation, and generations to come!

For the day: Stop, and choose! What words do you want to pass on to the next generation? What words would you take back if you had the opportunity?

Prayer: God, for all of our imperfections, you give enough love and enough forgiveness to cover each one. Thanks for the gift of a new day to start out fresh, anew, and forgiven! Amen.

Gail Erisman Valeta

∅

August 13

Corralling the Tongue

Reading: James 3:5-9

And the tongue is a fire. . . . With it we bless the Lord and Father, and with it we curse those who are made in the likeness of God (James 3:6, 9).

Meditation: As a young child growing up I often heard my mother say, "If you can't say something nice, just don't say anything at all." The older I become, the more I realize the wisdom in that saying. The writer of James admonishes us to remember what a powerful tool (or weapon) the tongue can be. He uses strong language to describe the destructiveness wrought by the things we sometimes say. James reminds us that every species of animal can be tamed, "but no one can tame the tongue—a restless evil, full of deadly poison" (v. 8).

Think about a time when the words of another person cut you deeply. Perhaps without even intending to, another person's words became the source of deep pain for you. Now think about a time when your words hurt someone else. Maybe you wished afterwards that you could call the words back, but they were already "out there" and caused pain. I once heard a children's story in which the pastor had a tube of toothpaste that she invited the children to squeeze out onto a plate. Then she asked them to "put the toothpaste back into the tube." The children quickly realized they couldn't get it to go back in— like our words once they are spoken. We can't take them back.

For the day: Before you open your mouth to speak each time today, quietly ask yourself whether what you are about to say brings blessing to others.

Prayer: Loving God, help me to "tame" my tongue, so that I might speak your words of blessing to each one with whom I converse today. May my words speak of your love and grace, in the name of the One whose very words were healing to those he met, Jesus Christ, Amen.

Chris Douglas

⊘

August 14

Speaking from the Heart

Readings: James 3:10-12; Matthew 12:34c

From the same mouth come blessing and cursing. My brothers and sisters, this ought not to be so (James 3:10).

Meditation: We need to watch our mouths. As children we said, "Sticks and stones may break my bones, but words will never hurt me." But that's not true. Words can hurt—or give life. God spoke the world into existence. God spoke blessing over creation. Jesus cursed the fig tree, and it died. Jesus, and later Paul, taught us to bless even our enemies and not curse them (Luke 6:27-36; Rom. 12:14). Our words are powerful. James says that a spring will not pour forth both fresh and brackish water from the same opening; a fig tree doesn't yield olives or a grapevine figs. Yet our mouths can speak both blessing and cursing. What is going on? The spring, the tree, and the vine are the source, but our mouths are not the source. Jesus said, "Out of the abundance of the heart the mouth speaks" (Matt. 12:34c). We need to watch our mouths because they show us our hearts. If our hearts are not right, we need to cry out to God to forgive us, cleanse us, and heal us.

For the day: Get alone with Jesus today. He has already paid the price for you to be forgiven. He wants to empower you to live for God. With Jesus' help, review the events of yesterday. Did you bless or curse others with your words? Did your words encourage? Did they show high regard? Did you tease or use sarcasm to belittle? What was going on in your heart? What do you need to do today?

Prayer: "Lord, make me an instrument of your peace . . ." (Attributed to St. Francis of Assisi).

James O. Eikenberry

August 15

Bearing Gentleness

Reading: James 3:13-16

Show by your good life that your works are done with gentleness born of wisdom (James 3:13b).

Meditation: Gentleness is an attribute that does not appear on many resumes. It is not trumpeted by politicians, automobile ads, or radio talk-show hosts. In fact, the world generally values the opposite. Instead of gentleness, the powers and principalities of this world seem to esteem shock and awe.

The brother of Jesus, however, sees humble gentleness as the attribute of the good life. Envy and selfish ambition are paths to disorder and wickedness; so give birth to gentleness in wisdom throughout your life, says James. True wisdom is shown in works of gentleness.

James is particularly interested in the life of the community of faith. We suspect that he is dealing with a church (or churches) with problems. Perhaps there are divisions around issues of wealth or status or envy or righteous superiority. Perhaps people in the church are dealing so harshly with each other that the life of Christ cannot be seen.

We know the feeling. It is easier to divide a church than unite it.

Christian gentleness is not necessarily an automatic or instinctive response. As do others, we often respond with violence, wrath, or retribution instead of loving gentleness. Sometimes our response is simply one of superiority or self-righteousness. Sometimes an even darker emotion emerges.

For the day: Find a way to give birth to gentleness in your life today, and work to plant seeds of kindness in your church.

Prayer: Our Father in Heaven, help us to deal with each other with gentleness and wisdom. Help us to deal with each other with the grace you have shown to us. Amen.

Christopher D. Bowman

ᘓ

August 16

It's Hard Work

Reading: James 3:17-18

The wisdom from above is first pure, then peaceable, gentle, willing to yield, full of mercy and good fruits . . . (James 3:17).

Meditation: "Real wisdom, God's wisdom, begins with a holy life and is characterized by getting along with others" is Eugene Peterson's paraphrase of James 3:17 in *The Message.* And in verse 18 he states: "You can develop a healthy, robust community that lives right with God and enjoys its results only if you do the hard work of getting along with each other, trusting each other with dignity and honor."

What a challenge to Brethren whose history knows discord and division firsthand. And what a challenge to congregations at those times when misunderstanding and mistrust seem to rule the day.

Those who seek wisdom from above and strive to apply it in moments of contention will do well to hear the counsel of Brazilian bishop Dom Helder Camara: "We must have no illusions. We must not be naïve. If we listen to the voice of God, we make our choice, get out of ourselves and fight nonviolently for a better world. We must not expect to find it easy; we shall not walk on roses; people will not throng to hear us and applaud; and we shall not always be aware of divine protection.

If we are to be pilgrims of justice and peace, we must expect the desert."

Desert moments are a reality, yes, but as James says, good fruits await.

For the day: Name an aspect of brokenness in your life and ask if "getting out of yourself" may be an essential step toward wholeness.

Prayer: God, energize us for the hard work of getting along with one another. Infuse our lives with gentleness born of wisdom, passion tempered with humility, and holiness overflowing with mercy. In the name of the Redeemer Christ. Amen.

Howard E. Royer

August 17

Wise and Pleasant Speech

Readings: Proverbs 16:21-24; James 1:5-8

The wise in heart are called discerning, and pleasant words promote instruction (Prov. 16:21 NIV).

Meditation: Once upon a time, a young man approached an old gentleman who was revered for his wisdom. After a proper greeting, he asked, "How may I become like you, respected for my wisdom?"

The old man thought for a moment and then replied, "By not making mistakes."

"How can I avoid making mistakes?" asked the young man.

The old man leaned back in his chair and responded firmly, "By having good judgment."

Not satisfied, the young man pressed his question. "How can I develop good judgment?"

The old man smiled and answered, "By making mistakes."

When faced with alternative choices, many of us can affirm that "experience is the best teacher." Hopefully, we learn from our mistakes and share our wisdom with others, offering "pleasant words" to those who come behind us in the journey of life. We are urged in the New Testament to ask God for wisdom. However, we ought not to think that God supplies wisdom with a lightning stroke from heaven. Through the crucible of life, he gives us understanding and insight. Sometimes we are crushed in the process; sometimes not. But through it all, the God of all wisdom offers us an opportunity to learn from him.

For the day: The Pennsylvania Dutch have a saying: "Ve get too soon oldt and too late schmart!" However, it is possible to grow old without getting smart. Today, make it your goal to ponder at least one experience and learn from it.

Prayer: Father in heaven, today I ask for wisdom from above. Remind me to connect my experiences with what I know about the spirit of Jesus. Teach me to be like him. Amen.

Jerry R. Young

August 18

Wooing Wisdom

Reading: Proverbs 3:13-18

You're blessed when you meet Lady Wisdom, when you make friends with Madame Insight. . . . Her manner is beautiful, her life wonderfully complete (Prov. 3:13, 17 The Message).

Meditation: In this Information Age, knowledge and data are easily found commodities. Yet biblical wisdom is much more than these. Wisdom, Eugene Peterson says, "is the art of living skillfully in whatever conditions we find ourselves," with "robust sanity" in these insane times. Wisdom helps us to raise our children, conduct our business, and relate to our neighbors in ways that allow for the flourishing of all.

Proverbs portrays wisdom as a real and living personality. Wisdom is personified as a woman worth courting—beautiful, mannerly, accompanied by a rich dowry. Yet Wisdom also woos human beings, seeking their attention, desiring to bestow on us the favors of insight and understanding that will make our lives complete.

Often I have needed—and prayed for—wisdom in some dilemma of life: whom to hire, where to live, how to conduct a relationship. On a few rare occasions, wisdom has come to me in a burst of insight. More often, I muddle through, less certain of the path. Frequently, wisdom comes only in the hindsight of regret. Sometimes I wish Ms. Wisdom were a bit more outspoken!

Proverbs offers us a new understanding of our relationship with Wisdom. It is a life-long courtship in which we are both pursued, and must pursue; in which we are courted, and must court; are sought, and must seek. If we desire God's wisdom, we must devote ourselves to seeking it throughout our lives—through the study of God's Word, through prayerful reflection, through attention to our God-given insight, and through the guidance of others who are wise. Yet Wisdom has a mind of her own—of God's own—and does not schedule revelations on our timing. Instead, Wisdom delightfully and graciously surprises us—then coyly hides until we come seeking again.

Scripture tells us that God made the world with wisdom (Jer. 10:12) and that Christ "became for us the wisdom from God" (1 Cor. 1:30). Won't you walk with Wisdom today?

For the day: In what do you need God's wisdom today?

Prayer: Wise, eternal God, in Jesus Christ you have courted us, and found us. Help us to seek your wisdom and to lovingly embrace it as our own. Amen.

Melanie Jones

&

August 19

Asking the Right Questions

Readings: James 4:1-3; Psalm 34:14

You ask and do not receive, because you ask wrongly (James 4:3).

Meditation: Brethren want peace. Whether it is peace in our daily lives, in our families, our churches, and our neighborhoods, or in the many worlds beyond our own, we all want peace of some kind. God grants us peace, but the daily work of sustaining this peace, of remaining open to God's graceful presence, is, in part, up to us. The psalmist charges us to "depart from evil and do good; seek peace and pursue it" (Ps. 34:14). But try as we might, we often falter.

"What is wrong with us?" we may ask. The key to exploring this dilemma is in the way we ask this question. Do we say "What is *wrong* with us?" or "What is wrong with *us*?" Asking the question the first way, we focus on how to improve the behavior of ourselves or that of others. This sometimes heavy-handed approach leaves us with little energy to listen for the leading of God. We may "depart from evil," but can we "do good" when we are always thinking about how bad we or others are? On the other hand, asking the question the second way may lead us to constructive action in the face of struggle. If we focus on the ways in which all of us interact together as Brethren, as fellow Christians who are loved by God, we may be more inclined to see ways of living that nurture both us and them. God loves all of us. Let us "seek peace and pursue it" together.

For the day: Recall someone with whom you have disagreed in the recent past, and tell yourself, God loves this person. Remember this in your encounters today.

Prayer: Creator God who loves us all, allow our hearts to seek your peace and our lives to pursue it, whenever we encounter people who need your love more than our judging. Amen.

Travis E. Poling

Agusta 20

August 20 in Hausa

Abota da duniya gaba ce da Allah

Wurin Karatu: Yakubu 4:4-7

Ku marasa aminci! Baku sani ba cewa zama abokin duniya yana daidai da gaba da Allah? Gama duk mai kaunar duniya ya maida kansa mai gaba da Allah ke nan (Yakubu 4:4).

Abincin Yini: Menene abuta da duniya? Ta yaya muna iya gane cewa muna abuta da duniya? Me ya sa Yakubu ya yi wannan magana? Ko akwai wata damuwa da ta tashi? Menene duniya?

Aya hudu yana nuna mana idan mun bar Allah mun juya masa baya muna abuta da duniya kuma mun ci amanar Allah ke nan. Yakubu yana ganin dangantakar da ke tsakanin Allah da mutanensa yana nan kamar dangataka da ke tsakanin miji da mace (Ishaya 54:5; Irimiya 3:20; Fitowa 34:15-16; Hosea 4:12; 5:4; 9:1). A nan, Yakubu yana tunashe jama'ar Allah cewa idan mun juya baya wa Allah, Allah zai ji kishi, kamar yadda miji zai ji kishi idan matarsa ta juya masa baya ta kama karuwanci da wini mutum. Haka nan kasancewar dangataka mai kyau a tsakanin mu da Allah tana nan kamar kasancewar dangantaka mai kyau a tsakanin miji da mace. Idan muka juya ga duniya muka kyale Allah, zamu kawo damuwa a cikin dan-gantakar mu da Allah.

Dangantakar mu da Allah ta rataya ne akan kauna da alherin Allah. Duniya tana da kyau domin Allah ne ya hallici kome, domin duk abin da Allah ne ya yi ta tana da kyau. Abinda ya bata dangantakar mu da Allah shine zunubi da tana kasancewa a cikin mu. Idan muna rayuwa a cikin zunubai kamar su karya, sata, zina, kiyaya, muna rayuwa ne rabe da Allah. Haka nan kuma idan muka ba wani abu daraja fiye da Allah, muna bautar gumaka ne. Idan muna kasancewa da sonkai, ba dama mu yi tunani akan Allah ba, balle tunani akan neman gafara daga Allah madaukaki (Eze.14:5; 44:10).

Abincin Yini: Ko kana aminci da Allah dare da rana?

Addua: Allah muna rokonka ka sa mu zama da ruhun aminci gareka kulayomin. Amin.

Filibus K. Gwama

August 20

Friendship with the World Is Enmity with God

Reading: James 4:4-7

Adulterers! Do you not know that friendship with the world is enmity with God? Therefore whoever wishes to be a friend of the world becomes an enemy of God (James 4:4).

Meditation: What does it mean to be a friend to the world? How can I know that I am a friend to the world and not to God? What was in James' mind when he wrote this passage?

Verse four tells us that if we turn our backs on God and enter into friendship with the world, we become unfaithful to God. James seems to see the relationship between God and his people as a husband-wife relationship (see Isa. 54:5; Jer. 3:20; Exod. 34:15-16; and Hosea 4:12; 5:4; 9:1). Here James is reminding God's people that when we turn our back on God, God will feel jealous, just as a husband will feel jealous when his wife is unfaithful. Also, a good relationship between us and God is like a good relationship between a husband and wife. But when we turn to the world in rejection of God, we bring problems into our relationship with God.

Our relationship with God depends solely on the love and grace of God. The world is good because it was created by God and anything created by God is good and perfect. But our sinful nature contaminates our relationship with God. When we live in sin, such as lying, fornication, adultery, killing, hypocrisy, stealing, self-centeredness, we are separated from God. Whenever we respect something more than God, it becomes an idol. In our self-centeredness, we seldom think of God and consequently may not think of repenting or seeking forgiveness from the Almighty God (see Ezek. 14:5; 44:10).

For the day: Are you faithful unto God day and night?

Prayer: Almighty God, please fill me with the spirit of faithfulness.

Filibus K. Gwama

August 21

Drawing Near to God

Reading: James 4:8-10

Draw near to God, and he will draw near to you (James 4:8).

Meditation: All around us we see conflicts of church and culture, people torn between being in the world and being of the world. It is no longer possible for us to be isolated from the influences that surround us or to live in a vacuum cut off from civilization. Each week as faithful Christians we make our regular trek to our local churches to encounter the presence of God amidst a body of believers with whom we have made a commitment as fellow seekers. For the past six days, we have been in and of the world participating in the daily grind of business practices and principles that at times seem to fly in the face of selfless dedication, preferring others, and loving our enemies. Families have faced the demands of culture shock, conflict of relationships, tensions of finances, struggles of power among peers, and keeping up with the Joneses. Now as we enter the house of worship, the hope and prayer is to lay it all at the door (or, as a last resort, at the altar) and stand free to face the power of God for redemption and forgiveness. Sixty minutes later we re-emerge into the conflict of the soul. The tension of living in the world is a daily threat to drawing near to the presence of God, but it is not impossible. Balancing life's demands and keeping God at the center of our core is different than simply "compartmentalizing" faith and work. When our identity originates out of our relationship with God, then and only then can harmony at home, at work, and at church become a reality.

For the day: Today, stop trying to control the world around you, and simply trust God by living with him in the core of your being.

Prayer: Father, I draw near to you, and with the strength of your presence I will stay committed to all you want me to be and do. Amen.

Frederick J. Finks

August 22

Do Not Judge

Reading: James 4:11-14

There is one lawgiver and judge (James 4:12).

Meditation: While working in Iraq with Christian Peacemaker Teams during the winter of 2004, a man from the village of Abu Hishma invited us to visit his home. We decided to go to this village, which the U. S. military had surrounded with razor-wire because there had been attacks on U. S. soldiers on the road outside. First we went to the U. S. military base nearby, where soldiers told us not to go there: They are terrorists. They will kill you. We prayerfully considered their warning, but still felt led to go. When we got to Abu Hishma, the residents warmly received us, and we listened to their stories of homes being bombed or raided by U. S. forces and men being rounded up and put in Abu Ghraib Prison. We ended up staying overnight and felt quite safe among these simple people. Had we accepted the label of the residents as terrorists and acted out of fear, we would have missed the gift of fellowship and love that we received from them.

Judgment can take the form of speaking evil or carrying inwardly evil thoughts. Judgment of an individual can lead to a broken relationship. Judging a particular group of people can lead to distrust and suspicion. This closes the door on the gifts of love and friendship God wants to give us and to the possibilities of God breaking in to transform us in our encounters.

For the day: Walk through the day with openness to each person you encounter, and keep your expectation that God will break into and transform difficult relationships or situations.

Prayer: God, give me the gift of love that refuses to judge or hurt another. Free my heart of fear or malice that prevents coming together with others in fellowship.

Peggy Gish

∅

Agosto 23

August 23 in Spanish

Buscando la Voluntad de Dios

Lectura: Santiago 4:15-17

Pero ahora os jactáis en vuestras soberbias. Toda jactancia semejante es mala (Sant. 4:16).

Meditación: La humildad y la sencillez son cualidades de una persona que busca la voluntad de Dios. Buscamos la voluntad de Dios para vivir y hacer todo lo que tengamos que hacer en nuestro diario vivir. Realizar nuestros logros confiando en nuestros propios esfuerzos, sin buscar la voluntad de Dios, es jactancia y soberbia. La jactancia y la soberbia son malas cuando quitamos a Dios de nuestros logros y éxitos. El verdadero éxito es realizar nuestros logros con sencillez y humildad, así engrandecemos a Dios y El nos engrandece a nosotros. Nuestro vivir y nuestro hacer es buscar la voluntad de Dios, servir al prójimo y hacer el bien, de esta forma seguimos las enseñanzas de nuestro Señor Jesucristo.

Para el día: Viva hoy expresando con su boca y su corazón, "Si es la voluntad de Dios, voy a vivir y hacer todo lo que pueda hacer, para la Gloria de Dios. Lo haré con humildad y simplicidad siguiendo las enseñanzas de Jesucristo."

Oración: Dios Soberano y Dios de la Vida, te pedimos que se haga tu voluntad como tu Hijo Jesucristo nos enseñó en el

Padre Nuestro. Líbrame de la jactancia y la soberbia en mi vivir y en mi hacer, sino que busque siempre tu voluntad para vivir en humildad y simplicidad para hacer siempre el bien. Amen.

Hector Perez-Borges

August 23

Seeking God's Will

Reading: James 4:15-17

But now ye rejoice in your boastings; all such rejoicing is evil (James 4:16 KJV).

Meditation: Humility and simplicity are qualities of the human being who seeks God's will. We seek God's will in all that we do in our daily lives. To rejoice in our boastings is to take credit for life's accomplishments and capabilities without seeking God's will. Rejoicing in boasting is evil when we leave God out of our accomplishments. The true aim is to achieve our goals humbly and simply; thus we glorify God, and God will glorify us. The purpose of our daily living and doing is to seek God's will, to serve our neighbor, and to do good works. In this way we follow the teachings of our Lord Jesus Christ.

For the day: Live today saying with mouth and heart, "If it is the Lord's will, I will live and do all the works I have to do for the glory of God. I will do my works with humility and simplicity following the teachings of our Lord Jesus Christ."

Prayer: Almighty God, God of life, as the Lord Jesus Christ taught us in the Lord's Prayer, I pray your will be done, as in heaven, so on earth. Free me from rejoicing in my boasting in life and works, that I may seek your will and live in humility and simplicity and do good works. Amen.

Hector Perez-Borges

August 24

The Fruit of the Light

Readings: Ephesians 5:8-11; John 1:5

Live as children of light—for the fruit of the light is found in all that is good and right and true (Eph. 5:8b-9).

Meditation: On a cool and sunny fall day, my family and I piled into the car and drove thirty miles or so to a small, family-run apple orchard for our very first apple-picking adventure. When we arrived we were given a bushel basket and set free to roam the grassy rows between the heavy-laden trees. "Look at all the apples, Mom! Aren't they beautiful?" my son shouted gleefully as he darted from tree to tree. I had to agree; the bounty was breathtaking. Up close, the individual apples were just as lovely—dusky red and streaked with yellow, gleaming in the sunlight, the most fragrant ornaments to ever grace a tree. As we munched apples on the ride home, we discovered that they tasted every bit as good as they looked—sweet-tart and crisp, with enough juice that some dribbled down our chins. Delicious.

There isn't much about fruit that doesn't please the senses, so it seems fitting that the writers of the Bible and Jesus himself often employed the metaphor of fruit when describing those good works and acts of love by which the followers of Christ should be known. For when we walk in God's light, something astonishing happens: we produce fruit, tangible evidence of our commitment to leave the darkness behind and embrace a new way of living. Together with our brothers and sisters, we become a veritable orchard of breathtaking bounty, offering a harvest that is altogether delicious to a world that hungers for what is good and right and true.

For the day: Live as a child of the light and remember these words from the Gospel of John: "The light shines in the darkness, and the darkness did not overcome it" (John 1:5).

Prayer: God of light and life, grant that I may be a bearer of fruit today as I seek to walk with you. Amen.

Karen Allred McKeever

$\mathscr{E}$

August 25

Pray Without Ceasing

Readings: 1 Thessalonians 5:16-22; Romans 12:12; Luke 18:1

Rejoice evermore. Pray without ceasing. In every thing give thanks: for this is the will of God in Christ Jesus concerning you (1 Thess. 5:16-18 KJV).

Meditation: We need to maintain a spirit of prayer continually and be in a proper frame of mind to lift up our hearts to God for his blessing. We need to persevere in prayer and not grow weary even though it seems our prayers are not being answered. We need to cherish the spirit of prayer and live near to the heart of God. We must not allow trifling causes to keep us from our regular prayer time, including personal devotions, family prayer time, or prayer in the assembly of the believers in Christ. We must always be mentally prepared to pray publicly or privately when the need arises. We must diligently guard against allowing worldly cares, frivolous conversation, vanity, reading an improper book, feelings of bitterness, lustful thoughts, or inappropriate companions to prevent us from being able to instantly engage in prayer. Nothing should stand between us and the Lord. We need to diligently test everything and hold on to those things that are good. Our soul and spirit ought to be in such a state that we can engage in prayer and communion with God at any time and find pleasure and fulfillment in approaching his holy throne.

For the day: Prayer is similar to conversing with an ever-present friend, sharing in the happy moments as well as in those moments of perplexity and despair. Be ready to converse with God during the course of your routine activities, just as you would talk with a friend.

Prayer: Dear Lord, keep my heart in a continual state of readiness to commune with you. Help me to stay in tune with your Holy Spirit and not repress your voice. In Jesus' precious name, Amen.

Robert S. Lehigh

August 26

The Cries of the Harvesters

Reading: James 5:1-6

The cries of the harvesters have reached the ears of the Lord Almighty (James 5:4b NIV).

Meditation: The General Board meeting was rolling along through a full but not overly exciting agenda when the general secretary announced a "holy interruption." Two Guatemalan workers from Imokalee, Florida, and their translator had stopped by the offices unexpectedly as part of a tour through the Midwest, campaigning for fair wages for their work in the sultry central Florida fields. They were asking some of America's fast-food giants for an additional penny a pound for the tomatoes they picked. It didn't sound like much, but they said it would make a world of difference to them. Even if it would cause a five-cent increase in the price of our hamburgers, would that be so much to ask for a bit of economic justice? Until confronted with the face of poverty, it's easy for most of us to forget that we're relatively rich. One example came on a trip to Latin America when a translation error led a local booking agent to think I was looking for a hotel room for about 50 pesos a night rather than $50 a night. So my room, which was simple but clean and comfortable, cost me about $11. It seemed an incredible bargain until I saw some of the statistics of wages in that region and strolled through a neighborhood market. Those "bargain-basement" deals would be great luxuries for many of the local people. Keeping the blinders off our relatively rich eyes is a constant task if we are to seek justice for all God's children.

For the day: Find a globe or a world map and locate some countries that struggle economically, praying for each of them. Remember, too, the poor and the overlooked in your own country.

Prayer: God of all nations, prevent us from gazing so narrowly within our own lives that we look past those in need. Open our eyes to their challenges and our ears to their cries, so that we might be motivated into action. Amen.

Walt Wiltschek

August 27

Patience

Reading: James 5:7-12

Be patient, therefore, beloved, until the coming of the Lord (James 5:7).

Meditation from our past: Sunday, July 14 (1850). Meeting at Liberty schoolhouse. Isaac N. Walter is there. He is a well-known and very popular preacher in the Christian church. This is the first time I have ever met with him. He is very friendly and sociable, and will carry an influence wherever he goes. He was at one time a very strong Adventist. He professed to believe in our foreknowing the day of our Lord's coming, and announced it as being very near at hand. Brother Benjamin Bowman told me that on one occasion friend Walter announced that he would preach a sermon on the second advent of Christ, and therein tell the day on which we might confidently expect the Lord to appear in glory, and give the scripture evidences on which his proofs rested. This sermon was announced for Antioch, a brick meetinghouse belonging to the Christian connection, and stood four miles north of Harrisonburg, and not far from where Brother Bowman lived. He told me that a large concourse of people was present to hear, and he with the rest. The discourse was eloquent, but with the thoughtful not very convincing. But the day, which Mr. Walter had so confidently set for the appearing of the Lord in glory, passed by as all other days pass by, in harmony with all the other notes that make the music of the spheres. Not long after this, the two met in the road. Walter looked a little bashful, but spoke first, and said: "Well, Brother Bowman, I was mistaken." "Yes," Brother Bowman replied, "but I had discovered that before you told me." —*John Kline*

From Life and Labors of Elder John Kline, *Benjamin Funk, coll. Brethren Publishing House, 1900, pp. 274-75.*

For the day: Resolve to test Christian fads with the community of faith.

Prayer: May I wait with patient endurance for your coming, O Lord. Set my heart and will on the tasks of the kingdom while I wait for you to establish it perfectly. Amen.

$\mathscr{O}$

August 28

The Prayer of Faith

Reading: James 5:13-15

And the prayer of faith shall save the sick, and the Lord shall raise him up . . . (James 5:15a KJV).

Meditation: It is a basic trait of man. Why pray when you can worry? A common attitude is this: We sing "Safe in the Arms of Jesus," but we are not there yet, so we will worry things along until we leave this veil of tears. But as Christians we are to keep our eyes on God and not on men. This is made possible through Jesus Christ, whose blood atones for us and whose intercession puts us in a right relationship with God. With this in mind, we find two kinds of prayer related in scripture.

First, in Matthew Jesus talks of private prayer: "When thou prayest, enter into thy closet, and when thou hast shut thy door, pray to thy Father" (6:6 KJV). In today's text we have the example of corporate or public prayer: "Let him call for the elders of the church; and let them pray over him, anointing him with oil in the name of the Lord" (James 5:14 KJV).

Of utmost importance is that we pray in faith. "Without faith it is impossible to please him" (Heb. 11:6). When our prayers, whether private or public, give honor and glory to God through our obedience to his Word, then we are fulfilling the defining goal of the Christian life.

For the day: Our church traditions must be biblical and they must be practical. Seek to glorify God in prayer, whether in public or in private.

Prayer: Dear Lord, allow me to seek you first in trials and troubles, and let me glorify your Blessed Name in all things. We pray this in the Adorable Name of Jesus. Amen.

Lynn Hayes Miller

August 29

The Sin of Self-Reliance

Reading: James 5:16-18

Therefore confess your sins to one another, and pray for one another, so that you may be healed (James 5:16a).

Meditation: One of the ways pride manifests itself in my life—and I expect I am not alone in this—is the desire to be able to handle on my own whatever life dishes out. I like to be thought of as a capable and strong person. I would prefer to be the person others come to when they need help or support. The idea of sharing my hurts with others is foreign to me. I justify my position: I can handle it; they don't need to know my pain; am I not a mature Christian with considerable spiritual resources available to me? Yet James would have us confess our sins and our needs to trusted friends in the faith and ask them to pray for us! Why is this so hard to do? Actually as I think back, I recall that some of the most meaningful moments in my walk have been in small groups in which deep sharing occurred, where we were willing to let our hair down and "be real." Could it be that I need to cultivate this level of trusted sharing and mutual support anew?

For the day: It is said that many Brethren are humble folk, not wanting to "toot our own horn." Yet frequently we are not humble but proud, as we defiantly go our own way. How can we walk in a more authentic humility?

Prayer: God, help me swallow my pride and reach out to trusted Christian friends, sharing my pain and my need with them and asking them to pray for me. Push me on this, God, until we get it done. Amen.

Dale E. Minnich

✑

August 30

Stay with the Truth

Readings: James 5:19-20; 1 Peter 4:8

My brothers and sisters, if anyone among you wanders from the truth and is brought back by another, you should know that whoever brings back a sinner from wandering will save the sinner's soul from death and will cover a multitude of sins (James 5:19-20).

Meditation: James concludes his letter with a word of hope. One may wander from the truth, one may be brought back, one may bring another back. The community is to live by the word of truth by which God has birthed us (1:18). These closing verses remind us that we must work together against self-deception and deviation from the truth. And the good news is that bringing one back to the truth brings salvation and covers a multitude of sins. What does truth mean to James? In chapter 2 he turns to Torah and the teaching of Jesus: "You do well if you really fulfill the royal law according to the scripture, 'you shall love your neighbor as yourself'" (2:8). James calls us to live this out in every aspect of our lives, in our speech and in our relations with others—with a single-minded devotion to God. This is the truth he calls us to live out, and to bring back those who wander. He calls us to do this in a way that is not judgmental, but merciful (2:13). In fact, James calls us not to judge (4:11). Rather, we are to show by our good life that our works are done with gentleness born of wisdom (3:13). Done in this spirit, mutual correction and exhortation are an expression of love of neighbor. And love, 1 Peter tells us, also covers a multitude of sins (4:8).

For the day: Stay the path of truth. Live today in gentleness, mercy, and love.

Prayer: God, fill me with the spirit of truth and love. Help me to live out the command of Jesus that we love one another. Amen.

Pamela K. Brubaker

August 31

Rooting for the Kingdom

Reading: Ephesians 3:14-21

. . . that Christ may dwell in your hearts through faith, as you are being rooted and grounded in love (Eph. 3:17).

Meditation: That Paul—he doesn't miss much.

In his day or in ours, it's easy to want our faith to soar to some higher plane. You see it in the words to the music on the front screen during a contemporary worship service—all those songs about reveling in Jesus and offering up one's devotion in praise of the Lord. We find it in our theology, where things are generally boiled down to the salvation equation—get Jesus, get saved, get to heaven. I found it during visits to South Korean congregations some years back, as there was a near-fixation on the vertical dimension of our faith—so much so that sermons about our responsibility to our neighbors were received as some new gospel (and often much appreciated!).

I suppose that's an appealing place to be—soaring up there. But in this text, the Apostle reminds us to keep our feet on the ground—or better, to keep our faith rooted in love. Indeed, immediately following this text, he flashes something else on our screen—a litany of another sort calling us to another way of living with our neighbors. You remember the words: humility, gentleness, patience, love, peace, and hope. Paul is calling us not only to communion with our Lord, but to community with our neighbors.

Some Christians already get it. While praying the Lord's Prayer at a worship service in Sudan, I'll never forget the way they ran together the words: ". . . thy-kingdom-come-thy-will-be-done-on-earth as it is in heaven." Those weary-from-war Christians wanted dearly for God's kingdom to become rooted in daily life, manifested in tangible expressions of peace, love, patience, and hope.

For the day: What about you—how are you "rooting for the kingdom"?

Prayer: Sink my roots into the good ground of your love and justice, Lord.

David R. Radcliff

Part 4

The New Testament Community

The Birth
of a
New Community

September 1–September 28

*I*nasmuch, we deem it our duty, obligation, and office to see to it that union, tranquillity, and peace be maintained, that all should be united and of one mind, so that we may, according to the commandment of our Lord and Savior Jesus Christ, love one another sincerely, and be enabled to love as he has given us a commandment, by which it shall be known that we are his disciples.

Annual Meeting Minutes of 1789
Great Conestoga, Pennsylvania

𝒪

September 1

The Messenger

Readings: Malachi 3:1-5; Matthew 3:1-12

See, I am sending my messenger to prepare the way before me, and the Lord whom you seek will suddenly come to his temple. The messenger of the covenant in whom you delight—indeed, he is coming, says the Lord of hosts (Mal. 3:1).

Meditation: To be sure, life can sometimes appear grim. To be sure, there seems no way to solve the conflict in Iraq. To be sure, your church may be losing members. To be sure, the cost of medical care may be more than you can afford. Oh yes, we can work with these problems. Yes, we can send conflict resolution experts to Iraq. Yes, we can adopt new strategies in church growth. Yes, we can urge Congress to put a cap on medical costs. Oh yes, we can do something. But we may also be surprised! The prophet Malachi promised God would send a messenger, someone to announce a coming change. In the midst of oppressive, insoluble Roman domination of the Jews, the messenger John the Baptist pointed to Jesus who would bring a new kind of life (Matt. 3:11). In the midst of military conflict with the British, God sent a messenger, Gandhi, to speak for a coming life of nonviolence. In the midst of racial antagonism, God sent a messenger, Martin Luther King, Jr., to speak for love of neighbor. Regardless of how difficult the situation, there may be a messenger of God right on our doorstep.

For the day: Even though your times might be difficult, or our common life together may seem hopeless, remember the words "a messenger in whom you delight is coming." Remain open for a surprise!

Prayer: O Lord, in the midst of everyday trials, decisions, and conflicts, keep our hearts and minds open to the possibility of a messenger who can show us a different way and bring us unexpected joy.

Graydon F. Snyder

∂

September 2

Building a Level Road

Reading: Isaiah 40:1-5

Comfort, O comfort my people, says your God. . . . Every valley shall be lifted up, and every mountain and hill be made low; the uneven ground shall become level (Isa. 40:1, 4).

Meditation: This passage is a message of comfort to an exiled and alienated people. The Israelites had suffered in Babylon long enough, and God was preparing a way through the wilderness of their separation, pain, brokenness, and fear. To a people who had been exiled from their homeland and estranged from God for generations, the promise of comfort and a level road back into God's embrace signified new life. All of us, no matter how hard we try to be faithful, feel separated from God at times in our lives. The frightened child within us longs for God to call us back into God's loving embrace and to bridge the distance with a level path. What I find most intriguing about this passage, however, is Isaiah's command to "*comfort*, O comfort my people" rather than to "*be comforted*, O my people." We are invited to feel the grace of God's acceptance, but we are also challenged to share that grace and become conduits of God's comfort. Where are there valleys of discouragement and brokenness that we can fill? Where are there mountains of oppression obstructing God's promise of hope? There are places in the world yearning for level roads to God's compassion; we are called to construct those roads and prepare the way for God's grace.

For the day: Look at the world around you through new eyes. Seek out the exiled and alienated in your community. Knowing that God is strengthening and embracing you, share God's comfort, grace, and promise of new life.

Prayer: Gracious and loving God, I am grateful for your comfort in my times of pain, encouragement when I struggle, guidance when I am lost, strength when I feel like I cannot go on, forgiveness when I disappoint you, and the joy and hope that comes from living in your loving embrace. Empower me to share those gifts with others as I seek to comfort your people, lift up valleys, move mountains, and prepare level paths to your grace. Amen.

Beth Rhodes

℘

September 3

No More Negative Ads

Readings: Isaiah 40:6-11; Romans 15:4-13

Get you up to a high mountain, O Zion, herald of good tidings; . . . lift it up, do not fear; say to the cities of Judah, "Here is your God!" (Isa. 40:9).

Meditation: Recent political campaigns have seen a barrage of negative ads. The reason? Negativity works, pollsters say. Even voters who say they don't like mudslinging end up believing at least part of an attack ad's message. Where is the candidate with the courage to stay positive when ugly is the name of the game?

Though we might think the Bible would never get down 'n dirty, the Old Testament prophets didn't hesitate to go negative. "For from the least to the greatest of them, everyone is greedy for unjust gain," speaks Jeremiah, "and from prophet to priest, everyone deals falsely. They . . . [say], 'Peace, peace,' when there is no peace" (Jer. 6:13, 14).

Isaiah, by contrast, brings words of comfort and hope to a repentant Israel brought out of exile. "What shall I cry?" the writer asks rhetorically. "The word of our God will stand forever" (Isa. 40:6, 8). We who believe in a mighty God need not surrender to those who play on our fears with the message that things are bad and getting worse. Things may be bad, but we know that with repentance they can change for the better. Because God is in charge.

In a cynical world, it takes courage to be a voice of hope. But we are called to be a "herald of good tidings." Isaiah tells his people: Get you up to a high mountain. Lift up your voice with strength. Lift it up, do not fear. Say to everyone, the Lord God comes with might!

For the day: Speak up. Say there is a better way. Shout it from the mountain. We can build a brighter tomorrow.

Prayer: May the God of hope fill you with all joy and peace in believing, so that you may abound in hope by the power of the Holy Spirit (Rom. 15:13).

Fletcher Farrar

♔

September 4

Proclaiming Good News

Reading: Matthew 3:4-10

Bear fruit worthy of repentance. Do not presume to say to your-selves, "We have Abraham as our ancestor" (Matt. 3:8-9a).

Meditation: John was an inside-out prophet, through and through! He was a revolutionary, an outlandish character with primeval garments and a barbaric diet. Over the generations, it's been easy to contain him—to keep him boxed in Bible times—to serve one very specific purpose: preparing the way for Jesus' earthly ministry.

Indeed John the Baptist's role did serve a pivotal point in the biblical account. Not only was he the one who set the stage for Jesus to usher in the upside-down kingdom, he was there to ceremonially launch Jesus on his way through baptism. He called people to three things: true repentance, *inwardly* in their hearts and minds; baptism, *outwardly* marking this change of heart; and he called them to behavior that *overtly* reflected that change by bearing fruit. A true inside-out movement.

But John's call really transcends time. It is a call to all generations, including ours. His harsh words to the established church of that day are also harsh words for us, the established church of our day. He warned the Pharisees and Sadducees against complacency and hypocrisy; they were resting on their Hebrew laurels. Might we be resting on our Brethren laurels? The earliest Brethren responded to John's call as they inwardly repented and as they outwardly marked that change of heart by baptizing in the Eder River. And they overtly reflected that change, as in the words of Alexander Mack, that all would know them "by the manner of their living."

John still calls us today to join his inside-out movement, to truly repent and turn our priorities inside out. It's a reorientation to life. This is not easy news—but it is the only good news!

For the day: John is still calling you—calling us—to repentance. What are the areas of complacency and hypocrisy in your life and in the life of the church? What is he calling you to turn inside out?

Prayer: O God of the upside-down kingdom, move us from our complacency and hypocrisy. Help us to live an inside-out life, here and now. Call us to true repentance and re-orientation. May we bear fruit worthy of your kingdom. Amen.

Pamela A. Reist

September 5

The Chaff He Will Burn

Reading: Matthew 3:11-17

He will baptize you with the Holy Spirit and fire. His winnowing fork is in his hand, and he will clear his threshing floor and will gather his wheat into the granary; but the chaff he will burn with unquenchable fire (Matt. 3:11b-12).

Meditation: Our Brethren founders understood this chaff metaphor clearly. They even quoted it twice in the first paragraph of their first tract in 1708. Chaff is the discarded shell that covers the grain; it is the worthless byproduct of the harvest. To separate grain from chaff, one pitches the mixture into a gentle wind with a winnowing fork. As they fall, the wind separates the two. The chaff drifts in the leeward direction; the weightier grain falls to the floor. Thus, the harvest is naturally divided between valuable and worthless.

It is messy work, but life does not arrive chaff-free. If we want the grain, we suffer the chaff. Today, a new definition creates another illustration. Chaff is also the name for the lightweight reflective material ejected into the wind to attract radar. Military planes use modern chaff to trick enemy missiles into chasing the chaff instead of the plane.

Both the old and new metaphors hold true. Baptism in Christ removes the worthless chaff so the real life is set free. Also, baptism in Christ guides us away from the illusionary fluff of life and returns us to the real goal. Christ reveals the true life and feeds us with the true bread.

In every life, there is a mixture of chaff and grain. How wonderful it is that the chaff is removed and the grain is redeemed in Christ Jesus.

For the day: Are there places in life where you chase glittering, worthless chaff? Recommit yourself today to Christ; stop eating the chaff and start feasting on the bread of life.

Prayer: God, remove the empty shell and redeem the precious grain within. Amen.

Christopher D. Bowman

⊘

September 6

God's Own People

Readings: 1 Peter 2:1-10; Revelation 21:3

But you are a chosen race, a royal priesthood, a holy nation, God's own people, in order that you may proclaim the mighty acts of him who called you out of darkness into his marvelous light (1 Pet. 2:9).

354

Meditation: Most of us have an inner desire to belong. Isolation is unhealthy and is even used as punishment (e.g., "Go to your room!"). As children we would form clubs so we could belong. We made some rules so we could feel it was an exclusive club. We strengthened our sense of belonging by making sure others could not belong! We grew out of that, we hope, but we continue to desire to belong. We may join various organizations in an attempt to belong as well as provide some worthwhile service to humanity. We also hope that the church in which we hold membership provides us with a deep sense of belonging. The ultimate answer to that very human and natural need is God's own provision of forming a people for himself, people who belong to him. From the early promise to Abram (Gen. 12:1-2) to the closing of the drama of redemption, God's desire was to create a people for himself. Those who stand in the stream of Abram's faith are those people, a unique people who belong to God. But the belonging is not for the sake of belonging; the belonging, while it meets our natural hunger, is in order to represent the God who formed the people for his own. We have been chosen by God to proclaim his mighty acts expressed in Jesus Christ. With this marvelous privilege comes a tremendous responsibility!

For the day: While delighting in the privilege of belonging to God's people, are you accepting the responsibility of proclaiming his mighty acts?

Prayer: Thank you, God, for calling me to belong to you and your people. Help me today to faithfully represent you in my world. Amen.

Brian H. Moore

&

September 7

John Prepares the Way

Readings: Mark 1:1-8; Matthew 3:1-3

John the baptizer appeared in the wilderness, proclaiming a baptism of repentance for the forgiveness of sins (Mark 1:4).

Meditation from our past: [Someone said he] cannot believe that John the Baptist could have baptized all the people by immersion. For, he says, he was no Samson, nor made of steel or iron, so that he could have constantly stood in water. . . .

    If we consider the matter merely with natural understanding, it is known that natural fishermen spend almost night and day for months at a time mostly in water, just for the sake of their temporal nourishment. Some have such constitutions that it does not harm them in the least, even though in these Occidental lands the water in the winter is much more penetrated by cold than in the warm Orient. I find therefore not the slightest reason to doubt that John, in the time that he had had, could have baptized as many people here in Pennsylvania as he did in the East.

    . . . I must testify here before God that in these cold Western lands, during the brief time of my pilgrimage, over one thousand people of various constitutions have been baptized in this manner by immersion and many in cold winter at that. I have not heard of a single one who has suffered the slightest harm or discomfort in the health of his body by this. On the contrary, there are conscientious people who will testify that they had periods of ill-

ness which were cured in the water bath through the
Word. —*Alexander Mack, Jr.*

From The Brethren in Colonial America, *Donald F. Durnbaugh, ed.*
The Brethren Press, 1967, pp. 522-23.

For the day: If you have been baptized, reflect on that day and
what it has meant to you. If you have not been baptized,
prayerfully consider the offer made to you by Christ and the
church.

Prayer: We thank you for the waters of life that surround us,
God of glory, from the waters that surrounded us before our
birth, the waters that flow through our daily lives, and the
water we have surrendered to in baptism. Amen.

September 8

Birth-Day

Reading: Hosea 11:1-7

My people are determined to turn from me (Hosea 11:7a NIV).

Meditation: Today is my daughter's birthday. Not only is it a
special day to celebrate her life, but it is also a time of reflection for me, her mother, as I recall this birth-day.

After thirteen well-used hours, Elena entered the world amid
tears and laughter—hers and ours. As any first-time mom, I
was eager to see her, to smell her, to simply embrace the beautiful body that had formed so delicately within mine. I was
thankful for the skillful birthing process that allowed her to be
born without complication. I was thankful for the care and
concern of nurses and family members as I adjusted to her
presence. I was thankful to God for the blessing of her life.

From those first moments, I knew my life would never be

the same; becoming a parent was the most selfless act of my life. And, oh, how she needed me in those first months, for diaper changes and food, warmth and love. But as she celebrates another year of life, I hear her emphatic words: "I'll do it myself, Mommy." I know that she is capable of so much, yet I worry about the times when her decisions will be in direct opposition to my desires.

In this passage, God laments the disobedience of Israel. It is a struggle of love and despair that can only be resolved through grace that is shared freely and fully with the children that God loves—grace for each of us.

May it be so in my own parenting as well.

For the day: Consider your own birthday or birth-day. In what ways do you show grace as a parent? In what ways have you received grace as a child?

Prayer: Father and Mother of us all, we are humbled by your gracefulness. We are grateful that, despite our rebellion, you sent Jesus for our salvation and example. May we also show grace to others in our lives with your strength. Amen.

Angela Lahman Yoder

✑

September 9

A Child of God

Reading: John 1:10-14

But to all who received him, who believed in his name, he gave power to become children of God (John 1:12).

Meditation: In many ways it seems like only yesterday. The preschoolers in Mrs. Kanode's Sunday school class were singing enthusiastically the childhood favorite: "Come into my heart, Lord Jesus. Come in today. Come in to stay. Come into my heart, Lord Jesus." And in a flash, over a half-century later, I am sitting in Sunday worship with the pastor playing her guitar and leading the congregation in the singing of that same precious children's chorus. As a sixty-something, the memory of being a preschooler in Mrs. Kanode's classroom and singing the children's chorus gave me goose pimples. The pastor's challenge this day is for each of us to enter into the presence of the triune God as a child. My mind wandered to the story in Matthew's Gospel where Jesus encourages the children to come to him (19:13-15). As I observe our eight-year-old grandson and his friends, they model how to live with gusto; how to disagree, yet stay in community; how not to judge; how not to hold a grudge; how to forgive; how to look forward! Are these traits that our Lord Jesus Christ is asking us to live today inside and outside of the church? The pastor's words from that Sunday morning worship continue to ring in my ears: "The words of this simple children's chorus are all we need to say to God in order to receive Christ's saving grace." Wow! Powerful! This gift of grace brings a lifelong commitment of living our discipleship in childlikeness.

For the day: As a child of God, always seek to follow Jesus' teachings in all you say and do.

Prayer: God, as our loving parent, teach us to be childlike as we walk our Christian journey. Forgive our childish behavior. Nudge us to respond to and trust your leading as we relate to our loved ones, our community, and the global village. Amen.

Judy Mills Reimer

𝒞

September 10

Consider Your Call

Reading: 1 Corinthians 1:26-31

Consider your own call, brothers and sisters: not many of you were wise by human standards, not many were powerful, not many were of noble birth. But God chose what is foolish in the world to shame the wise; God chose what is weak in the world to shame the strong; God chose what is low and despised in the world, things that are not, to reduce to nothing things that are, so that no one might boast in the presence of God (1 Cor. 1:26-29).

Meditation: Consider your call. What is it that God would have you do? What is it about "the call" that we want to avoid? And why do we struggle so in bearing witness to the good news of Jesus Christ? Perhaps the struggle lies within the many stories of those great people in our lives and traditions who have shared their experiences of hearing their call and responding with great accomplishments. We could never measure up to the acts of these great people of faith because we do not envision ourselves as God's great people. The folly of our consideration may rest in the assumption that God calls only those with the ability to accomplish great things. We simply believe we are not part of that crowd of people!

And yet it seems that not a day goes by without someone interrupting this lofty pondering by inviting us into the human experience: a family member in crisis; a fellow traveler lamenting too many days away from family; an invitation into another's pain and suffering of soul or body; a survivor of the earth's turmoil asking, "Why do you care about my plight by rebuilding my home?"

It was in the 1960s. I was only eight years old when a church leader from the Soviet Union, whom my family was hosting, took me on his knee and told me to "never cease in asking God to bring peace on earth, for only God's peace is capable of bringing to an end the words and weapons that nations use to frighten each other." It was then that I took on my heart, through prayer, a life-long hope and passion for God's peace to come on earth.

Paul's words to the Corinthians are a reminder to us that God does not call only the gifted, talented, and the equipped, but rather, equips the called.

For the day: So listen, and be ready to be interrupted into the service of your call, by God's grace.

Prayer: God, bring peace to this day that I might be attentive to those interruptions that invite me into your service and calling.

Stanley J. Noffsinger

Satumba 11

September 11 in Hausa

Kiyaye Dayantaka Cikin Ruhu

Nassi: 1 Korintiyawa 12:4-13; Afisawa 4:3-13

Wato kamar yadda jiki yake guda, yake kuma da gabobi dayawa, su gabobin kuwa ko da yake suna da yawa, jiki guda ne, to, haka yake ga Almasihu (1 Kor. 12:12).

Abin Tunani: Kokarin kiyaye dayantaka cikin rayuwan iyali, abu ne wanda yana da muhimmanci ga kowane miji da mace a Africa. Domin nacewar dangantakan nan na jini, kowa a cikin iyalin mutumin Africa suna kokari su tsare dayantakan nan ba makawa. A zaman dayantakar iyali nan ta wuriin jinni, ana bukatan kowa ya yi aiki cikin iyalin nan gwargwadon karfinsa domin inganta iyalin. Duk wanda bai yarda ya yi aiki don ci gaban iyalin nan ba, zai zama abin kunya ga dukan iyali. A zahiri, duk wanda ya bijire daga zaman dangantaka nan, ta wurin ayyukan sa, ana iya yashe shi gaba daya.

Haka nan yake a cikin ekklisiyar sabon iyali ne, ba a cikin jini ba amma a cikin Ruhun Allah. Ekklisiya tana da baye baye da yawa, da ayyuka masu yawa, amma dukkan su da ruhu daya ne, kuma an bayar ne domin inganta ekklisiya. A cikin ekklisiyar, jikin Kristi, babu mutum wanda zai buga kirji cewa ya isa don kansa ba. Domin duk abinda mutum ke da shi an bashi/ta domin inganta ekklisiya ne. Hakin kowa ne ya yi aiki da baiwarsa gwargodon iyawarsa. Dukkan membobi masu hidima ne ga junansu a cikinn Kristi. Kowane memba kuma an hatimce shi/ta ta wurin baptisma cikin ruhu (Afisawa 1:13).

Duk wanda ya/ta ki yin aiki da baiwa da Allah ya bashi a cikin ekklisiya yana kasadar rasa kasancewar sa/ta a cikin jikin Kristi kenan. Kamar yadda dangantaka cikin jini yana sa mu kwarginin kiyaye dayantaka cikin rayuwar mu a cikin iyali da kabila, haka nan ya kamata mu darajanta dayantuwar mu cikin ruhu domin inganta ekklisiyar Kristi.

Tambaya: Yaya kake amfani da baiwa da Allah ya ba ka/ki a cikin ekklisiya?

Addu'a: Ya Ubangiji Allah, ka taimake ni domin in kiyaye dayantakan nan na ruhu chikin Kristi, ka kuma bani zarafi domin in yi aiki da baiwa da ka bani domin inganta ekklisiya.

Patrick K. Bugu

September 11

Maintaining Unity in the Spirit

Readings: 1 Corinthians 12:4-13; Ephesians 4:3-13

For just as the body is one and has many members, and all the members of the body, though many, are one body, so it is with Christ (1 Cor. 12:12).

Meditation: The desire to maintain family unity is a very important endeavor in the life of every African man and woman. Everybody in the African family is aware of the importance of maintaining the unity of this blood tie because that is what gives prestige to everyone in the family. Because of the uncompromising drive of this blood tie, everybody in the African family tries earnestly to maintain this tie without hesitation. Every member of the family is expected to contribute toward the edification of the entire family, and failure to contribute as one is able is shameful. In fact, any member of the family who mistakenly deviates from this blood tie and corresponding communal service risks being deserted by the family members.

In the same manner, the church of Christ is a family united not through blood relation, but through the uniting influence of the Spirit of God. The church is a body with diverse gifts, diverse kinds of services, and different kinds of works that all come from the same Spirit and are mainly for the edification of the church.

In the church—the body Christ—there is no one who can claim being independent of the other members of the body. Every member is given a gift by God for the edification of the church. Every member is called to serve in the capacity of his or her gift. All members are servants to one another for Christ's sake. All are members of Christ's body sealed by the Spirit of

God (Eph. 1:13). Therefore, any member who fails to use his or her gifts for the edification of the whole church risks being alienated from the body of Christ in the same way one is alienated from being a member of a blood family tie.

As we unflinchingly and earnestly try to maintain the blood relationship in our families and clans, we should courageously and earnestly maintain the unity of the spirit in the body of Christ by serving others using the gifts we have received from God.

For the day: How do you use your giftedness as a member of the body of Christ?

Prayer: O God, help me to maintain the unity of the spirit in Christ, and enable me to serve the church faithfully. Amen.

Patrick K. Bugu

September 12

Members of the Body

Reading: 1 Corinthians 12:14-27

The way God designed our bodies is a model for understanding our lives together as a church: every part dependent on every other part, the parts we mention and the parts we don't, the parts we see and the parts we don't. If one part hurts, every other part is involved in the hurt, and in the healing. If one part flourishes, every other part enters into the exuberance (1 Cor. 12:27 The Message).

Meditation: My dad loved apple butter! As a boy growing up, I remember my mom and the aunts gathering apples, peeling them, and cutting them into small sections. The big copper kettle was retrieved from storage, cleaned, and put over the fire. Cooking and stirring took many people, but the end product was good!

Roma Jo and I continued the tradition, and now our eldest son has his own copper kettle—the tradition continues. At the last "apple butter weekend," I was reminded of today's scripture as I observed the many different people doing the various tasks: keeping the fire going; preparing the canning jars; cooking for the "crew"; setting up the work tables; young Willie, age 6, stirring with Uncle David; and the young people canning the finished product. Many parts of the body, all working together to make delicious apple butter.

The church is like making apple butter. Some collect materials, some prepare the lessons, some provide the energy, some stir the pot, but when the job is finished, the world appreciates the final product. It makes life better. As we celebrate our three hundredth birthday, let us remember that each one of us is a part of the whole. We have different tasks or ways of approaching these tasks, yet we are working toward the same goal of making life better for ourselves and for the world.

For the day: Live each day with the knowledge that you are an important part of the larger body of Christ.

Prayer: Creator God, channel our energies so that our individual contributions and lives will strengthen the witness of our church. May the message of Peace and Justice, as lived by Jesus, be seen by the world through our individual and corporate example. Amen.

R. Jan Thompson

ℰ

September 13

Sharing in the Inheritance

Readings: Colossians 1:9-14; Ephesians 2:10

He has rescued us from the power of darkness and transferred us into the kingdom of his beloved Son (Col. 1:13).

Meditation: When I was growing up as an only child, I often felt left out when seasonal holidays rolled around and family members traveled from near and far to be together. Frequently I shared in a meal or participated in a round of games that almost everyone knew, except me. There was a sense of welcome, but a definite understanding that I was not one of them. I grew up with that haunting feeling of being almost, but not quite, a part of the family. All of that changed when I committed my life to Christ and became a member of the family of God.

I began to realize that through the adoption of Jesus Christ, I had become a child of God. I was rescued from the feeling of aloneness and transferred into a new knowledge of life in the kingdom plan. This new knowledge brought with it an understanding that my life has a purpose. As children of God, we are granted the privilege to share in the inheritance of mercy, love, and grace. We are called to live a life that is not our own. We are challenged to become more and more like Jesus. We are charged with the responsibility to act as he did—to make a difference in this world as he did. We have been "called out of darkness into his marvelous light" to share the good news of salvation and the forgiveness of sins.

For the day: Live in the fullness of knowledge that you are a child of God, seeking his will for your life. Be strong with the strength that comes from his power, and give thanks for all that God is revealing in your life.

Prayer: God of mercy and grace, thank you for the generous love you have poured out upon us that we should be called children of God. Help us to lead lives that bear fruit and are pleasing to you.

Belita D. Mitchell

✐

September 14

God at Work

Readings: Matthew 1:18-25; 2:13-15

Joseph, son of David, do not be afraid to take Mary as your wife, for the child conceived in her is from the Holy Spirit (Matt. 1:20b).

Meditation: Whether the virgin birth is a vehicle or an obstacle for your faith, it is clear that Matthew is attesting to God's authority and work in Jesus.

Authority. Matthew is claiming that Jesus, not Caesar, speaks for God, and that his followers, a splinter group from the synagogue, are true heirs of Abraham, Joseph, Moses, David, and the prophets, all of whom are referenced here, much as the early Anabaptists, splitting from the Catholics, claimed to be the true heirs of the primitive church.

God at work. Here is Mary, betrothed and pregnant, but not by Joseph. It is a disaster. She looks like an adulteress. She will be an outcast, an unmarriageable woman with a child to support. How can she put bread on the table? But Joseph has a visitation: An angel posts a sign on Mary's tummy, "God At Work," and tells him to marry her and to name the child "God Saves." So Joseph embraces Mary, and they begin the wild ride of their lives: running in the dark from a murderous Herod, incubating in Egypt the salvation of their people.

We do not manage the outcomes of our lives. We do not

know what will come in this day, nor what will ultimately come of it—for the ripples of our doings carry far beyond the horizon of our lives. But an angel has posted a sign, "God at Work." It is as if the angel is saying to us, "Give God something to work with: just show up."

For the day: Live your life. Embrace your situation. God is at work.

Prayer: God, grant me the faith to walk into this day. Even if I do not see you at work, let me move as partner rather than manager. Let me be unafraid. Let me embrace this day. Amen.

Harry L. Sheller, Jr.

September 15

Pronouncing Blessings on Others

Readings: Numbers 6:22-27; James 3:8-12; Romans 12:10, 14

And the LORD spoke to Moses, saying, "Speak to Aaron and his sons, saying, 'This is the way you shall bless the children of Israel. Say to them: "The LORD bless you and keep you; The LORD make His face shine upon you, and be gracious to you; The LORD lift up His countenance upon you, And give you peace." ' " (Num. 6:22-26 NKJV).

Meditation: The Levitical priests were instructed to minister to and for the people of God as they served before God in the tabernacle. This included the specific duty to pronounce a blessing upon these people whom God loved so much. God promised that he would apply the blessing upon the people that his appointed priest pronounced. Peter tells us that every Christian is also a God-appointed member of a "royal priesthood" and entitled to a role of offering spiritual sacrifices. This includes pronouncement of blessings upon fellow Christians. Unfortunately, as James tells us, it is extremely easy to use our tongue to put down others rather than build them up. It's entirely possible that today's church is lacking her real potential for growth and power, because the average Christian fails to carry out his or her official duty to pronounce a blessing upon fellow brethren. Take a few moments and dream of the possibilities of blessing other Christians, and then as a God-ordained priest, why not get started right now. Let's change the world by unleashing the power of God through our blessings on others.

For the day: On Sunday our tongues are quick to offer blessings and praises to our heavenly Father, unto Jesus Christ, and to the Holy Spirit. Let us be just as quick to heap blessings upon each and every one of God's children every day of the week. Your tongue can have a powerful impact as God applies the actual blessing that you pronounce.

Prayer: Father in heaven, may your face shine on your children as you bless them and keep them and give them peace.

John E. Bryant

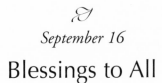

September 16

Blessings to All

Readings: Matthew 25:31-40; Job 31:13-32

Come, O blessed of my Father, inherit the kingdom prepared for you from the foundation of the world; . . . Then the righteous will answer him, "Lord, when did we see thee hungry and feed thee, or thirsty and give thee drink? . . . or naked and clothe thee?" (Matt. 25:34-38 RSV).

Meditation: In the hills and hollows of the southern Blue Ridge Mountains the folklore favorites are often stories of "moonshining," the making, consuming, and selling of homemade brews. This clandestine activity by "the light of the moon" is made possible by the abundant grain and fruit of the region, and it touches the lives of many mountain folk. The area is also known for its devout, Bible-believing and God-fearing Christians who distance themselves from the "bootleggers." They petition against the sale of alcoholic beverages and are sometimes quick to label as "drunks" those who aren't teetotalers. In Matthew's text these folks would be among the righteous.

Booker was a well-known community "drunk." He had a long-suffering wife, a passel of kids, and a succession of jobs he couldn't keep because of his frequent insobriety. His limited income, which could have been used to fix holes in the roof and feed his family, was too often spent on booze. During a weekend of drunkenness, one of the righteous neighbors from the adjoining ridge came to see Booker and his family. Booker expected a sermon. Instead, he received two bags of groceries including buttermilk, which was a standard Blue Ridge remedy to get one sober. Similar trips followed with sacks of food, but never a sermon. The neighbor invited Booker and his family to come over for a visit and to attend the church on top of the ridge. Booker never came for either, but his children did. Later, as an adult, one of the children expressed deep appreciation for the kindness of the neighbors and the acceptance by the church.

For the day: The neighbor never spoke to others about his kindness to "the least of these"; he knew that being "blessed by the Father" was equally available to Booker and his family as to himself. Look for your opportunity today to follow the neighbor's example.

Prayer: Dear God, help us to receive your gracious blessing by showing acts of kindness to others, that they may also be blessed. Amen.

Wilfred E. Nolen

☙

September 17

How Firm a Foundation

Reading: Matthew 7:24-27

Everyone then who hears these words of mine and acts on them will be like a wise man who built his house on rock (Matt. 7:24).

Meditation: Jesus' story of the wise and foolish builders is addressed to hearers of the Sermon on the Mount. It is a story we may have first learned as a children's song, which starts off with the words, "The wise man built his house upon the rock." Combining music and hand gestures, the song is fun to sing. For adults, however, the story poses a serious question: On what will we build our lives? Some foundations are clearly not up to code—an acquisitive lifestyle, the politics of fear, a self-serving agenda. The list goes on and on. Building our lives on such a basis can only lead to calamity for others and ourselves. By contrast, the words of Jesus provide a firm foundation. His words take their cue from God's vision for our lives. They call us to strive for God's reign, a reign that seeks the welfare of the least and the last, a reign in which compassion and mercy abound, a reign in which status is measured by service. And this reign is the real thing. To build on Jesus then is to build securely. The only question is, Will we? Will we act on what we hear as we listen to Jesus? As Alexander Mack put it in the hymn "Count Well the Cost," let us "have the mind of Christ," whose "word at all times has sufficed."

For the day: In what ways can you identify with both the foolish builder and the wise builder in Jesus' story? What might need to change for you to build more wisely?

Prayer: Gracious God, we acknowledge that we live in a world with many faulty foundations. Help us to learn afresh from the words of Jesus, which offer us a solid and dependable foundation, and then to act on those words as individuals and as a church. Amen.

Richard B. Gardner

September 18

Returning Evil with Good

Reading: Romans 12:9-13, 21

Do not be overcome by evil, but overcome evil with good (Rom. 12:21).

Meditation: It was ten days into the "Shock and Awe" bombing of Baghdad. Those of us in Christian Peacemaker Teams had entered Iraq five months earlier, asking ourselves the question, "What would it take to stop a war for a change?" Now, with U. S. troops on the outskirts of Baghdad, Iraqi security assumed that anyone from the U. S. still in the city was working with the CIA. We were ordered west toward the Jordanian border, three hundred miles away.

We passed the burned-out chassis of pickup trucks and buses and saw U. S. fighter jets in the air on either side of the road. Passing the village of Rutbah on a bombed bridge, we apparently picked up some shrapnel in the rear tire of our taxi. Four kilometers further that tire blew and we were in the ditch, all five injured, and the first two cars in our caravan didn't look back for another forty-five minutes!

An eastbound Iraqi driver stopped, hollered across the median of the six-lane highway, "Can I help?" He loaded us into his car and took us back to a first aid room in Rutbah. There they assured us that it did not matter if we were Christian instead of Muslim, Usonian instead of Iraqi. They started to bandage our wounds.

I was last. I think they were doing triage and thought I wouldn't live, with my head split open and my body drenched in blood. As the doctor sewed up my head wound, he said, "Three days ago a U. S. pilot bombed and destroyed the children's hospital here in Rutbah." Then it hit me: for this physician, I was the enemy! I am alive today because he saved the life of his enemy!

For the day: You can be surprised. We can be surprised.

Prayer: Graceful God, grant that we might love as much as our enemies.

Cliff Kindy

September 19

Living in Harmony

Readings: Romans 12:14-21; Philippians 2:1-8

Bless those who persecute you; bless and do not curse them (Rom. 12:14).

Meditation: One of my greatest joys is helping believers to identify their spiritual gifts. Our uniqueness is God's plan to enrich the body of Christ and we are all needed. But God also uses our different gifts to refine us. The very gifts that bless the Body also predispose us to see, interpret, and react differently. Just when we are ready to throw a party to celebrate ourselves, we find that walking in harmony requires us to lay aside our own perspective so we can see another's. This is frustrating. Why aren't you upset with what upsets me? Why can't you see what needs to be done like I can? Why can't you see the real issues? Why do you talk when you need to act? Why don't you care about people's feelings? Does God's perspective even interest you? Ouch. Our gifts enrich us, but they also separate us. I don't think it is a stretch to view these dynamics as persecution. In congregational life, we may agree about doctrine and mission, but in the daily process of working and worshiping, we struggle and often marginalize each other. And Paul is clear. He urges us past merely tolerating, to blessing, honoring, and preferring. We are to make wide spaces for those whose perspectives have stepped on our last nerve! And why would we want their gifts to have more space when there's not enough room for ours now? Because the likeness of Christ will be worked in us.

For the day: Today you can follow Jesus in laying aside your unique perspective—when you feel misunderstood, dismissed, overlooked, unappreciated, accused, judged, ignored, controlled, manipulated, undermined, or forgotten.

Prayer: Father, I want to walk in harmony with my brothers and sisters. Challenge me when I think that my gifts and contribution are too important. Give me the courage and humility to bless and honor those I do not always understand. Amen.

Susan L. Eikenberry

ℐ

September 20

Inheriting a Blessing

Reading: 1 Peter 3:8-15

Finally, all of you, have unity of spirit, sympathy, love for one another, a tender heart, and a humble mind (1 Pet. 3:8).

Meditation: In *The Living Bible* paraphrase, 1 Peter 3:8 reads this way: "And now this word to all of you: You should be like one big happy family, full of sympathy toward each other, loving one another with tender hearts and humble minds." "One big happy family" is an interesting parallel for "unity of spirit." Is it really possible for a family, whether based on biology or faith, to live together happily in unity of spirit?

God must laugh at our use of the word *possible*. Could it be that God is as incredulous at us for questioning the possibility of unity as we are at God for expecting unity?

The words in Peter make it plain. If we were to truly follow the guidance given in scripture, unity would be possible. So rather than being a question of ability, it's a question of desire. Do we really desire to live as one big happy family? Too often that desire is conditional, based on whether or not the family agrees with us on point X, Y, or Z.

"Do not repay evil for evil or abuse for abuse; but, on the contrary, repay with a blessing. It is for this that you were called—that you might inherit a blessing" (1 Pet. 3:9, 10). What if the blessing is the built-in motivation to work at creating and maintaining unity? Our families, our local faith communities, our denomination, and indeed the world would certainly be blessed if we would strive to live in unity.

For the day: Choose to approach one difficult person today with love, sympathy, a tender heart, and a humble mind.

Prayer: God, help me release my stinging words, anger, indignation, and desire to be the unchallenged expert. May I choose relationship over isolation, grace over perfection, and love over ambivalence.

Becky Ullom

A

September 21

Inside and Outside

Reading: Matthew 5:1-16

. . . let your light shine before others, so that they may see your good works and give glory to your Father in heaven (Matt. 5:16).

Meditation: It's a basic component of life, and attested to in Scripture throughout. We all know it to be true. What we do on the outside is a result of who we are on the inside. In this greatest of all sermons, Jesus begins with the inside of us. Meekness, mercy, and purity all lead to inward happiness. But these inward qualities or attitudes will also show up in our outward behavior toward others. The behaviors of showing mercy and making peace are powerful expressions of our inner character and have an equally powerful impact on others. Salt is salty, and it speaks of the inner character of who we are. But our saltiness also has an outward impact as we are the salt of the earth. Light shines out, and it is descriptive of the outward expression of what we do and the effect we have on our world. But our light must emanate from the Spirit of Christ that resides on the inside. Emptiness on the inside results in a life of outward uselessness. However, if our lives are lived in this inside-out order, our good deeds are recognized as having come from the Father who receives the glory!

For the day: Take time to consider who you are on the inside, and then determine to make the necessary heart adjustments for maximum impact in our world and in the lives of others.

Prayer: Lord, help me to be like Jesus. May the qualities of his life be seen in me. Thank you for the happiness that comes from seeking you and your kingdom. May my life be a blessing to someone today. Father, let me live to give you glory and seek my neighbor's good. Thank you for allowing me to join you in your work! Amen.

Kenneth D. Hunn

September 22

Power, Prestige, and the Awesome Dating Life

Readings: Philippians 2:1-11; James 3:13-18

Do nothing from selfish ambition or conceit, but in humility regard others as better than yourselves. Let each of you look not to your own interests, but to the interests of others. Let the same mind be in you that was in Christ Jesus (Phil. 2:3-5).

Meditation: The values of the world and the values of the kingdom of God tend to be in conflict, don't they? Some pastor friends and I had a good laugh over an article claiming people could be drawn to ministry due to the power, the prestige, and the awesome dating life. Yet all laughing aside, for us in the Anabaptist traditions, I believe this temptation is very real. The temptations to be "big fish in small ponds," to keep a surname that is recognized for generations, to wield the power over financial decisions of a congregation or denomination—these and many others are alive and well in our fellowship. All of us from the denominational head, elders, deacons, pastors, board members, to Sunday school teachers, secretaries, pianists, janitors, every member and attendee—if we claim to be Christians—must examine our motivations for being involved. Can you imagine the world, can you imagine the church, where we all live by kingdom values and not by selfish ambition? It's a beautiful image and the dating life isn't all that bad either.

For the day: Make a list of all the ways you would like to be or are involved with the ministry of your church or denomination. Examine your heart and make a list of the reasons why you are involved. Share your lists with a friend who will pray with you and help keep you accountable to the example of Christ.

Prayer: God of all compassion and grace, search me and know me. Let my life be guided by the example of your Son and the wisdom of heaven. Forgive me when I seek my own recognition over yours. You are the reason I am here, and you deserve all the glory and the praise. Amen.

Brandan E. Liepelt

September 23

Back to the Future of the Church

Readings: Matthew 18:1-5; 1 Peter 2:1-3

I'm telling you, once and for all, that unless you return to square one and start over like children, you're not even going to get a look at the kingdom, let alone get in (Matt. 18:3 The Message).

Meditation: Years ago I saw the popular movie *Back to the Future*, where the plot involved the main character, Marty McFly, going back in time to fix the past—so that the future

378

would be the way it was *supposed* to be. Making sure the future would be the way it was *supposed* to be was also on the minds of the disciples. When asked about it, Jesus responded in Matthew 18:4 (*The Message*), "Whoever becomes simple and elemental again, like this child, will rank high in God's kingdom." I am sure the disciples felt the same way about that response as you do now. What does it mean to become like a child again? Does Jesus want us to be ignorant of the knowledge and wisdom we have acquired in our adulthood? Certainly not! We are being told that our spirit must be constantly restored to the health and wholeness of our childhood. The unfortunate truth is that often stiffness and atrophy come with the aging and scarring of our spirits after a lifetime of walking with God through this broken and seeking world. In Peter's letter to struggling Christians, he gives us advice that guides us well back to wholeness, "So clean house! Make a clean sweep of malice and pretense, envy and hurtful talk. You've had a taste of God. Now, like infants at the breast, drink deep of God's pure kindness. Then you'll grow up mature and whole in God" (1 Pet. 2:1-3 *The Message*). Occasionally we hear of people claiming to have found the fountain of youth; Peter tells us that if we go back two thousand years to Jesus we can discover anew the fountain of a youthful spirit that will take the church into its future.

For the day: Knowing that God loves you and forgives you, ask God to help you sweep from your soul any malice, pretense, or envy that yields hurtful ways in your life. Then enjoy the youthful energy, vision, and hope that comes from your renewed spirit.

Prayer: Oh Healing and Restoring God, I confess that sometimes I confuse the wisdom of the ages with the pessimism and callousness that can come from age. I want to be part of the future of our church, not just a weathered member of its past.

Restore unto me the joy of my salvation and renew a right spirit within me. In Jesus' name, Amen.

Catherine B. Spire

September 24

Conformed or Transformed?

Readings: John 12:20-26; Romans 12:1-2

Those who love their life lose it, and those who hate their life in this world will keep it for eternal life (John 12:25).

Meditation: Through the years Brethren have emphasized nonconformity to the world. In the twenty-first century the strident voices of secular society surround and bombard us through a multitude of media. "Life's all about you!" the voices scream. "You're entitled. Power. Possessions. Wealth. Comfort. Pleasure. Acclaim. Everything you want. Right now. Demand it. Grab it. Consume it. Flaunt it."

Once when I found enough quiet to hear myself think—or perhaps it was to hear God speak—I recalled a shadow box on my mother's kitchen wall. Many kinds of beautiful seeds were artfully displayed in the box. Snug, smug, and secure, the seeds basked in self-glory. One day a powdery film clouded the glass of the shadow box. Weevils had invaded the display. Some seeds had been completely devoured. Other seeds were empty shells—the latent life within them forever lost. Buried in the earth, each of those seeds could have produced much fruit with new seeds to continue the cycle of life.

We are like those seeds. If we conform to the world's call to pamper and protect life, we will lose it. But there's good news. A calm, gentle voice calls us to another way: Let your life be transformed. Commit your life to Christ. Bury yourself in a loving, caring community of faith. Give your life in selfless service to those in need. Others will see Jesus through you; and you will be with God eternally. That's Life!

For the day: Be still. Listen. Where and how is Jesus calling you to serve "for the glory of God and your neighbor's good"?

Prayer: Loving and merciful God, set me free from selfish individualism. Embed me in a fellowship of Christ's followers. Make me a loyal servant through whose words and deeds others find your grace and love. Amen.

Geraldine N. Plunkett

⌀

September 25

Serving Fearlessly

Reading: Matthew 10:24-33

A disciple is not above the teacher, nor a slave above the master; it is enough for the disciple to be like the teacher, and the slave like the master (Matt. 10:24).

Meditation: Sometimes it would be nice to sit around and just learn the good stuff about discipleship. Just soak it up and enjoy all that new-found knowledge. Perhaps the course could be titled "The Amazing Road to Discipleship." But I guess that wouldn't be real discipleship, because that would be like studying to be a doctor and never seeing a patient. The real test in the Christian life comes when we have to put the course into action. To live out what we so bravely said yes to in the classroom. We are often tempted to believe that answering Jesus' call to follow him, living in relationship with him, somehow or another creates for us a zone of acceptance, a zone of comfort, so that we will not have to live with the challenges that Jesus had to live with. Unfortunately, fear often surfaces. Oh, how fear can paralyze any action on behalf of our faith, especially when we must face the challenges of everyday living. You know the situations: Should I speak up when someone gossips about another person at work? Do I allow an unethical situation to just slip by this once? Perhaps when we struggle and fear grips our ability to do what we believe is right, then we need to see ourselves in the company of Jesus and all the disciples that claim him so that we can speak and act boldly on his behalf. Fear is a powerful thing that can lead us down the road of losing our integrity and, most importantly, our relationship with Jesus Christ.

For the day: As a disciple of Jesus Christ, combat any fear that might limit your ability to witness to your faith.

Prayer: O God, as a servant of Jesus Christ, help me today to see my value and place in the work of living out my faith with conviction. When any fear surfaces, may your presence sustain me. Amen.

Dale W. Dowdy

September 26

Serving One Another

Readings: 1 Peter 4:7-11; Romans 12:4-13; 1 Corinthians 12:1-11

Whoever speaks . . . whoever serves is to do so . . . that in all things God may be glorified . . . to whom belongs the glory and dominion forever (1 Pet. 4:11 NASB).

Meditation: When we recall that Peter's first letter was written to God's people who were scattered with no place to call home, we can appreciate the significance of his writing. He instructs them in how to live and serve in the knowledge that the end of things is near. Today's church is certainly living in end times, so Peter's instructions are insightful for us, too. Such times call for sound judgment and a sober mind. Why? So we can pray. "The effective prayer of a righteous man can accomplish much" (James 5:16 NASB). Effective service must begin and be sustained with prayer.

Our service is to be characterized by fervent love for the brethren, that is, acting toward our brothers and sisters in their best interest. Such love overlooks personal failures and seeks to provide what another needs. In the circumstances of Peter's day, it very likely required the practice of gracious hospitality, the sharing of what one possessed and another needed. That remains a grace worth practicing today.

God's people are stewards (trustees) of his grace gifts. As in Peter's day, twenty-first-century Christians are to use those gifts—whether speaking or serving—in ministry to one another. How? With the strength God gives. We are not able, but he is (Phil. 4:13). Why? Obviously, to meet one another's needs, but ultimately, so that God will be glorified throughout eternity through Jesus Christ, whose servants we are.

For the day: Are you—and I—using the gifts God has given us to serve his people and to glorify him?

Prayer: God, teach us to be people of prayer, known by our love for our brothers and sisters and our faithful ministry to each other, serving in your strength and bringing glory to Jesus.

Jesse B. Deloe

_∅_

September 27

The Last Will Be First

Readings: Matthew 20:1-16; John 3:17

And so it is, that many who are first now will be last then; and those who are last now will be first then (Matt. 20:16 New Living Translation).

Meditation: A little boy was at a restaurant with his mother. When the waitress asked for their order, the mother told her what she and her son wanted. At this point, the waitress deliberately turned to the boy and asked him to confirm his choice. When she left, he turned to his mother and said, "Wow! She thinks I'm real." The parable of the vineyard workers in Matthew 20 reminds us of the tremendous love God has for all his children. In addition to the lesson about those who push to the front of the line, it tells us that he is willing to go beyond fair to welcome folks into the kingdom. It's likely that those not hired by the end of the day were less desirable workers. Perhaps they were weak, disabled in some way, or lacked the motivation to show up early in the morning. But, when they said yes to the owner, they were rewarded in the same way as those who had it together. We often believe that because we're feeling insignificant or aren't at our best, God's favor toward us is diminished. Today, may you know that all of God's blessings are yours regardless of your place in line. Even when you've failed to meet the challenges of the day or find yourself at the far end of the line, he thinks you're real.

For the day: Remember that you don't have to have it all together to receive God's blessings. Even when we consider ourselves to be among the less desirable, we get the full measure of his love.

384

Prayer: Father, thank you for your abundant love no matter how far short we fall. We rejoice at your goodness to us even when we find ourselves at the end of the line. Thank you for your passion for those who feel insignificant or less desirable.

John Shultz

September 28

Surrender

Reading: Mark 10:23-31

Jesus said, "Truly I tell you, there is no one who has left house or brothers or sisters or mother or father or children or fields, for my sake and for the sake of the good news, who will not receive a hundredfold now in this age—houses, brothers and sisters, mothers and children, and fields with persecutions—and in the age to come eternal life" (Mark 10:29-30).

Meditation from our past: Just two things in the higher spiritual life,—TRUST and OBEY; surrender and faith, surrender of all. Brethren, have you ever taken an inventory of everything that belongs to you—your clothes, your books, your time, your talents, your voice, your friends, your houses, your lands, your cattle, your children, your parents, your wishes, your hopes, your fears,— have you ever done it, and have you made a quit-claim deed of the whole business, without reserve, to the Lord? Have you surrendered everything that belongs to you, so far as you are concerned, over to the Lord? If you have not done that, I beg of you, do it. Get alone with God the first chance you get and ask yourself solemnly, "Am I willing from now on to let God have control of my life in everything?" "Am I willing to let him manage my time,

my occupation, my business? Am I willing? WILLING?"
And then, when you have surrendered, do you believe he
will? Do you believe he will take it? Are you trusting him
moment by moment, day by day, and hour by hour, that
he is taking, and using, and when you get into a pinch,
can you and will you trust him that he will bring salvation out of the difficulty? —*Albert Cassel Wieand*

From Two Centuries of the Church of the Brethren: Bicentennial Addresses
at the Annual Conference, held at Des Moines, Iowa, June 3-11, 1908.
Brethren Publishing House, 1909, pp. 176-77.

For the day: Consider what you would be willing to give up
for Jesus. How great is your trust?

Prayer: Am I willing, Lord, to surrender all? I believe. Help
my unbelief. Amen.

The Development and Work of the New Community

September 29–October 26

*E*ven if . . . outwardly one could not live together but rather be quite scattered, one here, and another there, yet pure love will not be parted or scattered, but rather through the wind of the Spirit blow the fire of love quickly to all places where there is need and do everything together.

Michael Frantz (1687–1748)

       ℘

September 29

Hands-on Ministry

Reading: 1 John 1:1-4

*[T]his life was revealed, and we have seen it and testify to it
(1 John 1:2a).*

Meditation: In 1983 the North Liberty Church of the
Brethren in Indiana caught a vision that inspired the congregation. A new, low-income housing complex had brought new
neighbors into town. Single moms, disabled folks, struggling
families, lots of children. How could a small church reach out
to these new neighbors? The answer came as simply "The
Christmas Project." The congregation had many gifted wood-
workers among the men. And there were many women talented in the areas of sewing and crafts. What if they produced
toys for the parents to give to their children? The men met one
night each week at one man's wood shop. The women worked
at church. By Christmas time the congregation had produced a
wonderful assortment of gifts. Parents were invited to come
and choose items for their children. Many eyes were wide and
tear-filled as they looked over the gifts. People who might
never have shared in door-to-door evangelism ministered with
joy in the toy-making project. It is not an exaggeration to say
that nearly everyone in the congregation got involved in one
way or another. It was hands-on ministry!

 John begins his letter by saying that he has heard and seen
and even touched "the Word of Life." John was making a case
for folks to listen to his words about Jesus. But when a follower of Jesus *sees* the need in the face of one of Christ's dear children, *hears* a vision for making a difference in Jesus' name, and
gets his or her *hands* involved in ministry—this opens the door

to true fellowship with God and Christ the Son! As John says in verse 4, and as the North Liberty folks would echo, this makes joy complete!

For the day: How might you *see*, *hear*, and *touch* the Word of Life today?

Prayer: Word of Life, help me *see* with your eyes today. Help me *hear* your call upon my life. Guide my *hands* that they might be about ministry for you today! Amen.

Larry M. Dentler

September 30

Living in Hope

Reading: Acts 2:22-35

But God raised [Jesus] up, having freed him from death, because it was impossible for him to be held in its power (Acts 2:24).

Meditation: It is good news in a nutshell. Death is feeble in the face of the power of Jesus Christ. God freed him from death, Peter insists. And he continues in verse 33 with the proclamation that Jesus, having received the promise of the Holy Spirit from the Father, has poured it out for his followers to see and hear. And that is our reminder that as we receive that gift of the Holy Spirit, we too can know the power that is stronger than death. We live in a death-obsessed culture. Some take gigantic risks to defy their fear. Many devote themselves to avoiding the reality of aging. The media offer a smorgasbord of products to achieve that goal. And when we die, we have the option of asking the undertaker to create an image of the way we were at age forty. But that is clearly not what Peter means when he speaks of the impossibility of death holding

Jesus in its power. Instead, it is the availability of the Spirit's power, as verse 28 tells us, to make known to us the ways of life—make us full of gladness with God's presence. It is not just the power of God to face death without fear, but the power of God to live free from crippling anxiety over what tomorrow will hold. Why waste time fretting? Instead, live in hope. Watch the continual unfolding of God's promise. Imagine what wonders will yet unfold.

For the day: Greet each day on tiptoe, never knowing how God will exhibit the Spirit's power in you and in those around you. Believe in life.

Prayer: Generous God, continue to open my eyes to the evidences of your life-giving power. Focus my attention on the amazing possibilities in each day as I accept the gift of your Spirit being poured out upon me. Amen.

Joan G. Deeter

◯

October 1

Living in Fellowship

Readings: Acts 2:37-47; 1 John 5:1

Then they that gladly received his word were baptized: and the same day there were added unto them about three thousand souls. And they continued steadfastly in the apostles' doctrine and fellowship, and in breaking of bread, and in prayers (Acts 2:41-42 KJV).

Meditation: Pentecost was a marvelous day. The Holy Spirit of God had come to dwell within his people. By the Spirit's power thousands had heard and responded to the gospel. But the benefits of Pentecost did not end that day. The joy of the day was continued through the fellowship of those who had received the Holy Spirit. They had a common experience, which would bond them together. The Spirit's work within each one led them to give of their means and their talents for the good of each other. Today we can share our common experience as recipients of God's gift. We have not only a precious past to share, but also an even more glorious future. As members together in Christ Jesus, we can share in prayer, the ordinances, service, study, and worship. We have become brethren and sisters in the family of God. Our fellowship is more than the tasks that we accomplish together; it is the attitude of shared love that we have in our hearts and minds. How can we fulfill our individual and corporate tasks to the glory of God and for the good of our brothers and sisters? Together we can move from the baptismal stream toward heaven's gate as we labor together doing the task we have before us.

For the day: Today think of the benefits of salvation not only as it applies to yourself, but also as it applies to those who have shared the same experience. Enjoy that shared experience through fellowship.

Prayer: Our Kind Heavenly Father, open our hearts to one another. We thank you for the plan of salvation. We also thank you for those who make our journey more pleasant through our shared experiences. Help us to be good journey-mates. In Jesus' name, Amen.

Milton Cook

October 2

Receive the Holy Spirit

Readings: John 20:19-23; Genesis 2:7; Galatians 5:22-23

. . . He breathed on them and said to them, "Receive the Holy Spirit" (John 20:22).

Meditation: As God so tenderly breathed life into the first human, so now the risen Christ breathes the Holy Spirit into his followers. These are the very ones who felt sad and discouraged for failing to support Jesus in his hour of agony. However, rather than criticizing or condemning them, Christ blesses them with his spirit of peace. In spite of their failings, Jesus confidently breathes on them the Holy Spirit of God, including the power to discern who is forgiven and who not. As believers we can also receive the Holy Spirit into our lives as we realize that every drawn breath is God's gift of life that enables us to practice the spiritual gifts that promote God's kingdom on earth.

We in the West generally fail to see the connection between respiration and health, whereas in the East it has long been known that how we breathe correlates directly with our emotional state and general well-being. We learn to breathe shallowly, using only the upper portion of our lungs as we struggle to maintain the rapid pace of modern living with increasing shortness of breath. It has been shown that consciously taking deep, slow abdominal breaths promotes a feeling of relaxation and tranquility. The inner peace that we then sense can be associated with a feeling of love and joy as we contemplate the blessing of life bestowed upon us by our Heavenly Father. Having this intimate (every breath) relationship with our Creator can give us a carefree attitude to bravely fulfill the mission to which we feel called.

For the day: Try starting the new day by simply becoming conscious of breath, taking a few deep, purposeful breaths before launching into your first practical thoughts. Rather than counting your projects, take a moment to count your blessings and thank God. Also, end the day with conscious breathing as you surrender to the mystery of sleep. Again, you can accompany this with a review of things for which you are grateful, recognizing the comforting presence of the Holy Spirit in every breath.

Prayer: Creator God, help us to know the presence of the Holy Spirit in our lives so that we will become bold witnesses to your forgiving love that is available to all for the asking. Amen.

David Fouts

Octubre 3
October 3 in Spanish

Un Cuerpo en Cristo

Lectura: Romanos 12:3-8; 1ra Corintios 12:27

Porque de la manera que en un cuerpo tenemos muchos miembros, pero no todos los miembros tienen la misma función, así nosotros, siendo muchos, somos un cuerpo en Cristo, y todos miembros los unos de los otros (Rom. 12:4-5).

Meditación: En esta sociedad tenemos hombres y mujeres que por los estudios universitarios que han alcanzado creen que pueden revolucionar al mundo. Por eso tenemos lucha de poder en todos los ámbitos sociales. Esto pasaba en la época de Pablo y en las congregaciones de aquella época. En Romanos 12, Pablo señala unos deberes para el cristiano. No importa cuanto hayas estudiado y cuanto hayas recibido en cuestión económica, la palabra dice que "no puedes o no debes tener mayor concepto de si que el que debes tener." Nosotros somos todos miembros del cuerpo de Cristo. Tal vez, sea las manos, o los pies, o los ojos, por lo tanto todos tienen diferentes funciones. ¿Qué te gustaría ser en el cuerpo de Cristo? ¿Qué función estas dispuesto a ejercer?

Hay tanto que hacer en nuestras comunidades, en nuestras iglesias que nos faltarían miembros del cuerpo de Cristo. Es hora de poner el cuerpo de Cristo a funcionar. Cada uno de nosotros tiene un don, que es un regalo de Dios algo para hacer en la viña del Señor. ¿Qué quieres hacer? ¿Qué dones tienes? Tienes que descubrir tus dones. ¿Te gusta servir? La bíblia dice que es mejor servir que ser servido. Sirve con mucho amor, desinteresadamente y veras cambios en tu vida. Te gusta enseñar? No esperes tener grupos grandes, comienza con uno en tu hogar, o en tu comunidad y hazlo con responsabilidad. En tu oración pregúntale qué El desea de ti y recibirás respuestas a través de la palabra de Dios.

Pensamiento del día: Comprender lo que es el cuerpo de Cristo nos hará mejores servidores de El.

Oración: Señor, somos tan volubles que a veces no podemos comprender qué grande que eres y lo que quieres hacer de nosotros. Perdónanos y ayúdanos a responderte.

Isabel Martinez

October 3

One Body in Christ

Readings: Romans 12:3-8; 1 Corinthians 12:27

For as in one body we have many members, and not all the members have the same function, so we, who are many, are one body in Christ, and individually we are members one of another (Rom. 12:4-5).

Meditation: In society today we have men and women who think that because of their university studies, they can change the world. Because of this, we have power struggles in every social area. There were similar struggles during Paul's time and in the congregations of that time. But in Romans 12, Paul says there are responsibilities for all Christians. No matter how much we have studied or how much wealth we have, God's Word tells us, "You [are] not to think of yourself more highly than you ought to think." We are all members of the body of Christ, serving as Jesus' hands, feet, or eyes, each of us having a different purpose. Ask yourself this question: What function of Christ's body am I willing to assume?

There is much to be done in our communities and congregations everywhere, in places where we are missing some of the parts of the body of Christ. As a member of Christ's body, it is time to get the body of Christ in working order again. We each have a gift from God, something to do in the Lord's vineyard. What do you want to do? What gifts do you have? You must discover your gifts. Do you enjoy service? The Bible says that it is better to serve than to be served. Serve with love, without reward, and you'll see changes in your life. Do you like to teach? You don't need a large group; you can begin by starting a Bible study group in your home or in your community and do it with commitment. In your prayer ask God what it is that he wants from you and receive answers through the Word of God.

For the day: Understanding the body of Christ will help you become a better servant.

Prayer: Lord, we speak so much that sometimes we fail to comprehend how great you are and what you desire for us. Forgive us, and help us respond to you.

Isabel Martinez de Figueroa

October 4

Spirit/Life

Readings: Acts 2:1-13; John 3:8

And suddenly a sound came from heaven like the rush of a mighty wind, and it filled all the house where they were sitting (Acts 2:2 RSV).

Meditation: The Hebrew word *ruach* can be translated wind, breath, or spirit. The Greek word *pneuma*, as in the word *pneumatic* (filled with air) can also be translated wind, breath, or spirit. Someone who is spiritually stimulated has received inspiration. Breathing in is also called inspiration. When someone dies, we might say "they expired." Yet to expire also means to breathe out. John's Gospel says Jesus bowed his head and gave up his spirit. Matthew reads, "Jesus cried . . . with a loud voice and yielded up his spirit." Luke says, "He breathed his last." Spirit is breath is life. At Pentecost, the mighty wind indicated strong presence of Spirit/Life. It was audible, just like the spirit/winds that hovered creatively over the abyss in the beginning. Something big was happening, a new creation was emerging. That creation was the church of Jesus Christ. Spirit-born, the church must forever remain spirit-filled to survive. Without the presence of the Holy Spirit, our souls begin to expire, discipleship becomes slavish drudgery, and congregations weaken. Three hundred years ago our forebears were spirit-led as they entered the baptismal waters of the Eder River at Schwarzenau, Germany. We are no less in need of Pentecost-power for the living of our Brethren faith today!

For the day: On the birthday of the church, God caused the Holy Spirit to pour out blessings, gifts, and graces. Meditate upon the gifts that you earnestly desire. Consider what gifts and graces are present or lacking in your congregation or fellowship.

Prayer: Be silent for some minutes. Pay attention to the rise (in-spiriting) and fall (ex-spiriting) of every breath. Note your dependence upon the atmosphere around you. Find in each breath the hint of life and of death. Express gratitude for life, so fragile and yet so vital. Pray for inspiration, thanking God for the gift of the Spirit. Ask God for a new outpouring of the Spirit upon Christ's body, the church.

Wallace B. Landes

October 5

Seized by Prayer

Reading: Acts 2:13-21

This is what was spoken through the prophet Joel: "In the last days . . . God declares . . . I will pour out my Spirit upon all flesh . . ." (Acts 2:16-17a).

Meditation: The early Christian movement has been characterized as a community seized by prayer. Certainly this description fits the Luke-Acts story.

Being seized by prayer became powerfully real for me recently. In late summer a worship service was held at our pastor's home (the invitation read liturgy first, food second). Near the end of worship our pastor announced that she had been diagnosed with late stage cancer and that she was ready for whatever God wanted. Through an image of poet Mary Oliver, our pastor's words were like an iceberg between the shoulder blades. Grief and tears ripped through us like that cyclone of Spirit-breath described in Acts. Then we began to pray. In a month our pastor was dead. We miss her so much. We are still praying, now from a place of loss and gratitude for who she was.

The church has always said *both* that the Spirit comes where she will *and* that the gift of Spirit is given to all who are baptized. The Spirit cannot be manipulated; yet, she is close at hand. The Spirit is in the wildly profligate love of God *and* in the ordinary, incarnate grandeur of God's presence.

We are called to be open to Spirit wherever, however Spirit may come (or has already arrived). Such a way involves practice, a persistent, patient willingness to be astounded, amazed, graced amidst the joy and wonder of life even if (especially if) suffering and loss are in the wonder. Such a way is to be seized by prayer.

For the day: Take time today to drink in and be amazed by God's presence.

Prayer: *Come, Holy Ghost, Creator blest, Vouchsafe within our souls to rest. Come with thy power and heavenly aid, and fill the hearts which thou hast made* (attrib. Rabunus Maurus).

Tom Kinzie

℘

October 6

No Other Name

Reading: Acts 4:1-12

There is salvation in no one else, for there is no other name under heaven given among mortals by which we must be saved (Acts 4:12).

Meditation: After I lost more than sixty pounds in 1983, I took up running as a hobby. Eventually that meant buying the proper gear: shoes, shorts, and, of course, shirts. I found a nice running shirt in a discount bin, but it had a Nike logo on it. This was at the beginning of what I call the Loco Logo Craze. People were willing to pay big bucks to wear clothing with the logo of the manufacturer so prominently displayed that they became, in effect, walking billboards. The logo bugged me. Nike wasn't paying me to advertise their company. Why should I do their work for them? So I took a razor and very carefully scraped away the symbol.

I'm picky about what symbols I display. I have four or five Brethren t-shirts and that's about it. For me the essence of being Brethren is being willing to follow Jesus by studying scripture together. We might enjoy a particular brand of potato chips or motor oil, but there is salvation in no other name under heaven except Jesus Christ. That's it.

For the day: Walk around your home, look through the drawers, glance at the bumper stickers on your car. What do they say about your allegiances? If someone were to accuse you of being Christian, is there enough evidence in your home or on your person to convict you?

Prayer: You, Creator, are the Lord, our God. We shall have no other gods before you. In your name, you who are the One God, we worship and serve. Amen.

Frank R. Ramirez

October 7

What We Have Seen and Heard

Reading: Acts 4:13-22

[F]or we cannot keep from speaking about what we have seen and heard (Acts 4:20).

Meditation: It isn't the Brethren way to be loud and proud. At least among those of us with a heavy dose of German in our blood. We would rather serve Jesus in our own quiet and dedicated way. For most of our three-hundred-year history this emphasis on walking the talk (with a heavy emphasis on the walk) has served us well. But we also know that there are moments in a faith journey when it simply isn't possible to walk and not talk. One such moment is when we are told to "be quiet" about our faith. For it is one thing to choose to quietly and humbly serve Jesus; it is another thing entirely to be told to "not speak or teach at all in the name of Jesus" (v. 18), as Peter and John were told by the Sadducees in the Jerusalem Council. Peter and John responded to this threat in the only way that a person can who has walked with Jesus and experienced the love and forgiveness of God healing broken lives. They gave their testimony: "We cannot keep from speaking about what we have seen and heard" (v. 20). Some 1700 years later our Brethren ancestors who gathered along the banks of the Eder River made the same public testimony. Facing a similar threat of persecution, they would not, they could not, keep silent about what God was doing in their midst. Most of us, of course, have been blessed with the freedom to serve God in the quiet way we Brethren seem to prefer. But we too have walked with Jesus; we have seen the love of God healing broken hearts and lives. And we know what Peter and John knew, what Alexander Mack and our Brethren ancestors knew: there are moments in our lives when it isn't enough just to walk the talk; there are moments when we simply cannot keep from speaking about what we have seen and heard.

For the day: Remember with gratitude the courage of those who would not keep silent about what Jesus was doing in their lives.

Prayer: Gracious God, may we be ever amazed at what your love has done, and is doing, in our lives and in our midst. May

your Spirit give us a voice to tell all what we have seen and
heard.

Jay H. Steele

Octubre 8

October 8 in Spanish

Hablar con todo denuedo

Lectura: Hechos 4:23-31; San Juan 13:12-17

*Y ahora, Señor, mira sus amenazas, y concede a tus siervos que con
todo denuedo hablen tu palabra . . . (Hechos 4:29).*

Meditación: Jesús nos dice en su palabra "Porque ejemplo os
he dado, para que como yo os he hecho, nosotros también
hagáis." Pues nosotros nos sentimos muy agradecidos de Dios,
por las tantas almas que han sido salvas y las que restan por ser
salva a través de este credo que es el "Nuevo Testamento."
Aunque hoy en día los primeros Hermanos fundadores no
estén pero nos han dejado el ejemplo. Nos sentimos agradecido
por Dios que nos ha dado la oportunidad de pertenecer a la
familia de la fe. Pues nosotros debemos trabajar, seguir el ejemplo, anunciar las buenas nuevas de Cristo, plantar nuevas iglesias, trabajar en conjuntos, enseñar a nuestros hijos el ejemplo
de Cristo (Tim. 3:5).

Nos dice el Salmista: Bienaventurado el varón que en la ley de
Jehová está su delicia, y en ella medita de día y de noche (Salmo
1). La meditación en su palabra nos hace vivir confiado, con la
confianza que tenemos en el Señor podemos lograr la meta que
tenemos. No es con nuestro esfuerzo, sino con la fuerza del
Espíritu Santo. Jesús dijo recibiréis poder cuando haya venido
el Espíritu Santo. Pues debemos de depender de él para tener
éxito en nuestra meta, y la meta es ganar el mundo para Cristo.

Porque para esto fuimos llamados. Al padecer Cristo por nosotros, dejando como ejemplo para que sigamos su pisada (1 Pedro
2:21). Cristo nos ofrece vida eterna para los que las siguen y los
que le aman. Cristo sufrió por nosotros una muerta tan cruel,
pagó el precio por nosotros, y fue un precio de sangre.

1 Timoteo nos dice, pero por esto fui recibido a misericordia
para que Jesucristo mostrace en mi el primero toda su clemencia
para ejemplo de los que habrán de creer en él para vida eterna.

Para el día: Por eso debemos de decirle al mundo que la misericordia de Dios sigue en vigencia. Y que Cristo salva, Cristo
sana, Cristo liberta, Cristo viene, y que un día volverá a buscar
a su pueblo, para gozar de una vida eternal, Jesús dijo alentaos
unos a otros con esta palabra.

Oración: Dios mió gracias te doy por tu perdón, ayúdanos
también a alcanzar aquellos que no te conocen. Para decirle que
tú los quieres perdonar en el nombre de Jesús. Amen, Amen.

Anastacia Bueno

October 8

Speak the Word Boldly

Readings: Acts 4:23-31; John 13:12-17

*. . . and grant to your servants to speak your word with all
boldness (Acts 4:30).*

Meditation: Jesus tells us in his Word, "I have set you an
example, that you also should do as I have done to you" (John
13:15). We are grateful to God, on behalf of so many souls
who have been saved and those who remain to be saved
through this creed which is the New Testament. Although the
founding Brethren are not with us today, they too have left an

example. We are grateful to God that he has given us the opportunity to belong to the family of faith. We ought to follow the example of our forebears and announce the good news of Christ, plant new churches, work in harmony, and teach our children the example of Christ (see 1 Tim. 3:5).

The psalmist tells us: "Happy are those . . . [whose] delight is in the law of the Lord, and on his law they meditate day and night" (Ps. 1:2). The meditation on the Word enables us to live trustingly, with confidence in the Lord that we can reach our goal. This is not with our strength, but with the strength of the Holy Spirit. Jesus said that we would receive power when the Holy Spirit arrives. And so we too must depend on the Spirit in order to have success in reaching our goal. The goal to which we have been called is to gain the world for Christ. Christ suffered on our behalf, giving us an example in order that we would follow in his footsteps (1 Pet. 2:21). Christ offers eternal life to those who follow in his footsteps and who love him.

Christ suffered such a cruel death for us, paying the price for us with his blood. "But for that very reason I received mercy, so that in me, as the foremost [sinner], Christ Jesus might display the utmost patience, making me an example to those who would come to believe in him for eternal life" (1 Tim. 1:16).

For the day: In this way we should tell the world that the mercy of God continues to be valid and that Christ saves, Christ heals, Christ liberates, Christ is coming again, and that one day he will return to seek his people, in order that they might rejoice in eternal life. Jesus said to encourage one another with this word.

Prayer: My God, I give you thanks for your forgiveness. Help me to reach out to those who do not know you in order to tell them that you want to forgive them in the name of Jesus. Amen! Amen!

Anastacia Bueno

♂
October 9

Breaking Community Trust

Reading: Acts 5:1-11

But a certain man named Ananias, with Sapphira his wife, sold a possession, and kept back part of the price, his wife also being privy to it, and brought a certain part, and laid it at the apostles' feet (Acts 5:1-2 KJV).

Meditation: O, my! Can't you just see the headlines in the *Jerusalem Daily News*: MEMBERS OF THE NEW CHRISTIAN CHURCH DIE AFTER BEING CHARGED WITH EMBEZZLEMENT.

No doubt the impact of this announcement rolled like a tsunami through the community of faith. Within the camp of fellow believers, there was a breach in the bond that had encircled the family. Trust was broken. The impact was enormous!

As members of the body of Christ, together we comprise the community of faith, the family of God. In any community, the quality of relationships found therein leans heavily upon the issue of trust.

Trust is a powerful quality that undergirds the ups and downs that every family unit faces. Trust preserves, but like a cancer, broken trust will siphon away the strength, unity, and vitality of the body. Broken trust will bring discouragement to the weak, downward momentum to the backslider, and additional winds of adversity to the faithful. Trust is a product of faithfulness in our relationships. Trust takes time to build, but it can be reduced to ashes with one selfish, careless choice or action. When we allow our selfish pursuits to rise above our concern for the community of faith or the reputation of the kingdom, like Ananias and Sapphira, we will breach the precious bond of trust!

For the day: Life is full of choices that affect you, your family, and the community of faith. Have your actions today reinforced or eroded that precious bond of trust?

Prayer: Heavenly Father, help me to remember that I am part of a community and to lay aside self for the good of the kingdom. By your grace, let my faithfulness add another brick to that solid wall of trust. In Christ's name, Amen.

Jim Meyers

☙

October 10

Obedience

Reading: Acts 5:27-39

We must obey God rather than any human authority. The God of our ancestors raised up Jesus . . . as Leader and Savior. . . . And we are witnesses to these things, and so is the Holy Spirit whom God has given to those who obey him (Acts 5:29b-32).

Meditation: The parent pleaded, "Please listen to me." The child responded with crossed arms and a pout. "Do as I say; it's for your own good," continued the parent.

"You're not the boss of me!" responded the child. Regardless of the issue or the person's age, there is often resistance to obedience. And yet . . .

Those who trace their spiritual roots to Schwarzenau are aware of the importance of obedience. Our forebears gathered to read God's Word and discern God's will. Their decision to be rebaptized in the Eder River was in opposition to civil and church authority. Based on Jesus' model of reconciliation and self-giving, they risked punishment and their lives in order to love God and serve others. The ordinances that we practice today (believers' baptism, love feast, and anointing for healing) are acts of obedience from the New Testament.

In a society that values individualism and self-interest, there is One who offers an alternative. In a time when faithful leadership is needed, there is One who empowers those who will obey and follow. As disciples in the twenty-first century, let us affirm, "Yes, God, you *are* the boss of us!"

For the day: *Take my life and let it be, consecrated, Lord, to thee. Take myself, and I will be ever, only, all for thee* (Frances R. Havergal).

Prayer: Gracious God, in you we find our redemption and hope. When distracted by competing priorities, help us to obey your voice and focus on your will for our lives. When faced with difficult decisions, open us to the Holy Spirit, the powerful presence promised to those who obey you. In Christ's name we pray. Amen.

Julie M. Hostetter

October 11

Believing, Trusting, and Proclaiming

Reading: Acts 8:1-8

That set off a terrific persecution of the church in Jerusalem. The believers were all scattered throughout Judea and Samaria. All, that is, but the apostles. Good and brave men buried Stephen, giving him a solemn funeral—not many dry eyes that day!

And Saul just went wild, devastating the church, entering house after house after house, dragging men and women off to jail. Forced to leave home base, the Christians all became missionaries. Wherever they were scattered, they preached the Message about Jesus. Going down to a Samaritan city, Philip proclaimed the

Message of the Messiah. When the people heard what he had to say and saw the miracles, the clear signs of God's action, they hung on his every word. Many who could neither stand nor walk were healed that day. The evil spirits protested loudly as they were sent on their way. And what joy in the city! (Acts 8:1-8 The Message).

Meditation: In a world where we are constantly moving, how can one be expected to proclaim the Message wherever he/she is? All of us can proclaim the Word, even scattered as we are. Philip proclaimed the Message and miracles occurred. Today miracles still happen and believing in God is just the first step. Believing, trusting, and proclaiming his Message will lead to joy wherever one may be.

For the day: Spread the Word of Jesus to those around you. Put your trust in the Lord, that he will care for you, keep you safe, and bring you joy, scattered wherever you may live.

Prayer: God all-powerful, teach me to be a true believer and a missionary of your Word. Help me to proclaim your Message in this fast-paced world, bringing purpose, peace, and joy to my life. Show me the miracles you have in store for me wherever you choose to send me.

Rebecca M. Lipscomb

October 12

Open to the Spirit . . .
Ready for Change

Reading: Acts 6:1-15

And the twelve called together the whole community of the disciples and said, ". . . select from among yourselves seven men of good

407

standing, full of the Spirit and of wisdom, whom we may appoint to this task" (Acts 6:2-3).

Meditation: "Ask me to do anything, but don't ask me to change." Have you ever heard anyone say that? Change can be hard to cope with, especially when it challenges the accepted and familiar way of doing things. We resist change when it threatens our comfort zones and the status quo.

In this story of the early Jerusalem church, a big change takes place. In order to care for the needs of the Greek-speaking widows who have been neglected during the daily distribution of food, the Apostles respond by asking for help. Instead of becoming defensive and drawing the lines more tightly around their authority, they seek to broaden the base of leadership by asking the community to call out seven men, "full of the Spirit and wisdom," to take over the big job of administering the benevolence programs of the congregation. This wasn't change for the sake of change. Adding seven people to the leadership team freed the Apostles for their ministries of teaching and evangelizing, as well as caring for the needs of the rapidly growing community.

For the day: While the vision and insights of our Schwarzenau ancestors have shaped our communities of faith throughout the past three hundred years, our way of doing and being the church today is different than it was in 1708. How has your congregation changed it's vision for ministry in order to meet the needs of your community? How do you discern new directions for ministry within your congregation and within your own life?

Prayer: God of old and new, steady us with courage and insight to walk with you into new ways of sharing the gospel with a hurting world. Grant us compassion as we discern our neighbors' needs, and give us the resolve to leave behind our fear of change so that they will know your love. Amen.

Michelle Grimm

☞

October 13

Revelation of Jesus Christ

Reading: Galatians 1:11-17

God . . . through his grace, was pleased to reveal his Son to me . . . (Gal. 1:15).

Meditation: How did you learn about Jesus? Writing to the Christians in Galatia, Paul tells them that his knowledge of Jesus Christ came by way of a dramatic revelation. (The most detailed account of that revelation is found in Acts 9:1-9). For many of us, however, getting to know Jesus takes place gradually, even quietly. For some of us it begins happening when we are children.

I remember visiting in the home of some friends and found myself sitting beside their son, a pre-schooler. Somewhat timidly he began showing me a book that was obviously one of his treasures. It was a Bible story book and, through the first half of it, the little fellow merely turned the pages without comment.

Finally he came to a picture that was a special favorite. "There's the baby," he said. He turned the page, and his eyes began to light up. "Here's Jesus in the temple." And from there to the end of the book, each picture was accompanied by a comment or a question. It was clear to me that he had begun a relationship with the one who stands at the center of the Christian faith: Jesus Christ.

Which is to say that there are revelations and there are revelations. Some people learn to know Jesus through reading about him, some have a dramatic moment of conversion, others hear stories of Jesus in Sunday school or at home. The "how" it happens isn't all that important. But no matter what form the revelation takes, the word Paul uses to explain it still applies—grace.

For the day: Try to remember how you learned to know Jesus. What songs or stories or pictures of him can you recall? Who were the people that introduced you to Jesus? Have you ever thanked them? If you haven't and you still can, why not do so?

Prayer: God, I thank you for my own revelations of Jesus Christ. Amen.

Kenneth L. Gibble

October 14

God Praised Because of Me

Reading: Galatians 1:18-24

They only heard the report: "The man who formerly persecuted us is now preaching the faith he once tried to destroy." And they praised God because of me (Gal. 1:23-24 NIV).

Meditation: God can and does use any of us to transmit his message, show his love, and demonstrate his power. Of all the most unlikely candidates to be God's dedicated and humble servant for Jesus, Paul must have ranked right at the top. Not even those disciples closest to Jesus, who now carried on his ministry, could believe Paul's conversion. So with the wisdom of God's timing, Paul waited three years before going to Jerusalem to confer with Peter and James. And in just fifteen days, he received their blessing and began his unprecedented ministry among the Gentiles, and, as they say, the rest is history. How many saintly people down through the ages has God used to accomplish his purposes, people who were considered unlikely by their peers! How shortsighted we are not to see God working in and through people around us whom we may judge unworthy! And how unprepared we may be when that distinct call comes to us to be God's messengers of love and encouragement or caring correction for a brother or sister. How blessed we would be to be able, like Paul, to say, "They praised God because of me!"

For the day: Be open to the ways God can work through you today, and give thanks to God for those around you who bring a blessing to you this day.

Prayer: O God of infinite possibilities, humble me to keep my agenda from superseding yours. Strengthen me to be more than my hesitant expectations. Purify my desire to be more like you, so that I may see through your eyes and so that I may love in the perfection of your love. In the name of Jesus Christ, Amen.

Donald L. Parker

October 15

Knowing Jesus

Reading: Philippians 3:2-11

Yet whatever gains I had, these I have come to regard as loss because of Christ. More than that, I regard everything as loss because of the surpassing value of knowing Christ Jesus my Lord (Phil. 3:7-8a).

Meditation: It is one thing to believe in Jesus Christ as your Lord and Savior. It is quite another to say firmly that you *know* Jesus, your Lord and Savior. Yet, as Christians, this intimate knowledge must supersede any of our other earthly relationships or desires.

Think of the people you know from work, school, childhood, adult Bible study, church, extended family. In what ways did you get to know each person? Was it through common interests, circumstance, same social circles, or chance?

Getting to know Jesus is a choice we make. It comes from prioritizing our lives to create space for Jesus, in much the same way that we make time for our friends and family. But this is not just about a healthy prayer and devotional life. More importantly, knowing Jesus comes from greeting him in all parts of our lives.

Many of us are eager to show our love for our family members, spouses, and close friends through physical touch and verbal communication. It is in these relationships that we practice skills necessary for deepening our spiritual connection with God. We can celebrate the joy of our faith in Jesus; there is no greater thing.

For the day: Be aware of strangers that you meet today; find Jesus within each of them and, thus, get to know Jesus better.

Prayer: God, forgive the ways that I have tried to claim human credit for life that can only come from you. As I learn to know you more nearly, I pray for humility and grace in my relationships. Amen.

Angela Lahman Yoder

♫

October 16

A Friend Like Barnabas

Reading: Acts 9:22-31

When he had come to Jerusalem, he attempted to join the disciples; and they were all afraid of him, for they did not believe that he was a disciple. But Barnabas took him, brought him to the apostles, and described for them how on the road he had seen the Lord, who had spoken to him, and how in Damascus he had spoken boldly in the name of Jesus (Acts 9:26-27).

Meditation: After Saul's transformation on the road to Damascus, he went from persecutor to proclaimer. As a persecutor, Saul literally hunted down the followers of Jesus. I can almost imagine Saul as a bounty hunter with a stack of "Most Wanted" posters, searching for disciples, leaving a wake of fear and death.

Once a believer, Saul (soon to be Paul) used the same intelligence, knowledge of the law, and determination to bring others to Christ. But, for the disciples, Saul the "bounty hunter" was hard to forget, to forgive, and to trust.

The transformed Saul needed the supportive network of the disciples. Even with his many gifts, he could not do it alone. Along came Barnabas, who introduced Saul to the apostles and convinced them that Saul was transformed. By believing in Saul, Barnabas opened a door that helped bring Jesus to the Gentiles.

How often do we encounter others needing a friend? We are not all blessed with the gifts of Paul, but we can all be a friend like Barnabas. We can support our pastors and their families. We can open the door and invite others into the community of believers. We can simply help someone in need.

For the day: Look for people needing a friend today. See how you can lend a hand or open a door that may lead to a transformation in their lives.

Prayer: God, you are always there for me. When rejoicing, when hurting, when longing, you are there. I pray that I can be present for others today. That I can be a friend who opens doors, gives a hug, encourages, and supports others. Amen.

Roy Winter

October 17

The Freedom of Contentment

Reading: Philippians 4:10-20

I have learned to be content with whatever I have. I know what it is to have little, and I know what it is to have plenty. In any and all circumstances I have learned the secret of being well-fed and of going hungry, of having plenty and of being in need. I can do all things through him who strengthens me (Phil. 4:11-13).

Meditation: "Friends, I am happy and grateful, and I find life very beautiful and meaningful. Yes, even as I stand here by the body of my dead companion, one who died much too soon, and just when I may be deported to some unknown destination. And yet, God, I am grateful for everything" (Etty Hillesum, Sept. 16, 1942, from *Etty: The Letters and Diaries of Etty Hillesum, 1941-1943*).

The Apostle Paul wrote the words of Philippians from prison. Etty Hillesum wrote many of her words from a concentration camp in the shadow of her eventual deportation to Auschwitz and the gas chamber (she died on Nov. 30, 1943). Both knew something of the freedom in contentment. We are not free because we can control our external circumstances. Real freedom comes when we know our sufficiency, our contentment in God, in life, no matter the external circumstances. So often as we face the chaos of our days, we focus our energy on managing, on trying to get on top of it all—reasserting our need for control. St. Paul and Etty offer another way—draw close to the presence of God in all things. Such presence in the day anchors our contentment and frees our living. In that freedom we can step lightly toward the myriad of ways we can embody the light, love, and peace of God's presence in our day.

For the day: Do something today for a neighbor. Contribute in some small way to justice in your community. Stay in your contentment; live in your freedom.

Prayer: Just and Merciful God, take my love of you and help it burn bright for others. May the circle of my contentment include all I do for my neighbor and the justice I proclaim for the world. Amen.

Glenn Mitchell

October 18

A Light from Heaven

Reading: Acts 9:1-9

As [Saul] was . . . approaching Damascus, suddenly a light from heaven flashed around him. He fell to the ground and heard a voice saying to him, "Saul, Saul, why do you persecute me?" (Acts 9:3-4).

Meditation: Talk about obsessive-compulsive people! Saul fits the personality type of people you may know—the kind of people who take everything they do quite seriously. When was the last time it took more than fifteen minutes to make your bed? Or when did you drive ten hours in bad weather so that you could keep a promise? Going overboard is what Saul did best. No job was left half done. As a student under the well-respected Jewish scholar of the Hillel school, Saul was well versed in Jewish law and gave great respect to the authority of tradition even when it conflicted with the law of the land. This zealot of a Jew had a passion that would make any teacher proud. He had all the makings of a great man: intelligence, drive, principle. He was fully in his element in his most recent mission to hunt down all those who belonged to this new movement called "the Way." Kicking up dust on the road to Damascus, it was quite a shock for him to be stopped dead in his tracks by a blinding light from heaven and hear a voice saying, "Why do you persecute me?" Saul in his religious zeal was blind to the horrible evil he was committing by threatening and persecuting those early converts to Christ's Way. In the strictest sense this passage isn't about seeing Jesus in others. It is about the conversion story of one of Christianity's most prolific writers. But perhaps seeing Jesus in others is a good point to emphasize so that we might do the same today. For those of us who really get into doing church, may we be careful not to miss seeing Christ in others.

For the day: Allow yourself to see the world in a new light.

Prayer: Forgive me, Lord, when my passion causes me to stumble and lose sight of your Way. Grant me the grace to lay aside self-centered thinking and turn my gaze upon your radiant purpose with the joy of a long overdue vacation.

Steven W. Bollinger

October 19

God's Chosen Instrument

Readings: Acts 9:10-21; 2 Corinthians 5:17-21

But the Lord said to him, "Go, for he is a chosen vessel of Mine to bear My name before Gentiles, kings, and the children of Israel" (Acts 9:15 NKJV).

Meditation: We often admire individuals who excel at a skill we practice. A young athlete will mimic a popular professional: his appearance, style, habits, and, hopefully, ability. It is even more likely that we marvel at those who have perfected a talent that we do not possess. I stand in awe of accomplished musicians. It is quite impressive to hear a saxophone player make melodious sense of all those buttons on his instrument, or a trumpeter produce such a vast array of sounds from a three-buttoned horn, and to listen to a pianist sort the musical notes written on the page with the left hand doing this and the right hand that. What talent, what skill that each musician must possess to command their instrument this way.

Likewise, we are impressed all the more with God, who has accomplished what no man has, who has performed the impossible in reconciling sinful man to himself through Christ and has transformed each believer into a new creation. Ananias was stunned that God could accomplish this feat in Saul of Tarsus; he found it nearly unbelievable. As a master musician picks up his instrument and plays to the delight of his audience, so God chose Saul and fashioned him into a sanctified instrument to perform his will and speak the truth to the glory of the Master. Saul preached the Christ, that he is the Son of God. All who heard were amazed not because of who Saul was, but because of who God had made him to be.

For the day: God has chosen you with intent and for purpose. Permit him to achieve his goals in your life as you live it for his glory.

Prayer: Lord, I give myself to thee. Wash and make me clean, holy. Use me, I pray, for thy glory. Lord, I thank you for choosing me.

Shawn M. Ostrander

October 20

More Folks Than You Think

Reading: Acts 1:15-26

. . . (together the crowd numbered about one hundred twenty persons) . . . (Acts 1:15).

Meditation: According to the joke, a minister once had to sit down with a total stranger at a local diner because there wasn't enough room for a single table. The stranger, noticing the minister's collar, began at once to tell him all about his church, what a great place it was, and all the wonderful people who went there.

"What church do you go to?" the minister asked.

"Oh, that white church on top of the hill."

The minister replied, "I've been pastor there for five years and I've never seen you."

"Well," replied the stranger, "I never said I was a fanatic."

The fact is, there are always more people in the fellowship than we realize. When we think about Jesus and his "church," we think of twelve apostles and their Master, but the New Testament paints a picture of a large group of men and women eating, drinking, and witnessing together. We don't even have names for a lot of these people. I'll bet that most of that one hundred and twenty believers didn't know everybody else's name. But God knew them and had called them into one fellowship—even a few who didn't consider themselves fanatics.

Your church probably has a few folks who consider themselves members, but not "fanatics." Maybe you've lost track of some of them. What's stopping you from reaching out to one of them today?

For the day: Glance through your church directory. Focus on the name of someone who is no longer attending. Pray for that person and for yourself. How will you reach out to that person today?

Prayer: Generous Lord, your fellowship is larger than we can imagine. Help us to reach out to each other in your name. Amen.

Frank R. Ramirez

October 21

Go, Proclaim the Good News

Reading: Matthew 10:1-15

Then Jesus . . . gave them authority . . . to cure every disease and every sickness. . . . As you go, proclaim the good news, "The kingdom of heaven has come near" (Matt. 10:1, 7).

Meditation: I recently read an article about "custom harvesters," folks who travel across the wide expanses of the West cutting wheat on a contract basis, following the wheat as it ripens. They travel from state to state, harvest until the job is done, and then they move on to the next field. Sound familiar?

Our scripture extends some blunt instruction that challenges what we normally consider as rational. Jesus tells the disciples (and us, by implication, as modern-day disciples) that they/we are to travel from town to town and have the "authority to cure every disease and sickness." And, as if that mind-bending charge weren't enough, Jesus directs them/us to take no money or provisions—not even a change of clothes! Come on, Jesus, cut us a break!

Now, I'll concede that most of us do not feel led to live a nomadic, penniless existence. But I won't so easily concede our

419

call to proclaim the good news. What would happen to us if we saw ourselves as "custom harvesters" when it comes to proclamation?

Would we be able to free ourselves from an "all or nothing attitude," which ends up in paralysis and inaction, and focus on those things that we do, and do well?

Might we complain a little less about the way others are proclaiming the gospel and focus a bit more on how we are called to proclaim it?

Would we take a step back to see what is really happening in our communities and the world and have the courage to hear anew how we are being called?

For the day: Given your interests, strengths, and God-given gifts, think about the ways that you can be a "custom harvester."

Prayer: God, I pray for the strength, confidence, and courage to boldly use the gifts you have given me to proclaim the good news. Amen.

Greg Davidson Laszakovits

October 22

Watch Out for Wolves

Reading: Matthew 10:16-25

See, I am sending you out like sheep into the midst of wolves; so be wise as serpents and innocent as doves (Matt. 10:16).

Meditation: Like the sergeant in the classic police drama *Hill Street Blues*, Jesus tells his disciples to be careful out there! The world can be a rather unfriendly place, and disciples must expect their share of hostility. It's bad enough to have a wolf in the midst of the sheep. But Jesus sends the sheep into the midst of wolves! Some wolves who cross our path may be hostile to faith as such. Naming the name of God is enough to provoke them. Other wolves, however, turn on us because we get in their way, because we stand in solidarity with the weak on whom they prey, because we threaten their ability to do what wolves do. Thus it was for Jesus, and thus it continues for his followers. So, what are we to do? Jesus' counsel is twofold: Be wise as serpents and innocent as doves. In other words, keep your eyes wide open, and keep your nose clean! Don't give wolves a chance to seize the advantage. Along with his advice, Jesus also offers assurance: You don't go it alone. Just when the wolves think they have rendered us speechless, the Holy Spirit gives us voice to say what needs to be said. And no matter what comes, the faithfulness of God will more than match our own.

For the day: How or where have we faced wolves at earlier times in the Brethren story? With what wolves are we contending at the present time?

Prayer: Faithful God of Jesus, give our faith enough of a cutting edge to provoke the wolves. And then, O God, walk with us through whatever hostility may come, and grant us the wisdom and courage we need. Amen.

Richard B. Gardner

October 23

Following Jesus; Finding Life

Readings: Matthew 10:32-39; 8:18-22

Those who find their life will lose it, and those who lose their life for my sake will find it (Matt. 10:39).

421

Meditation: For peace-loving Brethren, today's passage is hard to hear. First there's Jesus' language about being one who brings a sword—and with a direct reference to family relationships! And then there's "Whoever loves father or mother more than me is not worthy of me." So much for "family values" in this passage! Jesus' teaching proclaims a higher value than the bonds and love of family, placing highest value on the believer's love for God, for Jesus. If love for family is greater than love for God, then we've missed Jesus' point. And there are no "but first let me . . ." possibilities on this journey, as proposed by would-be followers in Matthew 8:18-22. Following Jesus is first. Finding life, the abundant life, may put us at odds with family members who don't also put discipleship first. Discipleship with Christ is radical, counter-cultural, and calls for our lives to be turned upside down in the most unexpected ways. Offering ourselves fully in Christian discipleship means letting go of the old life so that we can receive something greater, the new abundant life in Christ. There's a real paradox and mystery in this hard teaching.

For the day: Notice through your day times when you must choose between life with Christ over some other priority—such as family, worldly security, status, approval, job.

Prayer: Jesus, you call me to a lifelong process of finding life in following you. Help me to deepen my commitment to discipleship today. Help me to hold all the relationships in my life in balance in light of this high calling. Give me courage to follow. Amen.

Connie R. Burkholder

Outubro 24

October 24 in Portuguese

Seis Conselhos

Leitura: 1 Timóteo 4:6-16

Não negligencies o dom que há em ti (1 Tim. 4:14).

Meditaçao: Paulo escreve para seu discípulo Timóteo e, como um mentor, lhe dá seis conselhos. O primeiro é para exercitar a fé, não seguindo "lendas pagãs e tolas" e para progredir na fé (vv. 7, 8). O segundo é para ser modelo para outros, sendo um exemplo na maneira de falar, agir, no amor, fé e pureza (v. 12). Em terceiro lugar é para estudar a Palavra de Deus. O quarto é para pregar e ensinar o evangelho (v. 13). O quinto é para não descuidar do dom que tem, dado por Deus pela imposição das mãos do presbitério. O último, para cuidar de si mesmo.

A conseqüência de se observar estes conselhos é que se "salvará tanto você, como os que o escutam." Não é uma questão de escolha pessoal, não é algo que deve ser considerado como acessório para a vida cristã, um *addendum* para dar mais cor ou melhor reputação. Isto tem implicações eternas.

Algumas vezes nós nos esquecemos que há mais valor no estudar a Palavra de Deus que em ouvir fofocas e histórias ou lendas que não acrescentam valor. Temos que ter em mente que devemos ser exemplo para os outros, estudando e pregando a Palavra de Deus. Acima de tudo, devemos considerar que há um dom especial de Deus para aqueles que receberam a imposição de mãos do presbitério. Paulo não dá detalhes ou mais informações sobre o assunto. Ele somente afirma que isto acontece.

Por último, pede que cuidemos de nossos corpos e saúde. Há uma conexão entre a vida espiritual e a forma como cuidamos da nossa vida física.

Para o dia: Viver hoje dedicando tempo para estudar e pregar a Palavra de Deus, evitando lendas e fofocas, sendo um exemplo para os outros e cuidando do corpo e da saúde.

Oração: Senhor de todas as graças, perdoa-me por todas as vezes que dei ouvidos às lendas e fofocas. Dá-me a graça de andar na luz da tua Palavra, sendo exemplo para outros e dá-me também o cuidado por mim mesmo e pela minha saúde.

Suely Zanetti Inhauser

October 24

Advice with Eternal Implications

Reading: 1 Timothy 4:6-16

Do not neglect the gift that is in you . . . (1 Tim. 4:14a).

Meditation: Paul writes to his disciple Timothy and, as a mentor, he gives him six pieces of advice. The first is to exercise his faith not by following myths and old wives' tales, but by training to be godly (vv. 7, 8). The second is to be a model for others, being an example for the believers in speech, life, love, faith, and purity (v. 12). Third is to study the Word of God (v. 13). Fourth is to preach the gospel and to teach (v. 13). The fifth is to not neglect the gift that was given to him through a prophetic message when the body of elders laid their hands on him. The last is to care for himself.

The consequence of observing all this advice, for Timothy and us, is that we will save both ourselves and our hearers. It is not a matter of personal choice; it is not something that can be considered as an accessory to Christian life, an addendum to give it better color or nice reputation. This advice has eternal implications.

Sometimes we forget that it is of more value to study the

Word of God than to be involved with gossip, tales, and other stories that are worthless. We need to remember that we must be an example for others, studying and preaching the Word of God. Above of all, we need to remember always that there is a special gift from God for those who have received the laying on of hands from the body of elders. Paul does not give further or detailed information about it, he just says that it has happened through prophecy.

Last, Paul tells us to care about ourselves and the health of our bodies. There is connection between spiritual life and the way we care for our physical life.

For the day: Live today dedicating time to studying and preaching the Word of God, avoiding tales and gossip, being an example for others, and caring about the health of our bodies.

Prayer: Lord of all grace, forgive me for all the times I listened to tales and gossip. Give me the grace to walk in the light of your Word, being an example for others; and give me also the grace to care for myself and my health.

Suely Zanetti Inhauser

October 25

The Song Goes On

Readings: Acts 28:25-31; Matthew 28:16-20

He . . . welcomed all who came to him, proclaiming the kingdom of God and teaching about the Lord Jesus Christ with all boldness and without hindrance (Acts 28:30-31).

Meditation: What a marvelous finish to the Acts of the Apostles! In essence, the writer says it isn't finished! The story isn't complete, only becoming more so. The calling isn't fulfilled,

425

only in process. Apostle Paul continued to welcome, to proclaim, and to teach. In essence, the song of the story goes on.

As I entered the room, my spiritual director met me, extended his hand, and welcomed me with a smile and a greeting. The next hour was a refreshing time—listening, speaking, and discerning—and I left recognizing several new insights into my ministerial journey. The spiritual direction was not finished. It had only begun as I took with me fresh resources that centered my continuing ministry. God's story goes on through me.

When Jesus Christ was crucified, his executioners considered his life finished. Nothing more. Then, with Christ's resurrection, the song continues. The Book of Acts accentuates this continuing music. Despite persecution, imprisonment, challenging debates, martyrdom, and more, the song goes on. Nothing eradicates the Gospel of Jesus Christ. Human response, environmental catastrophes, and material devastation may impede the movement of the gospel, but that never stops the song. The closing verses of Acts sound like a new musical score for the Great Commission in Matthew: "As you are going, make disciples . . . baptizing . . . teaching. . . ." In Acts, this commission unfolds in living reality as the song goes on.

The song of God's good news in Jesus Christ continues whenever and however you and I welcome people and offer the presence of God in Jesus Christ.

For the day: How will your life be a welcoming presence to others? How will your faith community continue to announce and teach the good news of Jesus as it welcomes others into its life?

Prayer: O Holy One, as you surround me with your presence today, let that presence welcome others into my life. As you unveil the good news of Jesus Christ, may I share its story, its love, and its relevance with those I welcome. Amen.

Robert E. Alley

October 26

Set Apart for God's Work

Readings: Acts 13:1-12, 42-43; Matthew 7:15-20

The Holy Spirit said, "Set apart for me Barnabas and Saul for the work to which I have called them" (Acts 13:2).

Meditation: Sometimes life is confusing. How do we decide who to trust, who to vote for—whose voice is the one to trust?

When Rosa Parks sparked the Civil Rights movement in 1955 by refusing to give up her bus seat in the colored section to a white man, the Montgomery, Alabama, bus strike was born. During the first few hours of the incident, the people looked to the clergy of that town for leadership. The clergy gathered everyone to the Holt Street Baptist Church to introduce their newly chosen leader—the new preacher in town, twenty-seven years old. His name was Dr. Martin Luther King, Jr. One woman attending that service, Idessa Redden, who never before had become emotional in church, cried out during the service, "Lord, you have sent us a leader!"

Not always do we get a message sent directly from the Holy Spirit to guide us. Not always are the trusted leaders easy to distinguish from the popular ones who may let us down. The test that Jesus gave to the disciples is to "know them by their fruits." "A good tree cannot bear bad fruit, nor can a bad tree bear good fruit" (Matt. 7:18). Over the course of time, the hidden qualities will come to light.

The work of the Spirit is to set apart each person to do what is his or her calling. Not all in Montgomery were called to sit down on the bus. Some were called to hand out fliers about the boycott, some were called to provide car rides, others were called to sell home-cooked food to finance the movement. All were called to bear good fruit. As evangelical social justice leader Jim Wallis says, "If it isn't good news, it isn't the gospel."

For the day: You are the perfect person to do what God has set you apart to do!

Prayer: Help me to set apart time today to offer to God the good things that I have been given. Amen.

Gail Erisman Valeta

The New Community Faces Growing Pains

October 27–November 30

*U*p, sons of men! The time is right
To ward off ills impending,
For Christ himself joins in the fight,
His righteous realm defending.
To do this, have the mind of Christ
His Word at all times has sufficed.

Alexander Mack, Sr. (1679–1735)

$\mathscr{D}$

October 27

God's Magical Love

Reading: Acts 8:11-25

They followed [Simon] because he had amazed them for a long time with his magic. But when they believed Philip as he preached the good news of the kingdom of God and the name of Jesus Christ, they were baptized, both men and women. Simon himself believed and was baptized. . . . Peter and John placed their hands on them, and they received the Holy Spirit (Acts 8:11-13, 17 NIV).

Meditation: I once had the privilege of seeing David Copperfield in a live show. Sitting two rows back from the stage, I watched intently as he made himself disappear before my eyes. I didn't stop looking for one second, and yet he was suddenly behind me. I was amazed at this magical feat.

Even Simon, who practiced magic, was amazed when he saw the power of God in Philip. Philip's ministry led Simon, as well as other men and women, to believe in Jesus. It wasn't the magic that they saw; rather, it was the saving, healing power of Jesus working through his faithful servant. The coming of the Holy Spirit onto believers is so powerful that healing and hope is transmitted to others.

We too can amaze others when the power of God is revealed through us. We do not need to use trickery or showmanship to share Jesus. We just need to show them Jesus' love. No amount of flashy magic or human work is as powerful as the love of God expressed through the life and death of Jesus. When God fills us, transforms us, and uses us to touch others, something more powerful than any magic transforms the world around us. We just have to believe in the power of the Holy Spirit in our lives and ministry.

For the day: Share the love of God with someone in your life. It's a simple process that doesn't require special talents or abilities, just that you believe. The touch of God that you share may transform a life today.

Prayer: God of wonder, God of love, I pray for your healing power to permeate this world full of pain and hurt. Use me today as your instrument of healing for those around me. I know all I need is my faith in you to show your love to others. Give me courage, give me relentless faith, and give me your touch today. Amen.

Vickie Taylor

October 28

Being There

Reading: Acts 8:26-38

"How can I [understand]," he said, "unless someone explains it to me?" So he invited Philip to come up and sit with him (Acts 8:31 NIV).

Meditation: One of the more overlooked spiritual gifts may be that of accompaniment. As we trek along our often difficult spiritual journeys, few things can be more meaningful than having a trusted guide traveling alongside us. For some people, a dedicated pastor fills this role. For others, it occurs in the more formal relationship with a spiritual director. For many, it comes simply via a friend who is willing to be a bit vulnerable with us. The Ethiopian eunuch introduced to us in Acts engaged in such vulnerability when he encountered Philip in the desert. Philip, listening to the Holy Spirit, made the invitation, and this royal official accepted, asking Philip to teach him about the scripture he was reading. It led to deeper learning, a baptism, and, presumably, a changed life. Princeton Theological Seminary professor Kenda Creasy Dean describes this ministry of presence in the context of youth ministry as "fidelity." It is a community where "members are . . . committed to 'be there' for one another, and in so doing they make visible the faithfulness of Christ," she writes. This often isn't easy. Dean notes that "extending ourselves on behalf of others— bearing one another's burdens, especially for people we have never met—does not come naturally." Growing a heart with that sense of mission and compassion requires constant nurturing. We discover that no matter how hard we try, we cannot "be there" enough for others; we can, though, point the way to the One who always will be.

For the day: Think of a friend or neighbor who might need you to bear the presence of Jesus Christ to them in some way. Pray for them, and find ways to "be there" for that person.

Prayer: Meditate on the words of St. Teresa: "God has no body on earth but yours. Yours are the only hands with which he can do his work. . . . Yours are the only eyes through which his compassion can shine forth upon a troubled world."

Walt Wiltschek

October 29

What Are You Waiting For?

Readings: Acts 22:3-16; Micah 6:6-8

You are to be a key witness to everyone you meet of what you've seen and heard. So what are you waiting for? (Acts 22:15 The Message).

Meditation: "Telling everyone" what I have experienced and have seen in my life is fairly difficult, unless it is something I care about passionately. For instance, I admit that I have spent a good part of my life being silent about issues of justice. In the past it has been fine with me if someone else would do it.

Elie Wiesel, winner of the 1986 Nobel Peace Prize and chairman of the President's Commission on the Holocaust, said in his acceptance speech, ". . . I swore never to be silent whenever human beings endure suffering and humiliation. We must take sides. Neutrality helps the oppressor, never the victim. Silence encourages the tormentor, never the tormented. Sometimes we must interfere. . . ."

It must have been something like that for Paul. He realized through his encounter on the road to Damascus that he had no choice. He could not be silent about what he understood about the ministry of Jesus. Jesus spoke and lived out a ministry of caring for the poor and the outcasts. Jesus preached and lived what Micah spoke: "See that justice is done, let mercy be your first concern, and humbly obey your God."

Can you imagine how Paul felt when he heard the inner voice saying, "You are to be a key witness to everyone you meet of what you've seen and heard. So what are you waiting for?"

For the day: You have choices every day. Being silent is a choice. It's time to recognize that silence toward injustice is another injustice. Today look for the opportunity to "interfere" for justice.

Prayer: "Help us to live in truth. Grant that we may never speak or act a lie; that we may never evade the truth, even when we do not want to see it. Grant to us at all times to seek and to find; to know and to love; to obey and to live the truth. Amen" (William Barclay).

Ralph G. McFadden

433

October 30

What a Beautiful Name!

Reading: Acts 11:19-26

. . . and in Antioch the disciples were for the first time called Christians (Acts 11:26b RSV).

Meditation: In an early episode of *Little House on the Prairie*, Mary and Laura Ingalls return home from the first day at their new school with Laura proclaiming: "Nellie Olsen called us *country girls*!" Reassuringly, Ma agrees that they are, in fact, country girls. "But it was the *way* she said it," Laura sulks.

Nellie's intention was to scoff at the newcomers. But cloaked with Ma's wisdom in mind, Mary and Laura return to school the following day, heads held high, smiles on their faces, and wearing their country bonnets with delight.

I fondly remember when I was first called Christian. Christian—what a beautiful name! Christian! To be called as one who follows, who is devoted to, Christ. Christian! One who has made Jesus Savior and Lord of her life.

Some scholars say that Christian was first a term of reproach. Even now, we may find this to be true. Some choose to scoff at our Christlike beliefs and actions.

Upon my confession of Christ as Savior and Lord, just like the early believers, I knew I was a Christian. The world may scoff, but that does not change who I am.

I confess there have been days when I have failed to live up to this name, but God reassures me that I am, in fact, a Christian. Whether or not I wear a bonnet, I will hold my head high, smile, and go into the world knowing who (and whose) I am. Christian! What a beautiful name!

For the day: Have you chosen Jesus? Only then will you be called Christian.

Prayer: Father, I thank you for giving me a special name. I thank you for sending Jesus. I thank you for allowing me the privilege of carrying the name Christian. Help me, by your power, each day to be more Christlike. In Jesus' name, Amen.

Victoria J. Smith

October 31

Seekers Among All People

Reading: Acts 17:22-28

The God who made the world and everything in it is the Lord of heaven and earth and does not live in temples built by hands (Acts 17:24 NIV).

Meditation: On an Easter Sunday afternoon I was catching up with chores at the local self-service laundry. I noticed The Walker pacing out front. Though he would seldom talk to me, he would occasionally accept food from me. I bought a candy bar from the vending machine and walked out to see him. As I approached, I realized that he was in the midst of a heated debate with God. I sat on a nearby bench and listened. No sermon will ever stick with me the way The Walker's words did that day. He gave voice to my dearest hopes, my darkest fears, and my deepest yearning. In very simple, clear, and completely honest terms, he was declaring the fundamental human desire to know and be known. As the moment stretched into minutes, I moved from awareness of my own longing to a profound sense of the nearness of God. The air through which The Walker moved and which formed into words as it moved through him began to take on weight. Feeling both my own yearning and the nearness of the Spirit, I slipped the candy bar into my pocket. I had nothing The Walker needed on this day. He had what I needed and he had come to me both as fellow seeker and as gift. Many years later now, The Walker has gone to his rest. But his witness is alive in me to this day. As the poets still say, "We are all children of God."

For the day: Strive to be aware of the temperature, the smell, and even the taste of the air around you. Let this sensation remind you of the God in whom we live, and move, and have our being.

Prayer: Lord God, source of all, grant that I might be aware of your presence in everything I touch and in every one of your children that I meet this day. Amen.

Jonathan Hunter

November 1

A Worthy Calling

Reading: Ephesians 4:1-6

Lead a life worthy of the calling to which you have been called, with all humility and gentleness, with patience, bearing with one another in love (Eph. 4:1b-2).

Meditation: "She's a saint!" The parents thought Mrs. Gee was a wonderful Sunday school teacher for their young elementary children. Having no children of her own, she spent time weekly with theirs—including a group of squirmy, active boys. The children thought of her as a kind, soft-spoken woman who wore funny hats. In a dimly lit basement classroom, she taught children every Sunday. She told Bible stories, led activities, and sang songs with them. Her husband was a quiet man who served as an usher for every service, warmly welcoming members and visitors to worship. Though neither of them ever chaired committees, served on commissions, or were elected to "high" offices in the church, they led lives of humility, gentleness, patience—and she responded to inquisitive and energetic young ones with love!

Rufus P. Bucher, a Church of the Brethren farmer-preacher and evangelist, was once approached by a young man handing out a tract, "Brother, Are You Saved?" Brother Bucher invited the questioner to come to his home and ask the local hardware merchant, the grocer, his neighbors, and family to answer that question on his behalf (see *The Brethren Encyclopedia*, p. 461). Being saved means living every day a life worthy of the calling to which you have been called.

For the day: Remember those women and men who have modeled what it means to live a life of commitment to Christ and the church.

Prayer: *O God, our help in ages past* . . . we thank you for sisters and brothers who lived lives in faithful obedience to your will and in service to others. *O God, our hope for years to come* . . . give us courage to answer your call by living in humility, gentleness, and patience, showing love to all. In Christ's name, we pray. Amen.

Julie M. Hostetter

$\mathscr{O}$

November 2

Joined and Knit Together

Reading: Ephesians 4:7-16

But speaking the truth in love, we must grow up in every way into him who is the head, into Christ, from whom the whole body, joined and knit together by every ligament with which it is equipped, as each part is working properly, promotes the body's growth in building itself up in love (Eph 4:15-16).

Meditation: It was just a big floppy sock. Trusting the directions, I threw it in the washing machine with a little dish soap and ran it through a wash cycle. Sure enough, when it came out, the individual stitches had disappeared and the fabric was very tight. The floppy wool sock had been transformed into a warm slipper.

As a knitter, I'm often caught by the spiritual applications of my hobby. Learning to "full" yarn opens new insights into the concept of being knit together in Christ. Fulling transforms a loosely knitted piece of wool yarn into a dense fabric that will not unravel, even when cut. Just as the yarn is transformed by the action of the washing machine, so we are transformed and then formed into one body by Christ.

We are connected to each other in many ways, yet just as a plain piece of knitting can be unraveled, we can choose to disconnect ourselves from each other. It is when we are connected to each other through the grace of Christ that we are made into a fabric that cannot be torn apart easily. This is the kind of bonding that we need so that we can work together and support each other as we all mature in our faith.

For the day: Are you open to Christ working in you to help you become more like him? How are you letting Christ work through you to help others to mature?

Prayer: Jesus, thank you for your gift of grace, which transforms me into more than I am on my own. Help me to love you so that I can better love those to whom I am bonded in your name. Amen.

Kate Gandy

⊘
November 3

Dissension and Debate

Reading: Acts 15:1-5

And after Paul and Barnabas had no small dissension and debate with them, Paul and Barnabas and some of the others were appointed to go up to Jerusalem to discuss this question [of circumcision] with the apostles and the elders (Acts 15:2).

Meditation: Paul, in Romans 4, speaks to the issue of law as it relates to circumcision. He directs our attention to two passages in Genesis. The first is about circumcision itself (Gen. 16), and the second is about the promise made to Abram by the Lord regarding a male heir (Gen. 15:1-6). At the time of the promise, Abram was getting old and he and Sarah did not have a son. The Lord promised a son who would produce descendants as numerous as the stars in heaven, and Abram "believed the LORD; and the LORD reckoned it to him as righteousness" (Gen. 15:6). Paul argues that the phrase "reckoned it to him as righteousness" was a statement about Abram's faith. Paul goes on to ask, "How . . . was it reckoned to him? Was it before or after he had been circumcised?" (Rom. 4:10). Paul answers his own questions by saying, "It was not after, but before he was circumcised. He received the sign of circumcision as a seal of the righteousness that he had by faith while he was still uncircumcised" (Rom. 4:10-11). Paul believed the institutionalization of circumcision among the Gentiles placed too heavy a burden on the new church, and the leaders at Jerusalem agreed with him.

Every generation of Christians faces the same types of issues. It is easy to confuse a "sign of the faith" with faith itself. We are tempted to institutionalize our basic beliefs, doctrines, and even our beloved practices, and in so doing, we place needless burdens on people who are starving for the new life offered in Christ Jesus. While laws, traditions, and rules are important, we must see them as "signs" that point toward greater values— the "Glory of God and our Neighbor's Good."

For the day: Consider today that when law is in conflict with the gospel, the law must give way.

Prayer: Gracious God, help us to understand anew that our "good work" is a "sign of faith," but that we are not saved by the *sign*; we are saved by *faith*. Amen.

Allen T. Hansell

✑

November 4

In Higgi

Wsi ke necete tlene hyalatemwe

Tlene Mbelyi Ke Mne: Yesu 15:6-11

Hyalatemwe, tsa ke senata mni mbelyi pade, ke ncete date ye-nje te mbelyi kwa wdunya seke ke tsa ke nji nggereke mambeli hyalatemwe te hya, kala tsa ke nji ngge myi tsemi (Yesu 15:6-8).

Wsi ke zezi: Wenti tsenigwa tsa she zame va mbelyi ke mne Yesu le mbelyi kukule me kazeli tazhe ge vece mbweghe mbe, mbelyi kwa wdunya le vece tla pityi. Bitrus, madi ke mne Yesu, nje mdi kule mbweghe tsenigwa we, a nje mdi ke ge vece hya we, ndzara nje na, ndi ke ge dabe vece hya we. Ba mabeli hyalatemwe tlenete nje, a ba nje ge vece sekwa kwa mne hyalatemwe; kwe nje na, nda ka kele wamara mdi hyalatemwe me mbege nje seke ke mberesa kale. Tumbari, wuri hyalatemwe ke gereke mambeli nje te wamara mdi ke mbresa, tazhe ba hya ndza ka ngwase nje (Galatiya 4:6, 7). Hyalatemwe le zhihwe nje tsa ke mbe nkwa, ndaka kale wamara mdi nje kla nta ala. Ka nta ala hyalatemwe we. Wamara mdi ke mbresa na, mbele

440

hyalatemwe hya pade. Yesu kale, nje hukwa ndza me tlante mbe te, wal ka ka tlante pityi, kala zezi yahudawa we.

Zezi dashe: Temwi na fidlive ta tla pityi gwa na? Hyalatemwe, ke senata mne nee, tlante pityi mne me tsa ve nje. A mambeli hyalatemwe nje ngwe kye he le na.

Adewa: Hyalatemwe ke zhihwi, vwi tara bara senata na, a bara zelete hu nkwa ra nga, tsa ke mbekwa Vwi tara mwa ta zhie ra gere she te paede mbele le denama ra Mambeli ngga. Amin.

Suzan Mark

⌐

November 4

Evidence of God's Work

Reading: Acts 15:6-11

God, who knows the human heart, testified to the [Gentiles] by giving them the Holy Spirit, just as he did to us (Acts 15:8).

Meditation: There was a meeting of apostles and church elders on the issue of Gentile salvation and the necessity of circumcision. Peter, an apostle, was not the chairman of the meeting, he was not the spokesman, he was not there to sum up the talk. But led by the Holy Spirit, he spoke out of the mind of God, saying that everyone is welcomed into God's kingdom by faith alone. For God gave his Spirit to all who believe, to be his sons (Gal. 4:6-7). God's gracious work of salvation welcomes everyone with no discrimination. In God there is no favoritism. All who believe are God's people. Jesus is the only means of salvation—not circumcision as the Israelites thought.

For the day: Do you still value physical circumcision? God who sees our hearts is after the circumcision of the heart. Be guided by the Spirit of God.

441

Prayer: Gracious God, help me to understand and accept your only means of salvation, and help me to tell of it to all people, by the power of your Spirit. Amen.

Suzan Mark

November 5

Whose Way?

Readings: Acts 15:12-21; 1 John 3:23-24

. . . we should not trouble those Gentiles who are turning to God (Acts 15:19b).

Meditation: I have a bumper sticker that says "Think outside the box." The word *box* is superimposed over an outline of the United States. It is a reminder to me that we tend to think *our* way is *the* way, forgetting that Jesus' way calls us to love God and *all* our neighbors.

Most of us have experienced church business meetings where emotions ran high and tough decisions were made. The first church council meeting in Jerusalem was a doozy.

Most of the earliest Christians were Jews. Jews were known for their devotion to one God and their high ethical standards. Circumcision had been the mark of their belonging to God for more than a thousand years. They weren't perfect, but they were a proud people and had good reason to be. So it is not surprising that many believed that those who wanted to follow Jesus should be required to participate in this Jewish heritage.

But Peter, Paul, and Barnabas, though Jews, had a different idea. Each had felt led by God to share the faith with non-Jews. Each had seen non-Jews accept Jesus and receive God's Holy Spirit—and without first being circumcised or becoming students of the Jewish Law.

Two irreconcilable positions. Long and heated speeches. Scripture quoted by both sides. Prayers, both silent and loud. I expect stories were told about Jesus and the Pharisees.

Finally those assembled found not which side was right, but God's way.

For the day: Let's not make it hard for people who are different to join us. Jesus didn't. God hasn't. So let's not either. There is room at the table for all who love the Lord.

Prayer: Lord, your love is all-inclusive and overwhelming. Give us a poke in the ribs or a kick under the table when we start thinking it is up to us to make up the rules and guard the doors of your church.

Linda Logan

℘

November 6

Christ Alive in Us

Reading: Romans 10:5-9

The word is near you, on your lips and in your heart (Rom. 10:8b; see also Deut. 30:14).

Meditation: When my husband, Phil, and I served in Sudan during the war, many people gave witness to the way God's Word was truly alive in them. Mama (title of respect) Esther, a bishop's wife, told us stories of the suffering of her family during the war. Her husband was often absent, serving people in various places, which left her alone to care for the children. When the battle came to their town, she fled with her children to the forest, surviving on whatever they could find to eat. She spoke of her trust in God who helped her "live under the trees." She proclaimed her faith, but it was not from her lips only; it came from deep within her. Her belief in Christ lived in her so that in crisis, as well as in daily life, she had a Source to sustain her.

While we need to use words, the truth of our faith shows in our actions and attitudes, which come forth from our hearts. When Christ is alive in us, we live in the spirit of love and mercy, courage and peace, trust and grace. Christ's love motivates our words and actions.

When we spend time with God in prayer, contemplation, and Bible study, living in God's presence, then the Word comes alive in our hearts. It is that Word which is "on our lips," that belief which is seen in our attitudes and actions.

For the day: Spend time growing in love with God, and let that love spread to those you find difficult to love, so that you can be saved from rootless belief and grow into a faith from the heart and from the Living Christ.

Prayer: Loving God, thank you for your Word, which you offer for all our living. Let it be rooted deeply in our hearts to guide our thoughts, words, and actions in your great spirit of love. Amen.

Louise (Louie) Baldwin Rieman

November 7

Those Who Bring Good News

Reading: Romans 10:10-17

How beautiful are the feet of those who bring good news! (Rom. 10:15b).

Meditation: "Everything looks good!" The surgeon found us in the waiting room after our daughter's surgery. Until that moment, we didn't know what the future might hold for her or for us. But now, the tears flowed. I felt as if I could have anointed this man's beautiful scrub-covered feet with my tears and wiped them with my hair; he had brought the good news that our daughter's life was saved!

And how even more beautiful are the feet of those who bring the life-saving and life-giving good news of Jesus Christ. The incarnation of God came to bring abundant life to all. He came for the poor; he came to free the prisoner and to restore sight to the blind; he came to set the captives free and to let us know that God is at work in our world, even now! His gospel of peace and love is for you and for me and for everyone, regardless of who or where or what we are. And we must be compelled to share that good news so that no one will miss it and everyone will be saved.

Never is the gospel better illustrated than when we stoop to wash one another's beautiful feet at love feast. As our feet are washed, we are humbled to remember our need of God's grace and love. And in washing the feet of a sister or brother, we are offering forgiveness and loving service. We are reminded that there is no distinction—the good news is extended equally to each of us. And we are reminded that we are called to share that good news, for we are the body of Christ—his mouth to speak for him, his hands to work for him, and his feet to go for him.

Just as the surgeon came to the waiting room to share the good news with us, may we share the good news with those who wait for a word of hope and love.

For the day: Are you more concerned about the shoes you put on your feet than about the message they bring to an un-grace-filled world?

Prayer: Gracious God, you have done so much for us through giving your Son, Jesus Christ, for our redemption. Move us beyond our excuses to carry your message of good news to all we meet. Make our feet beautiful!

Pamela A. Reist

ℰ

November 8

Remember the Poor

Reading: Galatians 2:1-10

They asked only one thing, that we remember the poor, which was actually what I was eager to do (Gal. 2:10).

Meditation: Remember the poor. I'm glad that I am part of a church that has taken this commandment seriously. The early Germantown church received special collections for poorer members of the congregation and maintained a "poor book" that listed the recipients of their gifts (*The Brethren in Colonial America*, p. 210). Brethren responded to the needs of members in Virginia and Tennessee who suffered financially as a result of the Civil War *(Annual Meeting Minutes, 1865)*. As the Brethren became involved in foreign missions in India and China, members passionately responded to the needs of those suffering from famine. Following World War I, Brethren raised over $250,000 to support victims of genocide in Armenia. In response to the needs of Europe following World War II, Brethren Service was begun. Brethren continue to respond to the needs of the poor through Brethren Volunteer Service, Emergency Response, Church World Service, and Heifer International. Brethren also reach out to the poor in their communities through food pantries, emergency assistance, and Habitat for Humanity housing projects. Remember the poor—an important instruction for the early church. I'm glad that "remember the poor" is a commandment that is still important for us today!

For the day: Select one way that you can "remember the poor" today. Perhaps it is reaching out to somebody across the world—or maybe somebody next door.

Prayer: God, you call us to be good stewards of the gifts you give to us. Help us not to take your goodness to us for granted. We pray that we will find creative and generous ways to reach out beyond ourselves and "remember the poor." Amen.

Mark Flory Steury

$\mathscr{D}$

November 9

Living by Law or by Faith?

Reading: Galatians 2:11-21

I do not nullify the grace of God; for if justification comes through the law, then Christ died for nothing (Gal. 2:21).

Meditation: Picture this: Peter in Antioch, saying to the new believers who were recently rescued from hopeless heathenism: *We stand as brothers in the Lord! Gentile brothers and sisters, I embrace you as fellow sinners who have found the way to God in Jesus of Nazareth. We stand together here in Christ.* Peter wasn't thinking of the uncircumcised bodies, unkosher meals, unfringed tunics, or their bacon breakfast. He was focused on the Savior and walking on the waves of buoyant faith.

But then the folks from James show up. Peter's focus flashes to the waves of controversy around him. *What will they think? We can't let them see in the houses of these Gentiles. Looks like I better switch gears here and keep those Jerusalem boys happy. After they leave I'll get back to the truth and explain to these new believers what's going on. These men from James have a long and noble history and you can't really expect them to embrace the free-*

dom we enjoy in Christ. The relationship between us and the Jerusalem church is more important than the feelings of these new believers. Splash. Peter's going under.

But Jesus cares now, like he did on Galilee years before. Enter the Apostle Paul, who withstands Peter to his face. The Jerusalem group reluctantly listens to the truth, which they, too, need to hear. The wide eyes of the believing Gentiles begin to brim with tears of gratefulness. Peter weeps bitterly as his heart is struck by the rod of the Chief Shepherd and brought back to the truth of the gospel as he hears Paul say, *Through the law I am dead to the law, that I might live for God. This Christ, (remember we're called Christians here at Antioch) has included us in his death. I stand before you as one who has been crucified. Dead. My old life came to a final close when God included me in the execution of Jesus. Yes, obviously I'm still alive; I'm here talking to you. Yet it's not really me anymore; Jesus Christ lives in me, and my life is lived by the faith of the Son of God, who loved me and gave himself for me. I don't reject or despise God's grace (by pretending to keep the law and please the law-keepers) because I know that if my eternal destiny and good standing with God is based on my keeping of the law, then the awesome Christ who loves me died for no reason.*

For the day: Know that Jesus Christ by his death and resurrection repels the drizzling sheets of fear and the tidal wave of the cancelled condemnation of the law.

Prayer: Dear God, please take the triumph of the cross and magnify it until it reaches all considerations of my mind and emotions. Fill me with faith in this Christ crucified that I might be free from pretense and people-pleasing at the expense of truth. Amen.

Reuben Huffman

November 10

Stepping Out

Reading: Psalm 46

God is our refuge and strength, a very present help in trouble.
Therefore we will not fear, though the earth should change . . .
(Ps. 46:1-2a).

Meditation: In the climactic act of *Indiana Jones and the Last
Crusade*, Harrison Ford is faced with a series of obstacles that
can only be overcome by answering one-line riddles. Once he
understands the answer, he then must journey through the test
in the way described in the riddle. Upon entering the room of
his second test, he faces a floor of varying sized tiles inscribed
with letters. As he studies the floor and the riddle, it becomes
clear that his path is to follow the spelling of the name of God.
When he takes the first step, however, he starts on the wrong
opening letter to reveal that the floor is false and only the correct tiles are supported.

The world of the psalmist is a tumultuous one, seemingly
falling apart around the worshipers. Yet, in true liturgical fashion God speaks to the people and offers a firm grounding. "Be
still and know that I am God." This is a God whose very voice
orders and stabilizes the shifting sands, and yet speaks and
melts the same foundation. This is a God who works for the
end of conflicts and reorders a falling world. Our task then is
to hear God's direction to be still and to venture out knowing
that God grounds our lives together.

Just as Indiana Jones had to take steps in the name of God
so too are we to venture into our future trusting that God has
structured a firm foundation for our feet. Rather than retreat
in fatalism as the world crumbles beneath us, we are to hear

God's poetic words of comfort as we journey into a new century of life together.

For the day: Step out into a changing world knowing that God's presence rises above the shifting sands and firmly grounds each of our steps.

Prayer: God of our firm footing, you continue to speak and provide constancy in the midst of change. May your comforting words embolden us to step into a new century in your name that the world might become aware of your peaceful presence. Amen.

Joshua Brockway

November 11

Sharing God's Grace

Reading: Philippians 1:3-11

I thank my God every time I remember you. In all my prayers for all of you, I always pray with joy because of your partnership in the gospel from the first day until now, being confident of this, that he who began a good work in you will carry it on to completion until the day of Christ Jesus (Phil. 1:3-6 NIV).

Meditation: A community can make or break a person. Good community strengthens; bad community siphons. The community at Philippi is the good kind. This community supported Paul when he was in jail, through all his trials and tribulations, even when it seemed like there was no one by his side. And, as high and mighty as that sounds, that's what my church family does, too. Now, I haven't exactly been in jail, and maybe my trials and tribulations aren't quite biblical, but isn't that just the point? The Philippians were with Paul all the way, through the mundane and the magnificent, from the street to the stars. My church family is, too. That's the commitment we as a body of believers make every time someone joins the church. We agree to walk this journey together, even when it gets tough. We agree to make relationships and hold true to our promises. We agree to uphold each other. And what a model we have: The Philippians were everything Paul needed in his time of exile. Loving through Christ can be easier said than done, but the rewards are endless.

For the day: It has been said that you never know how you're affecting the people around you. Sometimes a word of encouragement is just what someone needs. Be the encouragement today; be the community.

Prayer: Lord of us all, let your love grant us the knowledge and understanding to see your will in our interactions with others throughout the day. Let us see you in ourselves and each other; let your love fill us with the righteousness of Jesus to your glory.

Cassidy McFadden

November 12

Rejoice

Reading: Philippians 1:12-18

The important thing is that in every way, whether from false motives or true, Christ is preached. And because of this I rejoice (Phil. 1:18b NIV).

Meditation: What Paul tells us in this passage is both incredibly honest and profoundly disturbing. Incredibly honest because he acknowledges that the motivation some people have for preaching the gospel is far from pure, but profoundly disturbing because he actually rejoices for these self-serving proclamations. How can anybody rejoice, one wonders, when the gospel is being preached by people with ulterior motives? How can the truth of the message come through?

The Christian scene around us, sadly, reminds us that Paul is right. Evangelists seem to want to outdo each other on their websites or TV shows by brandishing their many "conversions" as if they were hunting trophies. Even more disturbing is the history of Christian missions, which often reads like a story of rivalries: the Catholics versus the Orthodox, the Orthodox versus the Protestants, and to make it closer to home, different branches of Brethren exporting their differences on their respective mission fields.

But yet the message, miraculously, comes through. The gospel that was taught to the slaves to make them more docile became the message that liberated them. The gospel that was brought on the heels of colonization and economic imperialism produced a harvest that today is challenging the powerful dominations of the North. History shows us also that the message does indeed transcend its messengers, not just the insincere ones that Paul talked about, but you and me, who always will be unworthy of the message of the gospel of Jesus Christ.

For the day: Rejoice that the gospel of grace is greater than the sinfulness of its messengers.

Prayer: Lord, make us aware of our unworthiness to preach the gospel. But do not let our unworthiness be used as an excuse for refraining from sharing the good news.

Chantal Logan

ℰ

November 13

Living in the Material World

Reading: Philippians 1:19-26

My desire is to depart and be with Christ, for that is far better; but to remain in the flesh is more necessary for you. Since I am convinced of this, I know that I will remain and continue with all of you for your progress and joy in faith (Phil. 1:23b-25).

Meditation: Here we are, embodied in a physical world. The Apostle Paul admitted that he would have preferred to be united with Christ but felt the need to be present in the flesh to help others in their faith journey. This is a noble aspiration and has been echoed by those in other faith traditions, such as the Buddhist *bodhisattvas*, whose vow it is to return to human form until all sentient beings have achieved enlightenment. In our Christian striving for spiritual unity with God, we are sometimes led to dismiss our bodies and our physical surroundings as regrettable necessities. This doesn't seem right. God called the created world "good." This must include respect not just for the spirit but also for the body in which it is housed. Let us be present in this life, staying connected to our earthly bodies and to the physical realities of human existence. Let us find our spiritual fulfillment in and through the material world. This is the task of today.

For the day: Today, be fully present. Pay attention to your surroundings and to your body. What lessons does God offer you through your physical body and your material surroundings?

Prayer: Remind us, God, that this life is a gift. Let us cherish it. Let us experience fully all the joys and pains that accompa-

ny our earthly existence even as we strive to walk a spiritual
path in the footsteps of Jesus Christ. Amen.

Anna Speicher

November 14

Remain Steadfast in Suffering

Reading: Philippians 1:27-30

*Only, live your life in a manner worthy of the gospel of Christ, so
that . . . I will know that you are standing firm in one spirit,
striving side by side with one mind for the faith of the gospel. . . .
For [God] has graciously granted you the privilege not only of believing in Christ, but of suffering for him as well (Phil. 1:27-29).*

Meditation: Paul was writing from prison, urging Christians
to be faithful to Christ no matter what may take place in the
future. They were to live their lives in such a way that their testimony would bring honor to the One whose name they bore.
They were to strive to maintain unity even if they faced opposition and suffered for the cause of Christ.

God gives us the gift of salvation (believing in Christ); God
also gives us the gift of suffering (opposition because of faith in
Christ). We usually think of suffering as something hurtful and
ask God to take it away. But often God will use suffering to
develop character in us. We don't need to pray to lose it;
instead, pray that God will see fit to use it.

We do not normally consider suffering a blessing, but Paul
counted it a *privilege* to suffer for the cause of Christ. Suffering
has several benefits. It takes our eyes off of earthly comforts; it
strengthens the faith of those who endure; it serves as a helpful
example to those who follow. Physical suffering or suffering for
Christ does not mean that we have done something wrong; it

more likely indicates that we have *faithfully* represented the Lord Jesus. Suffering helps to build character; don't let it tear you down.

For the day: Let us praise God today for the grace that is supplied to those who suffer greatly.

Prayer: Loving God, I offer to you all that I suffer for striving side by side with brothers and sisters for the faith of the gospel.

Priscilla A. Martin

November 15

Stand Firm in the Lord

Reading: Philippians 3:17–4:1

He will transform the body of our humiliation that it may be conformed to the body of his glory, by the power that also enables him to make all things subject to himself (Phil. 3:21).

Meditation: What a hope! Paul touches the deepest desire of the human heart in this text. It is the desire to be changed and experience new life. We often experience our bodies as bodies of humiliation in which weakness, fear, addiction, brokenness, and sadness define our daily existence. In the midst of all this, Paul reminds us of the promise that our bodies of humiliation will be transformed so as to conform to the glorious body of Christ's resurrection. It is so easy to lose sight of this reality and become enemies of the cross through self-indulgence and undisciplined living.

How, then, can we live our lives so that God's power is released within us to transform our thinking and our actions? Paul suggests two realities. In Philippians 4:1, he invites us to "stand firm in the Lord in this way"—the "way" being the way of Christ, which he describes in Philippians 2:5-11: Christ does not grasp power or glory for himself but empties himself even unto the cross. This "standing firm in the Lord in this way" is made possible not only by imitating Paul, but by "observing those who live according to the example" (Phil. 3:17). The Spirit encourages and strengthens us inwardly for our daily walk when we pay attention to the example of Christ as seen in men and women of faith who have gone before us.

For the day: Think of someone who has influenced your life in a positive way. What is it about their life and faith that has challenged you? Carry this memory with you through the day, and be thankful.

Prayer: O God, help us to live out your love and justice as we see it in those who have walked before us. Amen.

Larry D. Fourman

November 16

Unexpected Trials

Readings: Philippians 4:2-9; 1 Thessalonians 5:16-18

Do not be anxious about anything, but in everything, by prayer and petition, with thanksgiving, present your requests to God. And the peace of God, which transcends all understanding, will guard your hearts and your minds in Christ Jesus (Phil. 4:6-7 NIV).

Meditation: I begin my morning by tucking an ugly yellow hot water bottle under my aching lower back. I am unable to walk the steep, twisting trail down to the garden below. I will not be weeding the fava beans today. Instead, I am in bed, challenged by Paul's words to the Philippians to let go of judgment and worry and to be thankful.

Life is full of unexpected trials: a pulled muscle, an expensive medical bill, a car accident or flat tire, an unannounced visitor, etc. Each day things happen that get in the way of carefully laid plans or general functioning. It is easy to name such things as bad, inconvenient, irritating, or damaging. It is easy to let feelings of frustration and anxiety well up inside.

At such moments of escalating worry, we are called to take a deep breath and to whisper a prayer of thanksgiving—for life; for family; for legs, arms, and eyes that work; for love; for nature; for being. In breathing deeply and allowing a shift in perspective, we find calm, we slow down, we reassess what is important, we let go of frustration, and we begin to feel the deep-reaching peace of God.

For the day: When you feel today's frustrations and challenges, close your eyes, breathe deeply, and raise your prayer of thanksgiving that you might be grounded in peace.

Prayer: Spirit of Life, I am grateful today for the quieting peace you bring when I open my heart to thanksgiving. Grant me the presence of mind to let go of frustration and irritation and prayerfully name my blessings. Calm me, ground me, and fill me with your peace.

Margo Royer-Miller

℘

November 17

Power, Love, Self-discipline

Reading: 2 Timothy 1:3-7

For this reason I remind you to rekindle the gift of God that is within you through the laying on of my hands; for God did not give us a spirit of cowardice, but rather a spirit of power and of love and of self-discipline (2 Tim. 1:6-7).

Meditation: Timothy's "faith-line" is traced through his mother and grandmother. That's true for me as well. While others have greatly influenced me, my faith is defined most by my mother and her mother. While not having great status by worldly standards, they are highly respected and have been inspirations to many. Life makes more sense to me when seen through their eyes.

When adversity and pains come, they still move forward, depending on God's spirit rather than giving in to their own fears. Power is defined as the ability to get things done. These two women have experienced that power in their life journeys, knowing that their human efforts are puny compared to the energy supplied by their gracious God. Love is evident as they move in positive ways, experiencing hope and joy and showering the same on others they encounter. They have lived out a gentle self-discipline that gives them the momentum to get up and do it all again.

For the day: Rekindle the gift of God's spirit this day. Step out in God's power and love, trusting that self-discipline comes in intentionally moving forward, one step at a time.

Prayer: Almighty and most gracious God, release me from fear. May I know your perfect love, which casts out all fear. Fill me with your power to get things done today. Help me to get up and get going one step at a time, seeking the mind of Christ in all I do. Amen.

Marlys A. Hershberger

November 18

Good Shame, Bad Shame

Readings: 2 Timothy 1:8-14; Romans 12:1-2

Do not be ashamed, then, of the testimony about our Lord or of me his prisoner, but join with me in suffering for the gospel (2 Tim. 1:8).

Meditation: If I'm not ashamed, I am sometimes embarrassed about being a Christian. Each year our peace group, made up mostly of Brethren, tries to organize a witness to the community about the use of our income tax dollars to pay for war. We stand in front of the post office on April 15 with placards, or we ask passersby to vote how they would spend the federal budget if given the chance. They often look a little disdainful of us, and I worry about what they think of me. It's a small town and we all know one another (I'd much rather attend a protest in New York City where no one knows me!). One time the newspaper interviewed us about our tax protest and plastered our pictures on the front page. My brother's friends thought we were a little kooky and a little pretentious. They were Christians, after all, and their faith didn't require them to speak out against the government, which, by the way, was ordained of God, thank you very much! I steered clear of them for a long time after that. Like Paul, I'm a prisoner, but unlike Paul, I'm a prisoner of what other people think. So occasionally I force myself to stand in front of the post office because I am more ashamed of injustices committed in my name with my money than I am of being identified as an oddball defender of the gospel of peace.

For the day: The things that should shame us as we stand before our God are things like wasting precious resources, turning a blind eye to injustice, ignoring the needs of the poor and the prisoner, and bearing grudges against fellow church members. Be ashamed for the right reason!

Prayer: Keep me from conforming to this world and believing that the opinions of others matter more than the gospel. Transform me and let my very life be my worship. Amen.

Julie Garber

&

November 19

Spiritual Gift Exchange

Reading: Romans 1:8-17

I am longing to see you so that I may share with you some spiritual gift to strengthen you—or rather so that we may be mutually encouraged by each other's faith, both yours and mine (Rom. 1:11-12).

Meditation: A burning desire of the Apostle Paul was to meet the followers of Jesus in Rome face to face. The depth of Paul's longing is captured by Eugene Peterson in *The Message* in this way: "I so want to be there to deliver God's gift in person and watch you grow stronger right before my eyes! But don't think I'm not expecting to get something out of this, too! You have as much to give me as I do to you."

Paul excelled in writing letters to scattered and often fragmented groups of Christians, explaining always that he praised God for them and held them in his prayers. But he did something more; he dispatched "living letters," himself and others, letters "written not with ink but with the Spirit of the living God, not on tablets of stone but on tablets of human hearts" (2 Cor. 3:3).

Often in traditional cultures, the only way to establish a

relationship is through oral communication face to face. Even in more complex societies, the wonders of technology do not supplant the warmth of human encounter.

The visits of John Kline to churches across enemy lines during the Civil War, Ted Studebaker's decision to go to Vietnam not with weapons but with tools, the hosting by Brethren congregations of Russian Orthodox Church leaders in the McCarthy/Cold War era—what bold and exemplary spiritual gift exchanges in our own history!

For the day: Arrange to visit someone you have long wanted to see, pray in advance for your time together, and as you meet, recount what God is doing in your lives.

Prayer: Grant, O Lord, that I may be open to the strength and fulfillment that come in receiving the gift of faith from others. Amen.

Howard E. Royer

November 20

The Unchained Word of God

Reading: 2 Timothy 2:8-13

Remember Jesus Christ, raised from the dead, descended from David. This is my gospel, for which I am suffering even to the point of being chained like a criminal. But God's word is not chained (2 Tim. 2:8-9 NIV).

Meditation: Given the many options that life presents to us, I don't know many people who would choose a pathway clearly leading to conflict and suffering. The Apostle Paul, however, was one who made such a choice. He had many opportunities to choose a course of ministry that would have been safe and comfortable, but for the sake of the gospel and the blessing of others, he chose to preach Christ crucified, buried, and raised from the dead. While a hostile world may treat us like common criminals and even imprison us, we have Paul's words: "But God's word is not chained." What a marvelous promise! The indestructibility of the Word of God, along with our love for Jesus, provide us with two compelling reasons to serve him faithfully. The motive for doing this, the apostle reminds us, is not just for our comfort and blessing, but for the eternal salvation of others. We may face adversity in this task, but we are never alone because he has promised to be with us even in the darkest valleys. With that assurance, let us even today move ahead with renewed confidence and joy.

For the day: Walk confidently today in your faith because he is with you and his Word will never be bound or destroyed. As our passage has admonished us, "If we endure, we will also reign with him."

Prayer: Precious Father, thank you for your presence and the enduring character of your precious Word. Help me to walk confidently today in the light of these truths, and may I do so not just for my personal satisfaction, but for the salvation of others. In his holy name, Amen.

John J. Davis

November 21

Realistic Expectations

Reading: 2 Timothy 2:14-19

Do your best to present yourself to God as one approved, a workman who does not need to be ashamed and who correctly handles the word of truth (2 Tim. 2:15 NIV).

Meditation: Do your best. As a student, I've often been reminded by teachers and professors to "do my best" when preparing for a test or writing a paper. But what do these words really mean? Doing our best often means setting standards of unattainable perfection in an effort to gain God's approval. Then when we fall short of our own lofty goals, we can be left feeling discouraged. However, we should see the text's words as encouraging another outlook on how to be a worker for God's kingdom. The author reminds Timothy to work diligently and eagerly as well as to be on his guard against rumors and quarreling among the believers that could destroy the community. Three times in 2 Timothy the author urges diligence in proclaiming the gospel truth. Instead of setting ourselves up for failure when we work for God or, on the other hand, underestimating our impact and gifts, we should trust that God will make provision for the work we should do. God does not demand an unattainable perfection. God asks that we be hardworking and attentive to the moving of the Spirit so that we can embrace opportunities to speak the truth to each other. We need to each be about the tasks that God presents to us on a daily basis so that, instead of quarreling among ourselves, we can all present ourselves as workers approved.

For the day: Be attentive to the opportunities that present themselves today to be about God's work.

Prayer: God of grace, free me from my unrealistic expectations to try to gain your approval. Help me to be a diligent worker for your kingdom and boldly embrace the work that you have set before me today. In the name of Jesus. Amen.

Denise Kettering

℘

November 22

A Personalized Faith

Reading: 2 Timothy 3:14-17

But as for you, continue in what you have learned and firmly believed, knowing from whom you learned it, and how from childhood you have known the sacred writings that are able to instruct you for salvation through faith in Christ Jesus (2 Tim. 3:14-15).

Meditation: When I was a fourth grader, I was given a *Good News Bible* by my congregation. It was a black, hardcover book. It had soft pages that whispered when I opened it. But I was most proud that my name had been embossed on the front.

I was hopeful that a new Bible would create a spirit of holiness within me, especially since now the Word of God bore my name. For awhile I carried my Bible with me to church, but at some point the novelty of this gift wore off and it started to collect dust on the bookshelf. Even though my Bible was personalized, I needed a model for personalizing my faith journey.

A voracious reader at a young age, I began to seek out Bible reading programs. My great-grandfather, an ordained minister, offered old resources that would inspire my success. I was thankful for the help and began the program with energy.

I soon realized how difficult it was going to be to read the entire Bible on my own, and I began to listen more carefully to our Sunday school lessons and apply them to my life. Through actively engaging in God's Word, I was inspired to deepen my journey, and within two years, I was baptized by my great-grandfather. I am grateful for his guidance to me, a little girl with a personalized Bible and hope for a personalized faith to go with it.

For the day: Write a letter of gratitude to a former Sunday school teacher. Send it or read it aloud to a current mentor as a memorial.

Prayer: O God, we pray for those who have walked with us on our faith journey, those who have walked ahead of us, and for those who are coming from behind.

Angela Lahman Yoder

☙

November 23

Proclaim the Message!

Reading: 2 Timothy 2:1-3; 4:1-5

In the presence of God and of Christ Jesus, who is to judge the living and the dead, and in view of his appearing and his kingdom, I solemnly urge you: proclaim the message . . . (2 Tim. 4:1-2).

Meditation: In these verses from 2 Timothy, the writer reflects a pronounced evangelistic emphasis. "Proclaim the message" (4:2). "Do the work of an evangelist" (4:5). "And what you have heard from me through many witnesses entrust to faithful people who will be able to teach others as well" (2:2). These passages among others in the New Testament underscore the fact that Christianity has been and is an evangelistic and missionary religion. While Brethren history has been marked by periods of evangelistic and missionary fervor, we have not excelled in these areas. We have been more comfortable with such activities as service, peacemaking, discipleship, and ethical living.

But these verses from 2 Timothy direct our attention to the centrality of evangelism and provide a theological and ethical context. The proclaimer of the message must "be strong in the grace that is in Christ Jesus" (2:1). The message is not the result of individual inspiration alone, but has come to us "through many witnesses" both past and present (2:2). There is an urgency about evangelism because it has both a present and future reference. It takes place in a time between the times, between Christ's coming and his coming again (4:1). The task will not be easy. Rather, the evangel will encounter indifference and even persecution and suffering (4:2-5; 2:3). Doing the work of an evangelist requires persistence and patience (4:2). But knowing that it is done in the presence and with the blessing of God and Christ Jesus marks it as one of the highest and noblest expressions of service and discipleship.

For the day: Reflect on why you find it difficult to witness and to speak about the person and work of Christ. How can and should you proclaim the message?

Prayer: Almighty God, we give thanks for those witnesses who in spite of dungeon, fire, and sword preserved the faith and passed it on to us. O thou who art at work within us and among us and can accomplish far more than we can ask or imagine, enable us as we attempt to proclaim your message of grace, reconciliation, and salvation. Amen.

Warren S. Kissinger

November 24

Trust Me

Reading: John 16:25-33

I have said these things to you in figures of speech. The hour is coming when I will no longer speak to you in figures, but will tell you plainly of the Father (John 16:25).

Meditation: Curiosity often makes me ask my husband how he has done something, such as fixed an electrical problem, or turned a wooden bowl on his woodworking lathe. He is often happy to share his interest and skill, and with much good will he explains and sometimes demonstrates the process. There are times when I actually think I understand, although I usually find that the knowledge hasn't stuck when the same situation comes around again. But with much patience, he always explains it again. Even though I don't always understand what he is doing, I trust that whatever he is working on will come out right.

I feel for the well-meaning disciples who tried hard to understand all that Jesus shared with them, and, perhaps in their desire to please, reassure Jesus that yes, indeed, they do understand. Jesus knows them better, however. He knows they will still react with much fear and will abandon him. But his words to them are ones of trust: Trust me and trust the Father. God is always present, even through the hardest times.

For the day: As you move through your day, note when trust—or lack of trust—affects your thoughts and actions. Think about your feelings. What would it mean to fully trust God?

Prayer: God, I am humbled by your love for me in spite of my fears, my weaknesses, my failure to understand. Let me take heart and move through this world in peace and confidence knowing that you are with me. Amen.

Sara Speicher

November 25

God's Word at Work Within Us

Readings: 1 Thessalonians 2:13-16; Acts 17:1-15

And we also thank God continually because, when you received the word of God, which you heard from us, you accepted it not as the word of men, but as it actually is, the word of God, which is at work in you who believe (1 Thess. 2:13 NIV).

Meditation: I have trouble praying for our adult children. And it's not for want of trying. It's just that when I lift them before God to ask that he strengthen them in matters of faith, my prayers for divine guidance in their decisions and spiritual power in their living tend to be eclipsed by a one-line prayer chorus that goes something like this: "Dear Jesus, please keep them safe!"

So it strikes me as incredibly significant that Paul, who considered the Thessalonians to be his *children* (2:11), was singularly unconcerned about the constant reality of persecution in their midst. Their suffering was mentioned just as a reference to validate the authenticity of their faith. The laser focus of Paul's prayer of thankfulness had to do with the pivot point of their conversion—that they had accepted the Word of God (i.e., that Jesus was indeed the Christ [Acts 17:3]) as being the sovereign Word of God and not some esoteric allegory of a culturally contrived religion.

With no heritage to draw upon and no experienced leader present, the suffering Thessalonian believers grew in faith by simply allowing the Word of God to do its work in them. The result was that the Lord's message rang out, and they became the Christians others looked to for guidance (see 1 Thess. 1:7-8).

For the day: Set aside the cultural pressure to be politically correct. If the Thessalonians could endure persecution from their own countrymen, surely we can live with a little criticism from ours. Embrace the Word of God as the Word of God, and let it do its work in you.

Prayer: Heavenly Father, forgive us for allowing safety and comfort to take precedence over faithfulness and courage. Thank you for your Word, which works in us. Amen.

Robin Wentworth Mayer

November 26

The Creation Groans

Reading: Romans 8:18-25

For the creation waits with eager longing for the revealing of the children of God (Rom. 8:19).

Meditation: When Paul wrote to the Romans, he presented an inconvenient truth: "We know that the whole creation has been groaning until now; and not only the creation, but we ourselves." The suffering of God's creation has taken on a new urgency in the twenty-first century, as the world recognizes that human activity has accelerated the pace of global warming, and environmental degradation continues unchecked. Paul recognized that when the earth suffers, we all suffer. In a 1965 speech at the United Nations, Adlai Stevenson would make the same point in a different way: "We travel together, passengers on a little space ship, dependent on its vulnerable reserves of air and soil; all committed for our safety to its security and peace; preserved from annihilation only by the care, the work, and, I will say, the love we give our fragile craft."

In his 2006 documentary, *An Inconvenient Truth*, Al Gore shows just how the earth is groaning. The ten warmest years in history were in the previous fourteen years. Glaciers are melting. Weather is changing. Japan and the Pacific are setting records for typhoons. The rising level of the oceans has grave implications for coastal areas.

The message about damage done through poor stewardship of the earth is disturbing. But the larger message is hopeful. It is not too late. If people take action, the earth can be saved. Science knows what to do; until now the will has been lacking to do it. But, as Al Gore tells us, human will is a renewable resource. We must act to save God's earth.

As believers we share Paul's great hope that "creation itself will be set free from its bondage to decay and will obtain the freedom of the glory of the children of God."

For the day: Strive to live as a better steward of God's creation by learning more, by praying for the earth, and by making lifestyle changes.

Prayer: The creation waits with eager longing to regain a vibrant ecosystem, to host a healthier human family, to provide a clean and peaceful home for our children. We pray for the earth to experience God's glory in these ways.

Fletcher Farrar

♂

November 27

Battered, Not Broken

Reading: Acts 14:21-23

There they strengthened the souls of the disciples and encouraged them to continue in the faith, saying, "It is through many persecutions that we must enter the kingdom of God" (Acts 14:22).

Meditation: My father used to play a mildly sadistic "game" with us kids—squeeze or pinch just to the point of real pain. We'd holler to be released. As he let go, he'd invariably say, "Doesn't that feel good when I stop? Don't you want me to do it again so it'll feel good when I stop?"

Nobody wants to experience pain just to experience the pleasure when the pain stops. And few would choose persecution as a way to God. Likely Paul still bore the marks of his recent stoning, even as he voiced this encouragement and strength. An eloquent message rendered dubious by its arrival in a battered container.

But as Quaker writer Parker Palmer observes, our spiritual journey may not be a climb into a rarefied experience of God's presence, but rather a descent to the inner circle of hell via the countryside of humiliation. For some, the path to God may be down.

It's a journey full of paradoxes, and one of them is that the humiliation that brings us down to the ground of our common human existence is bringing us down to ground on which it is safe to stand and to fall. Perhaps the energy we expend in trying to escape our pains would be more efficiently spent in mobilizing them into a common search for life among the ruins.

In truth, we're *all* battered containers, stuffed with a roiling mix of weakness and strength, burden and gift, courage and fear. Each of those pairings needs the other—we can't be brave unless we're scared. And we may not be able to get to God without facing the monsters of hell on the way.

For the day: "Claim the events of your life. . . . When you truly possess all you have been and done, you are fierce with reality." (Florida Scott Maxwell, *The Measure of My Days*).

Prayer: Weakness. Burden. Fear.
Giving way, giving way, giving way . . .
Through a crucible of monstrosity and beauty.
Releasing strength. Gift. Courage. Thank God.

Lee-Lani Wright

November 28

Sharing Christ's Sufferings

Reading: 1 Peter 4:12-19

But rejoice, inasmuch as ye are partakers of Christ's sufferings; that, when his glory shall be revealed, ye may be glad also with exceeding joy (1 Pet. 4:13 KJV).

Meditation: I had a dream. I was standing on Sandia Mountain above Albuquerque, New Mexico, and Jesus was standing beside me. Because of his presence, I could see what he could see.

Jesus looked toward the detention center, hospitals, and nursing homes. I remembered Christ's teaching in Matthew 25:43c, ". . . sick, and in prison, and ye visited me not." I looked at his face. He was weeping.

Jesus looked at the many shopping centers and saw the shopping bags filled with clothing. He pointed toward the poor countries of the world, and I saw people in tattered and scant clothing. Those in prison in frigid areas were very cold and some were dying. I remembered Christ's teaching in Matthew 25:43b, ". . . naked, and ye clothed me not. . . ." I looked at his face. He was weeping.

Jesus looked at the people at the eating places and grocery stores. He knew how full the garbage cans were at the eating places. I thought of the scripture in Matthew 25:42, "For I was an hungred, and ye gave me no meat: I was thirsty, and ye gave me no drink." I looked at his face. He was weeping.

My heart was broken, and I wept. My suffering in what I had been reminded of was insignificant compared to the ocean of Christ's suffering. I made no promises, but I did tell him I would try harder to live out his teachings in Matthew 25. He smiled through his tears. I was surrounded by his presence, and then I awoke.

For the day: Do you help meet the needs of those who are suffering? Do you give to the hurting? Do you visit those who are longing for a visitor? Take time today.

Prayer: Dear God, I praise you for all your blessings and benefits. Help me to be your vessel to share more, pray more, and see the needs of others more clearly. In Jesus' name, Amen.

Mildred (Kintner) Skiles

November 29

Turn to God

Reading: Psalm 44:17-26

Rise up and help us; redeem us because of your unfailing love (Ps. 44:26 NIV).

Meditation: The holidays are full of expectations for many of us. We plan for time away from work and time with family. Secretly we hope to find a moment of thrill or peaceful calm. But if the truth is told for many, Thanksgiving is the beginning of the season of dashed expectations. Too often the stranger at the grocery store squeezes into our place in the checkout line, or a friend doesn't call when we really just need someone to talk to. David, the psalm writer, is experiencing just one such depressive moment—and for good reason. No longer are the Israelites winning the wars they wage. And the consequences are not pleasant. There is insecurity about staying together as a people and possibly even existing at all. Where there was once pride, there is now only shame and ridicule from other nations.

Is there some reason for this sudden withholding of prosperity? The psalmist claims that even when the enemies are pushed back there is no self-centered pride in thinking these accomplishments are the result of their own strength. God is recognized as the reason for victory or defeat. Only God's name is praised, and yet . . . things are not going their way. If we seemingly do all the things God wants us to do, shouldn't there be prosperity? Our actions do not always give us the results we expect or want. In moments like this, perhaps the only way to remain faithful is to turn to God and cry out in pain.

For the day: Consider the lonely moments of your life. What is it that pushes you to the edge of faith, to the point of calling out in pain to God?

Prayer: Look upon me, O Source of my comfort and frustration. See my impatience; feel my anger and frustration. May I rest in your arms and find the peace I so desperately seek.

Steven W. Bollinger

November 30

Made Perfect in Weakness

Reading: 2 Corinthians 11:16-18, 21-30; 12:9-10

That is why, for Christ's sake, I delight in weaknesses, in insults, in hardships, in persecutions, in difficulties. For when I am weak, then I am strong (2 Cor. 12:10 NIV).

Meditation: Weakness and perfection rarely present themselves as complementary states. Our idea of the perfect is more likely to be defined by strength. We learn that wealth and the ability to make others suffer are what define strength. A strong person can defend the family. A strong person can retaliate for insults and injustice. A strong nation can kill its enemies. A strong business can drive out its competitors. Super-heroes are heroes because they are strong. There is no place in our culture for a caped weakling.

Of course, it is not just *our* culture that finds it impossible to see perfection in weakness. The Roman Empire and the religious establishment in Paul's world were determined to use their strength to stamp out the upstart community of believers who defined themselves by their relationship to Jesus of Nazareth—and to start with its most important leader. Beaten, jailed, robbed, starved, and stoned, Paul had legitimate weaknesses, and he was not above reminding his followers about them. But he also argued that the ability and even the willingness to accept suffering was actually a source of strength in the new community of God.

Paul taught what Gandhi and Martin Luther King, Jr., learned: truth can only be tested by nonviolence; change that moves us toward perfection will inevitably result in suffering; and only those who willingly accept that suffering, rather than visit it on others, will be ultimately victorious. The upstart community persists. The Roman Empire is distant history. What a delight!

For the day: Look for examples in the world around you where victory has come not through the exercise of worldly power, but through the application of love, compassion, and empathy.

Prayer: Temper my spirit, O God, with the fire of your truth that I might have the strength to delight in your weakness. Amen.

M. Andrew Murray

Commitment
to the Messiah

December 1–December 31

*A*lways take your understanding, will,
and imagination captive under the obedience
of the gospel; and always exercise and
associate with those that love peace,
and pursue it. . . . and if you love peace
and follow after it, the spirit of peace will
be with you.

William Knepper (1691–1755)

$\mathcal{O}$

December 1

Hannah's Prayer

Reading: 1 Samuel 2:1-10

My heart rejoices in the LORD. . . . My mouth boasts over my ene-mies, for I delight in your deliverance (1 Sam. 2:1 NIV).

Meditation: Hannah had been depressed and for good reasons! Although her husband loved her, she shared him with another woman in a polygamous marriage. She was barren and the other woman, who had children, ridiculed her. Even her priest had no sympathy!

However, when stripped of all earthly hope, Hannah still had faith that God would hear her plea and promise. He answered her prayer with the birth of her son, who became the prophet Samuel. Sorrow was turned to joy, weakness to power, and her exultant prayer expresses her gratitude.

Hannah's prayer includes a study in opposites: broken bows/armed with strength, hungry/full, death/life, poverty/wealth, humility/exaltation, poor/rulers, needy/rich, despised/honored. To Hannah, God is not only holy, but a rock, One who is always present. He is a God who knows all (v. 3). Like Hannah, we believe he's got the whole world in his hands and ultimately will provide justice, making all things right (vv. 8b-10a). Hannah ends her faith and praise statement with a prophetic reference to the "king" and "his anointed," other names for Christ, the Messiah. Jesus' mother, Mary, may have used Hannah's prayer as a model in composing her own song of joy, "The Magnificat," recorded in Luke 1:46-55.

Hannah's experience reveals God as caring, faithful, and in control. God keeps his promises and expects us to keep ours. God is seldom early, but he is never late. When God answers prayer and sends us blessings, like Hannah, we should always express our thanks and praise.

For the day: In life's darkest moments, your flickering rays of hope, prayer, and faith can reach the God of love, power, and miracles, and he will intervene in his time.

Prayer: Open our eyes, Lord, to see our life experiences from your perspective. Open our hearts to be willing to give our best and serve you in gratitude, giving you all the glory. Amen.

Vivian S. Ziegler

December 2

The Message of an Angel

Reading: Luke 1:26-33

The angel said to her, "Do not be afraid, Mary, for you have found favor with God" (Luke 1:30).

Meditation: The readers of this passage know who the angel Gabriel is because of his appearance to Zechariah earlier in this chapter. But Mary did not have this advantage and was "much perplexed."

Strange as Gabriel's actions may be, his words seem even stranger. "Do not be afraid"? My heart starts racing just imagining what my reaction would be to an angel dropping by! How would you know if this "guy" was for real, or just some prankster or whacko? Calling Mary by name was a huge point in Gabriel's favor (before the benefits of the Internet were available to help identify strangers by name).

Then Gabriel says something even stranger. "You will conceive and bear a son." Mary was too young. This was not going to be popular with her parents, or the neighbors, or with

Joseph! Mary's fear does not overwhelm her. She hears Gabriel out! She does not "shoot the messenger," but gives the angel a chance to be heard.

If I got to pick what message an angel would say to me, "Do not be afraid" would be near the top of my list. If I knew I could be free of fear, I could ask myself, "What can I do for God?"

For the day: If you could pick the message an angel would bring to you, what would you choose?

Prayer: I will not be afraid, for your love is stronger than my fear. I know this because you have promised always to be near.

Gail Erisman Valeta

December 3

A Sense of Calling

Reading: Luke 1:34-38

Mary said to the angel, "How can this be, since I am a virgin?" (Luke 1:34).

Meditation: It's happened many times over the course of my twenty-nine years in the pastorate. In person or on the phone, I'll be talking to a member of the church, describing an opening on the board or on a committee or an odd or perhaps new task within the church. There's a pause, and then an answer: *yes* or *no* or *maybe, let me think about it.* I like *yes.* I respect *maybe.* I understand *thinking about it.* And I trust *no.* When someone says no, then I can be certain that their yes will really mean yes.

And many times, before I get any answer, there are questions. I like questions. Asking questions means the person is taking the ministries of the church seriously and wants to know more about what's involved.

The way I look at it, if Mary, a young, unmarried, teen-aged Palestinian girl, found herself in the presence of Gabriel, who by his own admission stands in the presence of God and reflects the glory of the Almighty and announces that God has an unfathomable, unique, and world-altering task for her to perform—if Mary can stand in the face of a creature so awe-inspiring that he must utter "Do not be afraid" before they can settle down to business—if Mary can stand in the presence of the angel and have the guts to ask a clarifying question ("How can this be, since I am a virgin?")—then certainly everyone should have the peace of mind to ask me a few questions as well when I ask them to take part in our shared mission.

For the day: When was the last time someone called you to a task in ministry? When was the last time you called someone to engage in God's great work? How serious do we take the sense of calling in our fellowships?

Prayer: Here I am, Lord. Let it be with me according to your Word. Amen.

Frank R. Ramirez

December 4

Born Thy People to Deliver

Readings: Luke 2:25-35; Isaiah 52:10

[F]or my eyes have seen your salvation (Luke 2:30 KJV). The LORD hath made bare his holy arm in the eyes of all the nations; and all the ends of the earth shall see the salvation of our God (Isa. 52:10 KJV).

Meditation: I was about six years old when I wandered out to the pasture where our ram grazed with the sheep. The next thing I knew, a huge hard head had knocked me over, and that powerful sheep with his lethal horns stood over me. Terrified, I started to scream. I thought they would be my last moments alive. Then from the back door of the house my father came to my rescue—a man who loved me and would do anything to protect me. His very presence gave me hope and comfort. He got the ram to back off and I was safe. My father was my savior that day, and for the first time I experienced what it felt like to be saved.

In the time of Simeon, Israel was waiting for a Redeemer, the One who would set their people free. What joy it must have given Simeon to look into the face of the Lord Jesus who was to be the consolation of Israel! What hope we can have in the day we will see him face to face and what joy to spend eternity with him!

For the day: *Come, thou long-expected Jesus, born to set thy people free. From our fears and sins release us. Let us find our rest in Thee!* (Charles Wesley, 1744).

Prayer: Dear Lord, as I see troubles all around me, may I know the peace and quietness within that only you can give as we trust in you and look to you for that blessed hope. We know that someday you will come again and this time you won't have to go to Calvary. This time you will take us home to live with you forever. O, Lord Jesus, we look with longing for your coming!

Sally Meyers

♂

December 5

God Speaks Through People

Readings: John 2:1-11; Matthew 15:21-28

Do whatever he tells you (John 2:5 NIV).

Meditation: "They have no wine." Someone at the feast feels the sting of this—a lady who knows a thing or two about miracles. There's a private and rather tense exchange here between mother and son. Embedded in Mary's statement is a question. Could this be the hour? It's a question that carries a lot of freight. They both know there will be no phone calls to a wine vendor. If Jesus moves to meet this need, it will set in motion the most extraordinary series of events the world has ever seen. If he supplies the heavenly vintage, the veil that separates heaven and earth will be drawn aside and his disciples will see the in-breaking of God's glory. At first Jesus says no. "Why involve me? My hour has not yet come." He said no, but he must have thought better of it. Can we be that humble? God often speaks through people to reach us. What if this need—and Mary's request—is God's way of saying "Son, it's time"? It's not the only time in the Gospels wherein God uses a woman to help Jesus see something. For example, when Jesus hears the Canaanite mother's impassioned plea for her daughter, he expands his ministry to include the Gentiles (see Matt. 15).

Mary is wise. She knows Jesus won't be pushed into action before the appointed time. By summoning the servants, she involves other people and takes her request to the next level. But by saying "do whatever he tells you," she places the matter exactly where it should be—that is to say, in the hands of Jesus. And so, in response to both of his parents, Jesus acts. It is, after all, God's time.

For the day: Listen humbly and carefully to what others say to you today, yet place each decision in the hands of Jesus.

Prayer: God, help me to be truly open to the idea that your light can come through every person I meet.

Paula A. Bowser

&

December 6

Looking Up and Looking Down

Reading: Acts 1:6-14

They still had their eyes fixed on the sky as [Jesus] went away, when two men dressed in white suddenly stood beside them and said, "Galileans, why are you standing there looking up at the sky?" (Acts 1:10-11a TEV).

Meditation: The biblical account of Jesus' ascension has both an "upward" and a "downward" focus. The first is an upward focus. Jesus is taken from earth to heaven, rising through the air and disappearing into the clouds. It was never intended that Jesus would rule from a specific geographical location, such as Jerusalem. Jesus' kingdom is a spiritual one, and the ascension affirms that Jesus returned to the place from which he came. It is from that heavenly throne, not an earthly one, that Jesus reigns.

The ascension also has a downward focus. After Jesus ascends and disappears from sight behind a cloud, his followers stand there gazing into the sky. Perhaps they wanted to watch until there was nothing more to see, or maybe they were wondering if Jesus would turn around and return. Then two men dressed in white—suggesting an angelic presence—were suddenly beside them asking, "Why are you standing there looking up at the sky?" Jesus' followers are then prodded to focus on the everyday activities of life.

A life of faith involves focusing on both worlds:

• raising our prayers to God *and* speaking words of comfort and encouragement to the hurting beside us,

• lifting our hands in praise *and* extending our hands to help the needy,

• gazing heavenward toward God *and* looking into the eyes of the least and the lost.

For the day: Are you still here, looking up at the sky? Go on now, get going!

Prayer: Dear God, during this Advent season when we anticipate your coming among us in the Christ child, may we find you in our worship times *and* when we move out of the sanctuary to serve others. Amen.

J. D. Glick

December 7

Sing a Song of Praise

Reading: Luke 1:46-55

And Mary said: "My soul glorifies the Lord and my spirit rejoices in God my Savior" (Luke 1:46-47 NIV).

Meditation: I stand at the fork in the trail; steep steps wind up the hill behind me. I can choose to go left, gradually descending through the filazel trees and basket willow to the compost piles and tool shed. I can choose to go right, down an initial steep slope that levels out into steps passing the solar shower and entering the garden by way of the fragrant lavender stream.

Instead, I stop. This is my daily "mountaintop." I look out

at the vibrant, quilted garden below. Further down the slope, the valley spreads out north to south, a collage of pasture, trees, and buildings. The valley fades into a rolling ridge of evergreen trees that shelter the coast, hiding it from view. I breathe in and my spirit soars like the hawk rising on the wind toward the cloudless, turquoise sky.

I am filled with Life and Love in this moment. I am ready to glorify God, to raise my prayer of thanksgiving for the energy and mystery of creation, to affirm and claim my faith. I feel the deep joy of accepting and valuing my life path. I want to shout out in praise!

For the day: Where do you see or feel God's glory today? Follow Mary's lead. Claim your life, affirm your faith, and joyfully break into song!

Prayer: Creator of Life, I praise you for all you have done in my life, for the beauty with which you surround me, for the constant love and support you provide. Strengthen my faith each day through glimpses of your presence and your acts. Fill me with joy and move me to sing. Amen.

Margo Royer-Miller

December 8

Ready for the Unexpected

Reading: Genesis 18:1-8

Abraham looked up and saw three men standing nearby. When he saw them, he hurried from the entrance of his tent to meet them and bowed low to the ground. He said, "If I have found favor in your eyes, my lord, do not pass your servant by" (Gen. 18:2-3 NIV).

Meditation: We aren't told what Abraham had planned for the day, but how he responded to his unexpected guests is clear. Abraham greeted the men by offering food to eat, water to wash their feet, and a shaded place to rest. He appealed to his visitors to not pass him by, and they graciously accepted all he offered.

God had previously appeared to Abraham a number of times, but never with an empty stomach, dusty feet, and tired limbs. Jesus, too, came not as the expected conquering king, but as a baby delivered into human hands, needing to be fed and bathed and tucked in to rest. And this day, the Lord appeared to Abraham as a weary traveler grateful for these ministrations.

The God without whom we can never be filled allowed Abraham to feed him. The God who alone can truly cleanse us welcomed this offer of water for his dusty feet. The One who promises lasting rest to his weary and burdened children moved into the place of rest put before him. Our God receives our offerings of care and service and delights in our hospitality. How amazing to serve a God who longs to be welcomed, a God who will never pass us by!

For the day: Welcome God when he appears in the midst of your plans for the day. Rejoice in our intimate and loving Father who comes to us in unexpected ways!

Prayer: Lord, free me from a narrow focus that would make my plans for this day more important than welcoming you. Open my eyes to see you in each and every traveler who crosses my path. Make my heart an open invitation! Amen.

Judy V. Allison

⟨⟩

December 9

Barrenness to Birth

Readings: Genesis 18:9-14; Psalm 128

Why did Sarah laugh? . . . Is anything too wonderful for the LORD? *At the set time I will return to you, in due season, and Sarah shall have a son (Gen. 18:13-14).*

Meditation: Several of us middle-aged women giggled ourselves nearly to tears. Don't ask us to "be creative," we begged the leader, recalling another previous workshop event. We had been given colorful paper, magazines galore, scissors, glue, and sundry other craft objects. But our scheduled, professional adult lives had left us adrift as inspired artists, and now we could only be highly amused by the memory of someone demanding our creative juices on cue!

In ancient Israel, the creation called birth meant survival for the entire community, and survival was no laughing matter! When the social environment of famine, disease, and war means that very few children grow to maturity, then each gift of life becomes even more precious. Before people totally understood biological and growth processes, all new life was seen to be the consequence of God's direct intervention (John Otwell, *And Sarah Laughed*, p. 65). The more difficult or barren the situation was, the more powerful and impressive God's actions of bringing forth life became.

Remarkable Sarah, like other Israelites, did know *something* about life's beginnings. And when an impossibility confronted her, she, like many of us, coped by laughing. How could she be creative at her age and status? It's comedy! But the ongoing existence of Abraham and Sarah's offspring is no joke, for them or for the nation. The community depended upon the creation of life. Sarah also respected God's power and understood that "the birth of a child was a demonstration of God's active presence" (Otwell, p. 58).

When our lives feel unfruitful and desolate, can we laugh at ourselves? May we join Sarah in her barren situation and in her chuckled response to God's promise. May we also believe that God will provide for the world and bring forth new life in us.

For the day: Think of something lacking in your church, civic, or social community. What small action might you take to fill this void and thereby contribute to the health and well-being of your surroundings?

Prayer: God of creation, give me the courage to trust you when events seem ridiculous. God of new life, help me to smile at your power. God of humanity, show me my role in making the world a better place.

Jean L. Hendricks

December 10

Holy Imagination

Reading: Luke 1:5-11

Both of them were righteous before God. . . . But they had no children, because Elizabeth was barren, and both were getting on in years (Luke 1:6a, 7).

Meditation: Here is yet another story in the Bible where our human timelines don't match up with God's timeline. Zechariah and Elizabeth were "getting on in years." Their childbearing years were past, and it seemed their "holy imagination" had slipped away too. In verse 18, Zechariah asks how it could be possible for Elizabeth to bear a child—a reasonable question, it seems to me. Yet we should know by now that God's definition of "reasonable" is probably different from ours.

It is too easy to be like Zechariah. We are faithful servants. We send missionaries to be spiritual companions, give health care, and provide education, among other things. We help disaster victims rebuild their homes and care for their children. We grant micro-loans to help individuals create steady income for their families. Wells are dug, youth are called to greater commitment, and churches are planted. Young adults serve in a variety of settings for a year or more. Soup kitchens feed the hungry. Baptisms are held. Old, young, and those in the middle serve through lay and set-apart ministry. We are clear about faithful servanthood. But is our "holy imagination" as active as it should be?

Let us not forget to honor the undiscovered potential God has granted us as individuals, as local congregations, and as larger Brethren groups. Faith is not "knowing" something will happen; faith is trusting God, even if we are compelled to ask "how could it be?" when the Holy Spirit's movement startles us.

For the day: In your prayers today, invite God to surprise you.

Prayer: God we are impatient creatures. Surprise us with your blessings, and teach us to have faith. Amen.

Becky Ullom

December 11

The Promise of a Son

Reading: Luke 1:12-20

But the angel said to him: "Do not be afraid, Zechariah; your prayer has been heard. Your wife Elizabeth will bear you a son, and you are to give him the name John" (Luke 1:13 NIV).

Meditation: Zechariah and Elizabeth both were descendants of Obijah and Aaron. Both of them were upright in the sight of God and observed all the Lord's commandments and regulations blamelessly. But only one thing was missing. They had no child. They were very old, but they kept on praying for a child.

It happens to us also. Everything is going well, we are walking in God's path, we read the Bible daily, we pray regularly, but deep inside, we feel like our prayers are not being heard just yet. In Luke 18:1, Jesus tells us that we have to pray without ceasing—without giving up. God always listens to our prayers and answers in his own time in one of three ways: yes, no, or not now. Never give up on prayer, because prayer can change everything and anything. Pray in the name of Jesus, trusting him fully, and one day, sooner or later, we will get our answers.

Even though it was not humanly possible to bear a child, Zechariah and Elizabeth continued to pray. One day as Zechariah was praying in the temple and others were praying outside, God's angel Gabriel told him that his prayer has been heard.

We may not always know that others are praying for us. Not only our own prayers but the prayers of others are extremely important in our lives. In 2005 my father had a severe heart attack. A heart transplant was the only hope. But we all prayed together—as a community, as a family, and as a church. And our prayers were answered. My dad is alive and well and with me today without needing a heart transplant. Praise be to God!

For the day: Pray without ceasing. Trust God, and know that prayers can change everything. You will see that when you put yourself in his hands and tell him "Do as thou will, O God," the results are marvelous!

Prayer: Dear Lord! Help us to pray, trusting you just like Jesus has taught us to do. Help us to pray for others too. In Jesus' name, Amen.

Rachel Pandya

December 12

Waiting and Wondering

Reading: Luke 1:21-25

Meanwhile the people were waiting for Zechariah, and wondered at his delay in the sanctuary (Luke 1:21).

Meditation: I've never been very good at waiting, but have done a host of wondering. Waiting for Christmas to come was especially difficult for me as a child. While I loved all the Advent preparations, Christmas morning could not come soon enough. The wonder and awe of the celebration of Jesus' birth along with the anticipation and wonder of family gathered around the tree were exhilarating for me.

Waiting. Wondering. The people were waiting for Zechariah and wondering at his delay. In fact they had been waiting and wondering at the delay of the Messiah's arrival for many years! Zechariah gave the people a hint. He had seen a vision, but could not tell them about it. More waiting. More wondering.

Life is like that. Just when we think we're in control, know what's coming, and have all the answers, there's more waiting, more wondering. I still get caught up in the excitement of Christmas, but the more I mature the more I find myself relishing the time of waiting and anticipation. It somehow increases the wonder and awe of the gift that is to come.

For the day: What are you waiting for and wondering about this Advent season? Spend some time today waiting and wondering in quiet communion with God.

Prayer: God, wait with me today. Open my heart and mind to what you have in store for me. Fill my spirit with the joy and wonder and hope of this holy season. Amen.

Mary Jo Flory-Steury

December 13

Faith in God's Promises

Readings: Luke 1:39-45; Joshua 23:14

And blessed is she who believed that there would be a fulfillment of what had been spoken to her by the Lord (Luke 1:45 NASB).

Meditation: The responsibility is ours to believe whatever God speaks. Elizabeth witnessed two different responses to direct divine revelation, both delivered by the angel Gabriel. She saw her husband, Zechariah, struck dumb due to his unbelief in the promised birth of a son (Luke 1:18-20). In contrast, Mary responded to God's word of her virgin conception with complete trust and surrender, saying, "may it be done to me according to your word" (Luke 1:38). Elizabeth noted the difference, and her own personal faith is evident in her joyful greeting of Mary when she comes to visit. Both women are now pregnant, both anticipating joyous births of promised sons. Even unborn John leaps for joy in his mother's womb at the presence of the Messiah! They all know by faith that God's promise to send the Messiah, to bring deliverance for God's people, is in the process of being fulfilled. So Elizabeth acknowledges Mary as "the mother of my Lord" and twice pronounces her as "blessed" (Luke 1:42, 45). She sees in Mary a deep trust that what God has promised to her personally will be fulfilled. Do you believe the inspired message from the Bible that God has spoken to you? Are you trusting that all will come to pass just as Jesus says?

For the day: Even if you don't fully understand a passage of scripture, believe it anyway. For the path that leads to abundant blessing is marked with the signposts of God's promises and is walked by faith in whatever God says.

Prayer: Lord, may I fully believe all that you have spoken to me through your Word.

Scott Libby

December 14

He Is to Be Called John

Reading: Luke 1:57-63

. . . and they would have named him Zechariah after his father, but his mother said, "Not so; he shall be called John" (Luke 1:59b-60 RSV).

Meditation: After three years of infertility, my wife and I began the adoption process. We had discussed names throughout the ordeal, but without a definite selection. Eventually, and with a deep sense of blessing, we conceived. While still debating the name for a daughter, we settled quickly on the name for a son: Matthew, from the Greek, meaning "gift of God."

What's in a name? The ancients believed that a name assigned the nature of the being or captured some aspect of the person. Biblical parents often accorded names bearing spiritual significance. Hebrew matriarchs and patriarchs oriented their children in life by issuing a blessing through the naming process. In addition to holding the Brith Mila (circumcision ceremony) for sons, at which the Hebrew name of an honored relative is often given to the boy, modern Jewish families observe the Brita (naming ceremony) for their daughters as well. Names are carefully chosen, the announcement greatly anticipated, and the actual naming is cause for celebration. After the muted Zechariah wrote "His name is John," the old priest found his voice again. His son by Elizabeth would prepare the way for God's son. John derives from the Hebrew *Johanan* meaning

"God is gracious." Indeed, the grace of God was at work in John; as Luke says, "For the hand of the Lord was with him."

For the day: Do you have a namesake? In what ways do you resemble that person? How has the meaning of your given name informed your sense of being, character, or purpose in life? How might you bring honor to your name (or namesake) this day?

Prayer: God of blessing, your Word tells us, "Fear not, for I have redeemed you; I have called you by name, you are mine." May we come into deeper knowledge of our "name of grace," that true identity by which you alone know us. Amen.

Wallace B. Landes

December 15

God Finds a Way

Reading: Isaiah 46:8-13

. . . I am God, and there is no one like me, declaring the end from the beginning and from ancient times things not yet done, saying, "My purpose shall stand, and I will fulfill my intention" (Isa. 46:9c-10).

Meditation: Human beings can't see the End, and we can only guess at the Beginning. The chaos of daily life renders clear, long-range vision difficult. Wars and rumors of war, poverty and famine, school shootings and domestic violence all cloud our eyes with the gritty dust of despair. Our optimism rises and falls with the tide of history and the circumstances of daily life. Yet Christians hope. We hope not in what we may yet accomplish, for it seems that on the heels of every human success is a humiliating failure. Rather, we hope in God, the One and Only who sees and declares the End from the Beginning.

On the island of "Jurassic Park," one of the characters kneels beside a nest of broken dinosaur eggs from which scores of tiny, three-toed footprints lead. Since all the adult dinosaurs were created sterile, this is an amazing discovery. With a look of wonder in his eyes, he says, "Life finds a way!"

Christian hope is based on the historically-proven premise that *God finds a way*. Whether we are with God, against God, or completely unmindful of God, God finds a way to complete his purpose and fulfill his intention. Isaiah offered to help, though he felt like a voice crying in the wilderness. Jonah ran away but ended up saving a city. Cyrus ("the bird of prey") unknowingly freed God's people for a spell. But in Christ God freed us forever! God finds a way.

For the day: Whatever you are facing today, trust in God's deliverance. It is not far off.

Prayer: Dear Savior, not by our might nor by our power, but by your Spirit we are saved. Forgive us for thinking or acting otherwise. Let us rest in the assurance of the coming Messiah, for your salvation will not tarry. Amen.

Daniel M. Petry

December 16

The King of Glory

Reading: Psalm 24

The earth is the Lord's and all that is in it, the world, and those who live in it; for he has founded it on the seas, and established it on the rivers. Who shall ascend the hill of the Lord? And who shall stand in his holy place? Those who have clean hands and pure hearts, who do not lift up their souls to what is false, and do not swear deceitfully (Ps. 24:1-4).

Meditation: Just a few years ago, as I looked down on the Eder River and the village of Schwarzenau, Germany, I reflected on the beauty of the valley, the swift current of the high river, and the quick clouds moving through on that particular day of my visit. Our spiritual forefathers and mothers lived and worshiped high on the hill looking down. They looked down on this same valley and saw much more than my quick trip allowed. They saw storm clouds rolling by, rain showers passing, sunshine trailing across the scene, and nighttime slowly dimming the view. They saw winter, spring, summer, and fall.

In my everyday life, I am too busy to remember the earth and the nature around me. I am protected from the changing temperatures by my climate-controlled car and home. I am preoccupied by my daily tasks and assignments. All too often, I forget that the earth is the Lord's and all that is in it.

How can we approach God, the King of Glory, creator of heavens and earth? As the ancient people listened to the psalm, they asked, "Who shall be admitted to the temple?" and "Who shall ascend the hill of the Lord?" (v. 3). For the founders of our church who looked down on the valley where the gentle Eder River flowed, the question might have been, How can we live out our faith in God? We too ask, What does it take for me to be near? or What is required for us to be people of faith? The psalmist reminds us that we are all called to live ethical lives. We can only come to God with "clean hands and pure hearts." In other words, we can approach God because we try to live according to God's laws and Jesus' example.

For the day: We rejoice that God is the creator of heavens and earth. In addition, we rejoice that we are called to be God's people. Our response to God's power is to live our daily lives in accord with God's will.

Prayer: O God, the King of Glory, you seem so far away. When I think of the universe, I feel unimportant and small. Yet, I know that you care about each of us, as you care for the earth and all that is in it. I come to you with clean hands and a pure heart, a humble servant, seeking your strength and might. Amen.

Kathryn Goering Reid

December 17

Who Is Like the Lord?

Readings: Psalm 113; John 14:7-14

Who is like the LORD our God, who is seated on high, who looks far down on the heavens and the earth? (Ps. 113:5-6).

Meditation: The psalm begins as a cheerful praise to God. And then the psalmist asks the question: "Who is like the Lord?" What an incisive question! In our effort to answer that question, is the psalmist wanting us to remember God's awesome acts in the Exodus, that history-making story of liberation? Are we being challenged to consider God's call to us as we ponder God's call to Abraham and Sarah? Or are we to remember the God of Creation who made the worlds and us? Especially in this season, perhaps our hearts are touched most by the tenderness of God who became human in the coming of Jesus—who is the clearest and best answer to the psalmist's question, "Who is like the Lord?"

In John 14:9 Jesus says: "Whoever has seen me has seen the Father." Jesus, as no other, fulfills the last part of the psalm that offers hope for the needy and those who have had shattered dreams. Truly the work of Jesus continues, and we are challenged and encouraged to work together with him in the work of the Lord.

Through the stories of others whose lives reflect Jesus, increasingly I am being touched and moved and transformed by our Awesome God.

For the day: Are others able to see God reflected through your life and stories?

Prayer: Awesome God, we want the grace and love and joy and peace of Jesus to be reflected more and more through who we are and what we do. Amen.

Roger W. Eberly

December 18

Praise the Lord!

Reading: Psalm 148

Praise the Lord . . . fire and hail . . . stormy wind . . . mountains and hills; trees and cattle . . . creeping things and birds; kings and rulers . . . young men and women; old people and children. PRAISE THE LORD! *(Ps. 148:7-12, author's paraphrase).*

Meditation: I love to know that I am a part of all creation. It is a great comfort to me to realize that my body is composed of the same stuff that makes up the stars, the clouds, the oceans, and the wild animals. I am excited by the fact that my mind can be filled with the wisdom of the ages and the heavenly thoughts given to saints and angels. I treasure the experience of quiet contemplation and loud celebration as food for my spirit.

The psalmist who composed hymn 148 in the Hebrew hymnal (Ps. 148) includes all of creation— from stars, fire, wind, mountains, animals, birds, kings, to young people and children—as fit vehicles to praise the Lord.

My childhood in the mountains of Western Pennsylvania gave me an appreciation of hills as sacred places. (I was sure that God had ordained that the sun should rise up from the Tussey Mountain each morning.) Later, when I stood on Glacier Point in Yosemite National Park, I was "blown away" in awe of God. I am pleased that today young people have adopted the word *awesome* to describe stuff and events that point to God.

In this Advent season, we are reminded to add the coming of Jesus Christ to the list of praiseworthy events in Psalm 148. And we also need to add the whole family of Brethren on this our three hundredth birthday.

For the day: May we open our eyes to praiseworthy "stuff" in nature in all its forms, in people in all their behaviors, and in the frontiers of our souls' growing edges.

Prayer: God, creator of stars, angels, saints, and sinners, and everything else, we thank you for placing us in your vast playground. May we delight in all that we encounter, and may we welcome all our fellow passengers on Spaceship Earth on our way to the heaven above all heavens.

Dean A. Kagarise

✑

December 19

Part of the Choir

Reading: Romans 16:25-27

All of our praise rises to the One who is strong enough to make you strong, exactly as preached in Jesus Christ, precisely as revealed in the mystery kept secret for so long (Rom. 16:25 The Message).

Meditation: When I visited Italy, I was overwhelmed by the realization of how young we Brethren are in the broader history of Christianity. It was incredible to visit churches that were built during the third to fifth centuries, where worship has been continuous from that time to today, and on into the future. I marveled as I walked the streets of Assisi where nine hundred years ago a young man named Francis heard a call to rebuild the church. I saw with eyes of faith the chains that held Peter and the coffins that hold the remains of Zechariah (father of John the Baptist), St. Mark, and other saints of the faith. I saw paintings, sculptures, and other artworks that for centuries have tried to convey the good news of God as revealed in Jesus. Yes, I had studied this, but it was another thing altogether to experience it.

The song of praise to God of which Paul writes at the end of Romans is one that has been sung by Christians for nearly two thousand years. For the last three hundred years, we Brethren have added our voice to the mighty choir, lifting out the part that we have been called to sing. We should be humbled to be a part of this faithful choir. And we should sing God's song with boldness and beauty for as long as we have breath to offer praise.

For the day: Give thanks for those in your life, in our tradition, and the countless faithful who came before our tradition, for their song of praise "focused through Jesus on this incomparably wise God! Yes!" (Rom. 16:27 *The Message*).

Prayer: Wise God, I give thanks for the life of Jesus and for the ways in which your church has sought to be faithful for two thousand years. Give me the strength, hope, and faith to live and share your good news in our time and place. Amen.

Russell L. Matteson

℘

December 20

A New Understanding
of God's Love

Reading: Luke 2:1-7

And she gave birth to her firstborn son and wrapped him in bands of cloth, and laid him in a manger, because there was no place for them in the inn (Luke 2:7).

Meditation: It's time to change our attitude about the innkeeper's hospitality. Our images have him sending this poor couple to his dirty stable at the back end of the house. More accurately, this man and his family probably had several guest rooms, already rented for the night, and upon seeing Joseph and Mary, very tired and very pregnant, invited them into the simple living quarters of the family's private rooms of their home. Along one side of the cooking area would have been a long feeding trough built into the wall where newly weaned young lambs and calves were fed. The mother and grandmother of the household naturally would have stepped in to assist with the birth, as Mary's mother and sisters would have, had she been home in Nazareth. When the infant was born, bathed, and wrapped snugly in his swaddling strips, he would have been placed gently in the manger while the women attended to Mary's needs.

Mary and Joseph were welcomed into a household, which was able to care for her as she brought into this world a Savior. There are times in all of our lives when we have been away from the familiar, the comfortable, the usual, and someone has stepped into our lives to help us, to encourage us, and sometimes even to save us. This is the mission of the body of Christ. Somehow we need to find the courage to be open to the weary, very pregnant parts of our community that need a welcoming, helping hand.

For the day: Have you experienced the welcome of an innkeeper, or the help of a midwife, as you have journeyed to new levels of calling and commitment? Take some time this day to meditate, remember, and be grateful.

Prayer: O God, you know us better than we know ourselves. Guide us to be innkeepers and midwives; help us to birth a new understanding of God's love and grace in a weary world.

Rachel W. N. Brown

December 21

Glory to God!

Reading: Luke 2:8-20

So they went with haste and found Mary and Joseph, and the child lying in the manger. When they saw this, they made known what had been told them about this child; and all who heard it were amazed at what the shepherds told them (Luke 2:16-17).

Meditation: In the Christmas season, we can certainly empathize with the shepherds. Once December rolls around, my entire family picks up a shepherd's pace. "With haste" we shop, bake cookies, and visit family members. There are choir concerts to attend, trees to decorate, and friends to see as we bustle through the season. Christmas has become so busy with commitments and events that "with haste" may be the only way we know how to survive the Advent season.

While our hurriedness is perhaps the result of an over-commercialized holiday, the shepherds had just heard and seen amazing news. A multitude of angels, praising God and singing of God's glory, announced that a child was born who was to be the Messiah. The shepherds had good reason to rush to Bethlehem.

Once they arrived in Bethlehem and found Mary and Joseph and the baby, the shepherds went out and "made known what had been told them." In verse 20, the scripture mentions again that the shepherds returned "glorifying and praising God." Glory be to God for the gift of a son!

Let us go forth then, giving glory to God, sharing the joyful news of Jesus' birth.

For the day: Live today joyfully praising God for the gift of Christ Jesus. Remember the joy of the shepherds as they spread the news of what they had seen and heard.

Prayer: God, I rejoice with the angels, and with the shepherds I glorify you at the coming of your Son.

Cyndi Fecher

December 22

More Than a Prophet

Reading: Luke 7:24-29

What then did you go out to see? A prophet? Yes, I tell you, and more than a prophet (Luke 7:26).

Meditation: Jesus is talking about John "behind John's back!" Usually that's a troublesome experience that spreads rumor and causes pain. But when Jesus talks about his disciples, he always uses the conversation to build up. John was confused and discouraged. His confidence in Jesus' deity was melting. The kingdom John had expected was not happening. Does Jesus rebuke John's question or treat his servants harshly? No!

Instead, he provides great demonstrations that support his claims to deity, and he sends messengers back to share these evidences with John. Then Jesus begins to "brag about John" to the audience.

Just when we think we are worthless and ineffective in our witness about our Savior, Jesus affirms his grace to us and reminds us of his value in every effort we have given to him. While we may be frustrated with doubt, fear, and weakness, Jesus is ever mindful of his calling and purposes for our lives. When we wonder if there is any value to our efforts and service, Jesus speaks about how his purposes are being fulfilled in our same actions. If we feel we have failed to change our world or feel the frustration of the world's scorn and sneer, Jesus reminds us that in the kingdom of God these things do not mark success or determine value. Though John didn't see it or feel it, he was valued and significant in the workings of God. May we know the same about ourselves today and not let outward oppressions or inner fears steal our confidence and joy. Jesus knows and is talking about us "behind our backs," just like he did about John.

For the day: What Jesus says about me is the foundation of my value. Present circumstances are always temporary.

Prayer: Lord Jesus, tune my heart to hear what you have to say about me through your Word and by your Spirit. Help me not to measure my success or value by the standards of a fallen world. Increase my confidence in who you are, and give me grace to seek your pleasure. In your name, Amen.

James Custer

$\mathscr{Q}$

December 23

Witness to the Light

Reading: John 1:6-9

He himself was not the light, but he came to [bear witness] to the light. The true light, which enlightens everyone, was coming into the world (John 1:8-9).

Meditation: Moments before sunrise an amazing scene develops outside my front window in the pale gray pre-dawn sky. Needle-thin lines of gleaming silver-gold begin to pierce the cosmic canvas above and nearly parallel to the horizon. Rising slightly, they thread their way across the panorama, first one, then another, sometimes as many as five or six at a time. They begin to shimmer in peach and gold as the coming dawn begins to tint the sky.

My living room window faces toward the small but busy airport of Harrisburg, Pennsylvania, some thirty miles to the east. Just as the sun rises, busy travelers are taking off on their commuter flights for the day. The brilliant lines I see are the tail fumes of those small jets, exhaust fumes as arrow-straight as the course their pilots fly. For a moment, they are beautiful, gleaming—ascending angels taking off in flight.

These gleaming strands themselves are barely real—puffs of vapor that disintegrate quickly in the morning air. Yet in that moment they reflect something much greater: the still-hidden, but dawning presence of the sun's great light. When the sun is fully risen, they will disappear in its glare. But for the moment, they reflect its glory in brilliant minutiae. This was John's role, too. He was not the Light. But he came to bear witness to the Light, the Light that was coming into the world in Jesus Christ.

Our lives, too, are fleeting—barely a blip on the radar screen of time. But in the fleeing darkness of this winter world, may our lives, too, bear a reflecting witness—to the coming Light of God.

For the day: Where do you see the light of God present in your world today?

Prayer: Lord, in these dark days of winter, may our eyes be opened to the light of Jesus, and reflect the coming of your glorious reign. Amen.

Melanie Jones

December 24

A Voice in the Wilderness

Reading: John 1:19-27

Then they said to [John the Baptist], "Who are you? Let us have an answer for those who sent us. What do you say about yourself?" He said, "I am the voice of one crying out in the wilderness, 'Make straight the way of the Lord'. . . ." (John 1:22-23).

Meditation: It is the most precious of eves. Our eyes are open and ears tuned in. The children among us are at the edge of their waiting and are eager to make something out of everything. They teach us well on the eve of Christmas.

Our text paints the scene of another eve—the eve of Jesus' ministry. The struggle over John's identity settles on his confession that he is a voice in the wilderness. He proclaims what he has seen and heard. He points to what he knows. He looks to Jesus.

We all need a voice in the wilderness. If we listen deeply, we will discover that we are never without a voice. All of life holds God's presence and proclamation. Our work is anchored in our listening. We listen to all that speaks of God's incarnation in the world. As Brethren we have been listening for three hundred years. And we have also been adding our unique voice to the gospel's proclamation for those many years. There is a great gift in that, yet the wilderness is thick around us, and the work of listening and proclaiming goes on. Our future will unfold around the voice we hear and follow and the proclamation we become.

For the day: Listen today for the voice of God coming through all you do, and free the uniqueness of your voice to add to the chorus of wonder, praise, and gratitude. Become the Christmas proclamation.

Prayer: O God, from all my busyness gather me into the quiet so I might hear in my wilderness the clarity of your voice in the birth and life of Jesus. In this incarnational season, help form in me the good news you invite me to be and to share. Bathe my spirit in birth and keep me pondering the amazing advent of your Son. Amen.

Glenn Mitchell

December 25

Testimony

Reading: John 1:29-34

I myself have seen and have testified that this is the Son of God (John 1:34).

Meditation: One of my more unforgettable Christmases was spent in a motel room. My family had planned to stay in the assisted-living facility where my dad and mom had been living ever since her stroke the year before. But a virus was making its way around the building, so we decided it was best to get a room elsewhere.

On Christmas Eve we hung stockings on the drapery rod, and I used the laundry room across the hall as the workshop in which to fill the stockings and wrap presents. In the morning, nine of us crowded into the room for a makeshift celebration. Later in the day, when it became apparent that Christmas dinner had never quite gotten planned, we ended up eating canned miniature hotdogs from the one convenience store that we could find open. It felt rather pitiful.

But not completely. That morning we had awakened to an unusual sight for that part of Maryland—a white Christmas. Outside the world was silent and pure. The gray city wore new clothes. It was the most beautiful Christmas morning I could remember.

For my mother, celebrating Christmas on Christmas Day had always been important. That year we didn't know how much she was comprehending, but I'm sure she still understood what she had lived out every day of her life—that she had seen and knew the Son of God.

The day was a long way from our expectations. But I had to remind myself that we did indeed find room in the inn that year.

For the day: Now that Christmas is here and you cannot prepare anymore, slow down and look for Jesus. How can you make this holiday a holy day?

Prayer: O gift-giving God, may we both see and testify. May your Son be born in us today. Amen.

Wendy McFadden

⚘

December 26

A Shining Lamp

Reading: John 5:30-35

[John the Baptist] was a lamp that burned and gave light . . . (John 5:35 NIV).

Meditation: On Christmas Day 1795, a large sheep-skin deed, measuring 27" x 29", was signed by representatives of the German Lutheran, German Reformed, and German Baptist Brethren congregations on the wild frontier of Paradise Township, York County, Pennsylvania. The deed set aside one acre of farmland for the construction of a union house of worship to be used by the three congregations on a rotating basis, and to be used as a school. The old meetinghouse served faithfully until around 1920. In 1980 the youth of Bermudian Church of the Brethren began the major task of restoring Altland Meeting House. On Christmas Eve 1981, under the theme "A Light in the Window," a Christmas Eve candlelight worship was held. Each Christmas Eve since, by kerosene lamp and candlelight, the old meetinghouse windows shine with a welcoming light as the story of the first Christmas is told once more.

Jesus speaks of John the Baptist as a "lamp" that gave light as a testimony. Altland Meeting House still shines as a "lamp of testimony." In a time long before the modern ecumenical movement, Altland was a place where believers celebrated unity rather than differences. The old house of worship has a raised preaching platform, something unheard of in early Brethren meetinghouses, but obviously a testimony to being willing to work together. Today the windows shine as a testimony to the steadfastness of the gospel. A recent Christmas Eve saw a group of leather-clad "bikers" join the worshiping congregation. Neighbors gather at the old meetinghouse from many different denominational backgrounds. In the light of the old building, the true testimony of Christ's love being for all people still shines!

For the day: How can you "shine" for Jesus today?

Prayer: Lord of Light, in a world that so often is marked by darkness, the testimony of your love still shines brightly! May I, like John so long ago, be a "lamp of testimony" to who you are for all those with whom I come in contact today! Amen.

Larry M. Dentler

♔

December 27

In the Name of Jesus

Reading: John 3:22-30

He must increase, but I must decrease (John 3:30).

Meditation: C. S. Lewis once remarked that different characters in a story must play great parts without pride and small parts without shame. Today's text reveals that John the Baptist understood and lived that lesson well.

A challenge in being Christian, comments N. T. Wright, is taking into account the many sources of insight—the life, teachings, death, and resurrection of Jesus; the leading of the Spirit; the wisdom found in scripture; one's baptism and all that it means; the sense of God's presence and guidance through prayer; and fellowship with other Christians, present and past—and then weighing what we hear in one quarter alongside what is said in another and working it all together. But the essence, says Wright, is hearing "the voice of Jesus calling us to follow him into God's new world—the world in which the hints, signposts, and echoes of the present world turn into the reality of the next one."

The testimony of the Baptist to his followers is that Jesus is at the heart and center of God's new movement. And so he is to be for us. A metaphor attributed to Huston Smith and cited by Marcus Borg clinches the point: If you are looking for water, it is better to dig one well sixty feet deep than six wells ten feet deep.

The founders of the Brethren movement, like John the Baptist, had it figured right: As Christians, our calling is to be a living witness for Christ in the world.

For the day: Ministry is acting in the name of Jesus, J. M. Henri Nouwen has written, and to him that meant acting in intimate communion with Jesus. Assess your personal ministry by pondering the Nouwen question: Am I acting in the name of Jesus?

Prayer: God, keep ever before us an awareness that any good we do comes not of ourselves, but through your working in our lives. Keep us ever in the name of Jesus. Amen.

Howard E. Royer

℘

December 28

A Prophet's To-Do List

Reading: Luke 3:7-18

And the crowds asked him, "What then should we do?" (Luke 3:10).

Meditation: John the Baptist was a "hellfire and brimstone" preacher, if there ever was one! At the end of this passage from Luke, the writer somewhat ironically comments that "with many other exhortations, [John] proclaimed the good news to the people" (v. 18).

But was it good news? To be called a "brood of vipers"; to be told that "even now the ax is lying at the root of the trees"; to be informed that the long awaited Savior would arrive with winnowing fork in hand to burn the chaff as he gathered the wheat. It depends, doesn't it, on whether we confidently see ourselves among those who are fruit-bearing, or if we have a vision of the shriveled-up fruit that still hangs, metaphorically, from the branches of our lives.

When we read John's call to repentance, do we think of missed opportunities to help others, times we have kept that second coat for ourselves when others went coatless in the cold, selfish use of the world's precious resources like water and energy, days when we have not been satisfied with our wages even though so many survive on less than a few dollars a day?

John was as aware as we are of the inequities of the world. Many who heard him preach, and repented of their sins on the banks of the Jordan, must have come from the ranks of the poor and received his words as good news that justice was imminent. Others who were rich may have heard his words instead as fearful prophecies of judgment.

Whether we are poor or rich in today's terms, the question the crowd asked of John is the right one for us too: "What then should we do?" His answer is just as applicable today: Share with others, and be satisfied with what you have.

For the day: Consider the fruit you are bearing for Christ. Make a list of the things you have done today that are "good fruit."

Prayer: God, help me to be satisfied with what I have, and help me share what I have with others. Amen.

Cheryl Brumbaugh-Cayford

&

December 29

Step into the Tent

Readings: Psalm 15; Jeremiah 31:33-34

O LORD, who may abide in your tent? Who may dwell on your holy hill? (Ps. 15:1).

Meditation: O Lord, as I prepare for worship, I cannot check off everything on this list of righteousness and blamelessness the psalmist describes. If your tent had high security checkpoints, my swipecards would fail; my papers would not pass muster. But you are not like that, and here I am, turning toward you again. You have pitched your tent inside my heart, and I carry it around with me. Even though you have written your law upon my heart, I often choose to step outside your tent. I let go of an oath, or stand silent in the face of injustice. But you remind me that I can always step back inside. The song of the psalmist tells me that every act of loyalty, of generosity, of integrity, of solidarity—no matter how small—is a step into your tent. You are that close. Your promise sings to me: *Those who do these things shall never be moved.* That is my desire: to be firmly planted on your hill, to dwell in God's camp. Who does dwell in your camp all the time? Few people that I know. But I can tell those who have sojourned there by the way they act—courageously truth-telling, striving for justice; fiercely and lovingly defending their friends, the innocent, and other people of faith. Their actions are evidence of your work in them. I want to live where they live: with you. Yes, form my life into a witness to God-with-us.

For the day: Look back over the last twenty-four hours. How have you stepped into the Lord's tent today?

Prayer: God, I long to dwell with you. Help me to trust that even turning toward you right now is transforming me through grace. Help me take risks of faith today. I offer you my whole life as worship. Amen.

Sarah Kinsel

⌀

December 30

Fear or Faith? It's Your Choice!

Readings: Psalm 27:1-6; Numbers 13; 1 John 1:5-7

The LORD is my light and my salvation; whom shall I fear? The LORD is the stronghold of my life; of whom shall I be afraid? (Ps. 27:1-2).

Meditation: One of the scariest jobs a novice seaman was asked to do on old-time ships was to climb the mast and unfurl or repair the sails in the top rigging. The captains often advised young trainees, "If you lose your nerve and become afraid, don't look down, look up." That is what David did. When he was afraid, tested, or unsure, he trusted in his personal God—Jehovah. His Lord was personal! How personal is your Lord?

One of the most paralyzing emotions is fear. We experience many: fear of the unknown, of failure, of rejection, of death. Fear is faith in reverse. Remember those twelve spies sent by Moses to explore the Promised Land in Numbers 13? Ten came back afraid while two came back with courage. Fear won and resulted in another twenty years in the wilderness.

The answer to life's fears is in the Lord through the light, the salvation, and the strength that he gives. David, in the first six verses of Psalm 27, expresses praise, confidence, victory, and even singing. In 1 John 1:7, it is suggested that "we walk in the light as he is in the light." Can we? David lists the fears of his life and follows with a strong witness to the strength he gets through his intimate relationship with his Lord.

Rosa Parks changed the course of history when she refused to give up her seat to a white man on a bus in Montgomery, Alabama, in December 1955. She says, "I felt the Lord would give me the strength to endure whatever I had to face. God did away with all my fear. It was time for someone to stand up or, in this case, to sit down. I refused to move." Her faith triumphed over fear.

For the day: When the sun seems not to shine and a ground swell of fear invites panic, to whom do you turn? What a friend we have in Jesus!

Prayer: Lord, as I face a new year, send the light of Christ to expose my fears and immerse me in the joy of the Lord who is my strength.

Earl K. Ziegler

December 31

Facing Our Fears

Readings: Psalm 23; Luke 2:8-14

You prepare a table before me in the presence of my enemies; you anoint my head with oil; my cup overflows (Ps. 23:5).

Meditation: For generations we have used the 23rd Psalm as an amulet to ward off bad luck. It swings from rearview mirrors, printed on cardboard air fresheners. It's been written on little shards of paper and stuffed into a million wallets. Soldiers murmur it in the movies before they head into battle. The condemned ask for the psalm to shepherd them to the next world. It shows up on bookmarks, funeral home fans, coasters, plaques, and needlework, ever ready to soothe us and remind us God is near. We cannot go where it is not! It's true. The 23rd Psalm has been a great comfort for the world, but it's really courage the psalm is trying to impart, not safety. The Good Shepherd doesn't shelter us in the protective confines of the church. God leads us out into the world, which is both beautiful with its still waters and dangerous with its wolves in sheep's clothing, but the best grass is always in the beautiful, dangerous pasture. That's the right path. God doesn't give us a detour around death. We have to walk right into the valley of the shadow of death. God doesn't shield us from our enemies. God makes us sit right down at the table and break bread with them. God anoints us, perhaps for death, but also for courage as God anointed David the king. And only when we have faced our fears can we be restored to wholeness and grace. Only then does our cup overflow with fulfillment and peace.

For the day: Read the 23rd Psalm today and screw up your courage to confront an injustice, apologize to someone, write a letter to the editor, or tell the truth. See whether you do not feel restored.

Prayer: Shepherd, give us the courage we lack on our own to walk in the right path. Another path might be easier, but we know the right path leads to the peace that comes when we have done your will. Amen.

Julie Garber

Index of Contributors

Alley, Robert E. (1947–). Bridgewater, Virginia. Pastor. *Church of the Brethren.* 7/27, 10/25

Allison, Judy V. (1957–). Ashland, Ohio. Psychologist. *Brethren Church.* 12/8

Archbold, Phill Carlos (1936–). York, Pennsylvania. Interim pastor; Annual Conference moderator (2001). *Church of the Brethren.* 2/23

Augustin, Founa (1982–). Miami, Florida. Student; youth director at Eglise des Freres Haitiens. *Church of the Brethren.* 3/10

Bach, Jeffrey A. (1958–). Richmond, Indiana. Associate professor of Brethren and Historical Studies, Bethany Theological Seminary. *Church of the Brethren.* 2/20

Barlow, Martha Stover (1947–). Dayton, Virginia. Director of counseling, Bridgewater College. *Church of the Brethren.* 5/17

Beachler, Lowell H. (1931–). Modesto, California. Mortuary office manager. *Old German Baptist Brethren.* 7/23

Beachley, Ronald D. (1940–). Hollsopple, Pennsylvania. Executive/minister, Western Pennsylvania District; Annual Conference moderator (2006). *Church of the Brethren.* 1/21

Beahm, I. N. H. (1859–1950). Educator; evangelist; president, Elizabethtown College (1900–1901, 1904–1909). *Church of the Brethren.* 1/6

Beahm, Martha E. (1959–). Columbia, South Carolina. Counselor and therapist; ordained minister; spiritual director. *Church of the Brethren.* 1/30

Beckwith, James M. (1950–). Lebanon, Pennsylvania. Pastor; Annual Conference moderator (2008). *Church of the Brethren.* 4/30

Beekley, Charles (1945–). Frederick, Maryland. Pastor. *Church of the Brethren.* 7/16

Benedict, Fred W. (1930–). Union City, Ohio. Retired printer. *Old German Baptist Brethren.* 1/7, 7/3

Benedict, James L. (1959–). Union Bridge, Maryland. Pastor. *Church of the Brethren.* 3/23, 6/8

Benevento, Tom (1962–). Goshen, Indiana. Community sustainable development worker; Latin America specialist (General Board staff). *Church of the Brethren.* 2/26

Bennett, Melissa (1975–). Fort Wayne, Indiana. Pastor for worship and youth. *Church of the Brethren.* 2/17, 7/8

Brown, Kenneth L. (1933–). North Manchester, Indiana. Professor emeritus of Philosophy and Peace Studies, Manchester College; ordained minister. *Church of the Brethren.* 3/24

Brown, Rachel W. N. (1947–). Mount Sidney, Virginia. Author; designer; quilter; small business owner; workshop and retreat leader; Association for the Arts. *Church of the Brethren.* 12/20

Brubaker, Pamela K. (1946–). Thousand Oaks, California. Professor of Religion and Ethics, California Lutheran University. *Church of the Brethren.* 8/30

Brubaker, Paul W. (1943–). Ephrata, Pennsylvania. Ordained minister; bank executive. *Church of the Brethren.* 2/18

Brumbaugh-Cayford, Cheryl (1963–). Elgin, Illinois. Director of news services (General Board staff); ordained minister. *Church of the Brethren.* 1/15, 12/28

Brumfield, Larry L. (1948–). Westminster, Maryland. Retired businessman; licensed minister. *Church of the Brethren.* 1/8

Bryant, John E. (1951–). Mount Vernon, Ohio. Pastor; Brethren Encyclopedia board, treasurer. *Conservative Grace Brethren Churches International.* 1/18, 9/15

Bucher, Christina (1951–). Elizabethtown, Pennsylvania. Professor of Religion, Elizabethtown College. *Church of the Brethren.* 5/20

Bucher, L. Gene (1936–). East Petersburg, Pennsylvania. Retired pastor. *Church of the Brethren.* 3/9, 3/14

Bueno, Anastacia (1962–). Santo Domingo, Dominican Republic. Pastor; student. *Church of the Brethren.* 10/8

Bugu, Patrick K. (1960–). Mubi, Adamawa State, Nigeria. Director, EYN Theological Education by Extension. *Church of the Brethren in Nigeria.* 9/11

Burkholder, Connie R. (1956–). Great Bend, Kansas. Ordained minister; spiritual director. *Church of the Brethren.* 10/23

Camps, Michaela (1981–). Miami, Florida. Elementary school teacher; program director, Camp Ithiel. *Church of the Brethren.* 6/18

Carter, Jeffrey W. (1970–). Manassas, Virginia. Pastor. *Church of the Brethren.* 1/16

Chinworth, James H. (1957–). North Manchester, Indiana. Pastor. *Church of the Brethren.* 4/29

Colijn, Brenda B. (1952–). Columbus, Ohio. Associate professor of Biblical Interpretation and Theology, Ashland Theological Seminary. *Brethren Church.* 5/26

Cook, Milton (1943–). Beaumont, California. Elder; editor, *Bible Monitor. Dunkard Brethren.* 10/1

Crouse, Rebecca Baile (1959–). Warrensburg, Missouri. Team pastor; pediatric hospital chaplain. *Church of the Brethren.* 6/2

Crouse, Merle (1931–). Saint Cloud, Florida. Pastor; former missionary; former General Board staff; retired. *Church of the Brethren.* 7/9

Custer, James (1938-). Columbus, Ohio. Pastor. *Fellowship of Grace Brethren Churches.* 12/22

Daggett, Joan L. (1961–). Bridgewater, Virginia. Associate executive/minister, Shenandoah District. *Church of the Brethren.* 5/13, 5/14

Daté, Barbara (1946–). Eugene, Oregon. Educator; conflict transformation consultant. *Church of the Brethren.* 6/26

Davis, John J. (1936–). Winona Lake, Indiana. President/professor emeritus, Grace College and Theological Seminary. *Fellowship of Grace Brethren Churches.* 11/20

Deeter, Joan G. (1930–). North Manchester, Indiana. Chaplain, Timbercrest Senior Living Community; former General Board staff (1988–1997). *Church of the Brethren.* 9/30

Dell, Robert (1939–). Dallastown, Pennsylvania. Ordained minister, retired. *Church of the Brethren.* 2/11, 3/21, 5/10

Deloe, Jesse B. (1934–). Winona Lake, Indiana. Senior editor, BMH Books. *Fellowship of Grace Brethren Churches.* 6/13, 9/26

Dentler, Larry M. (1951–). East Berlin, Pennsylvania. Pastor; evangelist. *Church of the Brethren.* 9/29, 12/26

Douglas, Chris (1953–). Elgin, Illinois. Director of youth and young adult ministries (General Board staff); ordained minister. *Church of the Brethren.* 8/13

Dowdy, Christy L. (1954–). Huntingdon, Pennsylvania. Pastor. *Church of the Brethren.* 2/2

Dowdy, Dale W. (1949–). Huntingdon, Pennsylvania. Pastor. *Church of the Brethren.* 9/25

Eberly, Roger W. (1942–). Milford, Indiana. Pastor. *Church of the Brethren.* 12/17

Eberly, William R. (1926–). North Manchester, Indiana. Professor emeritus of Biology, Manchester College; Annual Conference moderator (1980). *Church of the Brethren.* 1/28

Eikenberry, James O. (1952–). Stockton, California. Ordained minister; pastoral staff; college instructor. *Church of the Brethren.* 4/26, 8/14

Eikenberry, Susan L. (1950–). Stockton, California. Director of women's ministries, counseling, and body life ministries, Quail Lakes Baptist Church. *Church of the Brethren.* 9/19

Eller, Vernard (1927–). Professor emeritus of Religion, University of La Verne; author. *Church of the Brethren.* 6/10

Encarnación, Gladys (1931–). Lancaster, Pennsylvania. Retired teacher; translator. *Church of the Brethren.* 4/23

Eshbach, Warren M. (1940–). Dover, Pennsylvania. Retired district executive/minister; adjunct faculty; General Board chair (2002–2003). *Church of the Brethren.* 2/22

Farrar, Fletcher (1949–). Springfield, Illinois. Journalist; neighborhood activist; former editor, *Messenger*. *Church of the Brethren*. 6/28, 9/3, 11/26

Faus-Mullen, Nancy R. (1934–). Richmond, Indiana. Professor emerita and adjunct faculty, Bethany Theological Seminary; leader of worship and preaching workshops and hymn festivals. *Church of the Brethren*. 2/1

Fecher, Cyndi (1982–). Elgin, Illinois. Project assistant, Gather 'Round curriculum (General Board staff). *Church of the Brethren*. 12/21

Fike, Earle W., Jr. (1930–). Bridgewater, Virginia. Retired pastor and seminary teacher; Annual Conference moderator (1982). *Church of the Brethren*. 6/4, 6/11

Finks, Frederick J. (1946–). Ashland, Ohio. President, Ashland University. *Brethren Church*. 8/21

Finney, Harriet Wenger (1940–). North Manchester, Indiana. Retired co-district executive/minister; Annual Conference moderator (2003). *Church of the Brethren*. 1/10

Fitzkee, Donald R. (1963–). Manheim, Pennsylvania. Free minister; writer. *Church of the Brethren*. 2/28, 2/29, 3/1, 3/2

Flora, Jerry (1933–). Ashland, Ohio. Professor emeritus, Ashland Theological Seminary. *Brethren Church*. 6/23

Flora, Julie (1932–). Ashland, Ohio. Library assistant, Ashland Theological Seminary. *Brethren Church*. 6/23

Flory-Steury, Mary Jo (1956–). Dayton, Ohio. Executive director of Ministry (General Board staff); ordained minister; General Board chair (1998–2001). *Church of the Brethren*. 12/12

Fourman, Larry D. (1942–). Nappanee, Indiana. Pastor; spiritual director; retreat leader. *Church of the Brethren*. 11/15

Fouts, David (1934–). Maysville, West Virginia. Retired physician. *Church of the Brethren*. 10/2

Franklin, Pam Warner (1953–). Modesto, California. Teacher. *Dunkard Brethren*. 8/9

Franklin, Philip (1950–). Modesto, California. Deacon. *Dunkard Brethren*. 8/8

Gandy, Kate (1972–). Mexico, Indiana. Youth/young adult pastor. *Church of the Brethren*. 11/2

Garber, Julie (1956–). North Manchester, Indiana. Editor, *Brethren Life & Thought*; managing editor, *Journal of Religion, Conflict, and Peace* (Earlham, Goshen, and Manchester Colleges). *Church of the Brethren*. 11/18, 12/31

Gardner, Richard B. (1940–). Richmond, Indiana. Professor emeritus of New Testament Studies, Bethany Theological Seminary. *Church of the Brethren*. 9/17, 10/22

Gibble, H. Lamar (1931–). Saint Charles, Illinois. Ordained minister; former peace and international affairs consultant (General Board staff 1969–1997); retired. *Church of the Brethren*. 6/5

Gibble, Kenneth L. (1941–). Greencastle, Pennsylvania. Ordained minister; writer. *Church of the Brethren.* 5/28, 6/24, 7/26, 10/13

Gilbert, Julia (1844–1934). Advocated equality of women in receiving communion; one of first women to speak at Annual Meeting (1909, 1910). 7/17

Gilmer, Arden E. (1943–). Ashland, Ohio. Pastor. *Brethren Church.* 4/22

Gish, Art (1939–). Athens, Ohio. Farmer; author; peace activist. *Church of the Brethren.* 1/9

Gish, Peggy (1942–). Athens, Ohio. Full-time worker with Christian Peacemaker Teams. *Church of the Brethren.* 8/22

Glick, J. D. (1941–). Bridgewater, Virginia. Pastor. *Church of the Brethren.* 12/6

Grady, Duane (1957–). Anderson, Indiana. Congregational life team (General Board staff); ordained minister. *Church of the Brethren.* 1/11

Grahe, Wilhelm (1693–1763). As one of the Solingen Brethren imprisoned at Jülich in 1717, authored an account of their persecution. 7/28

Gribble, James (1883–1923). Former streetcar conductor who began a mission in French Equatorial Africa. *Brethren Church.* 7/21

Griffith, Sonja Sherfy (1942–). Kansas City, Kansas. Registered nurse; pastor. *Church of the Brethren.* 3/31

Grimm, Michelle (1960–). Dayton, Ohio. Church musician. *Church of the Brethren.* 10/12

Groff, Warren F. (1924–). Bartlett, Illinois. President emeritus, Bethany Theological Seminary. *Church of the Brethren.* 7/25

Gross, Bob (1960–). North Manchester, Indiana. Co-executive director, On Earth Peace. *Church of the Brethren.* 2/3

Grout, Paul E. (1945–). Putney, Vermont. Ordained minister; A Place Apart; Annual Conference moderator (2002). *Church of the Brethren.* 1/31

Guynn, Matthew R. (1974–). Richmond, Indiana. Peace witness coordinator, On Earth Peace. *Church of the Brethren.* 5/15, 5/16

Gwama, Filibus K. (1944–). Mubi, Adamawa State, Nigeria. President, *Church of the Brethren in Nigeria (EYN).* 8/20

Hackman, Galen R. (1953–). Akron, Pennsylvania. Pastor; writer; Bible teacher, former missionary. *Church of the Brethren.* 4/1, 4/2, 4/3, 4/4, 4/5, 4/6

Hansell, Allen T. (1936–). Mountville, Pennsylvania. Director of church relations, Elizabethtown College; former district executive/minister; former director of ministry (General Board staff). *Church of the Brethren.* 11/3

Hardenbrook, James O. (1951–). Nampa, Idaho. Pastor; Annual Conference moderator (2005). *Church of the Brethren.* 2/6

Harmon, Gordy A. (1961–). Mount Vernon, Ohio. Pastor; elder; bishop. *Conservative Grace Brethren Churches International.* 3/6

Harvey, Timothy P. (1970–). Roanoke, Virginia. Pastor; General Board member (2003–2008). *Church of the Brethren.* 4/15, 4/16, 4/17, 4/18, 4/19, 4/20

Heishman, Nancy Sollenberger (1955–). Santo Domingo, Dominican Republic. Ordained minister; mission coordinator, Dominican Republic (General Board staff). *Church of the Brethren.* 3/13

Hendricks, Jean L. (1947–). Abilene, Kansas. Administrator; ordained minister. *Church of the Brethren.* 12/9

Hershberger, Marlys (1954–). Woodbury, Pennsylvania. Pastor. *Church of the Brethren.* 11/17

Hess, Reuben D. (1960–). Greencastle, Pennsylvania. A brother. *Old German Baptist Brethren.* 6/7

Hinshaw, Christopher J. (1958–). Elkhart, Indiana. Pastor. *Conservative Grace Brethren Churches International.* 3/30

Hipskind, Gene F. (1941–). Boise, Idaho. Retired; former district executive/minister. *Church of the Brethren.* 5/18

Hollinger, James E. (1943–). Goshen, Indiana. Surgeon; director of medical education, Goshen General Hospital. *Brethren Church.* 2/10

Holsinger, Henry R. (1833–1905). Leader of Progressive Brethren; pastor; publisher, *Christian Family Companion, The Progressive Christian, The Brethren Evangelist. Brethren Church.* 5/7

Hostetter, Julie M. (1951–). Dayton, Ohio. Ordained minister; director of academic and student services, United Theological Seminary. *Church of the Brethren.* 10/10, 11/1

Hostetter, Michael L. (1951–). Englewood, Ohio. Interim pastor. *Church of the Brethren.* 3/11, 3/12

Huffman, Bruce (1952–). Rocky Mount, Virginia. Pastor. *Church of the Brethren.* 7/24

Huffman, Reuben (1975–). Farmersville, Ohio. 2nd degree minister. *Old German Baptist Brethren.* 11/9

Hummer, Catharine (fl.1762–1763). Conestoga, Pennsylvania. Daughter of a pastor; caused controversy with her visions of heaven and angels. 4/21

Hunn, Kenneth D. (1955–). Ashland, Ohio. Ordained minister; executive director, the Brethren Church. *Brethren Church.* 9/21

Hunter, Jonathan (1950–). La Mesa, California. Ordained minister; California program director, Corporation for Supportive Housing. *Church of the Brethren.* 10/31

Inhauser, Suely Zanetti (1951–). São Paulo, Brazil. National co-coordinator, Church of the Brethren in Brazil (General Board staff); ordained minister. *Church of the Brethren.* 10/24

Jones, Melanie (1961–). Carlisle, Pennsylvania. Pastor. *Church of the Brethren.* 7/11, 8/18, 12/23

Julien, Thomas (1931–). Winona Lake, Indiana. Executive director emeritus, Grace Brethren International Missions. *Fellowship of Grace Brethren Churches.* 4/9

Kagarise, Dean (1932–). Milford, Indiana. Interim pastor. *Church of the Brethren.* 12/18

Keeney, Mervin B. (1951–). Elgin, Illinois. Executive director of Global Mission Partnerships (General Board staff). *Church of the Brethren.* 6/27

Kent, Homer A., Jr. (1926–). Winona Lake, Indiana. President emeritus, Grace College and Theological Seminary. *Fellowship of Grace Brethren Churches.* 5/19

Kettering, Denise (1978–). Iowa City, Iowa. Student; licensed minister. *Church of the Brethren.* 11/21

Kindy, Cliff (1949–). North Manchester, Indiana. Steering committee and full-time worker, Christian Peacemaker Teams; organic market gardener. *Church of the Brethren.* 9/18

Kinsel, Glenn E. (1922–). Hanover, Pennsylvania. Retired pastor; part-time administrative volunteer, Emergency Response/Service Ministries. *Church of the Brethren.* 5/31

Kinsel, Sarah (1978–). Richmond, Indiana. Writer; retreat facilitator. *Church of the Brethren.* 1/25, 12/29

Kinzie, Tom (1948–). Portland, Oregon. Health services coordinator for a refugee organization; workshop presenter; preaching/presider team of Journey Koinonia Catholic Community. *Church of the Brethren.* 10/5

Kirchner, Shawn (1970–). La Verne, California. Denominational music leader; composer; singer; pianist. *Church of the Brethren.* 8/5

Kissinger, Warren S. (1922–). University Park, Maryland. Ordained minister; retired religion cataloger, Library of Congress. *Church of the Brethren.* 11/23

Kline, Joel D. (1950–). Elgin, Illinois. Pastor. *Church of the Brethren.* 4/11

Kline, John (1797–1864). Church leader; Annual Meeting moderator (1861–1864); Civil War martyr. 1/20, 8/27

Kreider, J. Kenneth (1934–). Elizabethtown, Pennsylvania. Professor emeritus, Elizabethtown College; Germantown Trust chair. *Church of the Brethren.* 6/16

Kurtz, Henry (1796–1874). Pastor; publisher, editor, and printer; began *The Gospel Visiter*, the first Brethren periodical, in 1851. 5/23

Lahman, Aaron R. (1981–). Peoria, Arizona. Math teacher. *Church of the Brethren.* 5/29

Landes, Wallace B. (1952–). Palmyra, Pennsylvania. Pastor; Association of Brethren Caregivers board, chair (2006–2007); adjunct instructor in Religious Studies, Elizabethtown College. *Church of the Brethren.* 7/18, 10/4, 12/14

Laprade, Cindy E. (1981–). Rocky Mount, Virginia. Licensed minister; student, Princeton Theological Seminary. *Church of the Brethren.* 6/29

Laszakovits, Greg Davidson (1972–). Elizabethtown, Pennsylvania. Pastor. *Church of the Brethren.* 10/21

Lee, Verdena (1963–). Columbus, Ohio. Physician; On Earth Peace board, vice chair. *Church of the Brethren.* 4/28

Lehigh, Robert S. (1954–). Spring Grove, Pennsylvania. Editor, Bible Helps; presiding elder; Brethren Encyclopedia board. *Dunkard Brethren.* 1/13, 8/25

Lehman, James H. (1944–). Elgin, Illinois. Writer; publisher. *Church of the Brethren.* 5/22, 5/24, 7/13, 8/6

Leiter, David A. (1958–). Oaks, Pennsylvania. Pastor. *Church of the Brethren.* 6/3, 6/30

Lersch, Jean (1933–). St. Petersburg, Florida. Organist/choir director. *Church of the Brethren.* 7/12

Libby, Scott (1958–). Newport, Vermont. Pastor. *Conservative Grace Brethren Churches International.* 12/13

Liepelt, Brandan E. (1977–). Kwarhi, Nigeria. Ordained minister; lecturer, Kulp Bible College, Nigeria. *Church of the Brethren.* 9/22

Lipscomb, Rebecca M. (1988–). Springfield, Illinois. Student, Eastern Illinois University; district youth cabinet, co–president (2004–2006). *Church of the Brethren.* 10/11

Logan, Chantal (1948–). Bridgewater, Virginia. Missionary; university professor. *Brethren Church.* 11/12

Logan, Linda (1942–). Bridgewater, Virginia. Christian educator; writer. *Church of the Brethren.* 11/5

Logan, Mark (1943–). Bridgewater, Virginia. Missionary; mission pastor. *Brethren Church.* 5/12

Mack, Alexander (Sander), Jr. (1712–1803). Following ten-year stay at Ephrata Community, became elder and pastor in Germantown; produced first account of Brethren beginnings in Germany. 9/7

Mack, Alexander, Sr. (1679–1735). First minister and organizer of the Brethren movement at Schwarzenau in 1708. 4/10, 4/14

Major, Sarah Righter (1808–1884). First woman preacher among the Brethren. 1/24

Mark, Suzan (n.d.). Michika, Adamawa State, Nigeria. Principal, John Guli Bible School. *Church of the Brethren in Nigeria (EYN).* 11/4

Martin, Harold S. (1930–). Lititz, Pennsylvania. Ordained minister; non-salaried ministry; editor, *BRF Witness. Church of the Brethren.* 1/27

Martin, Priscilla A. (1934–). Lititz, Pennsylvania. Mother; homemaker; teacher of women's Bible classes. *Church of the Brethren.* 11/14

Martin-Adkins, Alice (1949–). Candler, North Carolina. Ordained minister. *Church of the Brethren.* 2/8

Martinez de Figueroa, Isabel (1938–). San Juan, Puerto Rico. Ordained minister, Caimito Christian Community Center. *Church of the Brethren.* 10/3

Morse, Kenneth I. (1913–1999). Editor, *Gospel Messenger* / *Messenger* (1950–1978); hymn writer; poet. *Church of the Brethren.* 2/27

Mow, Anna (1893–1985). Missionary to India; teacher at Bethany Biblical Seminary; author and popular retreat leader; one of the first women ordained in the Church of the Brethren. *Church of the Brethren.* 4/13

Mundey, Paul E. R. (1951–). Frederick, Maryland. Pastor. *Church of the Brethren.* 5/1

Murray, M. Andrew (1942–). Huntingdon, Pennsylvania. Elizabeth Evans Baker Professor of Peace and Conflict Studies and director, The Baker Institute, Juniata College; ordained minister. *Church of the Brethren.* 11/30

Myer, James F. (1939–). Lititz, Pennsylvania. Ordained minister; evangelist; non-salaried ministry. *Church of the Brethren.* 4/24

Naas, John (1669–1741). Preacher and evangelist among the Brethren in Europe and colonial America; hymn writer. 3/22

Nead, Peter (1796–1877). Elder; author; chief spokesman for traditional theological Brethren views in the 1800s. 3/15, 8/4

Neff, Robert W. (1936–). Alexandria, Pennsylvania. President emeritus, Juniata College; general secretary of the General Board (1978–1986); professor emeritus of Old Testament, Bethany Theological Seminary; associate for resource development, The Village at Morrisons Cove. *Church of the Brethren.* 1/1, 1/2

Noffsinger, Stanley J. (1954–). Elgin, Illinois. General secretary of the General Board (2003–). *Church of the Brethren.* 9/10

Nolen, Wilfred E. (1940–). Elgin, Illinois. President, Church of the Brethren Benefit Trust; ordained minister. *Church of the Brethren.* 9/16

Ostrander, Shawn M. (1967–). Jenners, Pennsylvania. Pastor. *Conservative Grace Brethren Churches International.* 10/19

Pandya, Rachel (1972–). Naperville, Illinois. Native of India; senior project controller, Deloitte, Chicago. *Church of the Brethren.* 12/11

Parker, Donald L. (1934–). West Salem, Ohio. Retired physician; Ministry of Reconciliation practitioner; General Board chair (2001–2002). *Church of the Brethren.* 10/14

Peña, Joel (1966–). Lancaster, Pennsylvania. Licensed minister; pastor, Hispanic ministries. *Church of the Brethren.* 2/7

Perez-Borges, Hector (1945–). Santa Isabel, Puerto Rico. Pastor; theology / Bible professor; General Board member (2006–2011). *Church of the Brethren.* 8/23

Person, F. Joyce (1936–). Polo, Illinois. Interim pastor; retired nurse. *Church of the Brethren.* 3/3

Petry, Daniel M. (1955–). Middlebury, Indiana. Pastor; author; artist; angler. *Church of the Brethren.* 1/4, 7/1, 8/7, 12/15

Plunkett, Geraldine N. (1925–). Roanoke, Virginia. Retired teacher; writer/ editor; former staff of General Brotherhood Board (1954–1960) and Bethany Theological Seminary (1977–1985). *Church of the Brethren.* 9/24

Poling, Edward L. (1947–). Hagerstown, Maryland. Pastor; spiritual director. *Church of the Brethren.* 7/15

Poling, Travis E. (1978–). Richmond, Indiana. Student, Bethany Theological Seminary; writer; licensed minister. *Church of the Brethren.* 8/19

Poulson, Israel, Sr. (1770–1856). Early English-speaking preacher; prominent community leader, Amwell, New Jersey. 1/12

Radcliff, David R. (1953–). Elgin, Illinois. Director, New Community Project; ordained minister. *Church of the Brethren.* 1/19, 1/22, 5/21, 6/1, 8/31

Ramirez, Frank R. (1954–). Everett, Pennsylvania. Pastor; author; General Board member (2002–2007). *Church of the Brethren.* 10/6, 10/20, 12/3

Reid, Kathryn Goering (1951–). Richmond, Indiana. Executive director, Association of Brethren Caregivers; ordained minister. *Church of the Brethren.* 6/9, 12/16

Reid, Stephen Breck (1952–). Richmond, Indiana. Academic dean and professor of Old Testament, Bethany Theological Seminary. *Church of the Brethren.* 3/4

Reimer, Judy Mills (1940–). Goodview, Virginia. General Board chair (1988–1990); Annual Conference moderator (1995); general secretary of the General Board (1998–2003); ordained minister; business woman. *Church of the Brethren.* 9/9

Reist, Pamela A. (1953–). Mount Joy, Pennsylvania. Pastor. *Church of the Brethren.* 9/4, 11/7

Replogle, Shawn Flory (1970–). McPherson, Kansas. Pastor. *Church of the Brethren.* 2/24

Rhodes, Amy R. (1984–). Elgin, Illinois. Assistant workcamp coordinator (2006–2007 BVS). *Church of the Brethren.* 1/29

Rhodes, Beth (1981–). Ann Arbor, Michigan. Doctoral student; former workcamp coordinator; National Youth Conference (2006) coordinator. *Church of the Brethren.* 9/2

Rhodes, Donna McKee (1962–). Huntingdon, Pennsylvania. Executive director, Susquehanna Valley Ministry Center; ordained minister. *Church of the Brethren.* 7/10

Rieman, Louise (Louie) Baldwin (1946–). Indianapolis, Indiana. Pastor. *Church of the Brethren.* 11/6

Roop, Eugene F. (1942–). Richmond, Indiana. President, Bethany Theological Seminary. *Church of the Brethren.* 3/25, 3/26, 3/27, 3/28, 3/29

Royer, Howard E. (1930–). Elgin, Illinois. Manager, Global Food Crisis Fund (General Board staff). *Church of the Brethren.* 8/16, 11/19, 12/27

Royer-Miller, Margo (1981–). Willits, California. Apprentice in sustainable agriculture, Ecology Action. *Church of the Brethren.* 11/16, 12/7

Satvedi, Valentina F. (1964–). Pasadena, California. Director of urban theological formation, Shalom Ministries; ordained minister. *Church of the Brethren.* 3/17

Sayler, D. P. (1811–1885). Prominent Brethren leader during the mid-1800s; three-time Annual Meeting moderator; forceful preacher sought after by Brethren and non-Brethren. 6/17

Scheppard, Carol A. (1957–). Mount Crawford, Virginia. Associate professor of Philosophy and Religion, Bridgewater College; ordained minister. *Church of the Brethren.* 3/18

Shaffer, Kenneth M., Jr. (1945–). Elgin, Illinois. Director, Brethren Historical Library and Archives (General Board staff); ordained minister. *Church of the Brethren.* 7/29, 7/30, 7/31, 8/1, 8/2, 8/3

Sheller, Harry L., Jr. (1941–). Hillsboro, Oregon. Semi-retired math professor; ordained minister. *Church of the Brethren.* 9/14

Shreckhise, Richard F. (1944–). Lancaster, Pennsylvania. Pastor. *Church of the Brethren.* 3/19, 3/20

Shultz, John (1950–). Ashland, Ohio. President, Ashland Theological Seminary. *Brethren Church.* 9/27

Shumate, David K. (1957–). Roanoke, Virginia. Executive/minister, Virlina District. *Church of the Brethren.* 5/25

Skiles, Mildred (Kintner) (1940–). Rio Rancho, New Mexico. Retired missionary, Torreon Navajo Mission. *Dunkard Brethren.* 11/28

Smeltzer, Bonnie Kline (1954–). Boalsburg, Pennsylvania. Pastor. *Church of the Brethren.* 4/7

Smith, Craig H. (1949–). Elizabethtown, Pennsylvania. Executive/minister, Atlantic Northeast District. *Church of the Brethren.* 4/8

Smith, Victoria J. (1950–). Elizabethtown, Pennsylvania. Executive director, Meant To Be Ministries, Inc. *Church of the Brethren.* 10/30

Snyder, Graydon F. (1930–). Chicago, Illinois. Ordained minister; retired seminary educator. *Church of the Brethren.* 9/1

Solanky, Asha (1957–). Richmond, Virginia. *Church of the Brethren.* 2/16

Sollenberger, Chrissy (1989–). Annville, Pennsylvania. Student. *Church of the Brethren.* 6/21

Sollenberger, Elaine M. (1931–). Everett, Pennsylvania. Annual Conference moderator (1989, 1998). *Church of the Brethren.* 5/6

Speicher, Anna (1958–). Elgin, Illinois. Director and editor, Gather 'Round curriculum project; historian of abolition, women's history, and religion. *Church of the Brethren.* 11/13

Speicher, Sara (1965–). Warton, Lancashire, United Kingdom. Media and communications consultant; former staff member, World Council of Churches (1997–2003). *Church of the Brethren.* 11/24

Spire, Catherine B. (1967–). Durham, North Carolina. Pastor; General Board member (2005–2010). *Church of the Brethren.* 9/23

Steele, Jay H. (1958–). Burnsville, Minnesota. Pastor. *Church of the Brethren.* 10/7

Steury, Mark Flory (1953–). Dayton, Ohio. Executive/minister, Southern Ohio District. *Church of the Brethren.* 11/8

Stokes-Buckles, James W. (1981–). New York, New York. Licensed minister; program assistant, World Council of Churches. *Church of the Brethren.* 2/5

Stone, Phillip C. (1942–). Bridgewater, Virginia. Lawyer; president, Bridgewater College; Annual Conference moderator (1991). *Church of the Brethren.* 8/11

Swartz, Fred W. (1938–). Bridgewater, Virginia. Retired pastor; former General Board staff (1977–1983); Annual Conference secretary (2003–). *Church of the Brethren.* 2/25

Taylor, Vickie (1958–). Ashland, Ohio. Director of technology services, Ashland Theological Seminary; United States Ministry Council; retreat leader; ordained elder. *Brethren Church.* 10/27

Thakor, Ernie (1948–). Woodridge, Illinois. Realtor. *Church of the Brethren.* 6/20

Thompson, R. Jan (1935–). Mesa, Arizona. Ordained minister; former General Board staff; missionary; educator. *Church of the Brethren.* 9/12

Trostle, Evelyn (1889–n.d.). Educator, McPherson College; relief worker in Armenia after World War I; lecturer and fundraiser for Armenia. 8/10

Ullom, Becky (1977–). Elgin, Illinois. Director of identity and relations (General Board staff). *Church of the Brethren.* 6/14, 9/20, 12/10

Valeta, Gail Erisman (1959–). Denver, Colorado. Associate coordinator of Justice and Peace Studies, Iliff School of Theology; ordained minister; conflict transformation professor. *Church of the Brethren.* 8/12, 10/26, 12/2

Wampler, Guy E., Jr. (1935–). Lancaster, Pennsylvania. Retired pastor; Annual Conference moderator (1987). *Church of the Brethren.* 1/3

Webb, Dennis (1963–). Aurora, Illinois. Pastor. *Church of the Brethren.* 7/20

Wenger, Dean (1961–). Petersburg, Pennsylvania. Co-executive director, Camp Blue Diamond Inc. *Church of the Brethren.* 6/25

Wenger, Jerriann Heiser (1959–). Petersburg, Pennsylvania. Co-executive director, Camp Blue Diamond Inc.; ordained minister. *Church of the Brethren.* 6/22

Whitten, David A. (1955–). Jos, Nigeria. Nigeria mission coordinator (General Board staff); ordained minister. *Church of the Brethren.* 2/19, 6/15

Wieand, Albert Cassel (1871–1954). Biblical scholar; founder and president, Bethany Bible School. *Church of the Brethren.* 9/28

Wiltschek, Walt (1970–). Saint Charles, Illinois. Ordained minister; youth advisor; editor, *Messenger* (General Board staff). *Church of the Brethren.* 7/4, 8/26, 10/28

Winter, Roy (1964–). Union Bridge, Maryland. Executive director, Brethren Service Center and Emergency Response (General Board staff). *Church of the Brethren.* 10/16

Witkovsky, L. David (1956–). Huntingdon, Pennsylvania. Chaplain, Juniata College. *Church of the Brethren.* 5/5, 5/11

Note: Biographical information is current as of 12/2006. Contributors identified as pastors, chaplains, district executive/ministers, and seminary faculty and administrators are also ordained.

Acknowledgments

The topical outline and daily scripture selections for this anniversary devotional are from the 2008–2009 Home Daily Bible Readings of the International Sunday School Lessons. Copyright 2005 by the Committee on the Uniform Series. Used by permission.

Annual Meeting Minutes of 1789, Great Conestoga, Pennsylvania. Minutes of the Annual Meetings of The Church of the Brethren 1778–1909, Brethren's Publishing House, 1909. Page 347

The Brethren in Colonial America, Donald F. Durnbaugh, ed. Brethren Press, Elgin, Illinois, 1967. Pages 387, 477

European Origins of the Brethren, Donald F. Durnbaugh, comp./trans. Brethren Press, Elgin, Illinois, 1958. Pages 39, 211, 429

Fruit of the Vine, Donald F. Durnbaugh. Brethren Press, Elgin, Illinois, 1997. Pages 3, 81, 131, 171

Theological Writings on Various Subjects, Peter Nead. B. F. Ells, Dayton, Ohio, 1850. Pages 259, 297

Index of Scripture Texts

Abbreviations used for translations quoted:
CEV—*Contemporary English Version*
KJV—*King James Version*
NASB—*New American Standard Bible (updated)*
NIV—*New International Version*
NKJV—*New King James Version*
REB—*Revised English Bible*
RSV—*Revised Standard Version*
TEV—*Today's English Version (The Good News Bible)*

Old Testament

GENESIS
2:7, 10/2
14:17-20, 6/4
18:1-8, 12/8
18:2-5, 6/25
18:9-14, 12/9

EXODUS
12:11-14, 1/2

LEVITICUS
19:17-19, 1/8
19:18, 8/7
23:33-43, 5/20
26:40-46, 3/27

NUMBERS
6:22-27, 9/15
9:1-5, 1/1
13, 12/30

DEUTERONOMY
16:13-17, 5/21
26:5-9, 1/2

JOSHUA
23:14, 12/13
24:15, 2/10

1 SAMUEL
2:1-10, 12/1
2:26, 1/5
16:7, 3/6

2 SAMUEL
8:6-9, 3/19
7, 3/4
7:12-16, 3/10

1 CHRONICLES
15:1-3, 2/26
15:11-15, 2/26
15:16-24, 2/27
15:25-29, 2/28
16:1-6, 2/29

16:7-36, 3/1
16:37-43, 3/2
17:1-6, 3/4
17:7-10, 3/5
17:11-15, 3/6
17:16-19, 3/7
17:20-22, 3/8
17:23-27, 3/9
28:1-5, 3/11
28:6-8, 3/12
28:9-10, 3/13
28:11-19, 3/14
28:20-21, 3/15

2 CHRONICLES
6:1-11, 3/18
6:12-17, 3/19
6:18-31, 3/20
6:36-39, 3/21
6:40-42, 3/22
34:1-7, 3/25
34:8-18, 3/26
34:19-21, 3/27